The Philosophy of J. L. Austin

The Philosophy of J. L. Austin

EDITED BY
Martin Gustafsson and Richard Sørli

OXFORD
UNIVERSITY PRESS

OXFORD
UNIVERSITY PRESS

Great Clarendon Street, Oxford, OX2 6DP,
United Kingdom

Oxford University Press is a department of the University of Oxford.
It furthers the University's objective of excellence in research, scholarship,
and education by publishing worldwide. Oxford is a registered trade mark of
Oxford University Press in the UK and in certain other countries

Published in the United States of America by Oxford University Press
198 Madison Avenue, New York, NY 10016, United States of America

British Library Cataloguing in Publication Data
Data available

Library of Congress Cataloging in Publication Data
Data available

ISBN 978-0-19-921975-9

Contents

Contributors   vi

1. Introduction: Inheriting Austin   1
   Martin Gustafsson

2. Unmasking the Tradition   32
   Simon Glendinning

3. Tales of the Unknown: Austin and the Argument from Ignorance   51
   Mark Kaplan

4. Austin, Dreams, and Scepticism   78
   Adam Leite

5. Believing what the Man Says about his own Feelings   114
   Benjamin McMyler

6. Knowing Knowing (that Such and Such)   146
   Avner Baz

7. Truth and Merit   175
   Charles Travis

8. 'There's Many a Slip between Cup and Lip': Dimension and
   Negation in Austin   204
   Jean-Philippe Narboux

Index   241

Contributors

AVNER BAZ, Tufts University

SIMON GLENDINNING, European Institute, London School of Economics

MARTIN GUSTAFSSON, Åbo Akademi University, Finland

MARK KAPLAN, Indiana University, Bloomington

ADAM LEITE, Indiana University, Bloomington

BENJAMIN MCMYLER, Texas A&M University

JEAN-PHILIPPE NARBOUX, Université de Bordeaux

CHARLES TRAVIS, King's College London

1

Introduction: Inheriting Austin

Martin Gustafsson

In a famous passage in *How to Do Things with Words*, J. L. Austin considers the question whether it is true or false to say of France that it is hexagonal. He refuses to give a straightforward answer. Instead, he notes that he can understand what it means to say that 'France is hexagonal' is 'true for certain intents and purposes. It is good enough for a top ranking general, perhaps, but not for a geographer.' He then makes the observation that the most natural thing would often be to say that the description is 'pretty rough', without ascribing to it any determinate truth-value. In such cases, insisting that it must be either true or false is a mistake: 'It is just rough, and that is the right and final answer to the question of the relation of "France is hexagonal" to France' (Austin 1975: 143).

Something similar might be said about the received picture of Austin. We are all familiar with the standard epithets: he was 'the doyen of Ordinary Language Philosophy', 'a master of observing minutiae of linguistic use', and, of course, 'the founder of speech act theory'.[1] The picture such epithets paint is not a mere fantasy, and it is perhaps impossible to avoid promulgating some version of it if one is writing a short presentation in a philosophical dictionary or in an introductory textbook. On the other hand, someone who seriously tries to find his way about in Austin's philosophical landscape will soon discover that this picture hides from view the diversity and variation that are in fact prominent characteristics of the terrain. It is true that Austin sometimes issues methodological recommendations, emphasizing the philosophical importance of 'the language of ordinary life' (1979: 189). But he does so only hesitantly, while making it clear that those recommendations are not universal rules and that their applicability to particular problems will have to be decided piecemeal, from one case to another. It is true that he is often concerned with subtleties of everyday usage and resists what he regards as unnecessary or unwitting employments of technical vocabulary. But he is open to the introduction of technical terms when

---

[1] These particular wordings are taken from Culler (1982: 111), Honderich (1991: 217), and Glock (2008: 43), but countless variations on them can be found in the literature.

they are helpful and does not hesitate to make use of simplified models if he finds them illuminating.[2] It is true that he initiated the study of ways in which 'to *say* something is to *do* something' (1975: 12). But it remains a controversial issue to what extent later developments of speech act theory deal with the issues that Austin thought of as central to his own project (Crary 2002; Sbisà 2007). With respect to Austin, as much as to any other important philosopher, the 'standard picture' is bound to be a caricature. Yet, such a picture has often controlled the reception of his thought, perhaps more so than with respect to any other important thinker of the twentieth century.

In fact, this tendency toward oversimplification seems particularly worrisome in the case of Austin. For one thing, taking the standard picture of him too seriously is to manifest precisely the sort of intellectual tendency that he was most concerned to combat. It is ironic that epithets like the ones given above are routinely allowed to shape our conception of a thinker whose whole work is permeated by a desire to make his audience aware of and lose confidence in the habitual imposition of preconceived categories.

More importantly, the received picture serves to confirm and strengthen a wide-spread view of Austin's work as effectively obsolete. For we all know—don't we?—that ordinary language philosophy, once so influential, was methodologically flawed. And we all know—don't we?—that even if *How To Do Things With Words* was a great achievement, the developments and revisions made by latter-day speech act theorists have made this pioneering effort outdated. Of course, no one denies that Austin's work is of considerable historical significance. We have to study it if we want to understand one important phase in the development of analytic philosophy. But is there really anything philosophically important to learn from him *today*?

If anything unites the contributors to this volume, it is the conviction that the answer to this question is 'Yes!' and, hence, that we should not let the standard picture of Austin lure us into treating him as a dusty figure of the past. This is not to say that the authors agree on *what* we can learn from him. There is much disagreement to be found in the pages of this book, with respect to both exegetical and philosophical points, with respect to questions of detail as well as to broader issues. The overall aim of the volume is not to present a new school of Austin interpretation. Rather it is to collect papers by philosophers who share the conviction that a serious engagement with Austin's work can be of real help in our struggle with contemporary questions. The papers deal with issues that are on the top of today's philosophical agenda, such as scepticism and contextualism, the epistemology of testimony, the generality of the conceptual, and the viability of the semantics/pragmatics distinction. The connections made between Austinian ideas and current debates provide both a deeper understanding of Austin's thought and a clear sense of why his work is still of genuine philosophical significance.

---

[2] The clearest example of Austin's willingness to make use of technical models is in his paper 'How to Talk' (1979: 134–53).

This is the first collection of essays on Austin's philosophy published by a major Anglophone press in almost forty years. Hence, it seems appropriate to provide it with a substantial introduction that describes the intellectual background and legacy of his thought and which, in doing so, gives a rich account of the character and rationale of this book as a whole. Section 1 discusses in some detail why a revival of Austin's philosophy requires a cross-fertilizing mode of interpretation that integrates exegesis and contemporary application, treating them as two sides of the same coin rather than as distinct aims. Section 2 provides background for the exegetical aspect of such interpretative cross-fertilization by describing Austin in his intellectual milieu, focusing in particular on the significance of his immediate predecessors, G. E. Moore and H. A. Prichard. Section 3 widens the perspective by tackling the unwieldy issue of the relation between Austin and the tradition of Western philosophy at large. Section 4 looks at Austin's legacy in contemporary thought, in all its astonishing variety. Finally, section 5 gives an overview of the contributions. Readers who just want a survey of the rest of the papers in order to be able to move on as quickly as possible to the chapters that seem of interest to them, can go directly to that final section.

1. Reading Austin today

In the forties and fifties, Austin was a revered, feared, and deeply controversial figure. In the sixties and seventies, he was posthumously dethroned. And then his work gradually 'slid into a state of respectable semi-obscurity' (Crary 2002: 59)—arguably the worst fate that can befall a philosophical corpus. Browsing through the most prestigious journals of Anglo-American philosophy, the mummification process is clearly visible. After 1980, Austin is present almost only in scattered footnotes where dutiful references are made to a few selected passages from 'Other Minds', 'A Plea for Excuses', and *How to Do Things with Words*. Even today, K. T. Fann's *Symposium on J. L. Austin* from 1969 remains the standard collection of papers on Austin's philosophy.[3] The second and (until now) last philosophical anthology published by a major Anglophone press and devoted exclusively to Austin is *Essays on J. L. Austin*, from 1973 (Berlin et al. 1973).

Many of the contributors to these two collections were Austin's students or colleagues, and it is striking how central a place they give to their experience of him as a teacher and discussion partner. In particular, they take their personal acquaintance with Austin to have provided them with a much better understanding of his philosophical intentions than what is possible to gather from his few publications. Thus, G. J. Warnock complains that many things written about his teacher are vitiated 'not merely [...] by ordinary misconstrual of what Austin wrote, but, more importantly, by apparent

---

[3] Most papers in Fann's volume were published even earlier, and many before 1965.

misunderstanding of him and his intentions, of what he had tried to do in philosophy, and of his reasons for so trying.' Hence, Warnock continues,

it would be desirable and useful to secure the comments of some of those who had had the advantage of, so to speak, observing at close quarters Austin in action, and of having themselves inhabited [. . .] the philosophical scene in which he was so conspicuous a figure. (Berlin et al. 1973: v)

Even if he is careful not to say that such first-hand experience guarantees correct understanding, Warnock seems to think that the advantage it gives is virtually irreplaceable. Indeed, he and the other contributors manage to convey a sense that even if their testimony regarding what it was like to experience Austin live and in person is indispensable for grasping what his philosophy is all about, it still does not suffice to provide an outsider with a full understanding of Austin's ideas and procedures. Or, as Warnock nostalgically puts it in his monographic study of Austin's philosophy:

[I]t is probably inevitable that in a case such as his—in which formal writing for publication played so comparatively small a part—the impression that he made as a philosopher upon those who knew him may be difficult fully to appreciate for those not included in that now diminishing number. (Warnock 1989: 2)

It would be futile to deny that there is a sense in which all this is quite true. In group-discussion, Austin could spend many hours probing some topic that, in a paper, was condensed into one or two short paragraphs. Indeed, most of what he did informally in front of small audiences did not enter his publications at all, and it has been said that it was precisely on such occasions that the nature of his philosophical talent and originality was most visible. We have the two reconstructed lecture series, *Sense and Sensibilia* and *How to Do Things with Words*, which are said to provide a somewhat better view of Austin's style as a teacher. But no one denies that these reconstructions, however carefully made, still only dimly reflect his actual performances.[4]

So, let it be granted that someone who reads only Austin's published works and ignores what his students and colleagues have to say about his teaching will have a distorted picture of his philosophical procedures, while someone who also reads the testimony of those students and colleagues will have a truer picture, though one which is still bound to be in certain respects incomplete and unreliable. Where does this leave us, late-born inheritors of Austin? Does this mean that our temporal distance only puts

---

[4] Isaiah Berlin even maintains that to fully appreciate Austin's philosophical gifts, you had to meet with him alone. Between four eyes, '[h]e understood what one said perfectly, talked about it with extreme acuteness and lucidity, and made one's thoughts race [. . .] and was not obviously trying to convert one to a particular point of view, wasn't either preaching to one or bullying one[.]' In groups, however, his strong competitive instincts took over, '[a]nd this desire to achieve victory sometimes led him into arguments which perhaps were slightly specious, at times. He was usually much cleverer than his interlocutors and usually did win. But the kind of way in which one wanted to talk to him was when he was entirely alone, face to face; then I think he was at his best' (Berlin 2006: 9).

us at a disadvantage, condemning us to uncertainty, speculation and misunderstanding in our reception of his thought?

Or are there perhaps ways in which this distance can be a blessing? Might there be certain respects in which the close quarters from which his contemporaries observed him were, so to speak, too close? Might there be features of Austin's philosophy that are in fact easier to register now that it has become *history*?

Answering the latter questions in the positive may seem to run counter to the aspiration not to treat Austin as a dusty figure of the past. It should be evident, however, that the sense of 'becoming history' that is relevant here is not to be identified with becoming outdated. The point is not that Austin's philosophy is now of 'merely historical interest', if that entails that it can safely be ignored by someone who is struggling with contemporary problems. Rather, the point is to question the necessity of that antiquarian notion of 'historical interest' which would seem to justify such a conclusion.

The crucial thing here is to recognize the possibility and legitimacy of a conception of past philosophical texts which is genuinely historical and yet not antiquarian. This is a conception according to which the achievement of a great philosopher can only come into clear view when the philosopher's thought is placed in relation to subsequent developments—developments which, though the philosopher himself would not have been aware of them, confer a special sort of significance on what he was able to do then and what we can still allow us to see now. The content of a philosophical achievement, measured in this way, is of the sort that unfolds and displays itself as time goes on.

While this approach is different from antiquarianism, it is also to be sharply distinguished from what Bernard Williams calls 'triumphant anachronism', exemplified by the view that 'we should approach the works of Plato as though they had appeared in last month's issue of *Mind*' (Williams 2006: 258). Triumphant anachronism is fundamentally *ahistorical*, as it operates on the assumption that the content and value of past ideas is determined by how well they can be made to fit with present views and modes of discourse.[5] In contrast, the sort of non-antiquarian history envisaged here does not use our present convictions as the touchstone of philosophical significance or intelligibility. Rather, it uses past ideas to gain a critical distance to our own preconceptions. In Williams's words, such history should 'help us in reviving a sense of strangeness or questionability about our own philosophical assumptions' (2006: 260).[6]

[5] In calling triumphant anachronism 'ahistorical', I am claiming that such purported history of philosophy does not deserve the name of history at all. Williams seems to take a similar view, arguing that such 'extreme forms of [. . .] history of philosophy', in removing the distance from the present altogether, 'lost the title to being any pointful form of historical activity' (2006: 259).

[6] What I call 'antiquarianism', Williams calls 'history of ideas', whereas his label for the sort of genuinely historical and yet not antiquarian approach I am describing is 'history of philosophy'. Williams's terminology is not entirely fortunate, since the important point is not that the work of actual historians of ideas always fits, or even aspires to fit, the antiquarian ideal. A fully satisfactory treatment of these and related issues would require a more extensive discussion than there is room for in an introduction such as this. An essay that comes

Consider again Warnock's worry, quoted earlier, that discussions of Austin's philosophy by people who have not seen him in action are vitiated by misunderstanding 'of him and his intentions, of what he had tried to do in philosophy, and of his reasons for so trying'. This worry gives rise to the question of what it is to understand 'what Austin tried to do in philosophy'. It is of course undeniable that his own articulations of his philosophical intentions are of central importance, and that those articulations must be interpreted in the light of the wider intellectual context in which he was situated. But there is also an important sense in which the full significance of some of the intentions of a past thinker might not be entirely clear to anyone of his contemporaries, including the philosopher himself.

To get a more concrete sense of what this might mean, consider an example. In his 1946 paper, 'Other Minds', Austin makes the notorious proposal that there is a close parallel between saying 'I know' and saying 'I promise'. He makes some suggestive remarks about the putative similarities between these two speech acts. But he also says things that seem quite confused, and he does admit that he fails to see his way clearly through the issues that arise in connection with the proposed parallel (Austin 1979: 99–103, 113–15). The parallel and its significance were much discussed in the fifties and sixties, but no one came up with a very satisfactory interpretation of what Austin might have been trying to get at. In his monograph on Austin, Warnock struggles with the issue but does not get very much further. Today, it is commonly thought that the parallel is fundamentally flawed.

A central question is obviously what speech act someone is actually performing in uttering 'I know'. Warnock takes Austin's parallel to mean that just as to utter 'I promise' is to perform an act of promising, to utter 'I know' is to perform an act of knowing. As Benjamin McMyler points out in his contribution to the present volume, this interpretation makes impossible any plausible and interesting development of Austin's proposal. After all, knowing is not an act but a state, and saying 'I know that p' is neither necessary nor sufficient for knowing that p. McMyler therefore offers a different interpretation. He claims that Austin's real point is that the speech act performed by someone who utters 'I know' is the act of *testifying*, where the notion of testifying is understood in a sense broad enough to include ordinary cases of telling someone something. According to McMyler, 'Austin's interest in the parallel is an interest in the way in which the act of testifying, one of the primary ways in which we communicate information to others, is in many ways analogous to the act of promising' (McMyler, this volume, p. 121).

The details of McMyler's reading need not concern us here. For present purposes, what matters is that McMyler is able to make sense of Austin's discussion not only by reflecting on the details of Austin's actual text but also by relating Austin's discussion to the contemporary debate on the epistemology of testimony. On the one hand, Austin's

much closer to providing such a satisfactory treatment, and which makes use of Williams's distinction between the history of philosophy and the history of ideas, is Kremer (forthcoming).

discussion is used to help us revive a sense of questionability about some of the philosophical assumptions that are usually made in the contemporary discussion. On the other hand, McMyler's viewpoint in the present helps him criticize and reject certain passages in Austin's text, by arguing that they fail to cohere with what we can now see as Austin's most valuable and basic objectives and insights.

If McMyler's reading is correct, he has managed to identify ideas which, on the one hand, can rightly be ascribed to Austin, but which, on the other hand, were not entirely clear to Austin himself or to his contemporaries. The striving for this sort of understanding can be found in all contributions to this volume, and makes them different from the contributions to the earlier volumes on Austin's philosophy mentioned above. Such striving is not only a legitimate sort of enterprise: the persistent vitality of a past thinker hangs precisely on our will and capacity to subject his ideas to this sort of inquiry.

We said earlier that the standard picture of Austin makes his philosophy seem obsolete. We can now understand better what this means. What the standard picture does is to thwart any expectation that Austin's work might have the power to revive in us a genuine sense of strangeness or questionability about our own philosophical assumptions. It fosters the tendency to assume that his work can be of *merely* historical interest, where this 'merely' implies that the sort of interest Austin's philosophy does have is only as an object of antiquarian history-writing.

Consider Colin McGinn's review of Warnock's monograph on Austin, a piece that was originally published in 1989 in the *London Review of Books*. Basing his claims entirely on a reading of Warnock, McGinn finds himself warranted to issue verdicts such as the following on the philosophical quality of Austin's work:

He may have initiated some fruitful lines of inquiry, later developed by others, but he himself seems to have been unable to pursue these lines with any surefootedness or perspicacity. You begin to understand why he wrote so little. (McGinn 1997: 165)

As an example of Austin's lack of perspicacity, McGinn considers the parallel between saying 'I know' and saying 'I promise':

Contrary to Austin's thesis, 'I know', unlike 'I promise', is as descriptive as any first-person attribution. And, I would add, knowing is not an *act* at all, which precludes its being effected by the utterance of a performative verb. These objections are (a) elementary and (b) definitive. Ten minutes reflection should have made it clear that the assimilation is simply a mistake, prompted by the most superficial of similarities between the two verbs as they (sometimes) occur in the first person. (McGinn 1997: 168–9)

Would the lack of charity manifested here seem at all acceptable if it were not simply taken for granted—by McGinn as well as by his intended audience—that we have very little of philosophical value to learn from Austin? Would not a serious engagement with a philosopher's work have to start from the quite contrary presumption, that an adequate appropriation and assessment of his ideas—especially when he is groping his way through unexplored territory while explicitly admitting that he does not see his way clearly—might in fact require not ten minutes but half a century or more of philosophical reflection?

The best way of contesting the habitual caricaturing of Austin's philosophy, and the resulting belittling of its contemporary significance, is by counterexample. The task, thus generally described, can be variously implemented, and this volume provides many illustrations of such variation. There are contributors who focus on some sharply delimited topic in Austin's work. They offer rational reconstructions that move at a level that throughout remains close to the details of Austin's texts. Others try to achieve unexpected syntheses that tie together seemingly disparate parts of his thinking. They give imaginative accounts of putatively implicit points and connections, in ways that take them beyond the mere letter of Austin's text. These different implementations of the task are each indispensable forms of the sort of history, and the sort of philosophy, that this book is meant to provide.

2. Austin, Moore, and Prichard

Probably the two then living thinkers who had the strongest influence on Austin's philosophical development were George Edward Moore and Harold Arthur Prichard (Hampshire 1969b: 91). Together with Russell, Moore had been the leading figure in the Cambridge revolt against the idealist school of Thomas Hill Green—a school often referred to by its opponents as an 'Hegelian' movement, even if its members repudiated that label.[7] Prichard was engaged in a similar revolt at Oxford, which had been the original home of Green's school and which housed some of its most prominent members. The original leader of the Oxford revolt had been Prichard's teacher and the front figure of Oxford 'realism', John Cook Wilson, who died in 1915.

Not that the Cambridge and the Oxford resistance movements formed a united front. Quite the contrary: Cook Wilson had an extremely dismissive attitude toward the logic of *Principia Mathematica* and thought that even Green's followers had a deeper understanding of logico-philosophical problems than Russell (Passmore 1957: 243). Prichard and Moore are both describable broadly as ethical intuitionists, but their forms of intuitionism differ considerably; and Prichard rejected other conceptions central to both Russell and Moore, such as the notion of a sense datum (Dancy 2009).

---

[7] See Collingwood (1939: 15). Bradley writes: 'For Hegel himself, assuredly I think him a great philosopher; but I never could have called myself an Hegelian, partly because I can not say that I have mastered his system, and partly because I could not accept what seems his main principle, or at least part of that principle' (1883: x; quoted in Candlish 2007: 8). It was said above that the reception of Austin's thinking has been shaped by a stereotype, perhaps to a larger extent than the reception of any other important twentieth-century thinker. The reception of Bradley and other members of Green's school is another instance of a similar phenomenon, even if in recent years a number of more nuanced and fair-minded readings have been published, such as Hylton (1990), Nicholson (1990), and Candlish (2007).

Still, C. D. Broad could say of Prichard that he was 'a man of immense ability whom I have always regarded as the Oxford Moore' (quoted in Cheney 1971, 14; cf. Dancy 2009). The similarity Broad saw between Moore and Prichard seems to have been a matter of philosophical attitude and procedure rather than of shared doctrines. In reaction to what they regarded as the speculative flights and inflated language of Green, Bradley, Bosanquet, Caird, and McTaggart, Moore and Prichard both aimed at breaking down unwieldy issues into well-demarcated questions suited for piecemeal treatment, using a clear-headed style that was meant to keep philosophy down to earth. Passmore describes Moore's approach as 'that minute philosophical procedure, with its careful distinction of issues, its insistence that *this*, not *that*, is the real question—where *this* and *that* had ordinarily been regarded as alternative formulations of the same problem' (1957: 210). Jim MacAdam talks of Prichard's 'methods of isolating small, manageable philosophical problems as exact questions, and insisting upon solutions in clear everyday English' (2002: xiv). The two descriptions can be swapped: they fit both thinkers equally well.

And they fit Austin too. Certainly there were a number of more specific points at which Moore and Prichard also influenced him. It seems, for example, that Austin started developing his conception of performatives in connection with a correspondence with Prichard in the thirties (Warnock 1989: 105). It seems fair to say, though, that Moore's and Prichard's deepest impact on Austin had to do with their resistance to oversimplification and sweeping apriorism. In their preference for slow, piecemeal inquiry over impatient generalization and pigeonholing, their investigations served for Austin as models of what lucidity and rationality may amount to in philosophy (cf. Warnock 1969: 5–7).[8]

And in being thus influenced, he was by no means alone in his generation. When he came to Oxford as an undergraduate in 1929, the old conflict between Green's and Cook Wilson's followers still retained some of its animus. It was pretty clear, however, that those of Green's followers who were still teaching there—amongst whom H. H. Joachim was the most prominent—had for a long time been unable to attract the ablest young minds. Not that those younger people wanted to fight in the realist trench either. They saw the old controversy as a senseless war that had been going on for far too long. What united them seems rather to have been a general sense of wanting to do something useful and manageable in philosophy, without the premature adoption of any particular 'ism'.

---

[8] Which is not to say that Austin found Prichard very open-minded or philosophically creative. According to J. O. Urmson, 'Prichard was no doubt a menace in many ways—dogmatic, repressive of all divergent thinking, and, on the whole, sterile' (Urmson 1988: 12). There is no reason to think Austin would have disagreed with this verdict. However, it should also be noted that Urmson goes on by making the following qualification: 'If he [Prichard] was dogmatically dismissive of heresy in debate, *in foro interno* he was endlessly questioning himself, and what at one time was publicly proclaimed to be obvious to anyone willing and able to think might later come to be equally firmly rejected' (ibid.).

This, however, did involve a sense of affinity with the philosophical temperament of old-school realism. As Isaiah Berlin says about the followers of Cook Wilson, 'before building an enormous building they wanted to test every brick'—and this was true of people in the younger generation as well (Berlin 2006: 2). 'The whole atmosphere', Berlin remembers, was

away from huge, not wholly intelligible, masses of words into something which was clear and distinct and honest and lucid and empirical, and provided one could sort of deflate the language, and get talking about something which one could really understand and operate with, one felt that perhaps there was a subject there worth discussing. (Berlin 2006: 4)

What Berlin describes here is an inchoate attitude rather than a well-developed conception of how philosophy ought to be done. Sharing this attitude seems to have been enough to induce a strong sense of common purpose among the people gathering around Austin in 1936–7, when he and Berlin began organizing weekly discussions on Thursday evenings.[9] With the exception of Ayer, who, under the influence of the logical positivists, had already formed a relatively determinate view of the nature of philosophy, these young men—the oldest was 27—had no clear program or method. Yet the sense of intellectual vitality was strong: 'we thought we were making progress, breaking through old categories, escaping from all kinds of cages, and this is of course an absolutely irreplaceable feeling. It's a thing which I've never had with the same intensity since' (Berlin 2006: 11).[10]

It appears to have been only after the war, when Green's and Cook Wilson's followers were all definitely gone, that Austin found his own, mature voice in philosophy. In 1946 he published 'Other Minds', and it is from this point on that there can be said to exist something like a developed, distinctively Austinian way of philosophizing—an approach to philosophy which would be further chiselled out during the remaining fifteen years of his life, and achieve its most paradigmatic expression in later papers such as 'Ifs and Cans' and 'A Plea for Excuses', both published in 1956.

---

[9] Besides Austin and Berlin, the regular members of this early discussion group were A. J. Ayer, Donald MacNabb, Anthony Woozley, Stuart Hampshire, and Donald MacKinnon (Berlin 1973: 9).

[10] It is interesting to compare Berlin's description with Collingwood's opposite assessments of the realists' impact on the younger generation: 'I have already said of "realism" that its positive doctrine was nugatory, its critical technique deadly: all the deadlier because its effectiveness did not depend on errors native to the doctrines criticized, but on a kind of disintegration produced by itself in whatever it touched. It was therefore inevitable that by degrees "realism" should part with all positive doctrines whatever, congratulating itself at each new jettison that it was rid of a knave. [. . .] In this process, by which anything that could be recognized as a philosophical doctrine was stuck up and shot to pieces by the "realistic" criticism, the "realists" little by little destroyed everything in the way of positive doctrine that they had ever possessed. Once more, I am concerned only with the effect on their pupils. It was (how could it not have been?) to convince them that philosophy was a silly and trifling game, and to give them a lifelong contempt for the subject and a life-long grudge against the men who had wasted their time by forcing it upon their attention' (Collingwood 1939: 46–50).

In the discussion group led by Austin—now, famously, on Saturday mornings—his coming to philosophical maturity had equally tangible effects.[11] Before the war, Stuart Hampshire recalls, '[w]e attended to words with exactness in the sort of way that Prichard and Moore did under Austin's guidance, but no more than that' (Berlin 2006: 12). After the war, there was a shift to a new, higher (or should one say lower, and slower?) gear in this pursuit of linguistic clarity. Patterns of usage were charted and distinguished with a meticulousness that made the efforts of Moore and Prichard look coarse and prejudiced in comparison. Moore's wish that analyses should take the form of traditional Socratic definitions appeared fraught with misguided philosophical assumptions, and Prichard's efforts to 'worry things out' seemed fruitlessly trapped within antiquated frameworks of thought (Berlin 1973: 3).

So, the relation between the mature Austin on the one hand and Moore and Prichard on the other is rather complicated. To someone unaccustomed to the mechanisms of intellectual influence it may seem paradoxical that the doyen of ordinary language philosophy should have been deeply influenced by 'the doyen of the old-style, non-linguistic Oxford philosophy' (this is Nicola Lacey's description of Prichard; see her 2004: 139). But remember that what Austin found exemplary in Prichard's work was his 'bubble-pricking' (Carritt 1948: 146), whereas he 'accepted neither Prichard's premises nor his conclusions' (Berlin 1973: 2). Similarly, as Ryle notes, 'Austin took [. . .] a lot after Moore—the un-muddler, not the definer' (Ryle 1971: 273). Of particular significance is to keep in mind that what Austin admired in the works of these two men was not their rejection of the systems of Green or Bradley or McTaggart in particular. Rather, what impressed him seems to have been their striving not to let *any* simplistic and prematurely invoked schema or system determine beforehand how things must be, or what possible views there are available on a given topic. Not that he thought they were entirely successful at this venture. On the contrary, it is clear that he thought they were unsuccessful. But he also thought it would be possible to reveal their failures, precisely by doing more consistently what they had managed to do only imperfectly.

In other words, Austin learnt from Prichard and Moore the art of philosophical criticism, but he thought of himself as having developed and radicalized this art so that it could now be turned against his own teachers. By Austin's lights, the admirable striving for non-dogmatic, unprejudiced clarity stands in internal conflict with many of Moore's and Prichard's most cherished views. According to Austin, doing full justice to what is most valuable in Moore's and Prichard's thinking therefore means rejecting many of the ideas that they themselves were most concerned to defend.[12]

---

[11] The classic description of these meetings is Warnock (1973). Among the regular participants were Paul Grice, R. M. Hare, H. L. A. Hart, David Pears, Peter Strawson, G. J. Warnock, Anthony Woozley, and J. O. Urmson.

[12] Lacey describes the relation between Austin's long-time discussion partner Herbert Hart and his teacher, H. W. B. Joseph (who, besides Prichard, was the most important realist at Oxford, albeit with a strongly Platonist bent), in similarly 'paradoxical' terms: 'Ironically it was Joseph, the man who must have felt most betrayed by Herbert's later turn from Platonism and espousal of the new linguistic philosophy, who

3. Austin and philosophy

At this point it is impossible to resist raising a related but rather unwieldy question that some commentators prefer not to consider at all, and which others tend to answer in one of two seemingly contradictory ways. The question is how Austin's mature thinking is related, not to a couple of teachers whose influence can be comparatively clearly identified, but to Western philosophy at large. Some say, with Juliet Floyd, that Austin 'hoped that philosophy teachers would teach something different, and differently, from much of what they had taught before. [. . .] He really believed, and more or less said, that most philosophers were just making mistakes and wasting students' time' (Floyd 2006: 140). Others would agree with Antony Flew that Austin's philosophy 'was not so new [. . .] as to constitute an abandonment of the activity pursued by the men of old' (Flew 1986: 80), and with J. O. Urmson that

[w]hat he conceived of as the central task, the careful elucidation of the forms and concepts of ordinary language [. . .] was, as Austin himself was well aware, not new but characteristic of countless philosophers from Socrates to G. E. Moore. [. . .] there was nothing essentially novel in Austin's philosophical aims; what was new was the skill, the rigor, and the patience with which he pursued these aims. (Urmson 1969: 23–4)

What is difficult here is that Austin's work seems to lend itself to either sort of interpretation. There seems to be something right both in Flew's and Urmson's claim that what Austin does is in an important sense similar to what others have done before, and in Floyd's claim that he is doing something very different from what earlier philosophers have done. Still it appears as if at least one of these readings must be wrong—for aren't they straightforwardly incompatible?

On second thoughts, things look less straightforward. The sense of incompatibility seems based on a superficial conception of how philosophical influence and criticism can function. In the previous section, an explanation was given of how Austin could have been both strongly influenced by and deeply critical of Moore and Prichard. His relation to Western philosophy at large can be conceived along similar lines. It was precisely by taking the traditional philosophical virtues of carefulness and clarity fully seriously that Austin claimed to be able to reach his subversive conclusions, undermining the tradition from within by taking its own alleged ideals *ad notam*, so to speak.

Austin conceived much of Western philosophy in its various forms, from grandiose idealism to tough-minded logical positivism, as being vitiated by the dogmatic, unquestioned, and often even unnoticed adherence to various oversimplified schemas of thought. As Simon Glendinning emphasizes in his contribution to this volume, Austin thought the function of such schematization was not to force everyone to agree unflinchingly on one single position, but, more subtly, to create a framework for the

helped to inspire him with the passion for clarity, accuracy, and detail which the linguistic approach promised to satisfy' (Lacey 2004: 27).

determination of a limited space of *possible* positions—positions that will then appear like the only ones over which one can meaningfully disagree.

A standard way of creating such a closed dialectical space is by invoking tidy dichotomies, thereby restricting the philosophical field of vision to theses and their anti-theses. But more complex patterns are also possible, and by the intermingling of various schemas the landscape of available options can become bewilderingly complex. Yet, according to Austin, the schematic, artificial character remains. And this schematic character is seductive because it provides philosophical discussions with a seemingly satisfying cogency. Even if we disagree, we are still players of the same tidy game, and it seems we can therefore agree on what our disagreement consists in and on how we should go about in resolving it. According to Austin, however, this apparent cogency is artificially created and hence achieved at the expense of genuine significance. His worry is precisely that philosophers tend to distort their own admirable ideals of clarity and rational argument by such premature schematizing. They are seduced into thinking that the formally rigorous though empty moves made within such a framework are what rational argumentation should look like, and that the oversimplified claims or analyses that come out of such argumentation are in fact prime examples of philosophical lucidity.

So, Austin may be read as trying to safeguard the ideals of clarity and rational argumentation precisely by exposing how this sort of imposed regimentation actually closes off and makes us blind to routes of investigation that might lead to genuine progress. He is trying to disentangle the ideals of clarity and rationality, central to Western thought, from the perhaps equally central but nonetheless misguided tendency toward premature schematization.

Now Flew and Urmson are certainly right that he is not the first philosopher whose work has tended toward such a goal. Part of the greatness of the great philosophers consists precisely in their exposing and criticizing hitherto unquestioned assumptions about what philosophical positions are available and what lines of argument can rationally be pursued. However, Austin can be read as suggesting that most such critics did not fully resist the temptation to oversimplify, but instead tended to replace one simplistic schema by another. By contrast, what Austin wants is to make us realize that we need not confine ourselves within *any* of those different frameworks of possibilities that various philosophers have thought of as compulsory and exhaustive. He wants consistently to disentangle the ideals of clarity and rational argumentation from the tendency to oversimplify. And it is perhaps not surprising if in this process of disentanglement, the ideals themselves will so to speak shed their traditional philosophical skins and take on a somewhat different, seemingly 'non-philosophical' appearance. Freed from their confinement within artificial frameworks, clarification and rational argumentation may look too unprincipled, too banal, or too philological for the traditional philosophical imagination to be willing to recognize them as properly philosophical at all.

At this point, we can begin to understand the rationale behind Austin's view that philosophy should proceed from ordinary language. His sense seems to have been that the sort of cogency that reflection on ordinary language can provide is *not* artificial in the sense indicated above. According to Austin, established linguistic practices do not just give us a well-structured but empty game of philosophical argumentation and counter-argumentation. Rather, the way ordinary language is anchored in our real-life circumstances and needs—the way it has developed from and become shaped by those circumstances and needs—ensures that there is something of substantial significance here that we can 'really understand and operate with'. He believed that it is precisely by contrasting such organically developed practices with the frameworks invoked by philosophers that we can reveal the latter's artificiality and arbitrariness.

But what, more precisely, does this mean? This is a very difficult question to answer. A satisfactory response would have to be based on detailed investigations of concrete instances of Austin's philosophical practice—investigations of a sort that several of the contributions to this volume provide. What I will do here is only to gesture at some main sources of perplexity. To begin with, as is often pointed out, Austin cannot be ascribed a conception of ordinary language as sacrosanct or as totally uncontaminated by philosophical views or theories. It would indeed be ironic if he had believed that one can abandon the philosophical tendency to dichotomize by invoking a new grand dichotomy between bad philosophical language (to be eradicated) and the good old vernacular (to be cherished and protected). In fact, Austin is well aware that everyday patterns of use might prove insufficient to handle various practical and theoretical needs that can arise, and that such ordinary forms of usage might therefore have to be revised or abandoned. He also notes that 'superstition and error and fantasy of all kinds do become incorporated in ordinary language', and that 'even "ordinary" language will often have become infected with the jargon of extinct theories, and our own prejudices too' (1979: 185, 182).

So it is clearly no part of Austin's conception that established habits of language use are to be just uncritically accepted and invoked as definite touchstones in the investigations of philosophical problems. Nor is it true to say that his thinking is 'resolutely anti-technical and anti-theoretical' (Hurka 2004: 249). His openness to the introduction of technical terms and models has already been mentioned. It is equally clear that he viewed the construction of theories as a highly desirable form of intellectual activity. In his famous image of philosophy as 'the initial central sun, seminal and tumultuous' which from time to time 'throws off some portion of itself to take station as a science, a planet, cool and well regulated', the latter state of coolness and regulation certainly figures as something that is worth striving for. Right after this comparison he even expresses the hope that 'the next century may see the birth, through the joint labours of philosophers, grammarians, and numerous other students of language, of a true and comprehensive *science of language*' (1979: 232, original emphasis).

Such brief and suggestive statements and analogies leave many questions unanswered. It remains an open issue what, exactly, Austin's conception of the relations between philosophy, ordinary language, and theory-construction amounts to. Clearly, much of his own work is being done on the tumultuous philosophical sun, rather than on some cool, scientific planet. His aim seems often to be to cool hot things down, perhaps as *preparation* for theory-construction. He would clearly regard it as a grave mistake to be impatient in this process and start theorizing prematurely, acting as if the relevant portion of the sun has *already* cooled off and taken station as a science. On the other hand, it is not clear that the two forms of activity—the preparatory clarification of established usage and the construction of theories—can be neatly separated, if Austin's just mentioned refusal to invoke an entirely sharp dichotomy between ordinary language and scientific theory is strictly thought through.

Warnock at one place says that Austin's conception of the philosophical significance of ordinary language 'is really quite simple' (Warnock 1969: 12). One aim of the present section has been to convey the opposite view—to provide some sense of how *difficult* it is to achieve a clear understanding of the character and point of Austin's philosophical procedures. It has to be admitted that his writings lend themselves to very different understandings of where he is going and what he is leaving behind. The aim here has not been to give a detailed account of his approach and its relation to more traditional kinds of philosophizing, but only to give the reader some idea of the vexed issues that such an account would have to address.

It is an interesting fact about Austin's work that it is hard to imagine a reading of it that is truly helpful and which at the same time just ignores these questions. All the contributors, including those whose main focus is on some much more specific philosophical point, have found it necessary to attend to these issues in one way or another. It is true that Austin himself seems to have found such philosophizing about his philosophy dubious or at least not very illuminating; he famously referred to his own attempts in this direction as 'cackle' (1979: 189). However, as long as those habits of thinking that Austin is criticizing retain their attraction, the character of his proce-dures, and their puzzling capacity both to engage with and differ from inquiries of a more paradigmatically philosophical kind—a capacity whose nature is the main theme of Glendinning's paper—will presumably make such 'cackling' an unavoidable element in the reception of his thought.

4. Austin's legacy

Given the difficulty of understanding exactly what Austin is trying to achieve in philosophy, it should not come as a surprise that those who take themselves to have learned something from him diverge substantially in their views of what he means and how his ideas are to be appropriated. Nonetheless, one can hardly avoid being astonished by the enormously different ways in which people have read and tried to make use of his work.

The most spectacular manifestation of such difference is the famous clash between John Searle and Jacques Derrida over Austin in the journal *Glyph* in the seventies, a painfully vivid illustration of the sort of acrimony that such different readings can excite. I will not say much about this particular fight as there is little to add to what has already been said elsewhere.[13] It is, however, worth mentioning that the influence of Derrida's reading and criticism of Austin has been considerable, indeed much greater than is visible from the confines of mainstream analytic philosophy where Derrida's discussion of Austin is often simply brushed aside as ridiculous. Stanley Fish's siding with Derrida played an important role (Fish 1980, 1989), but in the last couple of decades a more important figure has been Judith Butler. Combining Derrida's 'rewriting' of Austin (Osborne and Segal 1994: 33) with ideas from Michel Foucault about how power works through discourse, Butler's book *Gender Trouble* (1990) launched a notion of performativity that has played an enormously important role in theoretical debates within many branches of the humanities during the last two decades.

This use of Austin gives support to the claim that his influence has been greatest outside philosophy departments. However, it is a striking fact that in most work done by performativity theorists within Gay and Lesbian studies, cultural studies, cinema studies, post-colonial studies, and so on, there is little direct engagement with Austin's writings. This inheritance of Austin is very much second or third hand, via Derrida, or via Derrida and Butler. In fact, *Gender Trouble* itself contains no discussion of Austin's actual texts. Some important theorists, such as Shoshana Felman and Eve Kosofsky Sedgwick, do engage directly and in original ways with Austin's writings, and the same is true of Butler in some of her later works (Felman 1983; Sedgwick 1993, 2003; Butler 1997). However, it remains true of most people in these fields that they do not reflect in any detail on how their own use of the term 'performative' and its cognates is related to Austin's employment of such notions.

If the average analytic philosopher knows little about the Derridean and Butlerian ways of inheriting Austin, he is of course well acquainted with Searle's developments of Austin's ideas. Together with Paul Grice's 1967 lecture series, 'Logic and Conversation' (Grice 1989: 3–143), Searle's *Speech Acts* from 1969 set much of the agenda for subsequent developments of speech act theory and pragmatics in linguistics and in the philosophy of language. In fact, Searle's and Grice's importance for Austin's legacy in analytic philosophy can hardly be overrated, and, for all their mutual disagreements, their role in this story is similarly double-edged. On the one hand, they are both deeply influenced by and have great respect for Austin. On the other hand, it seems fair to say that their works have contributed more than anything else to the general sense that Austin's endeavours have become outdated. The spirit of both Searle's and Grice's engagements with Austin's philosophy is encapsulated in the idea that the greatest tribute one may pay to a theoretical pioneer is to criticize and develop the theory so that his pioneering efforts become obsolete.[14]

---

[13] Three interestingly different assessments are found in Cavell (1994), Glendinning (2001), and Glock (2008).

[14] The tendency to read Austin via Searle and Grice is strong also among philosophers outside the domain of analytic philosophy narrowly conceived. For example, even if Jürgen Habermas devotes much space in his

In sum, even if performativity theory and speech act theory are by far the most extensive and influential areas in which Austinian notions are of central importance today, Austin's own position in relation to these fields is mostly that of a dead predecessor rather than a living source of influence. Again, there are exceptions. The works of Felman and Sedgwick have already been mentioned. Within speech act theory and pragmatics, William Alston and Marina Sbisà are examples of writers who treat Austin as a philosopher to think with, rather than as a respectable but obsolete precursor (see, for example, Alston 2000; and Sbisà 2001, 2006, 2007). Nonetheless, if we want to gain a fuller understanding of how Austin's philosophy matters to contemporary thought, it will be necessary to look beyond its Derridean–Butlerian and Searlean–Gricean offspring.

Two other very significant examples of Austin's impact on areas at the interface between philosophy and neighbouring disciplines should be mentioned. First, there is the deep and direct influence he had on H. L. A. Hart, and thereby on legal theory in general and the post-war development of legal positivism in particular. (Classic works here are Hart 1961 and 1968, where Austin's influence is much more pervasive than the relatively few references may be taken to indicate. For an interesting account of Austin's influence on Hart, see Lacey 2004. A recent attempt to apply Austin's philosophy to legal theory is Yeager 2006.)

Second, there is Austin's impact on Quentin Skinner's development of a 'contextualist', 'Cambridge school' approach in intellectual history in general and the history of political thought in particular. According to Skinner, 'if we are to write the history of ideas in a properly historical style, we need to situate the texts we study within such intellectual contexts and frameworks of discourse as enable us to recognise what their authors were *doing* in writing them' (Skinner 2002, vii; original emphasis). Skinner's way of spelling out the 'doing' that we need to recognize, and the methods by means of which can come to recognize it, is deeply influenced by Austin's discussions of language, action, and intentionality. (Austin's impact is particularly visible in Skinner 2002, especially in chapters 5 and 6.)

The Theory of Communicative Action ostensibly discussing Austin, he freely acknowledges that 'I shall leave aside the development that speech act theory underwent in the hands of Austin himself [. . .] and take as my point of departure the interpretation that Searle has given to this theory' (Habermas 1984: 439, n. 32). Karl-Otto Apel's use of speech act theory is also influenced by Searle's interpretation, even if both he and Habermas have criticized what they regard as 'intentionalist' tendencies in Searle's later works (Apel 1991, Habermas 1991).

It seems that in the long run, Searle's and Grice's respectful criticisms have played a more important role for Austin's mummification process than the earlier vehement attacks on him by people such as Gellner, Russell, Ayer, Bergmann, and others. (The *locus classicus* here is Gellner 1959, with its preface by Russell (1959). An outsider's description of this quarrel over ordinary language philosophy, and of the Oxford scene more generally, can be found in Mehta 1963.) Those vehement attacks are indeed of 'merely historical interest' for us today. None of the contributors to this volume seem to see any use in dwelling on or responding to them, finding such polemics simply unhelpful if one is genuinely interested in understanding what is and is not valuable in Austin's philosophy.

However, if one is searching for a contemporary philosophical debate in which Austin still figures as a living and direct source of influence, an even better place to look is at the discussion of pornography and free speech. An igniting event took place in 1984, when Catharine MacKinnon and Andrea Dworkin tried to enact a civil rights ordinance in Indianapolis that would have made pornographers and those selling their wares vulnerable to civil action. The MacKinnon–Dworkin argument, which was ultimately unconvincing to an appeals court, was based in part on the claim that pornography is in effect a speech act that does not just *cause* the subordination of women but *constitutes* a kind of subordination. In the nineties, the debate took a decisively Austinian turn due to a series of papers by Jennifer Hornsby and Rae Langton (Hornsby 1993, 1995, 2000; Langton 1993; Hornsby and Langton 1998). Hornsby and Langton use Austin in their attempts to lend philosophical rigour and precision to MacKinnon's and Dworkin's argument, which some philosophers had argued was incoherent (see, for example, Parent 1990). Even if Hornsby and Langton differ on details, their basic and shared idea is that the alleged discrimination is not just a perlocutionary effect of the publication of pornography. Rather, they spell out MacKinnon's and Dworkin's claim as follows. In publishing pornography one performs an *illocutionary* act of subordination, and one also creates an environment in which the protests women may want to issue against sexual discrimination and violence will misfire. In these ways, the publication of pornography not just causes but constitutes discrimination of women. According to Hornsby and Langton, this is a perfectly coherent thesis that should be taken quite seriously.

Many different objections have been raised against this analysis (a collection of central papers is Dwyer 1995; more recent contributions include Jacobson 1995, Bird 2002, Bauer 2006, Saul 2006, Bianchi 2008, Mikkola 2008, De Gaynesford 2009). The details and validity of these objections need not concern us here. Rather, the relevant point is that most participants in this debate treat Austin differently from how he is usually treated by speech act theorists and performativity theorists. Within the pornography debate most participants actually read and discuss what Austin says, treating his writings as texts from which there is still something important to learn.

There seems to be no other similarly extensive debate in contemporary philosophy where Austin plays such a central role. However, there are important individual thinkers for whom his philosophy is of fundamental significance and very much alive. Stanley Cavell comes to mind here. His engagement with Austin's work is characterized by a deep clash of philosophical temperaments, and often takes the form of profound objections. What Cavell takes to be of sustaining value in Austin's work is not so much his specific philosophical theses as certain questions or themes, the forgetting of which Cavell regards not just as an accidental feature of contemporary philosophy but as a natural tendency and danger of all philosophizing. Austin's emphasis on language as something human beings use in real-life situations, his sense that it is characteristic of philosophy to overlook and distort the intricacy, adaptability, and contextual sensitivity of this usage by imposing preconceived and much cruder schemes, and his insistence that defying such schematization does *not* mean defying articulation altogether—these are all themes which are central to Cavell's thinking too, albeit ones that he develops in his own, sometimes rather un-Austinian fashion. Cavell maintains that the philosophical ignorance or falsification of our life with language— what he calls 'the flight from the ordinary'—is not a matter of mere carelessness or impatience, but an irredeemable human temptation. This gives rise to a more complex notion of 'the ordinary' than what seems possible to find in Austin, as something that cannot be neatly distinguished from the will to philosophize but contains a pull towards its own distortion (Cavell 1979, 2005; Gustafsson 2005).[15]

Another philosopher who for a long time has insisted that there are still important things to be learned from Austin is Charles Travis. In Travis's case, the Austinian inheritance takes the form of a questioning of presumptions central to much analytic philosophy of language. For example, Travis has argued that the radical sort of contextualism that he finds in Austin's work defuses Grice's claim that Austin's way of philosophizing often ignores the distinction between what is said and what is implicated. According to Travis, Grice's rejection of Austinian procedures is question begging, since the Gricean distinction between what is said and what is implicated presupposes that the context-sensitivity of natural language is restricted in ways that Austin would not admit (Travis 1985, 1991, 2008). In making this sort of point, Travis has not been entirely alone. For example, François Recanati is another important figure who has made Austinian objections against Grice (Recanati 1994), even if the so-called 'meaning eliminativist' conception that Recanati associates with Austin (Recanati 2004: 146ff.) is one which Travis rejects both as an interpretation of Austin and as a view in its own right.

Travis has also done much to clarify how he thinks the conception of language as pervaded by context-sensitivity shapes Austin's views on other issues such as knowledge and truth. In the last few years, Travis's Austin-inspired work on perception has gained much attention (see, for example, Travis 2004).

A third thinker to be mentioned here is Mark Kaplan. In a series of papers published over the last couple of decades, he has been clarifying and defending an Austinian approach to issues in epistemology, explaining its critical potential in relation to the views of Chisholm, Sosa, Stroud, and others (Kaplan 1991, 2000, 2006, 2008). Perhaps more than anyone else, Kaplan stresses Austin's openness to revision of established linguistic and justificatory practices. Being a defender of Bayesianism in epistemology and in the philosophy of science, Kaplan himself advocates such revision. What he takes to be the real target of Austin's criticism is rather the Chisholmian sort of project, characteristic of much contemporary epistemology, of looking for a theory of justification deprived of any real consequences for how everyday and scientific inquiry should actually be done. It is worth noting here the difference between Kaplan's and

[15] Cavell's recent autobiography (Cavell 2010) contains some very fine sketches of Austin, the man and the philosopher; see, in particular, pp. 322–6.

Cavell's conceptions: there is in Kaplan's work no trace of Cavell's view that the tendency toward such inert theorizing is in a sense made irresistible by our ordinary ways of talking and acting.[16]

In this introduction, a central theme has been the mummification of Austin's philosophy within mainstream Anglophone philosophy. It is appropriate, however, to end the discussion of Austin's legacy by qualifying precisely that point. It might be too early to tell, but perhaps the years around 1990 marked the low ebb of the reception of Austin. Since then, there have been signs that a revival is going on. One such sign is Hilary Putnam's 1994 John Dewey Lectures, where Austin plays a central role (Putnam 1994). Even more telling is the fact that Austin seems to be taken seriously again by many relatively young philosophers. Besides writings by the contributors to this volume, one might mention such diverse examples as Quassim Cassam's work in epistemology (Cassam 2007), Alice Crary's application of Austin to problems in moral philosophy (Crary 2007), Eugen Fischer's invoking Austin as an exemplary 'therapeutic' philosopher (Fischer 2005, 2011), M. G. F. Martin's work on perception (Martin, forthcoming), and José Medina's cross-disciplinary attempt to develop a new form of contextualism by interweaving Austin's philosophy with Wittgensteinian, neo-pragmatist, and feminist ideas (Medina 2006).[17]

Then there is also the fact that in recent years several recognizably Austinian themes have gained prominence in the philosophical discussion. Consider the enormous interest in the phenomenon of context-sensitivity. In this literature, Austin is often referred to as a precursor. One may quarrel with this reading of Austin—as Avner Baz does in his contribution to this volume, arguing that Austin's contextualism is quite different from most contemporary varieties—and one may note that few contemporary contextualists make any substantial use of Austin's work. Nevertheless, it would be surprising if the heated debates over contextualist views would not be conducive to a renewed interest in Austin's philosophy.

A second example is the extensive discussion of disjunctivist responses to the argument from illusion, in epistemology and in the philosophy of perception. Here, *Sense and Sensibilia* is sometimes referred to as an early example of a disjunctivist

---

[16] A fourth figure worth mentioning here is Burton Dreben, who knew Austin personally and regarded 'Other Minds' as one of the greatest philosophical essays of the twentieth century. Even if the Austinian influence is not immediately evident from his few published writings, in his teaching Dreben would convey to many students how important and radical he took Austin's challenge to more traditional forms of philosophy to be (Juliet Floyd, personal communication).

[17] This revival of interest in Austin goes hand in hand with a revival of interest in so-called ordinary language philosophy and its two other main representatives, Ryle and the later Wittgenstein. In the last decade, it has become clearer and clearer that the heated and extensive debate over whether Wittgenstein's *Tractatus* is to be read 'resolutely' or not is also a debate over how to interpret his later works (see, for example, several of the papers in Ammereller and Fischer 2004, and Kölbel and Weiss 2004). Examples of a renewed interest in Ryle include Tanney (2009) and Dolby (forthcoming). It would be very interesting to try to bring all this recent research together, in order to gain a new and better understanding of the character and significance of ordinary language philosophy, and of the similarities and differences between Austin, Ryle, and Wittgenstein.

analysis. Again, this reading may be questioned, and it is true that most contemporary disjunctivists do not make use of Austin's work. Still, the debate may well motivate people to actually read his texts and see what he has to say. (An interesting sketch of Austin's significance for contemporary philosophy of perception, in relation to the disjunctivist debate, is Schwartz 2004.)

A third example is the recent methodological debate, sparked by criticisms of the reliance on 'intuitions' in analytic philosophy. Linked to this criticism is an explosion of studies in so-called experimental philosophy where philosophical claims about what is intuitive and what is not are tested against how people actually respond in polls (a helpful introduction to this field is Knobe and Nichols 2008). It would certainly be absurd to describe Austin as an early proponent of such an experimental methodology. Indeed, his mode of investigation is sometimes described as one particularly pertinacious variety of the sort of armchair philosophy that the experimentalists reject. But that description does not seem fair either. In fact, Austin's emphasis on the importance of group discussions in philosophy, his criticism of the use of outlandish thought-experiments in philosophical arguments, and his insistence that reflections on what we should say in everyday cases require very detailed descriptions of the relevant speech situations, suggests that he shares some of the concerns of the experimentalists (Alexander and Weinberg 2007; Hansen, MS). What we have in Austin seems like an interesting and developable attempt to navigate between the rightly criticized habit of armchair intuition-mongering and the equally problematic reduction of linguistic practices to response-patterns charted in poll-based statistics.

Finally, it deserves to be repeated that the hope for an Austin renaissance expressed above is not the hope for an uncritical acceptance of Austin's views or of his way of doing philosophy. There is fortunately no indication that this sort of uncritical attitude is on the increase. What might be gaining ground is a sense that Austin's philosophy is still worth engaging with, critically and seriously. That is the sort of development that this book is meant to promote.

5. Overview of the contributions

The contributions are thematically organized. The first paper develops an original account of Austin's way of philosophizing. Then come four intricately interrelated and interestingly different papers on epistemological topics. The two final papers both discuss the relation between Austin and Frege, bringing up issues in the philosophy of language and logic that are rarely discussed in the secondary literature on Austin.

In 'Unmasking the Tradition', Simon Glendinning ponders the relation between Austin's procedures and the tradition of Western philosophy, as that tradition comes into view in Austin's own work. According to Glendinning, Austin's approach involves an intriguing sort of balancing act. On the one hand, Austin's aim is to free us from traditionally invoked frameworks of thought. This means that his mode of criticism has to be sufficiently distanced from those conceptual maelstroms not to be drawn into them. On the other hand, Austin's criticism cannot just isolate itself from traditional philosophical thinking. If so, it would lose all contact with it and become irrelevant. Thus, Austin must find a way between immersion and isolation. As Glendinning puts it, Austin has to situate his inquiries on the 'margins' of traditional philosophy. Instead of addressing the logic of statements, he explores performatives; instead of addressing the possibility of knowledge, he explores perception; instead of addressing the logic of reasons, he explores excuses; and so on and so forth. Glendinning explores this strategy in detail and argues that it is widely misrepresented and misunderstood, not only by critics such as Jonathan Bennett, but also by more friendly readers like Warnock and Cavell.

In the first of the four papers on epistemological issues, Mark Kaplan discusses how Austin can deal with the sceptical challenge posed by what is nowadays called 'the argument from ignorance'. Visiting the zoo, I claim to know that there is a zebra in the enclosure in front of me. But what if someone challenges my claim, arguing that I have done nothing to show that the animal is not just a cleverly painted mule? According to such a sceptic, I do not know that the animal is not a painted mule; and, if I do not know that the animal is not a painted mule, then I do not know that it is a zebra; so, by *modus ponens*, I do not know that the animal is a zebra.

As Kaplan notes, Austin thinks this challenge is faulty. But wherein lies the mistake? According to Kaplan, it is not enough to say that Austin thinks the sceptic would need some concrete positive reason to appropriately bring up the suspicion that the animal is just a painted mule. This is right, as far as it goes. But, Kaplan argues, it does not suffice to solve the problem. For Austin would still acknowledge that I cannot be said to know that the animal is not a painted mule. And it is hard to see how Austin could deny the conditional, that if I do not know that the animal is not a painted mule then I do not know that it is a zebra. But then, how can he avoid the sceptic's conclusion?

Kaplan's answer is that even if Austin acknowledges that I cannot be said to know that the animal is not a painted mule, he is not thereby committed to the claim that I do *not* know that the animal is not a painted mule. The key idea here is that the distinction between what one knows and what one does not know is not exhaustive. 'I do not know that *p*' is not simply the negation of 'I know that *p*'. Rather, there are instances of '*p*' such that my relation to those instances is neither one of knowing nor one of not knowing. Such cases are similar to knowledge in that I am entitled to act on *p*, but different from knowledge in that I cannot prove that *p* is true. These are things that are *in deed* not doubted—and *rightly* so—but for which we are nonetheless unable to give a proof if someone asks for it. According to Kaplan, it is a central idea of Austin's that such practical entitlements can exist even in the absence of an ability to prove the relevant belief.

Adam Leite offers a different interpretation of Austin's epistemological views. Drawing mainly on *Sense and Sensibilia*—or, rather, on unpublished notes from Austin's 1958 presentation of those lectures at Berkeley, notes that differ considerably from the published version—Leite discusses Austin's rejection of global sceptical arguments.

In particular, Leite considers the apparently question begging character of Austin's rejection of the Cartesian Dream Argument. Against the sceptic who makes use of this argument, Austin claims that there are in fact phenomenological differences between dream experiences and ordinary waking experiences, and that I can show that I am currently not dreaming by noting that my experiences are not dream-like. Leite shows in detail why such reliance on empirical background information about what dreams are like is not question begging, given certain general Austinian views on what it is for something to constitute a reason for believing something else. First, if there is no pro tanto reason in favour of a certain hypothesis—if the hypothesis expresses only a 'conceptual' or 'metaphysical' possibility—it constitutes no genuine reason to revise established beliefs. Second, epistemic priority relations are not determined once and for all and *a priori*, but depend upon the circumstances. Even in cases where there is some pro tanto reason in favour of a hypothesis, we have to look at the details of the case in order to become clear about what can and what cannot be used as arguments against the hypothesis. And, Leite argues, if we look at the claim that I am currently dreaming, there is a pro tanto reason in favour of it only if the dreaming is taken to be of the ordinary kind, viz. as involving experiences that differ phenomenologically from waking experiences. And if the dreaming is taken to be of the ordinary kind, we *can* without begging the question reject the hypothesis simply by noting that our experiences do in fact have the characteristic phenomenological features of waking experiences.

Leite generalizes this result so as to cover other global sceptical hypotheses, such as those about evil demons and brains in vats. According to Leite's Austin, it is possible to reject such hypotheses by noting that there are in fact no evil demons, and that we do not yet have the technology to create brains in vats. As Leite points out, this challenges a widespread conception of the task of epistemology found in the works of such prominent contemporary philosophers as Barry Stroud, Marie McGinn, and Laurence BonJour. Leite also notes that less global forms of sceptical arguments, such as the one with the painted mule, can be treated along similar lines. This puts his interpretation in explicit conflict with Kaplan's. According to Leite's Austin, just as the mere possibility that we are dreaming does not make it false to say that we know that we are not dreaming, the mere possibility that the animal in front of us is a painted mule does not make it false to say that we know that the animal is not a painted mule.

Benjamin McMyler's contribution has been mentioned earlier, and his account of the analogy between saying 'I know' and saying 'I promise' has been briefly sketched. What McMyler does in his paper is to explore the connection Austin sees between knowledge by testimony and the problem of other minds. According to McMyler, Austin thinks of testimony as a fundamental mode of access to the minds of other people, and his account of this mode of access emphasizes not only its non-inferential character, but, most of all, its irreducibly social nature. More precisely, McMyler's Austin thinks that testifying, like promising, is a matter of entering into a special kind of relationship with one's audience—a relationship characterized by the speaker's taking on responsibility for his words, and by the audience's acknowledging that responsibility. If I tell Paul, 'I know that Gloria was at the party', I thereby give Paul the entitlement to tell others that he knows that Gloria was at the party, and to act on that piece of information; and if someone challenges Paul's claim to know that Gloria was at the party, he has the right to defer that challenge back to me, expecting me to be able to provide an appropriate defence.

McMyler's Austin thinks of our preparedness to enter into such social relationships of responsibility and dependence as a fundamental feature of our lives as minded, language-using creatures. Moreover, he thinks of the philosophical problem of other minds as emerging from a theoretical unwillingness to fully acknowledge the necessity of such dependence. Furthermore, he thinks that this problem gains its depth from a sense of loneliness bound up precisely with this sort of unwillingness. If this is right, the philosophical tendency to try to solve the problem of other minds by reducing the reliance on testimony to the reliance on other epistemological sources, such as inference or perception, will in the end be counterproductive. Rather than liberating us from our worry, such a reductionist strategy will make it worse.

In his 'Knowing Knowing (that Such and Such)', Avner Baz criticizes the widespread idea that contemporary epistemological contextualism constitutes a continuation and development of Austin's most significant insights about language and knowledge. Baz mentions Keith DeRose's observation that Austin often seems to avoid the question whether epistemological claims are *true* or *false*, in favour of characterizations such as 'right', 'within reason', 'silly', 'outrageous', and so forth. According to Baz, it is no coincidence that this feature of Austin's discussion makes DeRose uncomfortable. For, Baz argues, it marks a very significant difference between Austin's philosophical viewpoint and that of DeRose and his contextualist peers. Indeed, Baz claims that this difference is much deeper than the difference between the contextualists and their anti-contextualist foes. According to Baz, the contextualist and the anti-contextualist both take it for granted that it is always a sensible and important task to determine the truth-value of an epistemological claim. What they disagree about is the extent to which contextual features are relevant for such determination. By contrast, Baz takes Austin to be questioning the shared presupposition that such determination is always in place. In fact, Baz claims, Austin thinks the philosophical demand for such determination itself means that the real-life significance of epistemological claims disappears from view. By agreeing with their alleged opponents about the general viability of asking whether epistemological claims are true or false, the contextualists miss the way in which such claims are anchored in the actual needs and circumstances of use. According to Baz, the contextualists bring in context-dependence too late in the discussion, for the very problem they want to solve is already a fundamentally de-contextualized, artificial question. Baz argues that the debate over this question is bound to end in stalemate: both sides rely on their favourite 'intuitions', but those intuitions have no clear connection with anything that matters to us outside the philosophical seminar room.

It is interesting to read Baz's paper together with Kaplan's and Leite's. These contributions work out in full detail three sharply different interpretations of how the contexts of real-life knowledge seeking matter to Austin's treatment of epistemological worries. Any future discussion of Austin's way with scepticism will have to situate itself in relation to these three interpretative possibilities.

However, the appropriation of Austin by contemporary epistemological contextualism figures in Baz's paper only as an example of a more general tendency to domesticate his philosophical radicalism. More precisely, Baz is reacting against the view that what is valuable in Austin has to be made compatible with the idea that the basic function of our words is to serve as instruments for *representation*. According to Baz, this is precisely to repress Austin's most challenging insight: that what we illocutionarily do with our words does not belong to a separable 'pragmatic' level of linguistic practice, but matters to the very meanings or concepts that our words serve to express.

Charles Travis's contribution is a detailed investigation of Austin's claim that statements and their truth, as philosophers have traditionally conceived them, are abstractions. Travis approaches Austin's conception by comparing it with what Frege has to say about truth. He notes that both Austin's and Frege's views are deep and persuasive, while also seemingly very different. The most immediately striking contrast is between Frege's and Austin's conceptions of what it is that constitutes the fundamental sort of truth-bearer. For Frege, anything that is perceivable is excluded from playing that sort of fundamental role. Instead, he thinks questions of truth and falsity arise in the first instance with respect to thoughts, and thoughts are not the sort of entities that can be perceived. By contrast, Austin thinks statements are what is most fundamentally true or false, and he thinks of the making of a statement as a concrete, observable historic event: it is an utterance made by a speaker to an audience in a particular, real-life situation.

According to Travis, what is really at stake here is how to understand the relation between the conceptual and the non-conceptual. In particular, the crucial issue is how to understand the sort of *generality* that characterizes the conceptual. Frege and Austin agree that the conceptual somehow looks beyond the particular case. If I say of a cat that it is on the mat, what I say of it may also be said by others, it may be true of other cats, and it may be true on other occasions of utterance. But how is this looking beyond the particular case to be understood, more exactly? Frege thinks of it in terms of the generality of a function mapping objects onto truth-values, and his conception means that once the function is determined it will not be left open how to apply it in a particular case. By contrast, Austin rejects the very idea of such determinacy. For him, a concept does determine something, but what it determines leaves its application in particular cases negotiable. What if the cat is in a box with cat litter, which is on the mat? What if most of the cat's body is outside the mat? What if the mat is rolled up, the cat being inside the roll? According to Travis's Austin, no rule can determine whether such cases are instances of the cat's being on the mat or not. No Fregean function can relieve us from the need to employ our human, unregularizable sensitivity in applying the conceptual to the non-conceptual, taking into consideration the needs and circumstances of the particular situation. Determining truth-value is, in this sense, like determining other values: it requires virtues of the same sort as those needed in giving a fitting advice or making a just verdict.

But now, how different from Frege does this make Austin? Travis argues that the difference is surprisingly slight. He claims that Austin retains many of Frege's central insights, such as the indefinability of truth, the shareability of content, the notion of a fundamental distinction between the generality of the conceptual and particularity of the non-conceptual, and a notion of truth as a matter of how the conceptual stands towards the non-conceptual. Indeed, in the final section of his paper, Travis even suggests that Frege's and Austin's views can be fully reconciled, in consideration of the quite different philosophical purposes for which those views were originally proposed.

According to Travis, Austin makes the fact-value dichotomy collapse, in that he rejects the sort of contrast between questions of truth and questions of value that this dichotomy requires. In this connection, Travis quotes Austin's claim that truth and falsity do not stand for anything simple, but for 'a general *dimension* for being a right or proper thing to say as opposed to a wrong thing' (Austin 1975: 145). This notion of 'dimension' is puzzling and rarely discussed. Yet it seems important to Austin, since it recurs at central moments in his works. Jean-Philippe Narboux explores this aspect of Austin's philosophy, and argues that the concept of dimension is a key tool for him in his attack on the philosophical tendency to structure thought by invoking oversimplified conceptual patterns. According to Narboux, Austin charges traditional philosophy with having given a few selected words such as 'truth', 'meaningfulness', 'goodness', 'freedom', and 'reality', an overly exalted status. Narboux's Austin thinks this sort of 'onomatolatry' has made philosophers forget about and do violence to the significance of whole arrays of other terms of assessment that fulfil equally important functions. Thus, Narboux reads Austin as holding that the notions of truth and falsity belong to a dimension that also includes words such as 'precise', 'exact', 'accurate', 'rough', 'exaggerated', and 'vague', each playing its own particular role, and none of which is more fundamental than any other. Similarly, the notions of meaningfulness and meaninglessness are just two words in a dimension that also includes terms such as 'void', 'vitiated', and 'hollow'; the notions of acting 'freely' and 'not freely' belong to a dimension that also involves terms such as 'tactlessly', 'spontaneously', and 'clumsily'; and so on and so forth.

Like Glendinning, Narboux portrays Austin as someone who wants to draw our attention to areas of language that have been unjustifiably marginalized by traditional philosophy. And Narboux's Austin is no less radical than Glendinning's: He wants to shake the very foundations of traditional Western philosophy. There is, however, one sense in which Narboux's Austin *is* traditional: He is in certain respects a deeply *systematic* thinker. Indeed, Narboux claims that it is only by bringing out the systematic structure of Austin's method and conceptual apparatus—and in this sense 'read him as a classic'—that it becomes possible to see clearly the radical consequences of his criticism.

Like Travis, Narboux thinks Austin is indebted to Frege and argues that he must be read against the background of Frege's work. Unlike Travis, Narboux thinks that, in the end, the difference between Austin and Frege is nonetheless fundamental and irreconcilable. It is impossible here even to begin to pinpoint the complexities involved in the disagreement between Travis and Narboux. What is clear is that investigating this disagreement will force the reader to explore very deep strata of both Austin's and Frege's thinking.

At the beginning of this introduction, it was emphasized that the aim of the present collection is not to promote a new school of Austin interpretation. The just given survey substantiates this claim. It should have become clear that the book contains a variety of readings that hang together, not by way of mutual agreement, but by way of deeply interesting differences and penetrating disputes. Evidently, these papers are not the last but the first steps in a discussion that is meant to continue beyond this volume, and give rise to further and unexpected suggestions for how to understand and explore the contemporary significance of Austin's philosophy.[18]

Bibliography

Alston, W. P. (2000), *Illocutionary Acts and Sentence Meaning*, Ithaca, NY: Cornell University Press.

Alexander, J., and Weinberg, J. M. (2007), 'Analytic Epistemology and Experimental Philosophy', *Philosophy Compass* 2: 56–80.

Ammereller, E., and Fischer, E. (eds.) (2004), *Wittgenstein at Work: Method in the Philosophical Investigations*, London: Routledge.

Apel, K.-O. (1991), 'Is Intentionality more Basic than Linguistic Meaning?', in LePore and Van Gulick 1991: 31–55.

Austin, J. L. (1962), *Sense and Sensibilia*, Warnock, G. J. (ed.), Oxford: Oxford University Press.

——(1975), *How to Do Things with Words*, 2nd ed., Urmson, J. O., Sbisà, M. (eds.), Oxford: Clarendon Press.

——(1979), *Philosophical Papers*, 3rd ed., Urmson, J. O., Warnock, G. J. (eds.), Oxford: Oxford University Press.

Bauer, N. (2006), 'How to Do Things with Pornography', in Crary, A., Shieh, S. (eds.), *Reading Cavell*, London: Routledge, pp. 68–97.

Berlin, I., et al. (1973), *Essays on J. L. Austin*, Oxford: Clarendon Press.

——(1973), 'Austin and the Early Beginnings of Oxford Philosophy', in Berlin et al. 1973: 1–16.

---

[18] Annette Baier, Nancy Bauer, Avner Baz, Alice Crary, Nat Hansen, and Richard Sørli have all made useful comments on earlier versions of this introduction. Special thanks to James Conant, whose careful and encouraging criticisms of a much earlier draft helped me see how to structure and express my ideas about Austin and his legacy.

Berlin, I. (2006), 'I'm Going to Tamper with Your Beliefs a Little', *The Isaiah Berlin Virtual Library*, http://berlin.wolf.ox.ac.uk/lists/nachlass/imgoing.pdf Transcript by Hardy, H., from the film, 'I'm Going to Tamper with Your Beliefs a Little', directed by Chanan, M., and produced by Chanan, N. Production year: 1972. The film is available at http://berlin.wolf.ox.ac.uk/lists/broadcasts/index.html#tamper (accessed 26 April 2011).

Bianchi, C. (2008), 'Indexicals, Speech Acts and Pornography', *Analysis* 68: 310–16.

Bird, A. (2002), 'Illocutionary Silencing', *Pacific Philosophical Quarterly* 83: 1–15.

Bradley, F. H. (1883), *The Principles of Logic*, London: Oxford University Press.

Butler, J. (1990), *Gender Trouble: Feminism and the Subversion of Identity*, New York: Routledge.

——(1997), *Excitable Speech: A Politics of the Performative*, New York: Routledge.

Candlish, S. (2007), *The Russell/Bradley Dispute and Its Significance for Twentieth-Century Philosophy*, Houndmills Basingstoke: Palgrave Macmillan.

Carritt, E. F. (1948), 'Professor H. A. Prichard. Personal Recollections', *Mind* 57: 146–8.

Cassam, Q. (2007), *The Possibility of Knowledge*, Oxford: Oxford University Press.

Cavell, S. (1979), *The Claim of Reason*, Oxford: Oxford University Press.

——(1994), *A Pitch of Philosophy: Autobiographical Excercises*, Cambridge, MA: Harvard University Press.

——(2005), 'Passionate and Performative Utterance: Morals of Encounter', in Goodman, R. B. (ed.), *Contending with Stanley Cavell*, Oxford: Oxford University Press, pp. 177–98.

——(2010), *Little Did I Know. Excerpts from Memory*, Cambridge, MA: Harvard University Press.

Cheney, D. (ed.) (1971), *Broad's Critical Essays in Moral Philosophy*, London: George Allen and Unwin.

Collingwood, R. G. (1939), *An Autobiography*, Oxford: Clarendon Press.

Crary, A. (2002), 'The Happy Truth: J. L. Austin's *How To Do Things With Words*', *Inquiry* 45: 59–80.

——(2007), *Beyond Moral Judgment*, Cambridge, MA: Harvard University Press.

Culler, J. D. (1982), *On Deconstruction. Theory and Criticism after Structuralism*, London: Routledge and Kegan Paul.

Dancy, J. (2009), 'Harold Arthur Prichard', *Stanford Encyclopedia of Philosophy*, http://plato.stanford.edu/entries/prichard/ (accessed 26 April 2011).

De Gaynesford, M. (2009), 'Illocutionary Acts, Subordination and Silencing', *Analysis* 69: 488–90.

Derrida, J. (1988), *Limited Inc*, Evanston, IL: Northwestern University Press.

Dolby, D. (ed.) (forthcoming), *Ryle on Mind*, London: Palgrave MacMillan.

Dwyer, S. (ed.) (1995), *The Problem of Pornography*, Belmont, CA: Wadsworth.

Fann, K. T. (ed.) (1969), *Symposium on J. L. Austin*, London: Routledge and Kegan Paul.

Felman, S. (1983), *The Literary Speech Act: Don Juan with J. L. Austin, or Seduction in Two Languages*, Ithaca, NY: Cornell University Press.

Fischer, E. (2005), 'Austin on Sense-Data: Ordinary Language Analysis as "Therapy"', *Grazer Philosophische Studien*, 70: 67–99.

——(2011), *Philosophical Delusion and Its Therapy: Outline of a Philosophical Revolution*, London: Routledge.

Fish, S. (1980), 'How to Do Things With Austin and Searle: Speech-Act Theory and Literary Criticism', in his *Is There a Text in This Class? The Authority of Interpretative Communities*, Cambridge, MA: Harvard University Press, pp. 197–245.

——(1989), 'With Compliments to the Author: Reflections on Austin and Derrida', in his *Doing What Comes Naturally: Change, Rhetoric and the Practice of Theory in Literary and Legal Studies*, Durham, NC: Duke University Press, pp. 37–67.

Flew, A. (1986), 'Apologia pro Philosophia Mea', in Shanker, S. G. (ed.), *Philosophy in Britain Today*, London: Croom Helm, pp. 72–97.

Floyd, J. (2006), 'Homage to Vienna: Feyerabend on Wittgenstein (and Austin and Quine)', in Stadler, F., Fischer, K. R. (eds.), *Paul Feyerabend: Ein Philosoph aus Wien*, Wien: Springer, pp. 99–151.

Gellner, E. (1959), *Words and Things*, London: Victor Gollancz.

Glendinning, S. (2001), 'Inheriting "Philosophy": The Case of Austin and Derrida Revisited', in Glendinning, S. (ed.), *Arguing with Derrida*, Oxford: Blackwell, pp. 9–35.

Glock, H.-J. (2008), *What Is Analytic Philosophy?*, Cambridge: Cambridge University Press.

Grice, P. (1986), 'Reply to Richards', in Grandy, R. E., Warner, R. (eds.), *Philosophical Grounds of Rationality*, Oxford: Clarendon Press, pp. 45–106.

——(1989), *Studies in the Ways of Words*, Cambridge, MA: Harvard University Press.

Gustafsson, M. (2005), 'Perfect Pitch and Austinian Examples: Cavell, McDowell, Wittgenstein and the Philosophical Significance of Ordinary Language', *Inquiry* 48: 356–89.

Habermas, J. (1984), *The Theory of Communicative Action. Vol. 1: Reason and the Rationalization of Society*, Boston: Beacon Press.

——(1991), 'Comments on John Searle: "Meaning, Communication, and Representation"', in LePore and Van Gulick (1991), pp. 17–29.

Hampshire, S. (1969a), 'J. L. Austin, 1911–1960', in Fann (1969), pp. 33–48.

——(1969b), 'A Symposium on Austin's Method', in Fann (1969), pp. 90–7.

Hansen, N. (MS.), 'A Slugfest of Intuitions: Reconsidering the Evidence for Contextualism'.

Hart, H. L. A. (1961), *The Concept of Law*, Oxford: Clarendon Press.

——(1968), *Punishment and Responsibility*, Oxford: Clarendon Press.

Honderich, T. (1991), 'An Interview with A. J. Ayer', in Griffiths, A. P. (ed.), *A. J. Ayer. Memorial Essays*, Cambridge: Cambridge University Press, pp. 209–26.

Hornsby, J. (1993), 'Speech Acts and Pornography', *Women's Philosophical Review*, November: 38–45.

——(1995), 'Disempowered Speech', *Philosophical Topics* 23: 127–47.

——(2000), 'Feminism in Philosophy of Language: Communicative Speech Acts', in Fricker, M., Hornsby, J. (eds.), *The Cambridge Companion to Feminism in Philosophy*, Cambridge: Cambridge University Press, pp. 87–106.

——Langton, R. (1998), 'Free Speech and Illocution', *Legal Theory* 4: 21–37.

Hurka, T. (2004), 'Normative Ethics: Back to the Future', in Leiter, B. (ed.), *The Future for Philosophy*, Oxford: Clarendon Press, pp. 246–64.

Hylton, P. (1990), *Russell, Idealism, and the Emergence of Analytic Philosophy*, Oxford: Clarendon Press.

Jacobson, D. (1995), 'Freedom of Speech Acts? A Response to Langton', *Philosophy and Public Affairs* 24: 65–79.

Kaplan, M. (1991), 'Epistemology on Holiday', *Journal of Philosophy* 88: 132–54.

Kaplan, M. (2000), 'To What Must an Epistemology be True?', *Philosophy and Phenomenological Research* 61: 279–304.

——(2006), 'If You Know You Can't be Wrong', in Hetherington, S. (ed.), *Epistemology Futures*, Oxford: Clarendon Press, pp. 180–98.

——(2008), 'Austin's Way with Skepticism', in Greco, J. (ed.), *The Oxford Handbook of Skepticism*, Oxford: Oxford University Press, pp. 348–71.

Knobe, J., Nichols, S. (eds.) (2008), *Experimental Philosophy*, Oxford: Oxford University Press.

Kremer, M. (forthcoming), 'What is the Good of Philosophical History?', in Reck, E. (ed.), *The Historical Turn in Analytic Philosophy*, London: Palgrave Macmillan.

Kölbel, M., Weiss, B. (eds.) (2004), *Wittgenstein's Lasting Significance*, London: Routledge.

Lacey, N. (2004), *A Life of H. L. A. Hart. The Nightmare and the Noble Dream*, Oxford: Oxford University Press.

Langton, R. (1993), 'Speech Acts and Unspeakable Acts', *Philosophy and Public Affairs* 22: 293–330.

LePore, E., Van Gulick, R. (eds.) (1991), *John Searle and His Critics*, Oxford: Blackwell.

MacAdam, Jim (2002), 'Editor's Introduction', in Prichard, H. A., *Moral Writings*, Oxford: Oxford University Press.

Martin, M. G. F. (forthcoming), *Uncovering Appearances*.

McGinn, C. (1997), 'Strawson and Warnock: Reputation', in his *Minds and Bodies*, Oxford: Oxford University Press, pp. 164–70.

Medina, J. (2006), *Speaking from Elsewhere*, Albany, NY: State University of New York Press.

Mehta, V. (1963), *Fly and the Fly Bottle: Encounters with British Intellectuals*, London: Weidenfeld & Nicholson.

Mikkola, M. (2008), 'Contexts and Pornography', *Analysis* 68: 316–20.

Nicholson, P. P. (1990), *The Political Philosophy of the British Idealists*, Cambridge: Cambridge University Press.

Osborn, P., Segal, L. (1994), 'Gender as Performance: An Interview with Judith Butler', *Radical Philosophy* 67: 32–9.

Parent, W. A. (1990), 'A Second Look at Pornography and the Subordination of Women', *Journal of Philosophy* 87: 205–11.

Passmore, J. (1957), *A Hundred Years of Philosophy*, London: Duckworth.

Putnam, H. (1994), 'Sense, Nonsense, and the Senses: An Inquiry into the Powers of the Human Mind', *Journal of Philosophy* 91: 445–517.

Recanati, F. (1994), 'Contextualism and Anti-Contextualism in the Philosophy of Language', in Tsohatzidis, S. L. (ed.), *Foundations of Speech Act Theory. Philosophical and Linguistic Perspectives*, London: Routledge, pp. 156–86.

——(2004), *Literal Meaning*, Cambridge: Cambridge University Press.

Russell, B. (1959), 'Introduction', in Gellner 1959: 13–15.

Ryle, G. (1971), 'Review of "Symposium on J. L. Austin"', in his *Collected Papers. Volume 1: Critical Essays*, London: Hutchinson, pp. 272–5.

Saul, J. (2006), 'Pornography, Speech Acts and Context', *Proceedings of the Aristotelian Society* 106: 229–48.

Sbisà, M. (2001), 'Illocutionary Force and Degrees of Strength in Language Use', *Journal of Pragmatics* 33: 1791–814.

——(2006), 'Speech Acts without Propositions?', *Grazer Philosophische Studien* 72: 155–78.

——(2007), 'How to Read Austin', *Pragmatics*, 17: 461–73.

Schwartz, R. (2004), 'To Austin or not to Austin, that's the Disjunction', *Philosophical Studies* 120: 255–63.

Searle, J. (1969), *Speech Acts: An Essay in the Philosophy of Language*, Cambridge: Cambridge University Press.

——(1977), 'Reiterating the Differences: a Reply to Derrida', *Glyph* 1: 198–208.

Sedgwick, E. K. (1993), 'Queer Performativity: Henry James's *The Art of the Novel*', *GLQ* 1: 1–16.

——(2003), *Touching Feeling: Affect, Pedagogy, Performativity*, Durham, NC: Duke University Press.

Skinner, Q. (2002), *Visions of Politics. Volume 1: Regarding Method*, Cambridge: Cambridge University Press.

Tanney, J. (2009), 'Rethinking Ryle: A Critical Discussion of *The Concept of Mind*', in Ryle, G., *The Concept of Mind*, 60th anniversary edition, London: Routledge, pp. ix–lvii.

Travis, C. (1985), 'On what is Strictly Speaking True', *Canadian Journal of Philosophy* 15: 187–229.

——(1991), 'Annals of Analysis', *Mind* 100: 451–66.

——(2004), 'The Silence of the Senses', *Mind* 113: 57–94.

——(2008), *Occasion-Sensitivity. Selected Essays*, Oxford: Oxford University Press.

Urmson, J. O. (1969), 'Austin's Philosophy', in Fann (1969), pp. 22–32.

——(1988), 'Prichard and Knowledge', in Dancy, J., Moravscik, J. M. E., Taylor, C. C. W. (eds.), *Human Agency: Language, Duty, and Value*, Stanford, CA: Stanford University Press, pp. 11–24.

Warnock, G. J. (1969), 'John Langshaw Austin, a Biographical Sketch', in Fann (1969), pp. 3–21.

——(1973), 'Saturday Mornings', in Berlin et al. (1973), pp. 31–45.

——(1989), *J. L. Austin*, London: Routledge.

Williams, B. (2006), 'Descartes and Historiography', in his *The Sense of the Past*, Oxford: Oxford University Press, pp. 257–64.

Yeager, D. (2006), *J. L. Austin and the Law*, Lewisburg, PA: Bucknell University Press.

2

Unmasking the Tradition

Simon Glendinning

1. Ecce Homo

This chapter is concerned with the relationship between Austin's own 'field work in philosophy' (1979: 183) and the ABCs of the philosophical tradition that is in view in that work—indeed, the philosophical tradition that for many readers first came into view with that work. The supplementary point here deserves stressing. Having passed half a century since Austin's death in 1960, we may now be so bred with familiarity that we already need Stanley Cavell's testamentary record, first published in 1965, concerning the renown that ought to be inherited by the name after the 'unfairness' of 'the early death' of what it names; namely, that Austin 'has done more than any philosopher in the Anglo-American tradition (excepting Wittgenstein) to make clear that there is a coherent tradition to be dealt with' (2002: 111). A tradition, however stable and well entrenched, can only be revealed to us through ways of thinking which represent (or in various ways uncover, discover, reclaim, recover, endorse, etc) it *as such*. A tradition is not simply given but must be *read*. And it is to a critical reader of just such a kind that Cavell's 'memorial' to J. L. Austin wants to 'testify'. Cavell approaches this idea with a presentation of Austin that will enable us to recall hereafter that Austin was a thinker 'devoted to unmasking' (2002: 112).

This was never simply a matter of identifying the false premises or invalid inferences in a way of going on in philosophy that Austin sought to get beyond. On the contrary, while Austin's readings are peppered with general remarks about philosophical failings, the unmasking effected by his criticism seems most often to proceed, Cavell suggests, through 'attacking' individual philosophers (2002: 109), and hence in terms that are 'quite particular, characteristic and finite' (2002: 105). What seems to bother Austin most, according to Cavell, is not that the philosophical texts he reads as representative of a tradition have, say, a recurrent faulty or invalid argument or line of thinking, but that they are altogether 'written inauthentically' (2002: 109). Cavell leaves this crucial term of assessment unexplained, and one might wonder at this point why authenticity has anything to do with the cogency of a philosophical argument or position. It seems at best to be an *ad hominem* attack.

Cavell's reading does little to remove this worry. Indeed, his presentation of Austin's criticism as enacting a shift 'from the character of a philosopher's argument to the character of the philosopher arguing' serves only to enforce it (2002: 110). I am sure that there is something right in Cavell's reading of Austin's approach, but I am concerned that the (not very Austinian) terms he uses here threatens to underestimate the extent to which the 'inauthentic' character (if we want to keep this word at all) of the philosophical writing that Austin wants to expose in his work of critical reading belongs to its status *as philosophy*, and is *not* the upshot of the particular or fallen character of the philosopher who produces it. The terms of criticism are, indeed, turned towards the author, but it is something to do with the author *qua* philosopher that concerns Austin, not his or her personality as an individual. Indeed, the author *qua* individual person is not the target of Austin's criticism at all. On the contrary, what Austin wants to show is that the 'persona' of the author one discovers in a text is the expression of a distinctively *philosophical voice*; a voice that is precisely *not* the author's own voice—and hence it is, in this sense, 'inauthentic'. What is revealed by Austin's unmasking is, that is to say, a mask, a *philosophical persona*. I will try to make good on this claim as we proceed.

Of course, Austin's writing is shot through with his personality and it would be absurd to think that he is somehow without a philosophical persona himself. Indeed, there is something both right and completely misleading in thinking that Austin 'at criticism' is a case of a philosopher who, as Geoffrey Warnock puts it, '*just argues*—just as anybody else might do, or try to do' (1989: 6). One might emphasize the anonymization after the dash to at least begin to chart the shift that marks Austin's turn to the philosopher arguing. A philosopher may take himself to be trying to 'just argue'— but, Austin will suggest, he is not entirely himself, not in charge of the words he writes, or the 'who' that writes them winds up a kind of anonymous 'I, philosopher', precisely an 'anybody'. In my view, it is the movement of an author becoming anonymous, becoming 'fully [master] of a certain special, happy style of blinkering philosophical English' (1962: 4), that should underlie any claim to see Austin's attacks on particular philosophers as involving the unmasking of an 'inauthentic' way of going on in philosophy.

The shape of an 'authentic' alternative will be sketched at the end of this essay. However, at least part of its measure lies in the fact that it cannot be a question of drawing attention to a 'method' that might be applied by just anybody. I have already cited Cavell's testimony to Austin's philosophical *singularity*. And it is not, I think, coincidental that the question of such singular unreplaceability (or near unreplaceability—there is always a complication here, a complication marked in Cavell's text by the parenthetical addition of the name 'Wittgenstein' in the epitaph) emerges in a quasi-memorial context in which one mourns the loss, the singular death, of the teacher or friend. On the other hand, Cavell is surely right to think that one cannot get very far reflecting on the Austinian shift to 'the philosopher arguing' without getting caught up with worries concerning the *general validity* of such singular criticism.

And it is not obviously reassuring to be told that a detailed study of Austin's own work helps to 'settle' these worries.[1]

Cavell does not attempt to provide the kind of study of Austin's criticisms of others that would respond to these worries, though he acknowledges that without it 'we cannot know the extent to which these criticisms are valid and the extent to which they project Austin's own temper' (2002: 110). Moreover, when he does turn in a summary way to this theme, his conclusion is, in my view, disappointing. Instead of finding in Austin's work grounds for thinking that his criticisms devolve from considerations which go beyond a temperamental dislike for the personal character of the author arguing, Cavell, in a gesture that is a mirror-image of Warnock's, brings everything back to the persona of the critic:

Austin was an Englishman, an English professor. If I say he *used* this as a mask, I mean to register my feeling that he must, somewhere, have known his criticisms to be as unjustified as they were radical, but felt them to be necessary in order that his work get free, and heard. It would have served him perfectly, because its Englishness made it unnoticeable as a pose, because what he wanted from his audience required patience and co-operation, not depth and upheaval, and because it served as a counterpoise to Wittgenstein's strategies of the sage and the ascetic. (2002: 112)

Even if one had doubts concerning the biographical accuracy of (any of) this explanation, it is clear that on this reading, the *persona* of the philosopher posing has completely taken over—just as the *person* of a philosopher arguing completely takes over in Warnock—and the possibility of providing an assessment of the general validity of Austin's criticism (which is, just as unsatisfactorily, the *only* issue that is visible in Warnock) of other philosophers has, it would seem, been completely forgone.

Austin's philosophical personality lends itself to both Cavell's and Warnock's assessments. The delightfully uncluttered, witty and largely untechnical style, rich in non-academic vocabulary, seems clearly designed to cultivate the pose of someone who, clearly without a pose, is 'just arguing'. Cavell the American takes it that the 'pose' of being an English Professor was conveniently invisible to those like Warnock who form part of Austin's (home) audience. If one is to get anywhere else with this scene, one has to get off the see-saw somewhere, and I would suggest that the success (if indeed Austin's teaching does reach the ears of his audience, if it does both 'get free, and heard') of Austin's unmasking—what he called the exposure of 'a wide variety of concealed motives' (1962: 5)—is not something that is facilitated by the counter-mask of his academic position but (and I think something like this is what struck Warnock) by his capacity to *escape* it; a capacity to immerse himself in philosophy while all the while leaving himself and all the while trying to lead others back 'in a sense, just where we began' (1962: 5), where we began ('the garden of the world we live in' (1962: 124), as he rather edenically put it) before, sadly, we underwent a distinctive kind of

---

[1] Cavell (2002: 109). I will return to the significance of this thought at the end of the chapter.

de-personalization or anonymization in a philosophical culture where election to the ranks of those deemed worthy of making a claim on our attention requires its novices to learn to put their own voice out of play and to become fluent in a special, and especially distorting, 'philosophese'. However, as I see it, for just the same reason, Austin's way of engaging with these philosophical-English-speaking philosophers can pass his readers by: his cultivation of an unblinkered alternative risks not being heard at all, or *almost*. In this essay I will both illustrate this risk and try to be more attentive to the details of, if not the method then, the procedures of Austin's singular criticism.

Cavell's recommendation that we read Austin as making a shift 'to the philosopher arguing' raises the worry (a worry that some have thought to be a recognition of how it is) that all he offers is *ad hominem* attacks on the arguments of others. However, if, as I am suggesting, Austin directs his attention always to particular examples of the blinkered philosophical voice, we need properly to acknowledge that the particular authors he chooses are chosen precisely because their ideas are *not* their own alone. What he is looking for is, as it were, something exemplary, and specifically texts that attest most powerfully to the movement and work of a *tradition* in the text of an individual thinker. I don't think Austin ever hides this ambition. Indeed, even in one of his most continuously polemical writings, the lecture notes posthumously published as *Sense and Sensibilia*, he is very careful to stress the generality of his target:

[V]ery numerous great philosophers have held these theories, and have propounded other doctrines resulting from them. The authors I have chosen to discuss may differ from each other over certain refinements [. . .] but I believe that they agree with each other, and with their predecessors, in all their major (and mostly unnoticed) assumptions. (1962: 1–2)

The mark of tradition is the way it organizes an inheritance into a matter of course, structuring framework whose operation on those working within it is, at least in part, not-conscious. And it is as insensible carriers of a traditional way of going on that Austin will read the authors he has chosen. I say carriers of *a* philosophical tradition, but Austin is sometimes rather more generally damning. On at least three occasions Austin simply identifies philosophy itself with the instituted and structuring ruts of tradition. Here is an example:[2]

My general opinion about this doctrine [viz., that we never directly perceive material objects] is that it is a typically *scholastic* view, attributable, first, to an obsession with a few particular words [. . .]; and second, to an obsession with a few (and nearly always the same) half-studied 'facts'. (I say 'scholastic', but I might just as well have said 'philosophical'; over simplification, schema-tization, and constant obsessive repetition of the same small range of jejune 'examples' are not only peculiar to this case, but far too common to be dismissed as an occasional weakness of philosophers.) (1962: 3)

---

[2] The same gesture can be found on p. 38 in *How to do Things With Words* (Austin 1975).

And here is another:

Life and truth and things do tend to be complicated. It's not things, it's philosophers that are simple. You have heard it said, I expect, that oversimplification is the occupational disease of philosophers, and in one way one might agree with that. But for the sneaking suspicion that it's their occupation. (1979: 252)[3]

If Austin's 'general opinion' of philosophy is plain and simple, his intended aim is equally so: namely, to shake off—and help others to shake off—these fruitless ways of thinking, to 'get free, and heard'. But, now, quite apart from the problem of getting heard by others, a clear problem faces him. Given this characterization of philosophy, how is one to *begin* in such a way that one does not *oneself* (perhaps more or less insensibly and unwittingly) repeat the very gestures that lead a thinker to produce texts that are, in the sense I am attributing to Austin's engagement with philosophy, 'written inauthentically'?[4]

What is needed, and what I think Austin consistently (if not altogether invariably) attempts in his work, is to find a way of engaging usefully with a topic that *disengages* from the rutted 'topos' of traditional philosophical discussion. When Austin is 'at criticism' he tends not situate his work—his chosen 'site for *field work* in philosophy' (1979: 183)—within *either* the boggy field of, *or* (more obviously) uncritically in the terms of, what he is attempting to disclose as the traditional account.

Certainly rather grandly, I will refer to this mode of engagement—this *avoidance* of the traditional field of engagement—as it shows itself in Austin's writing as the 'Disengagement Strategy' or simply 'Disengagement' and in the course of this essay I hope to show that it fairly characterizes a typically Austinian approach to philosophical criticism.[5]

---

[3] This might be the point to mention Myles Burnyeat's claim that Austin's view of the philosophical tradition is much more 'local' than Austin himself assumes (cf. Burnyeat 1979). I will identify the specific 'bugbear' that Austin identifies in (as) traditional epistemology in the final section, but the question of the reach of Austin's criticisms can be addressed in general terms now. The first point to note is that a way of going on in philosophy that takes its point of departure from 'the philosopher arguing' is always going to have a distinctively 'local' character: it is a work of reading specific texts. It is the claim that the selected texts are exemplary (good examples) of writing in a quasi-anonymous mode that broadens the horizon of Austin's reading. What Burnyeat's complaint brings to the fore is a methodological commitment on his own part to a distinction between (roughly) doing philosophy and reading philosophy that Austin rejects. But it is not simply that some of Austin's criticisms will be pertinent only relatively locally, whereas others are more widely relevant. If, as I suggested at the start, the 'tradition' is not simply given but must be *read*, we must accept that this work of reading takes its bearings from what is written in texts that are *always* also 'local'.

[4] See note 11 below for a suggestion that in the analysis of performative utterances Austin himself gets involved with the kind of insensible commitments that he finds in traditional philosophy.

[5] One may well wonder if this whole effort of coming to terms with Austin's procedures isn't a distinctively un-Austinian enterprise. Would it help to call the interpretive proposal I am defending—the idea of the Disengagement Strategy—a bit of what Austin called 'cackle'—which he hoped we might 'cut'? What is achieved by this elaboration? My answer is that what I say aims to provide something akin to the underlining that can orient an ongoing reading: it is (by my lights) a way of making salient noteworthy aspects of the way that Austin goes about his business even though he does not himself go about business in such a formally procedural or methodologically fixated way.

Tracking this shifting change in 'topos' is intended to provide a *fil conducteur* to a faithful reading of Austin's work. However, it also helps to shed light on certain prevailing interpretations of it. In particular, when Disengagement is accorded a privileged status, those moments where it is assumed by others that Austin's writings constitute the (traditional) attempt to engage directly on the terrain of certain (traditional) views take on a special significance. Implicitly operating with such an assumption I believe that they betray more than a personal failure to read Austin well, a failure that one might describe simply in terms of a reader's limited exegetical rigour. Indeed, with Austin, I want to stress that the reading I have chosen to discuss in this essay may differ from other readings over certain refinements but I believe that it agrees with many others in its major (and mostly unnoticed) assumptions. Such readings are committed to and dominated by the very ideas which Austin hoped to criticize, a commitment and domination that cannot but deliver an impoverished presentation of Austin's thinking and of a characteristically Austinian argument. The exemplary case that I want to look at in this essay is Jonathan Bennett's examination of Chapter VII of Austin's *Sense and Sensibilia* in ' "Real" ' (1969).[6]

2. The question of relevance

The relationship between the kind of inquiry pursued by Bennett in ' "Real" ' and that typically pursued by Austin is itself problematic. For although Bennett aims to defend 'the great tradition of modern epistemology' (1969: 280), he also claims that his central argument *against* what he takes to be Austin's view (namely, that 'the uses of "real" [. . .] are relevant to traditional epistemology') is itself a strictly 'Austinian' one (1969: 267). Furthermore, even when Bennett's criticisms of Austin are at their most vitriolic there is an (ironic) sense in which Austin might actually agree with them.

Bennett's reading is premised on the claim, laid down in the opening sentence of ' "Real" ', that Chapter VII of *Sense and Sensibilia* is an attempt to show that the traditional philosopher's 'views' concerning 'the criteria for distinguishing between appearance and reality' are 'misconceived' (1969: 267). Bennett's own argument consists in providing a classification of uses of the word 'real' that will show both that Austin's own handling of it is inadequate and that his own 'correct account' (1969: 267) makes perspicuous the irrelevance of such investigations to the traditional problem.

---

[6] The kind of objection Burnyeat (1979) raises against Austin's selection of exemplary texts can, of course, be raised against me here. Bennett's essay and its picture of Austin is most immediately representative of the 'local' situation in the late 1960s and early 1970s. As should be clear I take Cavell to be the main force behind another movement of evaluation of Austin's procedures (a movement that now includes, among others, Charles Travis, Hilary Putnam, Mark Kaplan, and most recently—and most recently influential on my own reading of Austin—Quassim Cassam). Perhaps Bennett will be thought a poor example today. However, what is so massively visible on its surface is a conception of Austin that I believe is now quietly dominant in mainstream analytic philosophy.

Although Bennett does not explicitly develop a conception of an 'Austinian argument', his claim is that his own work on the use of the word 'real' is 'a tighter and more Austinian' argument than Austin's. And that is revealing. For, while Bennett admits that other analyses are possible, he claims the strength of his own work, and what makes it 'more Austinian', is that it provides something approaching a classification of 'practically all idiomatic uses of the form "a real F"' (1969: 268). Bennett's view of Austinian arguments thus amounts to the idea that they are primarily attempts to render explicit the ordinary usage of certain key words so that the 'rules' for its normal application are fully clarified. Thus Bennett states that Austin's aim in the examination of the use of the word 'real' is to be understood as an attempt to give the 'rules which will tell us how to distinguish Fs from non-Fs for any F' (1969: 280). Such renditions would then be compared to what philosophers have said about these words or the criteria which they have employed to make this distinction.

It now becomes clear why Bennett can understand his own work as being itself 'Austinian' in character. For, given that Bennett is attacking Austin, this remark implies that Bennett takes (reads) Austinian arguments as deploying something like a method that is, in itself, *neutral* in respect of its relation to 'the great tradition of modern epistemology'. Whether an Austinian argument is critical, relevant, supportive, etc. is, in Bennett's view, independent of Austin's method. I do not think that my definition of Disengagement totally precludes such an assumption, but it should be noted that Bennett's conception of Austin's argumentation is limited to only one aspect of this definition which was twofold. Disengagement being, first, the refusal to engage on the terrain of and, second, the refusal uncritically to employ the terms of the traditional account. Based on the unexamined assumption in the opening sentence of '"Real"', Bennett conceives of Austin's procedures as merely a matter of turning away from concepts employed by or as employed by the traditional philosopher, and towards an examination of features of the ordinary use of language: i.e. the second aspect of Disengagement only. That aspect of Austin's work, the movement from philosophical-English to ordinary English, is not, of course, news. It is the first and to my mind more significant aspect which is (almost) unnoticed.

In order to determine whether Bennett's views of Austin's procedures and the argumentation of Chapter VII of *Sense and Sensibilia* can be maintained it is crucial that we gain a clear view of precisely what 'traditional account' Austin wants to bring into view in his inquiry into the use of 'real'. In what way, if any, does Austin think that the traditional inquiry represents itself as seeking criteria for distinguishing appearance and reality? And is it really Austin's aim to delimit the rules for the use of the word 'real' which tell us how to distinguish Fs from non-Fs for any F?

A summary of the general ambition of *Sense and Sensibilia* will be reserved for the conclusion to this essay but we may note, since Bennett also quotes it, that Austin's own description of his work in Chapter VII does not suggest that he is attempting to provide anything like an exhaustive account of the idiomatic uses of 'real'. Rather, he states that he is embarking upon 'a preliminary, no doubt rather haphazard, survey of some of the complexities in the use of "real"' which is followed by an attempt to 'tidy things up a little' by detailing what he considers to be the most 'salient features' of its use (1962: 65–8). Although it is of considerable significance if such (apparently) 'salient' features of the use of 'real' are of relevance to the inquiry he is criticizing, mere salience does not guarantee it, and relevance, as Bennett notes, is a dyadic relation (1969: 281). The crucial issue, for us as for Bennett, concerns what, in the field of concerns that belongs to the text he is reading, this survey of features is intended to be relevant to.

Even a cursory glance at the context of Austin's remarks on the usage of 'real' clearly shows that he does not think that 'the traditional philosopher' is concerned straight-forwardly with questions of criteria—but rather with a puzzle regarding their absence, or apparent absence. Indeed, Austin is quite explicit in his claim that the aim of his discussion will be to examine a philosopher's concern with understanding how we can (possibly) come to apprehend that something is real at all:[7]

Consider the expressions 'cricket ball', 'cricket bat', 'cricket pavilion', 'cricket weather'. If someone did not know about cricket and were obsessed with the use of such 'normal' words as 'yellow', he might gaze at the ball, the bat, the building, the weather, trying to detect the 'common quality' which (he assumes) is attributed to these things by the prefix 'cricket'. But no such quality meets his eye; and so he concludes that 'cricket' must designate a *non-natural* quality, a quality to be detected not in any ordinary way but by *intuition*. [. . .] [Similarly], many philosophers, failing to detect any ordinary quality common to real ducks, real cream, and real progress, have decided that Reality must be an *a priori* concept apprehended by reason alone. (1962: 64)

The point is that Austin is concerned here to disclose the ground-floor motivations of traditional inquiries in philosophy, in gaining an understanding of why such inquiries are elaborated in the distinctive ways they (traditionally) are. More precisely, Austin's investigation into the use of the word 'real' in Chapter VII of *Sense and Sensibilia* is carried out in order to draw attention to two features of the use of 'real' which he considers to be particularly important to an understanding of the traditional inquiry into the 'Nature of Reality'. The features he identifies are, first, that 'real' is an absolutely normal word: 'It is, that is to say, already firmly established in, and very frequently used in, the ordinary language we all use every day' (1962: 62). And, second, that 'real' is not a normal word at all, or at least is in a certain respect highly exceptional: 'exceptional in this respect that, unlike "yellow" or "horse" or "walk", it does not have one single, specifiable, always-the-same, *meaning*. [. . .] Nor does it have a large number of different meanings—it is not *ambiguous*, even "systematically"' (1962: 64).

It is this ordinary/extraordinary character of the word 'real' which Austin believes underpins the traditional philosopher's problematic theorizing about 'how possible' questions. For, on one level we seem to have no difficulty at all in confidently claiming

---

[7] The way I am putting Austin's thought here obviously owes a debt to John McDowell on 'how possible' questions in philosophy. My assumption is that McDowell's way of putting things already owes a good deal to Austin.

(very often) to apprehend a *real* such-and-such, and yet when we reflect on such claims there seems to be nothing (no feature or quality) in the appearance of a thing which would permit such a confident claim. However, and this is a crucial mark of an Austinian Disengaged argument, at no point does Austin attempt to supply what the traditional philosopher strives for: namely, an account which overcomes this aporia by showing or explaining how it is possible that we do come to apprehend real things. Rather his examination of the use of 'real' is intended to reveal, at least in part, why the problematic aporia arises in the way it does when a typical philosopher reflects on our ordinary practice. For instance, in the course of his discussion of the second salient feature of the concept 'real', Austin draws attention to the seemingly innocuous fact that, in the ordinary use of the word, 'it is the *negative* use that wears the trousers. That is, a definite sense attaches to the assertion that something is real, a real such-and-such, only in the light of a specific way in which it might be, or might have been, *not* real' (1962: 70). A philosopher seeking to explain how it is possible to apprehend reality takes it as unproblematic that one can, without more ado, sensibly speak of this or that as real. But this assumption is not only out of kilter with ordinary use, but having in this way gone insensibly out of kilter, a mystery emerges.

As Austin then goes on to argue, as long as one is thinking of the usage of 'real' on the model of substance and attribute (a spotty dog has spots, a real dog has reality), one (*anyone*) is forced into thinking that the apprehension of reality must be performed by a special intellectual faculty. According to Austin, the very idea of a search for a positive and invariably present sensible mark of the real is doomed to failure not because it is in fact—or *must* be—an a priori 'intellectual' addition to sensible experience but because, the function of 'real' is not to contribute positively to the characterization of anything at all, but to exclude possible ways of being not real.

Even these schematic remarks about Austin's argument in Chapter VII of *Sense and Sensibilia* should forewarn us against hastily thinking that Austin's inquiry into the uses of 'real' is merely a (defective) attempt to provide an account of the rules which will tell us how to distinguish Fs from non-Fs for any F in order to refute the traditional philosophers opinions on this matter. Indeed, the brief discussion of the chapter suggests that Austin's investigations should be understood as being fundamentally oriented towards features of our language which he believes are coordinated with confusions and misunderstandings arising in a typically philosophical discussion. In short, and *pace* Bennett, Austin's examination of the use of words is not intended to be a classification for the sake of accurate classification, nor does it presuppose that philosophers have thought of themselves as attempting to identify criteria or rules of some kind. On the contrary, as we have seen, the traditional philosopher's problem, as acknowledged by Austin, concerns the possibility of a subject's apprehension of anything as a real such-and-such—the apprehension of reality. Consequently Bennett's two step argument, claiming that his classification is both a 'tighter and more Austinian argument' in virtue of its being a more systematic and complete set of rules and yet still (almost) entirely irrelevant to the traditional problem cannot, unless Austin's examples are not even (real) examples, be to the point in terms of showing that Austin's efforts are irrelevant to the 'problem' explored in the text he is reading.

I noted at the beginning of the examination of Bennett's reading of Austin that Bennett's conception of Austin's procedures ('method') implies no prejudicial position vis-à-vis the traditional problem. Insofar as Disengagement requires the refusal uncritically to employ the terms of the traditional debate, Bennett's reading of Austin is uncontroversially Austinian. However, it was noted that this aspect corresponds (broadly speaking) with Disengagement only in its second moment. The first moment, the refusal to take a position within the 'topos' or site of the traditional discussion, is clearly absent from Bennett's reading since it is assumed from the outset that Austin (falsely) believes that the traditional philosopher is (in fact inadequately) attempting to provide something of the sort that Bennett reads Austin as (in fact inadequately) providing. We have already made a start in demonstrating that Bennett's view of Austin's examination of ordinary language is not Austin's. However, if we are to provide a conclusive refutation of Bennett's reading we need to deepen the understanding of Disengagement such that we can see whether Bennett's 'neutralist' reading of Austin's procedures can be maintained. To do so will require a far more general investigation of Austin's procedures than I have hitherto provided. In the following section I will briefly stand back from Bennett's reading in order to begin to justify the interpretative proposal I am advancing, and in particular to explore the underlying rationale of its first moment.

3. Habits of *Gleichschaltung*

Sticking with *Sense and Sensibilia* for the moment, it is worth emphasising again that its principle of organization is not the treatment of a philosophical problem but the reading of exemplary texts, texts that Austin identifies as works of traditional philosophy. The texts in question are A. J. Ayer's *Foundations of Empirical Knowledge* and H. H. Price's *Perception*. But Austin also has his own fish to fry, and it is equally important to note that he wants to do his own 'field work'. And Austin is explicit that it is, precisely, *perception* that he wants to work on. That is the topic or field that interests him (1962: 5). But now, and totally contrary to my interpretive proposal, it would seem then that Austin is engaging with precisely the same issue as the traditional philosopher. He is arguing, they are arguing, he is arguing against their arguments, but in the end everybody is just arguing about and trying to get completely clear and to solve philosophical problems about perception.[8] To suppose this would be quite wrong. Again Austin is explicit:

[8] Warnock gives a further word for this kind of reading—and attempts in doing so to hold Austin as far apart as possible from Wittgenstein—when he notes that Austin regarded the 'ideal of finality, of definite, clearly and fully stated solutions' that Wittgenstein deliberately rejected 'as alone worth seriously striving for' (1969: 11). Again there is something both right and completely misleading about this suggestion. On the one

> *It is of course knowledge, not perception at all, in which these philosophers are really interested.* In Ayer's case this shows itself in the title of his book, as well as, *passim,* in his text; Price is more seriously interested than Ayer is to the actual facts about perception, and pays more attention to them—but still, it is worth noticing that, after raising the initial question, 'What is it to *see* something?', his very next sentence runs, 'When I see a tomato there is much that I *can* doubt.' This suggests that he too is really interested, not so much in what seeing is, as in what one can't doubt. (1962: 104–5; first emphasis mine)

So the basic intention of the authors he is reading is to develop not an account of perception but about knowledge. And Austin takes a stand on what will shape the accounts in the two exemplary texts: not an observation or discovery, but a picture, an (ortho)*doxa*, a doctrine:

> In a nutshell, the doctrine about knowledge, 'empirical' knowledge, is that it has *foundations*. It is a structure the upper tiers of which are reached by inferences, and the foundations are the *data* on which these inferences are based. (So of course—as it appears—there just have to be sense-data.) (1962: 105)

Thus, unlike Austin himself, neither author Austin has chosen to read, is really interested in perception for its own sake, rather their interest is motivated and dictated by an epistemological conviction, a conviction 'descend[ing] directly from Descartes' (1962: 5). Indeed, the final parenthetical note in the quotation above indicates the real place of the facts of perception in the traditional problematic. One might say that *Austin's inquiry is situated in the parentheses or margins of his tradition.*[9]

'It is of course knowledge, not perception at all, in which these philosophers are really interested.' But Austin's Disengaged work in the margins of this interest is not intended to be irrelevant to what these philosophers are really interested in. On the contrary, it is the traditional philosopher's implicit doctrine about knowledge which is

---

hand, it represents Austin as endorsing a quasi-scientific view of the aim of his work in philosophy that he would reject, even in his sleep: 'I dreamt a line that would make a motto for a sober philosophy: *Neither a be-all nor an end-all be*' ('Pretending', in Austin 1979: 252–72, at p. 271, n. 1). On the other hand, there is a distinctive contrast to Wittgenstein—and to 'post-philosophical' philosophers like Rorty—to be had in the vicinity. For while Wittgenstein emphasized the distinction between philosophy and science, Austin regarded the non-scientific status of philosophy as a function of its *pre-scientific* character. Thus, rather like Husserl and Heidegger, Austin held that philosophy has a final 'end' through a kind of *aufgehoben* into science. As for this, see 'Ifs and Cans', where Austin writes: 'In the history of human inquiry, philosophy has the place of the initial central sun, seminal and tumultuous: from time to time it throws off some portion of itself to take station as a science, a planet, cool and well regulated, progressing steadily towards a distant final state. This happened long ago at the birth of mathematics, and again at the birth of physics: only in the last century we have witnessed the same process once again, slow and at the same time almost imperceptible, in the birth of the science of mathematical logic [. . .]. Is it not possible that the next century may see the birth [. . .] of a true and comprehensive *science of language*? Then we shall have rid ourselves of one more part of philosophy (there will still be plenty left) in the only way we ever can get rid of philosophy, by kicking it upstairs' (1979: 232). I discuss this conception of the 'end' of philosophy, and the contrast to Wittgenstein's conception of its fundamental interminability, in Glendinning (2003).

[9] It is important to note that in Austin's view the particular (distorted) view of perception found in the traditional text is *forced* upon these philosophers because of the epistemological (dis)orientation of their inquiry.

Austin's critical *target*, and that is intended to effect a transformation of our reflective self-understanding in this area. Thus, through attention to what we ordinarily or pre-philosophically say about *perception* the argumentation of *Sense and Sensibilia* aims to 'dismantle' the 'whole doctrine' about *knowledge* 'before it gets off the ground' (1962: 142).[10]

In other words, Austin's investigations at the margins of the tradition can be seen to belong but without (quite) belonging to the traditional framework which he seeks to dismantle. As Austin puts it in the penultimate chapter of *Sense and Sensibilia*, his field work on the topic of perception has the critical pay-off in showing that 'the general doctrine about knowledge which I sketched [the 'nutshell', quoted above], which is the real bugbear underlying doctrines of the kind we have been discussing, is *radically* and *in principle* misconceived' (1962: 123–4).

If Disengagement resulted in an inquiry which was entirely outside the space of traditional interests it would not be clear why it would have any critical bearing on them. Bennett's view that Austin's work is irrelevant to the traditional problematic would then seem to be about right. But Austin does not claim that his own work is totally remote from traditional concerns. On the contrary, one might say that it is an attempt to disclose them *as such*. That is, Austin's 'unhampered work' is carefully oriented towards assumptions in the texts he reads that are basic and internal to a particular way of going on in philosophy—the assumptions, that is, which lie at the bottom of traditional philosophy *as a tradition*. In a moment I will highlight and underline the Disengagement Strategy in Austin's most methodologically explicit text, 'A Plea for Excuses'. However, it is equally evident in his classic study of language, *How to Do Things with Words*. Austin's investigation into performative utterances simultaneously reveals and problematizes the traditional focus that makes assertions—'constative statements'—primary and the norm of language, treating other kinds of utterances as supplementary forms.[11]

---

[10] 'Austinian dismantling' is, for me, an appellation akin to (and, in its methodological formality, as misleading as) 'Derridean deconstruction'. What the two thinkers most obviously have in common is their suspicion of, and effort to disrupt, the functioning of certain binary or polar oppositions in the construction of philosophical theories. As Austin puts it, 'what is spurious is not one term of the pair, but the antithesis itself' (1962: 4). I discuss the pair 'Austin and Derrida' in more detail in Glendinning (2001). Derrida's own discussion of Austin in that book is well worth following up too. See also note 11 below.

[11] I discuss the role of the Disengagement Strategy in Austin's essay 'Other Minds' in Glendinning 1998: 25–31. Even Austin's earliest published essays have something of the Strategy about them. For example, 'Are there A Priori Concepts?' (from 1939) engages with a text by one Mr Maclagan but Austin explicitly 'decline[s] to pick the particular bones which he proffers to me' (1979: 32). Given that the particular bones that concern Austin in his most celebrated works are *philosophical commonplaces* not *personal lapses*, it bears stressing that what Austin seizes on in the case of Maclagan is the assumption that 'the word "concept" cannot be explained without using the word "universal"' (1979: 32), an assumption he (Austin) immediately identifies as 'the common view' (1979: 32). With this pattern of engagement in view, it is also worth noting that, while extremely grateful to Austin's dismantling of traditional approaches to language and convinced of its value, Derrida's main worry with Austin's procedures in *How to Do Things With Words* is precisely the recourse one finds there to the 'commonplace' antithetical distinction between 'serious' and 'non-serious' utterances in the

Thus, far from being independent from or neutral in respect of traditional philosophy, a crucial mark of Disengagement might thus be called a principle of maximal pertinence. This heuristic principle would state that when we are considering topics for investigation we should choose one which (critically) engages with the most deep-seated and hence typically unnoticed and unexpressed assumptions of the traditional problematic field, and hence without engaging with it in the terms which those assumptions underpin. Connecting to the ambition of *How to Do Things with Words*, this principle finds clear expression in 'A Plea for Excuses':

In ethics we study, I suppose, the good and the bad, the right and the wrong, and this must be for the most part in some connexion with [. . .] the doing of actions. Yet before we consider what actions are good or bad, right or wrong, it is proper to consider first what is meant by, and what not, and what is included under, and what not, the expression 'doing an action' or 'doing something'. These are expressions still too little examined on their own account and merits, just as the general notion of 'saying something' is still too lightly passed over in logic. (1979: 178)

Excuses are then assessed in the light of these considerations:

Excuses form an admirable topic; we can discuss at least clumsiness, or absence of mind, or inconsiderateness, even spontaneousness, without remembering what Kant thought, and so progress by degrees even to discussing deliberation, without for once remembering Aristotle or self-control without Plato. Granted that our subject is, as already claimed for it, *neighbouring, analogous or germane in some way to some notorious centre of philosophical trouble*, then [. . .] we should be certain of what we are after: a good site for *field work* in philosophy. Here at last we should be able to unfreeze, to loosen up and get going on agreeing about discoveries. (1979: 183; first emphasis mine)

As I mentioned in the first part of this essay, Cavell does not attend to the details of Austin's procedures. Cavell simply insists that Austin's 'radical' readings of exemplary texts of the tradition were 'necessary in order that his work get free'. However, once we see the connection of that freedom from tradition to the Disengagement Strategy it becomes clear that this is not a way of getting free which is 'ultimately unjustified' as Cavell supposes, but a form of criticism that steps beyond the tradition precisely by going to its heart. Disengagement, as a move which thus transforms the familiar and habitual space of inquiry, belongs without belonging to the framework which, in a manner which is now always 'by the way' (1979: 180), it seeks to undermine *from its roots*.

Let us return briefly to Bennett's reading of Austin in ' "Real" '. For while his 'neutral' view of Austin's procedures should not be sustained,[12] the kind of reading

---

analysis of the performative. This is a philosophical failure of just the sort that Austin identifies in the texts he reads elsewhere.

[12]   Austin's insistence that his topic selection aims to be 'neighbouring, analogous or germane in some way to some notorious centre of philosophical trouble' also pulls the rug under J. O. Urmson's suggestion that (unlike Wittgenstein who wanted to eliminate traditional problems) Austin 'wished to study ordinary

involved here is instructive. It is not just plain false and, as noted, Austin might actually agree with some of the ideas which Bennett considers to be criticisms of his (Austin's) work.

As we have seen, Bennett's reading is predicated on the claim that an 'Austinian argument' identifies a detailed set of rules for the ordinary use of a word or words which are then compared with traditional philosophical uses of or appeals to the concept in question. From this position Austin's work seems to show an almost complete lack of understanding of the aims and nature of the traditional inquiry; for it was never the traditional philosopher's aim to explicate such rules. (A grave nod. Bennett has not entirely missed the Disengagement Strategy, only he thinks Austin has.) On this reading even if Austin's descriptions of ordinary usage were actually correct (which is what Bennett claims for his own) it would still be irrelevant to the traditional epistemologist since it does not touch on what, in Bennett's view, is really at issue:

The great epistemologists have [. . .] not sought detailed rules for determining, of anything which seems (going by what one can see, feel, etc.) to be the case, whether it is really the case. They have enquired into what sort of thing we do when we ask and answer questions about what really is the case: what kinds of procedure we use, how these relate to one another, what there logical status is [. . .]. In short, they have sought high-level generalizations to cover extremely complex data. (1969: 280–81)

Ultimately, for Bennett, Austin's criticism of traditional philosophical theorizing as intrinsically or even just regularly prone to over-simplification, schematization, and obsessive repetition of a small range of 'examples' is a consequence of Austin's own lack of 'intellectual sympathy' for such high-level and abstract theoretical reflection, and his consequent failure properly to see or understand the nature of the problem at issue:

Someone who cannily suspends judgement on all the larger issues until he has probed every possible relevant detail may well fail to discover anything worth knowing. In philosophy, as in science, we need to carry *into* our investigations something in the nature of a hunch, a hypothesis, a general question, if we are to solve problems and not merely amass impeccably random data. [. . .] In order to show that philosophers are neglecting data relevant to their concerns, one needs to understand what their concerns are; and such understanding requires some measure of intellectual sympathy with modes of thought one may find distasteful. (1969: 281)

From this perspective, Austin's apparently hunch-free investigation of ordinary language is read as a dogmatism based on a personal or temperamental lack of sympathy for the texts he reads: 'It is mere dogmatism to say that unless the detailed work is done the results are bound to be wrong' (1969: 281). Bennett thus concludes that Austin's work cannot yield a satisfactory criticism of traditional epistemology at all. According

language' simply because 'he was interested in fine distinctions for their own sake and saw the application of his results to the traditional problems of philosophy as only a by-product' (1969: 32). As I explain in the main text, not setting his stall at the 'notorious centre' does not make Austin's work neutral with respect to it.

to Bennett, Austin simply has no answers on the 'important issues' and hence his (in fact 'erring') descriptions of the niceties of the English language are irrelevant to the traditional inquiry into the distinction between appearance and reality (1969: 267). But now, given our preceding discussion of Disengagement, if we take this claim in a slightly different key, if we register it slightly differently, we might not only agree but also think that this errancy with respect to the tradition is precisely what we should expect. That is, if, as Bennett claims, the important issues are 'concerned above all with the distinction between something's seeming to one (going by what one can see, feel, hear, etc.) to be the case and its really being the case' (1969: 280), then it is quite true that Austin doesn't provide any answers. For Bennett's remark just quoted shows quite clearly that what is really at issue for the traditional philosopher is precisely the issue identified by Austin: namely, the question of how it is possible for a subject to gain access to what is really the case, or apprehend reality. And Austin does not want to give an 'ordinary language' answer to such 'how possible' questions but to find a convincing way to dismantle the fabric of thinking which gives rise to the idea that we have asked a good question here in the first place.

This form of criticism does indeed 'carry into' it certain 'hunches'. Specifically, Austin has his hunches about traditional philosophy—and how to read texts of traditional philosophy. Indeed, what Austin's Disengaged readings of particular, exemplary texts wants to bring out are precisely the unnoticed and matter of course assumptions which structure the tradition as such. In the case of 'the great epistemologists' this matter of course background is, Austin suggests, a 'doctrine about knowledge' as having foundations, a doctrine which makes it seem plausible that we can rigorously distinguish between a subjective realm (perceptual data given to a 'subject' going by what one can see, feel, hear, etc.) and an objective realm (the 'world' as it is independently of the 'subject'). And it is this 'whole doctrine' which Austin is calling into question in *Sense and Sensibilia*, and specifically in the chapter that troubles Bennett. For in Austin's view the lack of general criteria, or rather their particularity and object specificity,[13] shows that there is something spurious about the traditional philosopher's unquestioned assumption that one can draw a completely general distinction here and hence something spurious about the idea of providing a general response to the epistemological 'how possible' question. So, of course Austin does not provide answers to what Bennett views as the really important issues, and to say it is irrelevant to them simply marks Bennett's failure to take into account Austin's attempt to Disengage from the traditional inquiry in anything but the most superficial manner ('Austin claims to show that the attempt to seek criteria for a general distinction between appearance and reality is misconceived.')

And yet it is not as if the Disengagement Strategy is left implicit in *Sense and Sensibilia*. On the contrary, the refusal to occupy a position within the standard range

---

[13] See Austin 1962: 76.

of responses is clearly and explicitly set out in the first chapter where, having just stated his intention to criticize the view that what we directly perceive are sense-data, he adds the following pointed remark:

I am *not* [...] going to maintain that we ought to be 'realists', to embrace, that is the doctrine that we *do* perceive material things (or objects). This doctrine would be no less scholastic and erroneous than its antithesis. [...] One of the most important points to grasp is that these two terms, 'sense-data' and 'material things', live by taking in each other's washing—what is spurious is not one term of the pair, but the antithesis itself. (1962: 3–4)

To take up an issue broached at the start of this essay, it is crucial to recognize that the problems I have identified in Bennett's reading involve more than mere exegetical inaccuracy. Bennett's misreading is motivated. And this must not be conceived as a personal matter. Following on from the passage in the first chapter of *Sense and Sensibilia* in which Austin complains about the tendency in traditional philosophy to simplify and schematize the functioning of ordinary concepts, Austin makes a telling remark on the necessity of a Disengagement from the traditional field of inquiry: 'It is essential, here as elsewhere, to abandon old habits of *Gleichschaltung*, the deeply ingrained worship of tidy-looking dichotomies' (1962: 3). '*Gleichschaltung*', meaning to bring something into line, to make something conform to a certain standard by force, represents, in its most general aspect, the kind of difficulty Austin identifies in (as) traditional philosophy and the kind of difficulty which he sought to overcome through Disengagement. It is worth noting, because, as Austin notes, 'a word never—well, hardly ever—shakes off its etymology and its formation' (1979: 201), that '*Gleichschaltung*', like '*Führer*' has been, since the 1930s, something of a poisoned word and is rarely used. Metaphorized by Hitler, '*Gleichschaltung*' was the name used for the (forced) integration of various previously autonomous bodies under the control of the National Socialist Party (e.g. Trade Unions, police, civil service, media). The word was subsequently co-opted and its meaning further displaced by anti-Nazi's to refer to those who became mentally integrated into the Party, particularly the intellectual elite (such as Heidegger). '*Gleichschaltung*' has, and certainly had at the time Austin was writing, enormous overtones of a ruling dogma or doctrine to which intellectuals capitulated or collaborated. That Austin accepts the word in the face of these connotations is indicative of the power and strength of control which he believes the traditional framework of inquiry holds over those who accede to it. Finally, it is arguable that it is simply Bennett's attachment to the traditional framework as providing the only legitimate space within which questions can be asked and answered which almost blinds him to the possibility of conducting researches pertinent to this issue in other ways. And hence almost blinds him to a reading of Austin which can see something different in his critical reading of exemplary texts of traditional philosophy. From within the perspective of traditional philosophy Austin's thought and his demand for Disengagement constitutes a dramatic form of heresy (cf. 'deeply ingrained worship') against the tradition. And, of course, given my characterization of the Strategy of

Disengagement, Austin's work will almost inevitably present itself as irrelevant to philosophers working within the traditional framework; appearing as nothing less than the abandonment of philosophy itself to impressionistic descriptions of the English language. The question is, then, whether a Disengaged inquiry can effectively intervene in and maintain a relation to the tradition or whether the very movement which was to provide an opening to an effective and critical intervention (Dis-engagement) actually forecloses the possibility. Austin may get free—but can he get heard too? 'What has all this to do with the old questions about appearance and reality? Almost nothing' (Bennett 1969: 280).

The sense of relevance (of having been touched) marked by Bennett's 'almost' marks the spot of penetration of Austin's procedures, a certain audibility of the appeal to ordinary language despite the traditional philosopher's commitment to the traditional framework. It is, Austin hopes, a call home. There is nothing 'unjustified' about this call, as Cavell suggests, but it remains true that however compelling such a call is—and no one is going to write in a way that they would regard as falling short of the most convincing expression of making a claim on our attention—Austin is ruefully sure that, for the reasons explained in this essay, it is not just 'an occasional weakness of philosophers' that they fail—or almost fail—to hear that call. However, they can't be completely deaf either. Willy-nilly and despite their mastery of blinkering philosophical-English, Austin wagers that they too must somehow feel that the traditional problematic is 'somehow spurious' (1962: 4). It is this residual sense that everything is *not* in order with the 'how possible' questions that Austin's Disengagement attempts to seize on and make vivid. Echoing the Husserlian rallying cry of phenomenology, that going *on* in philosophy requires that one 'go *back* to "things themselves"' (Husserl 1970: 252), Austin, in 'A Plea for Excuses', responds to the traditional philosopher's predicament by saying that his (Austin's) *positive* aim in philosophy, the mark we might say of its *authenticity*, is to see the world without blinkers:

Words are not (except in their own little corner) facts or things: we need therefore to prise them off the world, to hold them apart and against it, so that we can realize their inadequacies and arbitrariness, and so can re-look at the world without blinkers. (1979: 182)

A harmless formulation in some respects, this way of putting his ambition in philosophy has been seized on by others as marking an uncritical commitment to the 'myth of the given'.[14] Well, of course, one can see why. However, in the context of a discussion of the virtues of proceeding 'from "ordinary language"' (1979: 181), and flanked by a call to 'use clean [linguistic] tools', on the one hand, and to acknowledge the 'numerous' and 'subtle' distinctions embodied in our common stock of words on the other, I suspect that Austin is adverting here to a point that is brought out more transparently in the paragraph that follows: namely, that he is not setting out to look 'merely at words' but, precisely by recalling ourselves to 'what we should say when', to sharpen

[14] See, for example, Arrington 1975: 290.

our perception of 'the realities we use words to talk about (1979: 182). In short, 're-looking at the world without blinkers' is about the minimization of prejudices, especially philosophical prejudices, not about looking at the phenomena in a bizarre kind of concept-free way. On the contrary, Austin's return to the *words* of ordinary life is intended to be, as such, a return to the *world* of ordinary life. This is, as Austin notes himself, best understood as an attempt to pursue philosophy as 'linguistic phenomenology'. It is, that is to say, an attempt to find a way of getting *back in philosophy* to the native land of an understanding that is not dominated by traditional prejudices about, for example, the primary data for a theory of perception or meaning or whatever. For all the deviations that mark the later inheritance of phenomenology after Husserl, something of his call back to what we really know remains everywhere in the work of those who pursue philosophy, in one way or another, in the name of phenomenology. It is there in the effort to get rid of distorting presuppositions and assumptions not simply by constructing 'arguments'—and not by writing a novel or a poem either—but by way of descriptions which offer some other kind of *in their way* (aiming to be) convincing appeal to people's attention: through writing whose distinctive discipline resides in its capacity to bring people back to what they already know, to *turn people round* so that they can see clearly what (by the phenomenologist's lights) we typically find it hard to see.[15] How the linguistic phenomenology elaborated by Austin attempts to loosen the grip of tradition on our thinking in philosophy is, in my view, most strikingly presented in his work of reading exemplary texts of 'the philosopher arguing'. But, despite my talk of Disengagement, this is not just the application of a 'method', and we should not expect that a talent for such criticism will belong to everyone equally or that all who do attempt to pursue it will do so in the same way or even an especially convincing way. Can this be the right way to go on with philosophy? Cavell had suggested that Austin's work helps to settle the worries it raises. Although Cavell's own concern that there is, finally, a short-fall of justification in Austin's case seems to me fundamentally misplaced, what is right about his suggestion is that there is and can be no radical justification for phenomenology that is not itself phenomenological in character. Merleau-Ponty says: phenomenology 'rests on itself' (1962: xxiii). Austin adds: 'there is gold in them thar hills' (1979: 181). But to affirm this for yourself you must, as Austin put it, 'cut the cackle' (1975: 123). Indeed, you must move on to what I have suggested we should find Austin, through his Disengagement from traditional philosophy, brilliantly capable of: namely, of finding a future for philosophy not in a new theory but through field work in indigenous words.[16]

---

[15] I provide an introduction to this way of going on and with philosophy in the opening chapter of Glendinning 2007.

[16] I am grateful to the editors of this volume and to two anonymous referees for the publisher for giving helpfully constructive advice on the development and presentation of the ideas in this essay. I should also like to express my gratitude to Stephen Mulhall whose patience first made it possible for me to get going and get free with the great texts of J. L. Austin.

Bibliography

Arrington, R. L. (1975), 'Can there be a Linguistic Phenomenology?', *The Philosophical Quarterly*, 25 (101): 289–304.

Austin, J. L. (1962), *Sense and Sensibilia*, Warnock, G. J. (ed.), Oxford: Oxford University Press.

—— (1975), *How to Do things with Words*, 2nd ed., Urmson, J. O., Sbisà, M. (eds.), Oxford: Clarendon Press.

—— (1979), *Philosophical Papers*, 3rd ed., Urmson, J. O., Warnock, G. J. (eds.), Oxford: Oxford University Press.

Bennett, J. (1969), '"Real"', in Fann, 267–83.

Burnyeat, M. (1979), 'Conflicting Appearances', *Proceedings of the British Academy*, 65: 69–111.

Cavell, S. (2002), 'Austin at Criticism', in *Must We Mean What We Say?* (Updated edition), Cambridge: Cambridge University Press, 97–114.

Fann, K. T. (ed.) (1969), *Symposium on J .L. Austin*. London: Routledge.

Glendinning, S. (1998), *On Being with Others: Heidegger–Wittgenstein–Derrida*. London: Routledge.

—— (2001), 'Inheriting "Philosophy": The Case of Austin and Derrida Revisited', in Glendinning, S. (ed.), *Arguing with Derrida*, Oxford: Blackwell, 9–35.

—— (2003), 'The End of Philosophy as Metaphysics', in Baldwin, T. (ed.), *Cambridge History of Philosophy 1870–1945*, Cambridge: Cambridge University Press, 563–75.

—— (2007), *In the Name of Phenomenology*, Abingdon: Routledge.

Husserl, E. (1970), *Logical Investigations,* Vol. 2 (trans. J. N. Findlay), London: Routledge.

Merleau-Ponty, M. (1962), *Phenomenology of Perception*, trans. Colin Smith, London: Routledge.

Putnam, H. (1999), *The Threefold Cord*, New York: Columbia University Press.

Urmson, J. O. (1969), 'Austin's Method', in K. T. Fann (ed.) 1969: 76–86.

Warnock, G. (1969), 'John Langshaw Austin, a Biographical Sketch', in Fann, 3–21.

—— (1989). *J. L. Austin*. London: Routledge.

3

Tales of the Unknown: Austin and the Argument from Ignorance[1]

Mark Kaplan

1. The argument from ignorance

This chapter is an essay on what J. L. Austin has to say about knowledge—and on how what he says bears on a particular form of argument—what I am going to call (following DeRose 2005: 1) 'the argument from ignorance':

I don't know that not-q.
If I don't know that not-q, I don't know that p.
Therefore, I don't know that p.

I want to focus, in particular, on how what Austin has to say about knowledge bears on the propriety of deploying the argument from ignorance to establish scepticism of the philosophical variety. The following three arguments constitute well-known, and representative, examples of instances of the argument from ignorance that have been deployed to this end:

A. I don't know that I'm not dreaming.
   If I don't know I'm not dreaming, then I don't know that I have hands.
   Therefore, I don't know that I have hands.
B. I don't know that I'm not a brain in a vat.
   If I don't know I'm not a brain in a vat, then I don't know that I have hands.
   Therefore, I don't know that I have hands.

[1] I am very much in debt to the following people for their help as I wrote this chapter: Ken Gemes, Adam Leite, Ram Neta, Charles Travis, Jonathan Weinberg, the editors of this volume, two anonymous readers for Oxford University Press, and (especially) Joan Weiner. I am also grateful for comments I have received from audiences at the following universities to which I had the opportunity to read versions of this essay: the University of Illinois Urbana-Champaign, the University of London, Indiana University, Texas A&M University, the Ohio State University, the University of Chicago (the Wittgenstein Colloquium), and Hendrix College. My initial work on this essay was supported by fellowships from the Philosophy Programme of the School of Advanced Study at the University of London, and from the American Council of Learned Societies. They have my thanks.

C. I don't know that the animal in the enclosure is not a painted mule.
If I don't know that the animal in the enclosure is not a painted mule, then I don't know that it is a zebra.
Therefore, I don't know that it is a zebra.

A and B differ from C in an important respect. Both A and B substitute for q a proposition so constructed that, if it does the work it is meant to do by way of impeaching your claim to know that you have hands, it will do likewise for any claim to perceptual knowledge you might make. In contrast, C substitutes for q a proposition designed simply to effect the impeachment of the particular claim to knowledge at hand. It seems that most philosophers of sceptical bent find the first two instances more disturbing, because more radical. But it is worth noting that the subtituends for q of the C-type will clearly suffice to impeach (if the argument is a good one) all but those knowledge claims that we are best-placed to make—all the scientific ones and such.

We know that Austin would have disdained the first argument. He thought that the hypothesis that dreaming is indistinguishable from non-dreaming was an incoherent one. ('[H]ow otherwise', he wrote, 'should we know how to use and to contrast the words?' (1979: 87).) And, in any event, he thought there are recognized ways of telling whether one was dreaming or not (ibid.). The second argument is too new-fangled to have received his attention. But there is no question but that the first of his two reasons for disdaining argument A applies to argument B.

What interests me here is what he would say—and what there is available for him to say—about the third argument. Say what you like about whether the dream hypothesis really *is* coherent or whether dream states really *are* easily distinguishable from non-dream states. There can be no question as to the coherence of the hypothesis that the animal in the enclosure is a painted mule. And there can be no question but that (at least for many of us) it would not be easy to tell a zebra from a painted mule. So, whatever the propriety of Austin's way of dismissing the first two arguments, his way of dismissing them still leaves the third argument standing.

I mean to argue that a close examination of what Austin has to say about this third argument, and of the resources available to him for addressing it, reveals that he has at his disposal a response to the sceptical argument from ignorance that is novel,[2] and to this extent helpful: to those who are neither prepared to dismiss arguments A and B on grounds of incoherence nor are as sanguine as Austin about their ability to distinguish dream states from non-dream states (or sanguine about their ability to tell whether they are brains in a vat), this response to argument C will provide independent grounds for dismissing the other two.

---

[2] Though it has affinities (which I will not explore in this chapter) with a doctrine of Wittgenstein's.

2. Austin's way with the argument from ignorance: the case of the goldfinch

I don't mean to suggest that Austin actually wrote about argument C. He didn't. The argument first entered the literature in Fred Dretske's paper 'Epistemic Operators', published some nine years after Austin's death (Dretske 1970). But Austin did discuss a similar case in 'Other Minds': The case of the goldfinch. Austin there invites us to imagine that he has represented himself as knowing that there is a goldfinch in the garden. Consider a series of central passages, of which this is the first:

I. If you have asked 'How do you know it's a goldfinch?' then I may reply 'From its behaviour', 'By its markings', or, in more detail, 'By its red head', 'From its eating thistles'. That is, I indicate, or to some extent set out with some degree of precision, those features of the situation which enable me to recognize it as one to be described in the way I did describe it. Thereupon you may still object in several ways to my saying it's a goldfinch, without in the least 'disputing my facts' [. . .]. You may object: [. . .] But that's not enough: plenty of other birds have red heads. What you say doesn't prove it. For all you know it may be a woodpecker. [. . .]

It is in the case of [this] objection [. . .] that you would be more inclined to say right out 'Then you don't know'. Because it doesn't prove it, it's not enough to prove it. Several important points come out here:

   (a) If you say 'That's not enough', then you must have in mind some more or less definite lack. 'To be a goldfinch, besides having a red head it must also have the characteristic eye-markings': or 'How do you know it isn't a woodpecker? Woodpeckers have red heads too'. If there is no definite lack, which you are at least prepared to specify on being pressed, then it's silly (outrageous) just to go on saying 'That's not enough'.
   (b) Enough is enough: it doesn't mean everything. Enough means enough to show that (within reason, and for the present intents and purposes) it 'can't' be anything else, there is no room for an alternative, competing, description of it. It does *not* mean, for example, enough to show it isn't a *stuffed* goldfinch. (1979: 83–4)

Or, at least, it doesn't mean this in ordinary cases. Here is a second central passage:

II. Knowing it's a 'real' goldfinch isn't in question in the ordinary case when I say I know it's a goldfinch: reasonable precautions only are taken. But when it *is* called in question, in *special* cases, then I make sure it's a real goldfinch in ways essentially similar to those in which I made sure it was a goldfinch, though corroboration by other witnesses plays a specially important part in some cases. Once again the precautions cannot be more than reasonable, relative to current intents and purposes. (1979: 88)

And what does it take to call in question whether the goldfinch is real (as opposed to stuffed)? What makes for a special case? Writing directly of our knowledge of other minds, Austin says:

III. When to all appearance angry, might he not really be feeling no emotion at all? [. . .] There are (more or less roughly) established procedures for dealing with suspected cases of deception or of misunderstanding or of inadvertence. By these means we do very often establish (though we do not expect *always* to establish) that someone is acting, or that we were misunderstanding him, or that he is simply impervious to a certain emotion, or that he was not acting voluntarily. These special cases where doubts arise and require resolving, are contrasted with the normal cases which hold the field *unless* there is some special suggestion that deceit, &c., is involved. (1979: 112–13, note omitted)

And, writing of testimony, he says:

IV. Naturally we are judicious: we don't say we know (at second hand) if there is any special reason to doubt the testimony: but there has to be *some* reason. It is fundamental in talking (as in other matters) that we are entitled to trust others, except in so far as there is some concrete reason to distrust them. (1979: 82)

And, finally, writing about the notion that if one knows one can't be wrong:

V. 'When you know you can't be wrong' is perfectly good sense. You are prohibited from saying 'I know it is so, but I may be wrong', just as you are prohibited from saying 'I promise I will, but I may fail'. If you are aware you may be mistaken, you ought not say you know, just as, if you are aware you make break your word, you have no business to promise. But of course, being aware that you may be mistaken doesn't mean merely being aware that you are a fallible human being: it means that you have some concrete reason to suppose that you may be mistaken in this case. Just as 'but I may fail' does not mean merely 'but I am a weak human being' (in which case it would be no more exciting than adding 'D.V.'): it means that there is some concrete reason for me to suppose that I shall break my word. It is naturally *always* possible ('humanly' possible) that I may be mistaken or may break my word, but that by itself is no bar against using the expressions 'I know' and 'I promise' as we do in fact use them. (1979: 98)

Given this last passage, it would seem that Austin's idea is this. We are entitled to claim knowledge that *p* when we have done enough for present intents and purposes—and within reason—to establish that *p*. What counts as enough is rough to be sure. But doing enough doesn't require that we do enough to prove false every imaginable hypothesis whose truth is incompatible with our knowing that *p*.

What counts as enough is also somewhat routinized. One can, as Austin does, speak of normal cases and what is enough—what will do—in normal cases. So we can talk of what normally counts as doing enough to establish the propriety of a knowledge-claim of a particular sort (where both the content of the claim and the circumstances in which it is made contribute to determining that the claim is of that sort). It is presumably that of which Austin is thinking when he denies that he has to establish that it isn't a stuffed goldfinch. Only in special cases, cases in which we have a special reason to suppose, of some particular way things can go amiss, that things have gone amiss in this way, can we demand that more be done than normally counts as enough.

And what makes a reason special? Austin doesn't explicitly say. But this much would seem to be judicious: for a reason to count by Austin's lights as a special reason to think that something is amiss, it has to be, at the very least, a reason that one doesn't have in the normal cases—the cases in which it is not legitimate to demand, of some way of things' going amiss, that the claimant to knowledge do enough to show that things haven't gone amiss in that way, the cases in which we are (rightly) happy to grant the knowledge claimed without further ado. This way of thinking of special reasons is particularly consonant with the 'When you know you can't be wrong' passage, Quotation V. There Austin seems to tell us that we always have some reason to suppose we are mistaken: we are fallible beings. But that is no bar to our using 'know' as we do. Only when we have special/concrete reason to think we are mistaken—a reason we *don't* always have—can we legitimately say that we may be mistaken and, hence, cannot count as knowing.[3]

This way of describing things goes some considerable distance toward taking care of all the arguments. Consider argument C. We normally grant people the knowledge they claim when they appeal to general lay knowledge of how things differ from one another (zebras from other animals) and to what they see. So it is illegitimate to do otherwise in this case unless we have a special reason—a reason we haven't in the normal cases—to suppose that something has gone amiss. But we have no such reason. So it is illegitimate to demand, of some particular way of things' going amiss (it's really a painted mule), that I do enough to show that things haven't gone amiss in that way.

Now to arguments A and B. We normally grant people the knowledge they claim of familiar objects and surroundings when they claim to know by dint of having seen it to be so. So it is illegitimate to do otherwise in this case unless we have a special reason—a reason we don't have in the normal cases—to suppose that something has gone amiss. But we have no such reason. So it is illegitimate to demand, of some particular way of things' going amiss (I am dreaming, I am a brain in a vat), that I do enough to show that things haven't gone amiss in that way.

It goes a considerable distance toward taking care of all three arguments, but not all the way. What it doesn't do is give us marching orders as to how to go about the traditional way of disposing of a valid argument (as all these three arguments are) whose conclusion we reject. It doesn't tell us what premise or premises are to be rejected.

---

[3] I say that he *seems* to be saying that we always have a reason to think we are mistaken (we are fallible beings) because he doesn't *actually* say that. Rather, he says that it is always possible that we are mistaken. And that is not the same thing. But there is this much in favour of reading Austin here as I do. Were it Austin's view that our human fallibility is no reason whatsoever to suppose we are mistaken in any particular case, one wouldn't expect him to write that merely being aware that you are a fallible human being does not provide any *concrete reason* to suppose that you may be mistaken in this case; one would expect him to write that it provides *no reason whatsoever* to suppose that you may be mistaken in this case. That he makes (what would appear to be) the weaker claim would seem to indicate that he is willing to concede that our fallibility *is* a reason to suppose we are mistaken in this case—just not a *concrete* or *special* reason, not the sort of reason it would have to be to be a bar to saying (or, to its being the case that) we know in this case. For a detailed examination (and defence) of what Austin is saying in Quotation V, see Kaplan (2006b). For more details on (and, again, a defence of) Austin's appeal to special reasons, see Kaplan (2008).

3. An apparent problem with Austin's way

The problem is that what Austin actually says about the goldfinch case is not, at least on the surface, very comforting on this score. To see this, consider the following argument:

D. I don't know that it's not a stuffed goldfinch.
   If I don't know that it's not a stuffed goldfinch, then I don't know it's a goldfinch.
   Therefore, I don't know that it's a goldfinch.

What is there available for Austin to do by way of disposing in the traditional way of the challenge this argument would seem to pose to the propriety of his claim to know that the bird in his garden is a goldfinch? Austin holds the view that claiming to know carries with it a certain justificatory obligation. He writes:

VI. Whenever I say I know, I am always liable to be taken to claim that, in a certain sense appropriate to the kind of statement (and to present intents and purposes), I am able to *prove* it. In the present, very common, type of case, 'proving' seems to mean stating what are the features of the current case which are enough to constitute it one which is correctly describable in the way we have described it, and not in any other way relevantly variant. Generally speaking, cases where I can 'prove' are cases where we use the 'because' formula: cases where we 'know but can't prove' are cases in which we take refuge in the 'from' or 'by' formula. (1979: 85–6)

Now, it may at first appear that, in the last sentence, about cases in which we 'know but can't prove', Austin is taking back what he says in the first sentence. But I think this worry is easily addressed. Think of being able to prove a statement as being able to offer an adequate answer to the question, 'How do you know it?' Austin is simply reminding us that, in ordinary life, saying how one knows a proposition does not always require very much. To 'How do you know it's a Pakistani rug?' it might do to say 'By the way it feels', or 'From its feel' (1979: 84–5). In some cases (like 'How do you know this is a theorem?'), 'It's just obvious' may do. And that won't look very much like what one ordinarily thinks of as a proof—it won't have the appropriate sort of premises. Hence the scare quotes around 'prove' and 'know but can't prove'.[4] Context influences what needs saying, what constitutes saying enough to say how one knows. But this much is pretty clear: Austin thinks that we won't credit a person's claim to know that P unless she can say how she knows it. This is apparent in his account of the goldfinch case: it is what makes the 'How do you know it is a goldfinch?' question and the subsequent challenges legitimate.

He also appears, from his account of the goldfinch case, to think that if a claimant to knowledge is unable to carry the justificatory burden that comes with her claim to

---

[4] The idea that there are claims to which we are perfectly entitled and yet cannot count as being able to prove—not because we cannot say anything in their favour, but rather because we cannot supply anything (or enough things) to serve as straightforward premises—harkens back to Moore (1939: 299–300).

knowledge, then it is appropriate to say that she doesn't know what she has claimed to know. Recall Quotation I: if all Austin can say in response to 'How do you know it is a goldfinch?' is, 'By its red head', and if he has no response to the subsequent challenges ('But that's not enough: plenty of other birds have red heads. What you say doesn't prove it. For all you know it may be a woodpecker'), then, he writes, 'you would be more inclined to say right out "Then you don't know". Because it doesn't prove it, it's not enough to prove it.'

He also writes as if he thinks that, in most normal cases, the justificatory burden for the claim to know that it's not a stuffed goldfinch will be one he is not (or not yet) in a position to carry. He clearly doesn't think that he can meet that obligation simply by doing what is necessary to legitimize his claim to know it is a goldfinch. Recall again Quotation I. While he admits to his obligation to do enough (within reason and for present intents and purposes) to show that it 'can't' be anything else, he denies that this requires him to do enough to show that it isn't a stuffed goldfinch. If Austin thought that doing enough to show it's a goldfinch is always, in every normal case, sufficient to show that it isn't stuffed, he wouldn't dismiss the demand that he show that it's not a stuffed goldfinch on the grounds that he *doesn't need to show* this much; he would dismiss the demand on the grounds that, once he has done enough to show (within reason, and for the present intents and purposes) that it 'can't' be anything else, he *has already shown* this much.[5]

It is equally clear that it is not because he wants to say that he already knows that the bird isn't stuffed—it is not because he thinks the claim that it isn't stuffed doesn't require proof in order to be known in the normal case—that Austin thinks that he doesn't need to do enough to show the bird isn't stuffed. Remember: Austin holds that, whenever he claims to know something is the case, he will always be 'liable to be taken to claim that, in a certain sense appropriate to the kind of statement (and to

---

[5] It might be replied, however, that Austin is merely writing here of what he is *obliged* to do in response to the question, 'How do you know?', not of what he is *able* to do. That is, it might be replied that it is entirely compatible with what Austin says here that, while he thinks that in a normal case he has no obligation to do enough in response to the question, 'How do you know?' to show it isn't a stuffed goldfinch, he must nonetheless be *capable* of showing this much in any such case—he must be *capable* of shouldering the justificatory burden with which a claim to know that it's not stuffed would saddle him—if he is legitimately to claim to know that it's a goldfinch.

But this doesn't square with Quotation VI. There he *is* writing of what he must regard himself as capable of proving if he is legitimately to claim he knows that is a goldfinch. He must, he writes, regard himself (in this case) as capable of 'stating what are the features of the current case which are enough to constitute it one which is correctly describable in the way we have described it, and not in any other way *relevantly variant.*' (The italics are mine.) If Austin thought that, in order legitimately to claim to know it is a goldfinch, he must regard himself as capable of proving, for every wild hypothesis incompatible with its being a goldfinch, that this hypothesis is false, we would expect him to write that he must regard himself as capable of 'stating what are the features of the current case which are enough to constitute it one which is correctly describable in the way we have described it, and not in any other way' *full stop.* That he adds the words 'relevantly variant' would seem to indicate that he does *not* think that, before he can claim in a normal case that he knows it's a goldfinch he needs to be capable of stating, for *every conceivable* variant, no matter how far-fetched, what the features of the current case are that render it not describable as being variant in that way.

present intents and purposes), I am able to prove it' (1979: 85). That is, he holds that, if he claims to know the goldfinch isn't stuffed, he will be liable to be taken to claim that he can provide a good answer to the question, 'How do you know it isn't stuffed?' Austin also holds that, if he is asked how he knows that the goldfinch is real, then, while heroic measures are not called for, additional work—work beyond what is required for him to be able to explain how he know it is a goldfinch—will be required. He writes that the doubts expressed by the question are

to be allayed by means of recognized procedures (more or less roughly recognized, of course), appropriate to the particular type of case. There are recognized ways of distinguishing between dreaming and waking [. . .], and of deciding whether a thing is stuffed or live, and so forth. (1979: 87)

And, as we have seen, Austin thinks he can have done enough to have proved (within reason, and for present intents and purposes) that it 'can't' be anything other than a goldfinch *without* having deployed any of one of these recognized ways of deciding whether a thing is stuffed or live. Recall: for Austin, doing enough to have proved it can't be anything else does not require doing enough to have proved that it isn't a stuffed goldfinch.

One might be tempted to think it is still possible that Austin wants to count himself, in the normal case, as knowing that the bird is not stuffed. One might be tempted to think it is still possible that only special cases, cases in which there is a special reason to suspect the bird is stuffed, does Austin think it necessary, in order for him to be counted as knowing that the bird is not stuffed, that he have deployed a recognized procedure for deciding whether a thing is live or stuffed.[6]

But this is a temptation to be resisted. After all, there is likewise no special reason in the normal case to suspect, as Austin claims to know the bird is a goldfinch, that the bird actually belongs to some other species.[7] Yet, despite there being no special reason to suppose that he is mistaken in saying he knows the bird is a goldfinch, Austin holds (in Quotation VI) that he still has to be able to prove that it is a goldfinch—where he understands that to mean, in this 'very common' type of case, 'stating what are the features of the current case which are enough to constitute it one which is correctly describable in the way we have described it, and not in any other way relevantly variant'. That is, Austin holds that, even when there is no special reason to suspect that his claim to know isn't true, he must still be able to say, by appeal to recognized ways of distinguishing birds from one another, how he knows this bird is a goldfinch.

---

[6] Adam Leite suggests as much in his contribution to this volume.

[7] True, once he has said that he knows *by its red head* that it's a goldfinch, a special reason to suspect that he is mistaken arises: it is entirely compatible with the bird's having a red head that it is one of the woodpeckers that we have in these parts. But Austin is clear in his commitment to the view that his merely saying he knows it is a goldfinch cannot itself be a special reason for suspicion. '[W]e don't say we know (at second hand)', Austin writes (1979: 82), 'if there is any special reason to doubt the testimony: but there has to be *some* reason. It is fundamental in talking (as in other matters) that we are entitled to trust others, except in so far as there is some concrete reason to distrust them.'

Given this, he cannot think it sufficient, to legitimize his claiming to know the bird is not stuffed, that there is in the case under discussion no special reason to suspect that the bird is stuffed. Holding as he does that '[t]here are recognized ways of... deciding whether a thing is stuffed or live, and so forth', he cannot hold it sufficient, to waive the requirement that he be able to say (by appeal to recognized ways of making such decisions) *how* he knows the bird is not stuffed, that there is no special reason to suspect that he does not know that the bird is not stuffed.

All the same, one might think that Quotation II presents evidence that Austin *is* prepared to waive that requirement: he says there that '[k]nowing it's a "real" goldfinch isn't in question in the ordinary case when I say I know it's a goldfinch'. But the temptation to read this as meaning that *there is no question but that, in the ordinary case, he knows it is not stuffed* quickly disappears once one recalls how this passage is situated:

Knowing it's a 'real' goldfinch isn't in question in the ordinary case when I say I know it's a goldfinch: reasonable precautions only are taken. But when it *is* called into question, in *special* cases, then I make sure it's a real goldfinch in ways essentially similar to those in which I made sure it was a goldfinch, though corroboration by other witnesses plays a specially important part in some cases. Once again, the precautions cannot be more than reasonable, relative to current intents and purposes. (1979: 88)

Austin is here simply contrasting what he is called upon to do in two different cases: first, the ordinary case in which he claims to know the bird is a goldfinch, and the question, 'How do you know the goldfinch is real—e.g. that it isn't stuffed?' isn't (and properly isn't) raised; second, the special case in which he claims to know that the bird is a goldfinch, and the question as to how he knows it isn't stuffed *is* (and properly is) raised. In the former case, Austin maintains, he needs only take reasonable precautions that the bird is a goldfinch; in the second case, he needs to do somewhat more. Whether or not he counts as *knowing* in the ordinary case that the bird is not stuffed—that is a matter the passage simply does not address.

So Austin's doctrine seems to be this. In the ordinary case in which he claims to know the bird is a goldfinch, he has no call to explain how he knows it is not stuffed. But, of course, in the ordinary case he does not *claim* to know it isn't stuffed; the subject never arises. But were he to claim that it isn't stuffed, he would take on the liability of explaining how he knows it isn't stuffed—a liability he could not discharge simply by explaining how he knows it's a goldfinch. He would take on a liability that he could discharge only by having done something that he won't (yet) have done in many normal cases—only by having deployed one of the recognized ways of deciding whether a thing is live or stuffed. Thus it is that he cannot in the normal case—the case with which we are concerned—legitimately claim to know that the bird is not stuffed.[8]

---

[8] Might Austin maintain that he knows it all the same, but is merely unable legitimately to *claim in ordinary life* that he knows it? Only if he thought he might legitimately be able to make knowledge claims before his colleagues in the Aristotelian Society (to a meeting of which 'Other Minds' was first delivered) that would be illegitimate for him to make in ordinary life. But it was a fundamental methodological tenet of Austin's

What these considerations seem to suggest is that Austin is committed to there being cases in which the first premise of argument D is true and the conclusion is false. These are cases that are normal—there is no special reason to suggest that something is amiss. He has done enough (within reason and for present intents and purposes) to show that it is a goldfinch. But he is not (or not yet) in a position to prove that it's not stuffed—he hasn't had (or hasn't yet had) the opportunity to deploy one of the recognized way of deciding whether something it real or stuffed. A case of this sort is not hard to imagine. Austin looks up from his book, looks out his window and sees, standing still in a tree, a bird he can identify by its markings as a goldfinch. This being an unremarkable sighting, he goes back to his reading. The next time he has occasion to look up from his book, the bird is gone. He knows it is a goldfinch, but he doesn't know it isn't stuffed—but, because there is no special reason to suppose anything here is amiss, he doesn't *need* to know it's not stuffed to know it's a goldfinch.

This would seem to commit him to denying the second premise of argument D. But it is hard to see how he could possibly afford to do that. For all his apparent commitment to there being cases in which he knows it is a goldfinch but doesn't know it's not a stuffed goldfinch, he clearly is not prepared to say in such cases, 'I know it's a goldfinch, but for all I know it's just a stuffed goldfinch.' After all, to that we could justifiably say, 'In other words, what you are saying is that you know it's a goldfinch but you might be wrong.' And, of course, that is something that Austin (in quotation V) explicitly denies he can say.

Austin thus appears to fall right into the trap the sceptical argument has laid. He appears to be committed to there being cases in which he must affirm the premises of D and deny its conclusion—this despite the fact that the argument is patently valid.

4. A way out for Austin: a third category

But does he really fall into the trap? Think again about the first premise. I think that of this much there can be no question: Austin cannot think it legitimate to say (because it is essential to his understanding of the circumstances under which we make and challenge knowledge—claims in ordinary life that he not be permitted to say) that he knows it is not a stuffed goldfinch. If, as we are supposing, he has done no more than is necessary in the normal case to prove that it's a goldfinch, he hasn't proved (and is not currently in a position to prove) that it is not a stuffed goldfinch.

But, it seems to me, the trip (via Quotation I) to the conclusion that he is committed to the legitimacy of his saying that he doesn't know it isn't a stuffed goldfinch is too quick. After all, the only thing Austin *actually* says there is that, if he claims to know it is a goldfinch, and if he cannot meet (in a manner appropriate to the intents and purposes

ordinary language approach to epistemology that he could not legitimately keep two sets of books: that what we say when doing epistemology must be true to what we say and do, and are *right* to say and do, in ordinary life. I have more to say about this tenet, and its propriety, in section 6 below.

at hand) legitimate challenges to his claim to know that it is a goldfinch, then we would be inclined to say (and presumably he should agree) that he doesn't know that it is a goldfinch. The only thing to which Austin thereby commits himself is the legitimacy of saying, of this particular proposition in this particular case, that, by virtue of his being unable to meet the (legitimate) challenges raised, he doesn't know the proposition.

Now, I am prepared to concede—it seems to me patent in what Austin writes—that he thinks that, were he to claim to know that it's not a stuffed goldfinch, there would likewise in that case and with respect to that proposition be legitimate challenges he could not meet. But only by generalizing from the former case can one get from this a commitment on Austin's part to the legitimacy of his saying that he does not know that it's not a stuffed goldfinch. Only so long as one supposes that what goes for the former case goes for *every* case—only so long as one supposes that, for *all p* in *all* circumstances, if we think he could not shoulder the justificatory burden he would incur by claiming to know that *p*, then we should say he doesn't know that *p*—can one get the conclusion that Austin is committed to the legitimacy of saying he doesn't know that it's not a stuffed goldfinch. The facts that (a) we are not forced by the words on the page to attribute to him this general principle, and that (b) if we do attribute to him that principle, he ends up in the sceptic's snare, add up to a good reason to seek some other, better way of making sense of Austin's position.

It may seem that Austin has not left us much room in which to manoeuvre. After all, even if we don't attribute the offending principle to him, we are still reading him as committed to the illegitimacy of his saying, in the case we are imagining, that he knows it is not a stuffed goldfinch. Given that, what else is there left for him to say except that he *doesn't* know that it's not a stuffed goldfinch?

To be sure, it is not difficult to imagine how there could be a circumstance in which Austin felt—and felt with at least some justification—that he could neither legitimately say he knew a proposition nor legitimately say that he didn't know that proposition. Suppose that he knew that there was a rather specific procedure one needs to follow to come to know a certain proposition in his present circumstances and he wasn't quite sure whether he had done all the steps yet. He might then think that, while it would be clear to anyone who knew what steps he had done and what steps are required whether he knows the proposition in question, he was not himself in a position either to say that he knew it or to say that he didn't.

Alternatively, suppose that Austin found that, in a given circumstance and with respect to a particular proposition, he faced a borderline case of knowledge. Suppose that no amount of reflection on the meaning of 'know' seemed to him capable of deciding whether he had, at present, done quite enough for present intents and purposes to show that the proposition was true—and so to count as knowing it. Again, he might then think that he was not in a position either to say that he knew it or to say that he didn't.

The trouble is that Austin cannot plausibly think himself to be in either of these two situations with respect to the proposition that it's not a stuffed goldfinch, in the circumstances we are imagining—circumstances in which he has only done enough for present intents and purposes to show it's a goldfinch, where enough does not include enough to show it is not a stuffed goldfinch. Insofar as there is a procedure for telling that a goldfinch is not stuffed (and, as we have seen, Austin thinks there are more or less recognized procedures for doing this), he will know full well that he has not taken all the steps in that procedure. Far from its being a borderline case of doing enough, it will be clear to him that he has not done enough to prove that it is not a stuffed goldfinch.

But then, it would seem, since Austin cannot say he knows that it's not a stuffed goldfinch, and cannot claim to be on the fence as to whether he knows it or not, he has no option: he has to say that he doesn't know it's not a stuffed goldfinch, and he's back in the sceptical trap. The principle at work here is pretty simple: if you don't want to say that *p*, and it's not because you are on the fence as to whether it is the case that *p*, you have to say that not-*p*.

But, simple or not, this is a principle that Austin rejects. In 'The Meaning of a Word', written only a few years before 'Other Minds', Austin writes:

It seems, does it not, perfectly obvious that every proposition must have a contradictory? Yet it does not turn out so. Suppose that I live in harmony and friendship for four years with a cat: and then it delivers a philippic. We ask ourselves, perhaps, 'Is it a real cat? or is it *not* a real cat?' 'Either it *is*, or it is *not*, but we cannot be sure which.' Now actually, that is not so: *neither* 'It is a real cat' *nor* 'it is not a real cat' fits the facts semantically: each is designed for other situations than this one: you could not say the former of something which delivers philippics, nor yet the latter of something which has behaved as this has for four years. (1979: 67)

The moral he draws is that

[o]rdinary language breaks down in extraordinary cases. (In such cases, the cause of the break-down is semantical.) Now no doubt an *ideal* language would *not* break down, whatever happened. In doing physics, for example, where our language is tightened up in order precisely to describe complicated and unusual cases concisely, we *prepare linguistically for the worst*. In ordinary language we do not: *words fail us*. If we talk as though an ordinary must be like an ideal language, we shall misrepresent the facts. (1979: 68)

But it is not just in extraordinary cases that, Austin thinks, we may find ordinary language breaking down. He writes that

[a]lthough it will not do to force actual language to accord with some preconceived model: it *equally* will not do, having discovered the facts about 'ordinary usage' *to rest content* with that, as though there were nothing more to be discussed and discovered. There may be plenty that might happen and does happen which would need new and better language to describe it in. [. . .] There may be extraordinary facts, even about our everyday experience, which plain men and plain language overlook. (1979: 69)[9]

---

[9]   One may, of course, wonder how to understand Austin's demand that our philosophy be faithful to ordinary usage—to 'what we can and cannot say, and *precisely* why' (1979: 69)—in light of his admission that

Austin thus opens the door to the following possibility: that neither 'I know that it's not a stuffed goldfinch' nor 'I don't know it's not a stuffed goldfinch' is true of him in the circumstance we are imagining—neither fits the facts. If so, Austin can and should refuse to affirm either: the sceptical trap is avoided.

But *is* it so? Austin did not, as far as I know, ever address the question. But, if my reading of him is correct, then it is a condition on the coherence of his treatment of the goldfinch case—on the coherence of what he has to say about knowledge in 'Other Minds'—that the answer be affirmative. That is, if my reading of him is correct, then how we should assess Austin's contribution to our understanding of knowledge depends on whether there is available to him a convincing argument—on whether it can be established, by appeal to considerations we have reason to suppose Austin might be willing to accept—that neither 'I know that it's not a stuffed goldfinch' nor 'I don't know it's not a stuffed goldfinch' is true of him in the circumstance we are imagining.

One may think the suggestion that there *is* such an argument to be found an implausible one. After all, 'I don't know it's a stuffed goldfinch' appears to be nothing more or less than the negation of 'I know it's a stuffed goldfinch'. And if it is, then there simply is no way, short of abandoning classical logic, successfully to argue that there is a circumstance in which neither is true of Austin.

But Austin's suggestion, that ordinary language sometimes fails us in the way he describes, poses no challenge to classical logic—or, at least, no challenge to classical logic that isn't already posed by the well-known behaviour of 'I haven't stopped smoking' and 'I have stopped smoking'. The former sentence looks every bit as much the negation of the latter as 'I don't know it's not a stuffed goldfinch' looks to be the negation of 'I know it's not a stuffed goldfinch'. Yet we recognize that there is a circumstance in which (it is, at least, not obviously a mistake to say that) neither of 'I haven't stopped smoking' or 'I have stopped smoking' is true of Austin: the circumstance in which Austin has never smoked at all. All I mean to argue is that there is likewise a circumstance in which neither 'I know it's not a stuffed goldfinch' nor 'I don't know it's not a stuffed goldfinch' is true of Austin—and that it is in just such a circumstance that (in the case we are imagining) Austin is claiming to know that the bird in his backyard is a goldfinch. Thus it is that, in the circumstances in which we are imagining him, neither 'I don't know it's not a stuffed goldfinch' not 'I know it's a stuffed goldfinch' is true of Austin.

5. The case for a third category

My argument to that effect will turn on two observations—or, at least, I claim they count as observations—about our practice of knowledge attribution. The second of these observations is a generalization of one that Austin explicitly made—an

ordinary usage may be unfaithful to the facts, and his apparent willingness to override ordinary usage when it *is* unfaithful to the facts. I address this matter in section 6.

observation that we have taken note of already. The first, as far as I can tell, Austin did not explicitly make, though it is hard to see, given what he does explicitly say, why he would want to—and, indeed, how he could afford to—deny it.

Let me turn to the first.

Why do we care to distinguish what we know from what we don't? Why does it matter to us? The answer, I think, is that we want to distinguish questions that (at least, for the purposes we have at hand) we can consider closed from those we cannot—to distinguish propositions on whose truth (at least, for the purposes we have at hand) we can act from those on which we cannot. When we claim to know that p, we are claiming a certain entitlement, for present purposes, to act on p; when we claim not to know that p, we are claiming that we have no such entitlement for present purposes— that we cannot act on p for present purposes. Our interest in distinguishing what we know from what we don't know is an interest in determining with respect to which propositions we are currently so entitled, and which not.

And in what does this entitlement to act on p for present purposes—to regard the question as to p's truth as closed for these purposes—consist? Here is a fact about knowledge that suggests at least part of the answer: one cannot, without opening one's position to criticism, regard oneself (or, for that matter, anyone else) as knowing that p, yet be unwilling to act on p in one's current circumstances. That is, one cannot, without opening one's position to criticism, (a) regard oneself as knowing that p, (b) recognize, with respect to a decision one has to make, that there is no available option that will work out better if p than option A will, yet (c) be unwilling to choose option A. This fact explains why, when having claimed to know that p and having subsequently found out that the consequences of acting on p are far direr than one had thought, one will often withdraw one's claim to knowledge. And it suggests that knowing that p entails an entitlement—indeed, an obligation—to act on p.[10]

This, however, cannot be the full story of the entitlement that comes with knowing that p—at least, not if our interest in distinguishing what we know from what we don't know is to be understood as an interest in distinguishing propositions with respect to which we are so entitled from those to which we are not. Suppose that p is a proposition on which, as far as you are concerned, nothing good or bad hangs. You would, then, be perfectly entitled to act on p, even if you do not know, and do not regard yourself as knowing, that p.

---

[10] For more on this, see Kaplan (2006a). The relation between knowing that p and being entitled to act on p is actually more complicated than I have suggested here. In this respect, the entitlement that comes with knowing that p can be usefully compared to the entitlement that comes with owning a piece of property. Just as the entitlement to act with respect to a thing one owns is circumscribed, so is the entitlement to act on a proposition one knows to be true. There are limits to what one is entitled to do with a piece of land one owns: one isn't entitled to douse it with carcinogenic poisons, or to violate zoning regulations. Similarly, there are limits to how one is entitled to act on a proposition one knows. For example, a person opens her position to criticism if she treats her regarding herself as knowing that p as sufficient reason to adopt a policy of denying a hearing to any putative evidence that p is false. This suggests that knowing that p does not bring with it the entitlement to act in (at least) *that* way on p.

There is at least one more thing involved in the entitlement to act on p for present purposes (the entitlement to regard the question as to p's truth as closed for these purposes) that knowing p affords and not knowing p precludes. Suppose (to return to an earlier example) I claim to know that the rug I am examining is Pakistani. You ask me how I know. 'It has a cotton warp', I say by way of reply. Whatever the other merits of my explanation of how I know the rug is Pakistani (Is there really no other type of rug that has a cotton warp?), the explanation collapses if it can be legitimately replied, 'But you don't know that!' This suggests that part of the entitlement, that knowing that p provides and not knowing that p precludes, is the entitlement to appeal to p to explain how you know other propositions.[11]

The notion that to claim to know that p is (at least in part) to claim an entitlement to act on p (for the purposes at a hand) is not explicit in Austin's writings. But it is also not very far from the surface. Austin famously held that claims to knowledge have illocutionary force: 'When I say "I know",' he writes, 'I *give others my word: I give others my authority for saying* that "S is P" ' (1979: 99). And, a bit later, 'The right to say "I know" is transmissible, in the sort of way that other authority is transmissible. Hence, if I say it lightly, I may be *responsible* for getting *you* into trouble' (1979: 100). It would be odd, not to say morally monstrous, if Austin thought that he might legitimately say he

---

[11] A worry. Suppose Austin looks out his window and makes the knowledge claim we imagined, but (bad luck!) it turns out that the goldfinch is stuffed. We don't want to say he knows it's a goldfinch: he cannot prove it, as it isn't true. But it may not seem obvious that we want to deny his entitlement to act on its being a goldfinch. After all, he has made a responsible claim: we would have done no differently in his place. Isn't that enough to secure his entitlement to act on its being a goldfinch? And if so, doesn't this mean that one can have the entitlement to act on p even if one doesn't know that p? The answer is 'No'. Here again, the entitlement that comes with knowing that p is usefully thought of as being like the entitlement that comes with owning a piece of property. In the latter case, you have the entitlement to sell the piece of property if you own it, regardless of whether you are aware that you own it; and you lack the entitlement to sell it if you don't own it, even in circumstances (to which the circumstance described above is an analogue) in which you would be held entirely blameless for thinking it was yours to sell.

Of course, for this analogy to go through, it needs to be the case that, just as you can own a piece of property even if you are unaware that you own it (and even if you believe you don't own it), so you can know something even if you are unaware that you know it (and even if you believe you don't know it). But is this so far fetched? Suppose (I advert here to an example from Lemmon 1967: 63) I ask you if you know the ten decimal expansion of pi. You are convinced you do not. 'Oh, I knew it a long time ago', you say, 'but not anymore.' I ask you to think a minute. And, all of sudden and to your immense surprise, the number 3.1415936536 comes to you and you realize that this is the ten decimal expansion of pi. Don't we want to say that you knew all along that the ten decimal expansion of pi is 3.1415936536, but were, for a period of time, unaware that you did? Or, suppose that you have all the proof of p I have—proof on the basis of which I count myself as knowing that p—but, because you have (to my mind) unreasonably high standards of proof (or because you can't bring yourself to believe that p), you don't count yourself as knowing that p. Isn't it natural for me to say that you know as well as I do that p, but you just don't realize it (or, in the case in which you can't bring yourself to believe that p, are not willing to face up to it)?

For all that, the analogy will still fail to go through if there is any special difficulty in saying that—even though you are unaware that you have, or convinced you don't have, the knowledge in question—you have in these cases the entitlements that come with knowledge. Fortunately, there seems to be no such special difficulty—that is to say, no difficulty that isn't also present when we say (quite properly) that, if you own a piece of property, then you have the entitlements that come with owning that piece of property, even if you are unaware you own it, or are convinced you don't own it.

knows that p, thereby giving someone his word that p and taking on the responsibility for that person's getting into trouble on account of having taken his word that p, when he was not himself prepared to claim an entitlement to act on p (or, at least, an entitlement to act on p in the circumstances in which that person finds herself).[12]

As for the notion that explanations of how you know a proposition to be true preclude appeal to any proposition you do not know—this, too, is not explicit in Austin. But it is implicit in Quotation I. There Austin is suggesting that the enterprise of explaining how you know that p is not a matter of citing beliefs that support your claim to know that p (as Chisholm, amongst others, were later to assume—see, for example, his 1966: 25). Explaining how you know that p is a matter of citing *facts* that support your claim to know that p. In response to the question, 'How do you know it's a goldfinch?' Austin writes, 'I may reply "From its behaviour", "By its markings", or, in more detail, "By its red head", "From its eating thistles". That is, I indicate, or to some extent set out with some degree of precision, those features of the situation which enable me to recognize it as one to be described in the way I did describe it.'[13] These explanations of how he knows that it's a goldfinch collapse if it turns out that he has appealed to features he does not actually know the situation to have—if, for example, it can legitimately be replied, 'But the light wasn't good enough for you to know the colour of its head', or 'You cannot possibly know at this distance what the bird is eating'.

Now for the second of my two observations: when we are deciding whether a proposition belongs among the propositions we know, what settles the matter is whether we think we can (for present intents and purposes and within reason) prove that the proposition is true. It is understood here, as in our earlier discussion of Quotation VI, that being able to prove a proposition is true comes to no more or less than being able to offer an adequate answer (that is to say, adequate for present intents and purposes) to the question, 'How do you know it?' In some cases, the answers, 'It's obvious', or 'By the way it feels', or 'By the colour of its head', will do. This much said, however, if and only if we think we can prove that the proposition is true (i.e. explain how we know it is true) will we think we know it to be true. This observation, of course, is a generalization of Austin's, as a perusal of Quotations I and VI shows.

The upshot of the two observations, taken together, is then this. We distinguish between the propositions we know and those we don't know by way of trying to

---

[12] There is also Austin's talk, in Quotation I, of how a claimant to know the bird is a goldfinch has to do 'enough to show that (within reason, and for the present intents and purposes) it "can't" be anything else.' There is in this (at least) the suggestion that, amongst the present intents and purposes, there might be practical ones—and thus that doing enough to prove that p (and thus to be entitled to say 'I know that p') involves doing enough to be entitled to act on p. See, too, Quotation VI, where he writes, 'Whenever I say I know, I am always liable to be taken to claim that, in a certain sense appropriate to the kind of statement (and to present intents and purposes), I am able to prove it.'

[13] Notice, Austin does not write, 'I indicate [. . .] those features I *believe* the situation has and *believe* enable me to recognize it as one to be described the way I did describe it.'

determine on the truth of what propositions we are entitled to act. We count ourselves as knowing that *p* only if we can (for present intents and purposes and within reason) prove *p* to be true. We count ourselves as not knowing that *p* only if we *cannot* (for present intents and purposes and within reason) prove *p* to be true. We regard ourselves as entitled to act (in the respects described earlier) on the truth of the propositions we know. We regard ourselves as not entitled to act on the truth of the propositions we don't know.

These morals carry over to second- and third-person knowledge attribution. We will count another person as knowing that *p* only if we count her as able prove that *p* is true. We will count her as not knowing that *p* only if we count her as unable to prove *p* is true. In the former case we will regard her as entitled to act on *p*, in the latter case we will count her as not entitled to act on *p*. When it comes to young children and animals— creatures we are inclined to credit with knowledge but which are not up to the task of proving much of anything—we do the same, except that instead of focusing on whether *they* can adequately answer the question 'How do you know it?' we focus on whether *we* can adequately answer the question on their behalf. So we credit the dog with knowing his food has been set out in the next room because we can say, on his behalf, how he knows it: 'He smells it.' We doubtless practice this sort of permissiveness, as to what it is to be able to prove P is true, in other cases as well.

Is the distinction between what a person knows and what she doesn't know exhaustive? Not given the characterization I have just rehearsed. The propositions we know are ones we can (for present intents and purposes) prove true and on which we are entitled to act. The propositions we don't know are ones we cannot (for present intents and purposes) prove true and on which we are not entitled to act. This is not an exhaustive distinction. Suppose, for example, there are propositions that we cannot prove true, yet on which we are, all the same, entitled to act. Any such proposition will belong in a distinct third category: it will be a proposition that we neither know nor don't know. The distinction is exhaustive only on the assumption that, if and only if we can prove that *p* is true, are we entitled to act on *p*. Is that assumption true?

One will search in vain for any sign in ordinary practice of knowledge attribution of our *explicitly saying* anything that suggests we do not treat it as true. Cases of vagueness and uncertainty aside, we simply do not in ordinary life encounter any difficulty in deciding into which category a proposition belongs in a given a circumstance: in the category of ones we know or in the category of ones we don't know. Indeed, we don't even have an epithet for a proposition that doesn't fall in either category. So it can be little surprise that we find compelling the thought that 'I don't know that *p*' is simply the negation of 'I know that *p*', little surprise that we find compelling the thought that, for every *p*, either I know that *p* or I don't know that *p*. These are thoughts that serve us well. There is no cause, as we distinguish between what we know and what we don't know in ordinary life, to modify in any way our conviction that 'I know that *p*' and 'I don't know that *p*' are exhaustive.

Of course, one of the reasons that these thoughts serve us so well—one of the reasons we have no cause in ordinary life to modify our conviction that 'I know that p' and 'I don't know that p' are exhaustive—is that the arguments from ignorance that the sceptic advances have no place in that life. They issue challenges that are entirely illegitimate. They are challenges we would be embarrassed to voice ourselves in ordinary life, and that we would dismiss out of hand if someone were so misguided as actually to raise them.

Think again of Austin, looking briefly out his window at the motionless bird and telling us that he sees a goldfinch in the garden. Who among us would be willing seriously to reply (in enthymematic expression of argument D), 'You don't know that! For all you know it's a stuffed goldfinch!'? And who among us would be in the least inclined to take Austin to task if, in the face of someone who did issue this challenge, he simply grimaced and went on? Surely no one. Austin is right. The challenge would be outlandish. If raised, it would deserve no serious reply. Absent any special reason to suppose that he is subject to deception, it would be outrageous to demand, before we will grant him the knowledge he claims, that he do enough to show, with respect to this particular sort of deception, that he is not its victim. The question as to which, if either of 'Austin knows it's not a stuffed goldfinch', and 'Austin doesn't know it's not a stuffed goldfinch', is true in this case, simply does not arise. Things are never allowed to get that far.

This observation is, of course, double edged. On the one hand, it argues in favour of the idea that our regarding 'I know that p' and 'I don't know that p' as exhaustive may be due simply to the fact that there is no room in ordinary life to raise the question as to which, if either, Austin can say truly (in the circumstances we are imagining) when p is 'It's not a stuffed goldfinch.' On the other hand, the selfsame observation is part and parcel of a concession on my part to the effect that, with respect to those questions for which *is* room in ordinary life, the hypothesis that the two expressions are exhaustive is entirely adequate. In particular, I am conceding that, in part because sceptical arguments from ignorance have no place in ordinary life, we will not find in our ordinary practice of knowledge attribution any evidence of anyone's being uncomfortable (except in borderline cases, and cases of uncertainty) in being restricted to the options 'I know that p' and 'I don't know that p.' That is, I am conceding that the hypothesis that 'I know that p' and 'I don't know that p' are exhaustive is entirely adequate to what we say using those expressions (or, rather, their substituends) in ordinary life.

This second edge of my observation may seem worrying. It may seem to open me to the charge that, whatever I mean to go on to say in defence of the thesis that the two expressions are *not* exhaustive, it cannot possibly be something that Austin would endorse. Austin famously demanded that epistemology be scrupulously faithful to what we ordinarily say. (I leave to the next section a fuller discussion of what this demand entails.) Thus (one might think), in conceding what I have, I have conceded that it is a condition on any epistemology that Austin would consider adequate that it treat

'I know that *p*' and 'I don't know that *p*' as exhaustive. That is (one might think) I have conceded that I am about to embark on an enterprise unconstrained by the only evidence (ordinary usage) whose legitimacy Austin acknowledged.

But the charge won't stick—and for two reasons. First, as we have already seen, Austin thought that ordinary language can fail us in precisely the way I am suggesting it does here: it can lead us to think exhaustive a pair of propositions that, in light of reflection on a case that is out of the ordinary, is not actually exhaustive. Second, Austin was in any event not just concerned with being faithful to what we ordinarily say (where that is to be understood as what we ordinarily say frankly,[14] and think ourselves *right* to say frankly—Austin was not concerned to fashion a philosophy faithful to ordinary language in any other sense). The originator of the expression 'performative utterance' was just as famously concerned with faithfully making sense of what we *do* by saying what we ordinarily say—and what we do by other means. So it is entirely in the spirit of Austin's own approach to epistemology to suppose that, even if what we ordinarily say does not directly pin down whether 'Either he knows it or he doesn't' is true of Austin and the proposition that it's not a stuffed goldfinch, what we *do* in saying what we ordinarily say might pin it down.

And, in light of the two observations I highlighted earlier and Austin's own observations about our ordinary practice of knowledge attribution, it is clear that, what we do when we say what we ordinarily say, *does* indeed pin the matter down.

Let us return to Austin as he looks out the window into his garden and tells us that he sees a goldfinch. In saying this, he is claiming to know that it's a goldfinch. Insofar as we think he is able to prove (for present intents and purposes and within reason) that it can't be anything else, we will grant that he knows what he claims to know. Only if there is some special reason to think he is subject to deception, a reason that we don't have in the normal cases in which people claim to know things by virtue of having seen them to be so (the cases in which we grant without fuss the knowledge they claim), will it be in order to ask him to do more than we ordinarily require—for example, that he do enough to show that it isn't a stuffed goldfinch. Let us suppose that we have no such special reason. Then it will be a matter of indifference to us that he hasn't done enough to show it isn't a stuffed goldfinch. We will say that that he knows that it is a goldfinch.

In saying that, we are attributing to him an entitlement to act (for present intents and purposes, and in the sense described earlier) on its being a goldfinch. But, of course, to attribute to him an entitlement to act on its being a goldfinch is to attribute to him an entitlement to act on its not being stuffed. Thus, in saying that he knows that it is a goldfinch we are attributing to him an entitlement to act on its not being a stuffed goldfinch.

But if what I've just said is a correct description of what we will ordinarily say, and what we will be doing in saying this, then we have found in ordinary practice all we

---

[14] So there is no call for an epistemology to pay any attention to what we (for example) say simply out of politeness but know to be false as we say it.

need to warrant the conclusion that, in the circumstances imagined, it is neither correct to say that Austin knows it's not a stuffed goldfinch, nor correct to say that he doesn't know that it is not a stuffed goldfinch. It is not correct to say that he knows it because he cannot prove it—he hasn't gone up to it, he hasn't tested it, hasn't inspected it thoroughly enough. And it is not correct to say that he doesn't know it, because to say that would be to deny what we have already attributed to him in saying that he knows that it's a goldfinch: namely, an entitlement to act on its not being a stuffed goldfinch. That is, an examination of what we are doing when we say what we ordinarily say (and are *right* to say) about the case reveals that the thesis, that either one knows a proposition or one doesn't, is false. In the case at hand, what we are doing, when we say what we ordinarily say (and are right to say) about the case, is denying that he knows it and denying that he doesn't know it.

That is, the distinction between what we know and what we don't know is not exhaustive. The propositions we know are ones we are able (for present intents and purposes) to prove true and on which we are entitled to act. The propositions we don't know are ones we are unable (for present intents and purposes) to prove true and on which we are not entitled to act. But there are propositions that fit in neither category. They are propositions on which we are entitled to act, even though we are unable (for present intents and purposes) to prove them true. Only on the assumption, that if and only if we can prove p true are we entitled to act on p, is the distinction exhaustive and this last category empty. And this assumption is false. If it seems surprising that there should be this non-empty third category, it is because, though false, the assumption that this third category is empty is perfectly adequate to the task of classification in which we are engaged in ordinary life. The propositions that belong in the third category—the propositions that neither count as known nor as unknown—occupy this category in circumstances in which the question, 'But do I/you know it or not?' would, in ordinary life, strike us as bizarre.[15]

---

[15] It might be objected that the very novelty of my thesis, that 'I know that p' and 'I don't know that p' are not exhaustive, casts serious doubt on its truth. After all, no one needs to be told (we see right off) that 'I have stopped smoking' and 'I haven't stopped smoking' are exhaustive only under certain circumstances. We know that neither is true of Austin if he has never smoked. Isn't my thesis—that 'I know' and 'I don't know' are, similarly, exhaustive only under certain circumstances—seriously discredited by the fact that this thesis strikes us (at best) as surprising news? No. All this last shows is that my thesis cannot plausibly be thought to be supported by the sort of linguistic consideration that supports its smoky analogue—i.e. the reluctance of a person who has never smoked to assent either to 'I have stopped smoking' or to 'I have not stopped smoking'. But then I do not *claim* to find support for my thesis in linguistic considerations; I claim to find support in epistemological considerations. And, given this, it is of little moment whether we find the thesis surprising.

After all, the thesis, that 'I know that p' and 'I don't know that p' are exhaustive only under certain circumstances, comes to nothing more and nothing less than this: that the inference, from 'I do not satisfy the conditions I would have to satisfy in order for me to count as knowing that p' to 'I don't know that p', is fallacious. The inference preserves truth only in circumstances in which my being entitled to act on p (in the sense earlier described) requires my satisfying the conditions I would have to satisfy to count as knowing that p. And those circumstances do not always hold. Let us grant that it is a surprise to be told that this inference is fallacious. Does this show that what we are thereby being told isn't, in fact, true? Hardly. Consider the base rate fallacy. Studies show that most of us can be reliably induced to commit the base rate fallacy; that we are

Indeed, the sign that a proposition is in the third category is that, even as we recognize, with respect to a person, that she cannot know what she knows unless she is entitled to act on the proposition in question, and even as we recognize (or, at the very least, suspect) that she could not shoulder the justificatory burden she would take on were she to claim to know the proposition in question, we recognize that it would be outrageous to ask, we would be embarrassed to ask, we would in her place dismiss the question if it were asked, 'How do you know it is true?' It is a sign that (as we have already noted) is exhibited quite clearly by the proposition, 'It's not a stuffed goldfinch' in the case at hand. And it is a sign exhibited equally well by the propositions 'It's not a painted mule', 'I'm not a brain in a vat', and 'I'm not dreaming' in the cases in which we imagined arguments C, B, and A are raised.[16]

That is to say, each of the arguments A through D is defective in exactly the same way. In each, the first premise is false. It is not because (in the circumstances in which it is imagined the arguments are advanced) I know that I am not dreaming, I know that I am not a brain in a vat, I know that the animal in the enclosure is not a painted mule, Austin knows that the bird is not a stuffed goldfinch. It is, rather, because (in the circumstances in which it is imagined the arguments are advanced) the propositions in question—that I am not dreaming, that I am not a brain in a vat, that the animal is not a painted mule, that the bird is not a stuffed goldfinch—belong in the third category. They are propositions on which I am (Austin is) in those circumstances entitled to act, but of which it is neither true to say I know (Austin knows) nor true to say I don't know (Austin doesn't know).

But mightn't only a little modification of each argument suffice to repair the arguments? Consider, for example, argument D. Suppose we just replace the first premise with, 'It's not the case that I know that it's not a stuffed goldfinch' and then alter the antecedent of the second premise accordingly. The result is argument D':

---

surprised to be informed that we have thereby committed a fallacy; that we need to be taught the error of our ways; that we find it all too easy to fall back into our old, fallacious, patterns of reasoning. But we are not in the least tempted to regard this as showing that a deviant statistics is actually correct—that the base rate fallacy is really no fallacy at all.

[16] Note, however, that it is not a sign exhibited by *every* proposition p on which a person is entitled to act and of which it would be outrageous to ask, 'How do you know that p?' After all, there are cases in which the question is outrageous because p is an obvious consequence of some other proposition it is already granted one knows and by appeal to which p can be proven true. (For example, once it has been granted that I know there are exactly two bottles of milk in the refrigerator, it is outrageous to ask how I know there are not four.) There are also cases in which the question is outrageous because p is one of those propositions the claimant to knowledge *just knows*. (For example, it is outrageous to ask how I know that the woman who is standing before me in fine light is my wife.) But then both sorts of cases are ones in which the claimant to knowledge can perfectly well shoulder the justificatory burden imposed by the question 'How do you know that p?' What distinguishes third category propositions is that the question, 'How do you know that p?' is outrageous even though the justificatory burden of providing an adequate answer to the question is one the claimant cannot shoulder. As I have argued, Austin is committed to regarding 'It's not a stuffed goldfinch' as being (in the circumstances we are imagining) just such a proposition—as instantiating neither of the two sorts of cases described earlier.

D'. It's not the case that I know that it's not a stuffed goldfinch.
    If it's not the case that I know that it's not a stuffed goldfinch, then I don't know
    it's a goldfinch.
    Therefore, I don't know that it's a goldfinch.

Insofar as 'It's not a stuffed goldfinch' is in the third category (it is neither a proposition
Austin knows nor one he doesn't know), the first premise of D' is true.

The trouble is that, in rewriting the antecedent of the second premise so that it will
be identical to this new first premise (as we must do if the argument is to be valid), we
render the second premise false. To see this, think of why the second premise of the
original argument D is true. If I don't know it's not a stuffed goldfinch, then I'm not
entitled to act on its not being a stuffed goldfinch. But if I'm not entitled to act on that,
then I'm certainly not entitled to act on its being a goldfinch. But then that rules out
my knowing that it's a goldfinch and rules out my neither knowing nor not knowing
that it's a goldfinch, both of which carry with them the entitlement to act on its being a
goldfinch. So I must count as not knowing it's a goldfinch.[17]

But this line of argument is not available for the second premise of D'. From its not
being the case that I know it's not a stuffed goldfinch, nothing follows as to whether
I'm entitled to act on its not being a stuffed goldfinch. It's compatible with its not being
the case that I know it's not a stuffed goldfinch that I don't know it's not stuffed, in
which case I am not entitled to act on its not being stuffed. But it is also compatible
with its not being the case that I know it's not a stuffed goldfinch that I neither know
it's not stuffed nor don't know it's not stuffed. In that case the proposition is in the third
category and I'm entitled to act on its truth. That 'It's not a stuffed goldfinch' is in the
third category is entirely compatible with my knowing that it's a goldfinch. So the
repair won't work. Once we see that the propositions upon which the first premises of
arguments A through D focus—the propositions those premises classify as ones I do not
(Austin does not) know—actually belong in the third category, we have seen all we
need to see to see why the arguments cannot carry conviction.

6. Understanding Austin's method

But have we *really* seen that these propositions belong in a third category? In making
the case that they do, I have quite deliberately restricted myself to considerations to
which either Austin appealed or to which (by my best estimate) he would be happy to
see appeal made. My ambition has not just been to produce a good argument for the
thesis that 'I know that p' and 'I don't know that p' are not exhaustive, but also to
produce an argument that is (in the sense just described) available to Austin. But there
are doubtless some (and possibly many) who will think that these two parts of my

---

[17] One upshot of the view being promulgated here is, then, that while knowledge is not closed under
known entailment, the entitlement to act on a proposition is so closed.

ambition are not capable of being jointly satisfied—that, to the extent that I have succeeded in the second part of my ambition, I cannot but have failed in the first.

The thought would be this. I have followed Austin too closely. I have written (just as Austin did) as if the fact that it is by the lights of our ordinary practice perfectly appropriate and proper to say that *p* in a given circumstance means that it is true to say that *p* in that circumstance. And I have written (just as Austin did) as if the fact that it would by the lights of our ordinary practice be outrageous to say that *p* in a given circumstance means that it would be false to say that *p* in that circumstance. The trouble is that it is one thing for it to be *appropriate by the lights of our ordinary practice* to say that *p* in a given circumstance, quite another for it to be *true* to say that *p* in that circumstance. And it is one thing for it to be *outrageous by the lights of our ordinary practice* to say that *p* in a given circumstance, quite another for it to be *false* to say that *p* in that circumstance. As Grice taught us, there are factors having to do with the purposes of communication in ordinary life that have the effect of rendering inappropriate assertions that are nonetheless true. (You ask me where Helen is; I know she's in the dining room; but I say 'She's either in the dining room or she's in the garage.' What I said is inappropriate, because misleading—it leads to you to think I don't know in which of the two places she is. All the same, what I said is true.) There may likewise be factors, having to do with the practical purposes that knowledge attributions serve in ordinary life (perhaps the role knowledge attributions play in granting and claiming entitlements to act on propositions) that render it inappropriate in ordinary life to say, 'Austin does not know that it's not a stuffed goldfinch', even though it is true, and appropriate to say, 'Austin knows it is a goldfinch', even though it is false.

The thought would be that Austin failed to appreciate this, and so failed to appreciate that the unvarnished facts about what we would and wouldn't say in ordinary life, to which he (and I in his thrall) appeal to assess epistemological doctrines, are simply not probative in epistemological inquiry. Epistemological doctrines do not, in themselves, *have* any implications for what we should or should not say in ordinary life. It is thus a mistake to write, as Austin did, as if facts about what we would and wouldn't say and do in ordinary life are capable of undermining scepticism. The battle between the sceptic and his foe is not over what it is appropriate to say in ordinary life about what we know and why. The battle is over whether what we thereby say is actually *true*. That is to say, the thesis of philosophical scepticism is not a methodological one. It is not a call for reform of our ordinary practices. And so, when it comes to the matter of whether the thesis of philosophical scepticism is true, the sort of observation by which Austin (and I following him) set such store—that, were we to reform our ordinary practice of knowledge ascription so that we ascribed in ordinary life only such knowledge as the philosophical sceptic is prepared to ascribe while conducting a philosophy seminar, we would end up behaving quite outrageously—is simply beside the point.

The line of thought just rehearsed has had a long history. It has its origins in the early reception of Austin's work by Paul Grice, Roderick Chisholm, and Stanley Cavell in the 1960s (Grice 1961; Chisholm 1964: 1; Cavell 1965: 216–17; Cavell 1979: 57). And it is present in monographs on scepticism from the 1980s and 1990s by Barry Stroud, Marie McGinn, and Michael Williams (Stroud 1984: chapter 2; McGinn 1989: 62; Williams 1996: 147–8). It is a line of thought that I think is largely responsible for the fact that Austin's epistemological work is so little cited today and is virtually invisible in anthologies of epistemological writing.

But it is a line of thought that misunderstands why Austin wrote as he did. To see this, suppose that a philosophical theory of knowledge does not have to mirror the ways in which it is ordinarily appropriate to use 'know'. What exactly, then, is supposed to constrain such a theory? To what does it have to be true? The tempting answer is that we have a concept of knowledge and it is fidelity to that concept to which a philosophical theory of knowledge aspires. But what is supposed to convince us that a given theory really is faithful to our concept of knowledge? We cannot examine the way the theory tallies with everything we are ordinarily inclined to say using the word 'know', for we would then be testing the theory as if it meant simply to codify ordinary usage. We would be using just the sort of test that (according to the line of thought under discussion) is entirely inappropriate to apply to a philosophical theory of knowledge. And we cannot set aside as irrelevant to our inquiry everything we are ordinarily inclined to say using the word 'know'. How could we even motivate—let alone evaluate—any theory of knowledge were we unable to appeal to what we ordinarily, and appropriately, say people know and when we say it?

We could, of course, opt to make selective use of what we would ordinarily say—to treat only certain *aspects* of our ordinary practice as properly bearing on the propriety the theory in question. But what help would that be? It is an elementary rule of sound inquiry that one must evaluate the adequacy of a theory, not just on *some* of the available evidence, but on *all* the available evidence. After all, if *we* can pick and choose what aspects of our ordinary practice are to be considered salient to assessing the philosophical propriety of the theory of knowledge in question, so can anyone else—so can the philosophers who take as salient some of the aspects of our ordinary practice that the theory captures poorly, if at all. But then, with everyone free to pick and choose in this way, the philosophical enterprise, of determining what we know and by virtue of what we know it, degenerates into a game in which almost every move is legal and each participant plays according to her own fancy.

As his writings make clear (see, in particular, Austin 1962: 2), Austin felt that this sort of degeneration is inevitable once epistemology abandons fidelity to what we ordinarily say and do. He recognized that our ordinary practice is indispensible evidence as to the propriety of an epistemological theory. And he recognized that an epistemological theory (like any other) must be held accountable to *all* the evidence—and so to *all* of our ordinary practice in all its richness. It is for this reason, and this reason alone, that Austin devoted so much effort to describing our ordinary practice and why he attached such philosophical importance to the result.

Austin thus had no stake in denying that what it is appropriate to say in ordinary life in a given circumstance can, and sometimes does, diverge from what it would be true to say in that circumstance. He did not write as he did out of the conviction that no such divergence can, or does, occur. On the contrary, he admitted that 'we are often right to say we *know* even in cases where we turn out subsequently to have been mistaken—and indeed we seem always, or practically always, liable to be mistaken' (1979: 98). He wrote as he did because he thought that only by appeal to how things look by the lights of our ordinary assessment of our circumstances can one make the case that such a divergence is, in a particular instance, occurring.

This thought, it is worth noting, is in no way undermined by Grice's observations. Consider, again, the fact that, if I know that Helen is in the dining room, it is inappropriate, even though true, for me to say, when you ask her whereabouts, 'Helen is either in the dining room or in the garage.' To acknowledge as much does not require choosing a philosophical assessment of the case over an ordinary one. It is a commonplace that there are ways of misleading someone (and in so doing saying something it is inappropriate to say) by saying only what is true. This stands in stark contrast with what is required if one wants to endorse the claim—anything but a commonplace—that, outrageous as it may be to say so in ordinary life, Austin does not know that there is a goldfinch in his backyard (or much of anything else about the world around him).

Yet for all Austin's emphasis on the import of an epistemology's being faithful to our ordinary practices, he never claimed that our ordinary practices—the things we ordinarily say and do—constitute the last word on all matters. Quite the contrary. In 'A Plea for Excuses,' Austin conceded that the way ordinary language arranges matters 'is likely enough to be not the best way of arranging things if our interests are more extensive or intellectual than the ordinary' (1979: 185; see also 67–9). His view, he wrote, was that 'ordinary language is *not* the last word: in principle it can everywhere be supplemented and improved upon and superseded. Only remember, it *is* the *first* word' (ibid.). That is to say that Austin was (rightly) open to the possibility that sophisticated reflection on matters—even sophisticated *philosophical* reflection on matters—might lead us to the conclusion that our ordinary practices needed changing. What he was *not* open to—and hence his admonition that we remember that ordinary language *is* the *first* word—is the idea that our epistemology needn't take on our ordinary practices. What he was not open to was the idea—expressed so clearly in the line of thought under discussion—that our epistemological research might proceed with indifference to how its results tallied with ordinary practice.

Austin's requirement that epistemology be faithful to what we ordinarily say and do is thus more subtle than one might have thought. It does *not* demand that epistemology bend slavishly to the contours of ordinary practice. What it requires, rather, is that our philosophical assessment of our epistemic condition coincides with our ordinary assessment of that condition. Thus, when we find our epistemological inquiries leading us to views at odds with our ordinary practices, we have only two choices. We can either reconsider the path on which those inquiries have led us or change our ordinary practices to conform to our epistemological views. The position favoured by the advocates of the line of thought under discussion—a line of thought which would allow us to leave our ordinary practices as they are yet conclude that they are nonetheless unsatisfactory from a philosophical point of view—is unavailable.

Of course, even if Austin's fidelity requirement is more subtle than it has been thought, the requirement is by no means incontestable. The requirement's claim to command our assent rests on the proposition that there is no intellectually respectable way to steer a middle course between the following two views: (i) the view that *no fact* as to what we would ordinarily say and when is evidentially relevant to the evaluation of a theory of knowledge, and (ii) the view that *all the facts* as to what we would ordinarily say and when are evidentially relevant to the evaluation of a theory of knowledge. And, while Austin was clearly convinced that there is no intellectually respectable way to steer such a course, others will doubtless want persuading.

I think that Austin was right to be convinced that there is no such middle course. And elsewhere (Kaplan 1996, 2000, 2003, 2006b, 2008, and 2010) I have undertaken the task of saying *why* I think he was right—in particular, the task of saying why Austin's critics' pretensions, to have (in effect) charted various intellectually respectable middle courses between (i) and (ii), are false. It is because I think Austin was right that my argument, for the propriety of an epistemology that admits of propositions that we neither know nor don't know, has taken the form it has. For, if Austin is right, the sort of argument I have offered is the only sort of argument that can legitimately be offered for the propriety of an epistemology. It is an argument to the effect that this epistemology is true to our ordinary practices—to the things we do, and rightly do, in ordinary life.

But even if Austin *is* right to think there is not middle course to be steered between (i) and (ii), my argument goes only so far by way of establishing the propriety of the stance toward arguments A through D that (I have suggested) is available to Austin. Going the full distance would require comparing that stance with the others that are available *simpliciter*. It would require going beyond the present interpretive task to see whether there are other stances—stances I have not considered simply because they appear precluded by the words on the pages of 'Other Minds'—that are equally true (or more true) to our ordinary practices. Whether there *are* any such stances—and what the consequences are for our understanding of sceptical arguments from ignorance *if* there are such stances—these are matters that interest me greatly. But they constitute a topic for another essay.[18]

---

[18]   This essay is the seventh in a series (Kaplan 1996, 2000, 2003, 2006b, 2008, and 2010 are the other six) designed to explain and defend Austin's approach to the theory of knowledge. Since each is written to be a freestanding paper, there is necessarily some overlap between them. When writing here about some of the matters on which there *is* overlap, I have occasionally availed myself of passages from the other essays.

Bibliography

Austin, J. L. (1962), *Sense and Sensibilia*, ed. Warnock, G. J., Oxford: Oxford University Press.

—— (1979), *Philosophical Papers*, 3rd ed., eds. Urmson, J. O., Warnock, G. J., Oxford: Oxford University Press.

Cavell, S. (1965), 'Austin at Criticism', *The Philosophical Review* 74: 204–19.

—— (1979), *The Claim of Reason: Wittgenstein, Skepticism, Morality, and Tragedy*. Oxford: Oxford University Press.

Chisholm, R. M. (1964), 'Austin's *Philosophical Papers*', *Mind* 73: 1–26.

—— (1966), *Theory of Knowledge*. Englewood Cliffs, NJ: Prentice-Hall.

DeRose, K. (1995), 'Solving the Skeptical Problem', *The Philosophical Review* 104: 1–52.

Dretske, F. (1970), 'Epistemic Operators', *The Journal of Philosophy* 67: 1007–23.

Grice, H. P. (1961), 'The Causal Theory of Perception', *Proceedings of the Aristotelian Society: Supplementary Volume* 35: 121–52. Reprinted in Grice, H. P., *Studies in the Way of Words*, Cambridge, MA: Harvard University Press, 1991, pp. 224–47.

Kaplan, M. (1996). 'Skepticism and Pyrotechnics', *Acta Analytica* 16/17: 159–77.

—— (2000), 'To What Must an Epistemology Be True?', *Philosophy and Phenomenological Research* 61: 279–304.

—— (2003), 'Chisholm's Grand Move', *Metaphilosophy* 34: 563–81.

—— (2006a), 'Deciding What You Know', in Olsson, E. J. (ed.), *Knowledge and Inquiry: Essays on the Pragmatism of Isaac Levi*, Cambridge: Cambridge University Press, pp. 225–40.

—— (2006b), 'If You Know You Can't be Wrong', in Hetherington, S. (ed.), *Epistemology Futures,* Oxford: Oxford University Press, pp. 180–98.

—— (2008), 'Austin's Way with Skepticism', in Greco, J. (ed.), *Oxford Handbook of Skepticism*, Oxford: Oxford University Press, pp. 348–71.

—— (2010), 'John Langshaw Austin', in Bernecker, S., Pritchard, D. (eds.) *The Routledge Companion to Epistemology*, London: Routledge, pp. 798–810.

Leite, A. (this volume), 'Austin, Dreams, and Scepticism'.

Lemmon, E. J. (1967), 'If I Know, Do I Know That I Know?, in Stroll, A. (ed.), *Epistemology, New Essays in the Theory of Knowledge*, Evanston and London: Harper and Row, pp. 54–82.

McGinn, M. (1989), *Sense and Certainty: A Dissolution of Scepticism*, Oxford: Blackwell Publishers.

Moore, G. E. (1939), 'Proof of an External World', *Proceedings of the British Academy* 25: 273–300.

Stroud, B. (1984), *The Significance of Philosophical Scepticism*, Oxford: Clarendon Press.

Williams, M. (1996), *Unnatural Doubts: Epistemological Realism and the Basis of Scepticism*, Princeton: Princeton University Press.

4

Austin, Dreams, and Scepticism

Adam Leite

J. L. Austin's attitude towards traditional epistemological problems was largely
negative. They arise and are maintained, he charged, by 'sleight of hand', 'wile', 'concealed motives', 'seductive fallacies', fixation on a handful of 'jejune examples', and a host
of small errors, misinterpretations, and mistakes about matters of fact (1962: 3–6; 1979:
87). As these charges indicate, he did not offer a general critical theory of traditional
epistemological theorizing or of the intellectual motivations that lead to it. Instead, he
subjected individual arguments to piecemeal criticism, patiently showing how things
go awry in conception, motivation, argumentation, and plain fact. The work was
incremental, but the goal was radical: to reduce large edifices to rubble. As he put it
regarding certain sense datum theories, 'the right policy is to go back to a much earlier
stage, and to dismantle the whole doctrine before it gets off the ground' (1962: 142).

It is often said that Austin's criticisms were linguistic, but this is only partly right.
While he occasionally charges traditional epistemologists with misusing crucial words
and relying on unregulated and inadequately motivated technical terms, he also
charges them with factual errors and with distorting or misunderstanding the procedures involved in epistemically evaluating people's claims and beliefs. For this reason, it
is best to see Austin as criticizing traditional epistemological puzzles and projects from
the point of view of our ordinary lives (including our best scientific theories and
practices). He starts with a commitment to our ordinary ways of using words, our
ordinary convictions about what is the case and what we know or don't know, and our
ordinary epistemic practices. None of this is held sacrosanct; reason may emerge to
modify some of it. The point, however, is that this *is* our starting point, and a compelling
reason to modify it will have to come from or be appropriately related to the materials
with which we started.[1] We could consequently summarize Austin's approach like this.
Confronted with a surprising epistemological claim ('We never know anything about
other people's minds'; 'We never directly perceive material objects, but only sense-
data'), Austin's question is whether we, *starting from where we are*, could reasonably be

---

[1] As Austin put it, ordinary language is not the last word, but it is the first (1979: 185).

brought to believe it. What he tries to show is that the arguments that are supposed to do the trick turn out to be hopeless.[2]

My goal in this paper is to flesh out and provisionally defend this sort of Austinian response to the dream argument for external world scepticism.[3] On first encountering this argument, it is natural to reply like this:

Of course I can't know anything about what's going on around me, if I don't even have reason to believe that I'm not dreaming. If I granted that I didn't know or have reason to believe this wasn't a dream, it would be completely unreasonable for me to believe that there is a piece of paper before me right now. But I have good reason to believe that I'm not dreaming; I even know that I'm not. *This* is nothing like a dream.

As I will argue, Austin shows us—at least in outline—how this ordinary, pretheoretical response could succeed. My argument will proceed by stages. I will first explore Austin's arguments about dreaming and our ability to recognize that we are awake (section 1). These arguments rely upon contingent, empirical background information and are quite plausible when considered from the vantage point of ordinary life. The crucial philosophical question is how—if at all—Austin's argumentative strategy can be made to seem unsatisfactory. One tempting thought is that it is objectionable to rely upon empirical background knowledge to explain how one can tell that one is not dreaming. However, Austin provides compelling reasons for thinking this objection fails (section 2). It might be thought that the philosophical reflections leading to external world scepticism will reveal a shortcoming in Austin's position, so in section 3 I will bring Austin's remarks to bear on traditional sceptical concerns. I will argue that if his factual and epistemological claims are correct, then the dream argument for external world scepticism—and, by extension, several other prominent sceptical arguments—won't so much as get off the ground.

1. Austin on dreaming

When we are awake and our faculties are functioning properly, can we tell that we are not asleep and dreaming? Austin's answer is unequivocal.

---

[2] On this understanding of Austin's approach, Stroud's (1984, chapter 2) Grice-inspired objection is largely beside the point. Austin's primary method is not, as Stroud would have it, describing facts about 'what we say when' as data for a conclusion regarding what knowledge requires. Rather, he is standing within our practice, articulating epistemic principles and factual claims to which he is committed. For someone taking that approach, the ultimate question would be whether he can find reason to think that those principles or claims are incorrect. Stroud offers him no such reason. Of course, a further question could be asked: 'This is what I am committed to, and I have no reason to think it incorrect, but is it correct?' Perhaps the deepest split between Austin and more traditional epistemologists such as Stroud concerns their approach to this question. I will not directly broach this issue here. My concern is to get the main lines of Austin's position clearly in view.

[3] As found, e.g. in Descartes's *Meditations on First Philosophy* (1984: 13) and more recently elaborated by Barry Stroud (1984, chapter 1).

There are recognized ways of distinguishing between dreaming and waking [...]. (1979: 87)

I may have the experience [...] of dreaming that I am being presented to the Pope. Could it be seriously suggested that having this dream is 'qualitatively indistinguishable' from *actually being presented to the Pope?* Quite obviously not. (1962: 48, italics in original)

[W]e all know that dreams are *throughout un*like waking experiences. (1962: 42, italics in original)

As the lack of qualification in the last passage indicates, Austin's claim is a bold one: no dream is qualitatively indistinguishable from a waking experience had while one's faculties are functioning properly. If that is so, then it should be relatively straightforward to determine that one is not asleep and dreaming. Drawing on what 'we all know' about dreams, a person who is awake and whose faculties are functioning properly should be able to infer from what her present experience is like that she is awake, not dreaming. And this has an important explanatory pay-off. We would think it bizarre for someone to raise the question, 'Mightn't I be dreaming?' in the course of most everyday inquiry, reasoning, or epistemic appraisal. Austin can explain why that is so. If we all recognize that every competent adult in ordinary circumstances can plainly tell that he or she is not dreaming, then there is no point in bringing the issue up. That is why we don't bother to do so, and why doing so is silly even if knowledge or reasonable belief about the world requires adequate grounds for believing that one is not dreaming.

To see why Austin held this view, a fair bit of reconstruction is required.

In Warnock's published redaction of *Sense and Sensibilia*, the second claim quoted above is immediately followed by this:

After all, we have the phrase 'a dream-like quality'; some waking experiences are said to have this dream-like quality [...]. But of course, if the fact here alleged [that dreams are qualitatively indistinguishable from waking experiences] *were* a fact, the phrase would be perfectly meaningless. (1962: 49)[4]

On one natural interpretation, the argument here is as follows:

1. Our language contains the phrase, 'a dream-like quality', and this phrase is linguistically meaningful.
2. If we could never distinguish dreams from waking experiences, then this phrase would have no meaning.
3. So, we must be able to distinguish some dreams from waking experiences.
4. We could not do that if dreams and waking experiences were always qualitatively indistinguishable.
5. So dreams and waking experiences must always be qualitatively different.

---

[4] In the earlier paper, 'Other Minds', the first passage quoted above is followed by a similar comment: 'There are recognized ways of distinguishing between dreaming and waking (how otherwise should we know how to use and to contrast the words?)' (1979: 87).

Quite aside from its commitment to verificationism, however, this argument is patently inadequate: (5) manifestly doesn't follow from (3) and (4). The verificationist demand regarding the phrase 'a dream-like quality' does not require that *all* dreams have a distinctive 'feel' distinguishing them from waking experiences, only that there be a quality that typical or paradigmatic dreams have and that ordinary experiences lack. But for this reason the verificationist requirement leaves open the possibility that some dreams might be qualitatively indistinguishable from waking experiences.[5]

It would be a mistake to think that Austin merely intended to establish the weaker claim that *some* or even *most* dreams can be distinguished from waking experiences. For one thing, the weaker claim doesn't do the work the argument would need to do, since it doesn't support his confident claim that it 'quite obviously' cannot seriously be suggested that dreaming one is being presented to the Pope is qualitatively indistinguishable from actually being presented to the Pope. Moreover, the weaker claim is irrelevant in the dialectical context. A. J. Ayer had offered a standard argument for sense-data beginning with the premise that 'there is no intrinsic difference in kind between those of our perceptions that are veridical in their presentation of material things and those that are delusive' (1940: 5–6). What Ayer clearly meant—and all that he needed for the purposes of the argument—is that *some* 'delusive' perceptions do not differ from 'veridical' perceptions in what they are like from the relevant person's point of view; that is, that there are *some* cases in which it seems to the perceiver that she is in perceptual contact with objects around her, she isn't, and the situation is qualitatively indistinguishable by her from one in which she is. The suggestion on the table, then, is that some instances of dreaming are cases of this sort. The weaker conclusion yielded by the verificationist argument, that some or even most instances of dreaming *aren't* of this sort, is simply beside the point.[6]

Given the evident failure of the verificationist argument, it is noteworthy that Austin didn't actually think that his claim about dreams needed sophisticated philosophical defence. In his initial characterization of the failings of sense datum theories, he writes, 'The fact is [. . .] that the facts of perception, as discovered by, for instance, psychologists but also as noted by common mortals, are much more diverse and complicated than has been allowed for' (1962: 3). His strategy, then, is in part to remind his readers of the relevant facts. He thought that an honest look would reveal that Ayer had simply

---

[5] This failing is pointed out by Blumenfeld and Blumenfeld (1978: 238). It arises even if we interpret the argument as appealing instead to the weaker, non-verificationist idea that if there were never an aspect of dream experience that differed from waking experience, then there would be no *point* to the phrase 'a dream-like quality'.

[6] This interpretation might be challenged on the ground that Austin later grants that there may be some cases in which 'veridical perceptions' and 'delusive perceptions' are qualitatively indistinguishable, arguing that even this concession wouldn't require us to grant that we always perceive sense-data (since there is no reason why there shouldn't be cases in which perceiving one sort of thing is exactly like perceiving another (1962: 52)). However, the discussion of dreams appears at a moment in the text when the thesis of qualitative indistinguishability is itself under attack, and Austin's point there is that the example of dreams cannot be used to support this premise of the argument from illusion.

gotten them wrong. Ayer's argument, he writes, 'begins [. . .] with an alleged statement of fact [. . .]. Let us ask whether what is being alleged here is actually true [. . .].
Consider a few examples [. . .]' (1962: 48). His example of dreaming that one is being
presented to the Pope is offered as one such example. It is thus designed to remind us of
the relevant facts, to make vivid that Ayer is denying the 'obvious fact that the
"experiences" are *different*' (1962: 50, italics in original). Evidently, Austin intended
the example itself to do the necessary argumentative work.

Austin's last revision of the lectures later published as *Sense and Sensibilia* was
delivered at Berkeley in the fall of 1958. In those lectures the argument from the
meaningfulness of the phrase 'a dream-like quality' is conspicuously absent. In its place,
Austin offers a list of particular ways in which dreams differ from waking experience:

> But there are differences, e.g. in temporal and spatial boundaries. And it is like being told a story:
> one cannot ask for completeness—e.g. what the weather was—if it wasn't given. Also—as
> another aspect of 'having a dream-like quality'—things HAPPEN to the dreamer, often, rather
> than his doing these things. And not only is the sensuous balance different (e.g. few smells), but so
> also is the emotional balance quite different in dreams from that of real life. (1958: 8, Lecture
> VII.7)[7]

What Austin manifestly intended to be offering here are some of those facts that 'we all
know' about the ways in which dreaming is '*throughout un*like waking experiences'. In
hoping his example would carry conviction, he was banking on—and reminding us
of—our knowledge of what dreams are like.[8]

This strand of Austin's argument is thus ultimately empirical. He appeals to a set of
generalizations drawn from a lifetime of experiences with dreaming and with being
told things about dreams by other people. And it follows from those generalizations
that no dream is qualitatively indistinguishable from veridical waking experiences. This
underlying empirical argument is an instance of a style of argument that we all regard as
unexceptionable in ordinary life and science. Given a wide enough experience with
cats in a sufficient variety of circumstances, one can reasonably conclude that cats don't

---

[7] From notes taken at University of California, Berkeley, by R. Lawrence and W. Hayes. These notes—
covering in detail the entirety of the twenty-nine lectures Austin delivered at Berkeley—were kindly brought
to my attention by Wallace Matson, Professor Emeritus of Philosophy at UC Berkeley. (Matson was present
at the lectures and supplemented the Lawrence and Hayes typescript with his own notes.) I am in possession
of a copy of the Lawrence and Hayes typescript and will gladly make it available to other researchers. I do not
know whether other copies are in existence, as I have not had a chance to explore the Oxford Austin
archives. According to Matson, the Lawrence and Hayes notes were at Warnock's disposal when the
published edition of *Sense and Sensibilia* was prepared. I do not know Warnock's reasons for not including
this passage in the published edition.

[8] Given the obvious failure of the argument in the published version of *Sense and Sensibilia* and its
replacement in the Lawrence and Hayes notes by a set of empirical generalizations in support of the example,
I'm inclined to think that the text of *Sense and Sensibilia* would look quite different had Austin lived to rework
this material for publication. Archival work needs to be done to determine whether Austin had abandoned
the problematic argument by the time he prepared the Berkeley lectures. It is noteworthy, however, that the
verificationist themes that sometimes sound in the published version of *Sense and Sensibilia* are largely missing
from the Berkeley typescript.

talk, that is, that *no* cat will talk. One might go on to allow that it is in some sense conceivable or possible (conceptually possible, logically possible, or whatever) for a cat to talk. But still, one might quite reasonably insist, the data show that it won't happen. So in arguing as he does, Austin is taking up a position within our ordinary practices, making use of a type of argument that we would all ordinarily accept without a blink.[9]

To be sure, substantive questions might be raised. (1) Are dreams the right sort of phenomenon to be treated in this way? (2) Do the facts actually support Austin's conclusion? So far as I can see, there is no serious empirical dispute about these matters in ordinary life. (Again, the mere conceivability or possibility—in some sense—of alternatives is irrelevant.) And those who feel the need for something more might profitably look at contemporary scientific work on dreaming.[10]

[9] Of course, some philosophers have purported to raise doubts about whether such arguments actually support their conclusions, or to have provided arguments that such arguments are not reasonable, etc. These arguments, and possible Austinian responses to them, are beyond the scope of this paper.

[10] Here, for instance, is a quick pass through some relevant literature. Hobson (1988) provides extensive analysis of the phenomenology of dreaming as well as an attempt to link it with the known facts about the neurophysiological side of things circa the late 1980s. Here are just a few relevant phenomenological features catalogued by Hobson. Dreams are characterized by reduced visual acuity and reduced content in the non-visual sensory modalities (including physical sensations such as itches and tickles). One's ability to direct and focus one's attention is considerably hampered. The affective tone of dreaming differs sharply from that of waking life, as Austin notes. And dreams exhibit distinctive features in their formal structure, including incongruities (strange, unusual, or impossible combinations of elements), indeterminacies of identity and persistence conditions, and fundamental discontinuities in apparent space and time, as well as in the identities of objects and persons.

Neurophysiological research appears to support generalizing from these considerations. In fact, correlations between the phenomenology of dreams and neurophysiological functions are so tight that one researcher has urged using subjective dream reports as clinical diagnostic indicators of certain lesions and other neuro-pathologies (Solms 1997).

Researchers distinguish dreams, which are correlated with REM-sleep, from hypnogogic or hypnopompic imagery which can occur as one is falling asleep or awakening. (The latter imagery is extremely fragmentary, consisting mainly of shapes, colours, and sensations of movement and touch.) REM-sleep itself is a highly unified state of the brain, induced by distinctive changes in the brainstem and characterized by a number of significant differences from the brain's waking state. It involves a drastic shift in the relative proportions of the neurotransmitters norepinephrine, serotonin, and acetylcholine; a shift which, if produced pharmacologically in a waking person would result in artificially-induced psychosis (Hobson 1999). (Hobson, et al. (1998: R3–R7) provide a detailed discussion of the neuromodulatory control of the onset of REM sleep. Hobson himself goes so far as to suggest that during REM-sleep, the brain is in a psychotic state.) During REM-sleep, blood flow to several parts of the brain is sharply reduced; in particular, blood flow to the dorsolateral prefrontal cortex—an area widely accepted to be implicated in the planning of voluntary activity and in less well-defined functions termed 'executive functions' and 'reality checking'—is reduced roughly by half, in effect shutting this area down to a level adequate only for the preservation of the tissues involved. (The relevant imaging studies are surveyed by Hobson, et al. 1998). These findings dovetail with Solms' (1997: 222–3) observation that lesions in this region appear to have no essential effect upon dreaming. The activity of several important brain structures shifts during REM-sleep as well. The hippocampus—widely accepted to be implicated in the functioning of memory—shows a higher level of activity and appears to function in a way fundamentally different from the awake state (Stickgold, et al. 2001). Finally, during REM-sleep the brain processes signals which appear to be randomly generated by the brainstem and fed to the visual, motor, and emotional systems without any 'control' from the systems of the prefrontal cortex (Hobson, et al. 1998: R11). Computer models show that under these conditions patterns of neuron firing will shift in sudden and unpredictable ways (Stickgold 2001, citing Collins, et al. 1995: 236–8). Given the extremely strong correlation between dreaming and REM-sleep and the well-established ways in which brain states can affect

Even granting that Austin is right on this score, however, one might still have epistemological reservations about the further claim that we can tell that we are awake by considering whether our current experience has (or lacks) certain features.

First, Austin would have to concede that our judgements about whether we are awake are fallible. He grants that while dreaming we are often incorrectly convinced that we are awake.[11] Moreover, on his view error should be possible regarding the presence or absence of relevant phenomenological features, since he holds that error is generally possible in our judgements about what our current experience is like (1962: 112–13; 1979: 90ff.).[12] And he would have to grant that even if we have determined that our current experience has (or lacks) the relevant features, this would not *entail* that we are not dreaming. However, Austin would not regard these concessions to our fallibility as blocking our ability to know or reasonably believe that we are not dreaming, since he holds in general that our sometimes making mistakes does not preclude our ability to gain knowledge (1979: 98) and that evidence adequate for knowledge need not ensure against 'outrages of nature' (1979: 88).[13] Any fallibilist should be willing to follow him here.

Two worries might nonetheless arise regarding the concession that dreaming often brings an incorrect conviction that one is awake. First, it might be thought that if dreams have features that distinguish them from waking experiences, then we ought to recognize these features and their significance *while we are dreaming*. However, as Austin repeatedly stresses, the fact that under certain conditions we confuse two things does not show that there are no features that would enable us to distinguish them (1962: 51).

---

what one's experience is like, it is reasonable to take the brain's state during REM-sleep as constraining—and as helping to explain—what dreams are like. And given the extremely strong correlation between dreaming and REM-sleep, it strongly appears that dreams are the right sort of thing to be treated via an argument such as Austin's.

Would Austin be open to this appeal to science? It seems so. He himself appeals to psychology (1962: 3, 53), and the Lawrence/Hayes notes contain this: 'Insofar as some people (psychologists) ARE now paying attention to the phenomena of perception, they are discovering that there are many MORE "qualitative differences" than one ordinarily pays attention to (e.g. the work at Cornell)' (1958: 9, Lecture VIII.1).

[11]   In the Berkeley notes he comments, regarding delirium tremens, 'What produces the conviction is that the sufferer takes it for granted, in some odd sense (as in dreams), that this is a real experience' (1958: 8, Lecture VII.6). And the supplementary notes include this: 'It is characteristic of dreams that *at the time* one thinks they are actual' (p. 8a note 2a). In this regard, Austin differs from thinkers such as Ernest Sosa (2005) who hold that while dreaming one does not judge or believe, and is not convinced, that one is awake (and indeed, that while dreaming a dreamer does not judge or believe, and is not convinced, of the truth of the content of the dream).

[12]   This concession strongly suggests that Austin is committed to the possibility of one's current state having phenomenal features that one fails to recognize even when they are present. This possibility is crucial if we are to make sense of the idea that dreams have phenomenological features that distinguish them from waking experiences even though we often fail to recognize them or their significance while we are dreaming. (I am grateful to Fred Schmitt for highlighting the importance of this issue for the Austinian position.)

[13]   In Leite (2004a) I offer an Austin-inspired defence of a fallibilist view that I take to be similar to Austin's.

The trouble with dreaming is that while one is dreaming, one is (normally, often) not in a position to appreciate the relevant features.[14]

Second, it might be thought that the fact that we regularly get it wrong *when we are dreaming* somehow raises a problem regarding our ability to tell that we are not dreaming *when we are awake*. However, this is not so. In principle, the following situation is perfectly possible: there are two states A (the good state) and B (the bad state); when one is in B, one is unavoidably convinced (incorrectly) that one is in A, but when one is in A, one can tell that one is in A, not in B.[15] For example, someone who is drunk may slur his speech and yet be entirely convinced (incorrigibly so) that he is not doing so. Still, someone who is not drunk and not slurring his words can tell, on the basis of how his speech sounds, that he is not doing so. The difference is simply that in the bad state, he fails to correctly register and appreciate the features that indicate that he is in the bad state, while in the good state he correctly registers and appreciates the presence of the features that indicate that he is in the good state, not the bad one.[16]

Given these epistemological points, what evidence might one have—when one is awake and in full possession of one's faculties—that enables one to determine that one is not dreaming? A variety of phenomenological considerations will be relevant. But a striking consideration is brought out by Austin's comment that dreaming 'is like being told a story: one cannot ask for completeness' (1958: 8): one cannot expect to be able to press deeply at a variety of points for further narrative details; dreams do not include anything like a reasonably full 'backstory', an account of one's recent and more distant history that enables one to make sense—in the way one generally can in waking life—of where one is, why one is there, how one got there, what one is doing, and how all that relates to both one's more distant past and one's ongoing activities.

This is the feature of dreams that Descartes appealed to at the end of the Sixth Meditation to explain his knowledge that he was not dreaming. Hobbes, like many readers, thought that this appeal failed. He wrote:

---

[14] It is worth noting that with training some people appear to be able to learn to appreciate them, at least on occasion. A key step in learning to 'lucid dream' is learning to consider—while dreaming—whether one's state has certain phenomenological features that mark it as a dream.

[15] This general point has recently been stressed by Williamson (2000). Bernard Williams (1978) makes the point with regard to dreaming in particular.

[16] It might be objected that even when we are awake, we are not in a position to determine whether our experience has the relevant distinguishing features, because just as dreams can bring an incorrect conviction that one is awake, they can also involve incorrect convictions about what one's current subjective state is like. However, I might incorrigibly get it wrong when I am dreaming but still be able to determine that my experience has the relevant features when I am awake; this objection is a version of the objection just canvassed, and so is likewise mistaken in principle. (It is empirically dubious as well.) It is worth noting that Austin's position on this issue entails denial of Robert Nozick's (1981) 'sensitivity requirement'. Nozick maintained that one doesn't know that *p* unless the following condition is met: if *p* were false, one wouldn't believe that *p*. Austin's position requires denial of this requirement, since he holds that one can know that one is not dreaming *even though* if one were dreaming, one would still believe that one was not dreaming. (Nozick's requirement is vulnerable to pretty straightforward counterexamples (Williamson 2000; Sosa 2002; Leite 2004b).)

My question is whether [. . .] a man could not dream that his dream fits in with his ideas of a long series of past events. If this is possible, then what appear to the dreamer to be actions belonging to his past life could be judged to be true occurrences, just as if he were awake. (Hobbes 1984: 137)

We must distinguish two issues here, however. Hobbes could be suggesting that one might have a dream which includes a full complement of relevant dream-generated nonveridical memories, or he could be suggesting that even without any such full complement of apparent memories, one might merely be convinced, while dreaming, that one's current experience fits appropriately with one's past in a way that renders one's present intelligible. The latter suggestion is quite plausible (I regularly have dreams of this sort), but it is irrelevant in this context, since it does not impugn one's position while one is awake. The former suggestion, by contrast, would be to the point, were there evidence in its favour. (Its mere imaginability is irrelevant in this context.) And as Austin stresses, the evidence with which we are all familiar goes the other way. Dreams never involve a full complement of apparent memories sufficient to render one's apparent current situation and activities intelligible in the way that they generally are when one is awake.[17]

Now if it is true that dreams at best involve a streamlined backstory, then one can unproblematically determine whether one is awake even if dreams can generate a wide variety of false convictions. Try to recount or call to mind a reasonably full, rich story about where you are, how you got there, what you are doing there, and the many links between features of your situation and the rest of your life. If you manage to recount or call to mind such a story, then that provides you with good grounds for concluding that you are not dreaming. Might you merely be *dreaming* that you are recounting or calling to mind such a story? No. If you are currently recounting an appropriately rich history, then your current experience includes a backstory of the sort not found in dreams. Might your conviction that you are currently thinking about that history only be the product of a dream, and so be misleading? Again, no. For consider how the objection would have to go in detail. 'Might I only be dreaming that I started today with a shower and breakfast, then went to the office and answered e-mail, working on the paper I started yesterday, taught a class and am now listening to a song while revising yesterday's lecture notes and drinking the tea I bought last week—a song that I listened to while driving to Lake Superior seventeen years ago on my honeymoon with my spouse, who used to like it and who still likes other songs I like, such as . . . (and so on)?' If you manage to consider

---

[17] Contemporary research on the neurophysiology of dreaming, particularly on the REM-sleep functioning of brain systems associated with memory, might help explain why this would be.

It is true that while one is awake, one sometimes (temporarily) finds oneself seeming to remember doing a thing that one in fact only dreamed about doing. But this phenomenon doesn't support Hobbes' suggestion or suggest that dreams are at times indistinguishable from waking experiences; the phenomenon is straightforwardly explicable just given the familiar facts that (1) while one is dreaming one can acquire confused convictions and (2) confused convictions from whatever source can sometimes linger even when one could correct them after a moment's thought. (I am grateful here to a query from an anonymous referee for the press.)

an adequately ramified question like that then your current state involves thinking about an appropriately rich backstory, and so—the thought goes—you are not dreaming.

2. Can it really be this easy?

Austin's proposal—that if we freely make use of our empirical background knowledge of what dreams are like, then we can readily determine that we are awake, not dreaming—might give rise to a vague sense of epistemological unease. How could it be legitimate to make use of empirical background knowledge at this juncture? Isn't that knowledge placed out of play when we consider whether or not we are dreaming? Worries along some such lines can easily tempt us out of our ordinary confidence that we can tell that we are not dreaming. However, as I will argue in this section, if Austin's larger epistemological framework is right, then we shouldn't be too quick to leave our ordinary confidence behind.

First, a few words to orient the discussion. It is often assumed that Austin's main focus in epistemology is the use and meaning of epistemic terms such as 'knows'. This interpretation is not without some support. In 'Other Minds', Austin does describe key aspects of our practice of making knowledge claims, objecting to them, and responding to those objections, and part of his aim appears to be to draw conclusions about the conditions under which a knowledge claim is true. However, it is a mistake to think that his focus is limited to such matters. His target is both broader and more funda-mental. Whenever one claims to know something, he says, one is 'liable to be taken' to claim that one is able to prove it (1979: 85).[18] Much of his discussion consequently concerns the structure of attempts to establish that something is true by articulating reasons to believe it and responding to objections. This structure will be the focus of my discussion. It is shared by cases in which we attempt to defend a belief by providing reasons in its favour (whether in response to another's queries or in solitary meditation). It is perhaps best characterized as part of the structure of reasoning about what to believe.

2.1. Objections involving alternative possibilities

Suppose that someone has offered or is considering a set of reasons in defence of a claim. As Austin notes, there are several points at which an objection could in principle be lodged. Objections could be raised regarding (1) the *adequacy* of the offered considerations (assuming they are true), (2) the *truth* of the offered considerations, or (3) the reasoner's *ability to determine* the adequacy or truth of the offered considerations or of the claim in question.[19] In each of these cases, objecting can take the form of

---

[18] Austin allows, however, that there can be cases in which someone knows that something is the case but can't prove that it is (1979: 86).

[19] Austin's categories here are only roughly characterized. He identifies objections of the first sort in terms of cases in which one might respond, 'But that doesn't prove it!' The second he calls 'challenging our facts'; the third, challenging 'the reliability of our alleged "credentials"' (1979: 84, 86).

offering a suggestion about how the world could be—a particular way in which the evidence could be inadequate, the alleged evidence false, or the person unreliable—and asking what reason the person has for thinking that the world is not that way. An inability to respond adequately to the objection reflects negatively on the person's position.

Austin draws a crucial distinction in this regard. He indicates it as follows.

Enough is enough: it doesn't mean everything. Enough means enough to show that [. . .] it 'can't' be anything else, there is no room for an alternative, competing description of it. It does *not* mean, for example, enough to show it isn't a *stuffed* goldfinch. (1979: 84)

Suppose that I have claimed that there is a goldfinch in the garden and have supported my claim by noting that the bird in question has a red head.[20] We all sense that in any ordinary situation, there would be a significant difference between the objection, 'But woodpeckers have red heads too. What shows it isn't a woodpecker?', and the objection, 'Couldn't it just be stuffed?' The first must be taken seriously. The second is silly and shouldn't be. (For an even clearer example of the latter sort, consider the objection, 'But couldn't it be an intergalactic spying device cleverly disguised to look like a goldfinch?') Objections of the first sort are appropriately countered only by adducing specific additional evidence that things are not as the objection suggests they might be, for example, 'It can't be a woodpecker, because . . . '. By contrast, objections of the second sort may be summarily dismissed, for example, by saying, 'Don't be ridiculous. There's no reason to think that it is an intergalactic spying device cleverly disguised to look like a goldfinch!' In order to respond adequately to objections of this latter sort, one doesn't need to find or adduce additional specific evidence showing that things are not as the objection suggests they might be.

It might be thought that this difference is best explained by the practical context: different possibilities are made relevant to particular episodes of reasoning and inquiry, the thought would go, depending on our interests and purposes. In particular, it might be urged that the more concerned we are to attain the truth, and the more we ignore other interests and purposes, the wider we must cast the net of possibilities under consideration.[21] Austin at times seems to suggest some such view himself. For instance, he writes (italics indicating the text elided in the previous quote), 'Enough means enough to show that (*within reason, and for present intents and purposes*) it "can't" be anything else, there is no room for an alternative, competing description of it' (1979: 84, italics added). However, the proposed view fails as a description of our practice. Given things as they are, there is *no* set of purposes and interests that would make it reasonable to seriously consider the suggestion that the thing in the garden might be an intergalactic spying device. No matter what one's interests and purposes, it would be nothing but nutty to try to capture it and cut it open in search of an alien spying

---

[20] Austin's familiar example involves a European goldfinch, not an American one.
[21] Stroud (1984, chapter 2) suggests a view along these lines.

apparatus. Moreover, the suggested interpretation does not seem to capture Austin's considered view. Regarding our knowledge of other minds, he writes,

These special cases where doubts arise and require resolving, are contrasted with the normal cases which hold the field *unless* there is some suggestion that deceit, &c., is involved, and deceit, moreover, of an intelligible kind in the circumstances, that is, of a kind that can be looked into because motive, &c., is specially suggested. (1979: 113)

And again, regarding objections arising from human fallibility, he comments,

being aware that you may be mistaken doesn't mean merely being aware that you are a fallible human being: it means that you have some concrete reason to suppose that you may be mistaken in this case. Just as 'but I may fail' does not mean merely 'but I am a weak human being' [. . .]: it means that there is some concrete reason for me to suppose that I shall break my word. (1979: 98)

In both passages, Austin is concerned simply with epistemic reasons for thinking that the suggested possibility obtains. The proposal appears to be that if there is no reason in favour of a suggested possibility, then one may (and should) simply dismiss it, while if there is some reason in its favour, then one may not do so. One's interests or purposes simply don't come into the story in the suggested way. The presence or absence of relevant epistemic reasons is what matters.[22]

As the above passages make clear, on Austin's view the mere fact that a suggested possibility is compatible with one's evidence does not constitute a reason in its favour; a reason, in the relevant sense, is something that is the case that tells in favour of the suggested possibility. ('It might be stuffed' or 'he might be faking,' by itself, is thus not a reason in the intended sense.) To capture this notion, Austin talks of 'specific' and 'concrete' reasons. These formulations are also meant to capture an important additional distinction. That human beings are fallible and can make mistakes is not a consideration of the right sort; that one was not wearing one's glasses might well be, as might the considerations that one frequently makes mistakes about relevantly similar matters in relevantly similar circumstances, that red-headed woodpeckers are not uncommon in the area, or that one's neighbour often puts fake birds in nearby yards. Austin does not provide a theory or principle to explain this additional distinction, and it is difficult to know how such a theory would best be elaborated. But all that's needed here is that a distinction of this sort is embedded in our practice. (The suggestion that one might have made a mistake, since people do after all sometimes

[22] A subtle issue arises here regarding talk of 'epistemic reasons': our ordinary discourse in this regard involves a variety of related locutions. Austin himself uses a variety of expressions, and it is not at all apparent whether he means to distinguish them. As my preferred idiom, I will talk of there being or not being some reason in favour of a certain possibility (or in favour of the truth of a certain proposition). I will also occasionally use the word 'evidence' to do the same work. My talk of possibilities, propositions, and the like—that is, the things that can on occasion have reasons in their favour—is similarly idiomatic rather than technical. Nothing more is needed in this context.

make mistakes, is appropriately met with the rejoinder, 'Yes, but what reason is there to think that I have made a mistake *now*?')

Austin's proposal, then, is this. In a given context the possibilities that could in principle figure in objections to a given claim or argument can be fairly cleanly divided into those that have no epistemic reason in their favour and those that have some reason in their favour, where a reason is something that tells in favour of the obtaining of the suggested possibility and is appropriately specific and concrete. If there is some reason in favour of the suggested possibility, then to respond adequately one must obtain or provide additional reasons that defeat the reason(s) in question. If there is no reason in favour of the suggested possibility, however, then of course one needn't find defeating reasons, since there is no reason to defeat; the possibility hasn't even made it onto the field, as it were. In the latter case one is already in a position to reject the suggested possibility if one recognizes that there are no reasons in its favour, and explicitly or implicitly indicating this recognition will constitute an adequate response. It is this latter sort of rejection that I have in mind when I talk of 'summarily dismissing' a suggested possibility and of 'rejecting it out of hand'. The difference in required response reflects at bottom a difference in the sort of reasons one must possess, a difference that arises from a difference in the reasons that bear on the issue.

So on Austin's view the evidence necessary to substantiate the claim that there is a goldfinch in the garden must be sufficient to eliminate any 'alternative, competing' possibility—that is, any alternative that has some reason in its favour. What this requires is evidence defeating the reasons in favour of those competing possibilities. Such evidence—even in conjunction with positive evidence that it is a goldfinch—may not be enough to show that the bird isn't stuffed. But that doesn't matter, on Austin's view. Since there is no reason in its favour, that latter possibility isn't on the table to begin with. That is why 'enough is enough'.[23]

It should be emphasized that Austin's view is not that one may summarily dismiss an objection if one simply happens to lack any information in its favour. Mere ignorance is not so easily transmuted into epistemic strength. Rather, the proposal is that if one's background information enables one to recognize that there is nothing in a suggested possibility's favour, then one should summarily dismiss it even if one lacks additional specific evidence against it. Background ignorance would instead leave one unable to reach a reasonable conclusion about whether or not the suggested possibility may be so dismissed.

---

[23] What of the phrase 'within reason and for present intents and purposes' in the sentence 'Enough means enough to show that (*within reason and for present intents and purposes*) it "can't" be anything else' (italics added)? I read this phrase as calling attention to the importance of the actual circumstances in which the particular course of reasoning is placed. Austin is here emphasizing that what will count as adequate grounds for the purpose of *this* course of reasoning—given the reasons that bear on the issue here and now—may not count as adequate grounds elsewhere. That was a view which he clearly held, and he could have held it even without thinking that practical considerations played any role in this regard.

It is hard to see how one could be in a position to treat a possibility in this way without also possessing background information that tells against the possibility's obtaining and in favour of some other. This background information may well fall short of what would be required to show that the possibility does not obtain. For instance, the facts that no one would have any interest in deceiving me by putting a stuffed facsimile in my backyard, that nothing like that has happened around here before, and that nothing was on the branch five minutes ago all help underwrite my judgement that there is no reason in favour of the possibility that the seeming goldfinch is stuffed. But they hardly suffice to show that this possibility doesn't obtain. (Seeing the bird fly away would do so, as would cutting it open to reveal the usual mess.) However, knowing that something isn't the case needn't require an ability to *show* that it isn't. So I don't see anything to prevent Austin from holding that someone in such a position could thereby know that the bird isn't stuffed.[24]

---

[24] An interpretive digression. Austin is not entirely clear about our epistemic relation to possibilities that we recognize to have no reason in their favour. This has led some interpreters to read him as offering an early version of a 'relevant alternatives' theory of knowledge something like those later championed by Dretske (1970 and 1981) and Nozick (1981). The broad idea here would be that if there is no reason in favour of a possibility and we recognize that this is so but lack any further specific evidence against the possibility, then we are entitled to assume that the possibility does not obtain—we can reasonably ignore it, fail to investigate it, act and believe as if it doesn't obtain, and know other things that entail its non-obtaining—but may lack sufficient reason to believe that it doesn't obtain and may not know that it doesn't.

Though the texts are not probative, Austin says things strongly suggesting that he would reject such a view. For instance, in his discussion of Warnock's interpretation of Berkeley, he writes,

Although Warnock insists that neither he nor Berkeley has any intention of casting doubt on the judgments we ordinarily make, of arguing for any brand of philosophical scepticism [. . .]. To say, as Warnock does, that we are making assumptions and taking things for granted *whenever* we make an ordinary assertion, is of course to make ordinary assertions look somehow chancy, and it's no good his saying that he and Berkeley don't mean to do that. (1962: 138)

Austin strongly suggests here that he doesn't regard ordinary assertions as always being chancy in the way that they would be if we were always merely assuming and taking for granted that the sceptical possibilities do not obtain. It might be replied that we are making assumptions that we are *entitled* to make. But that would still leave our ordinary judgements looking 'chancy', only a chance that we are entitled to take. Austin's thought is rather that we are not taking a chance *at all*, and for that thought to make sense, he must have thought that we know the sceptical possibilities not to obtain.

Mark Kaplan, in his contribution to the present volume, offers a sophisticated version of this interpretive line that evades this objection. On Kaplan's reading, Austin holds that certain of our beliefs have a special status: all the entitlements of knowledge but without the obligations. We therefore neither know nor don't know that we are not brains in vats or deceived by an evil demon, or even that the seeming zebras in a pen at the zoo are not cleverly painted mules (though we do know that we have hands, are standing at the zoo, and seeing zebras in a pen), but we have precisely the entitlements regarding belief and practical reasoning that are involved in knowledge. Our ordinary judgements are thus no longer left looking 'chancy'.

Given the epistemological framework I have offered, this interpretation loses much of its philosophical motivation. If one recognizes that there is no reason in favour of the possibility that one is confronting cleverly painted mules, then one *is* in a position to satisfactorily defend one's attitude towards that possibility: one may summarily dismiss it on the ground that it has no reasons in its favour. One can thus fulfil the relevant epistemic obligation. I fail to see why we should not grant that under such circumstances, one knows that the possibility does not obtain. If the creature in a pen looks like a zebra, the pen is labelled 'zebra', and one knows that this is a reputable zoo dedicated to a scientific and educational mission and with no reason to deceive, then I see no reason not to grant that one knows that the animals in the pen are not merely cleverly painted mules. (I will discuss an Austinian response to the standard global sceptical hypotheses in section 3.)

Given these epistemological views, Austin could hold that *if* we recognize that there is no reason telling in favour of the possibility that we are dreaming, then we are thereby in a position to know that we are not dreaming and can dismiss this possibility out of hand. However, there is no straightforward application of this result to our overarching question. For one thing, it isn't at all obvious whether in ordinary conditions there is any reason in favour of the possibility that one is dreaming. Moreover, to dismiss the dreaming possibility in this way we would have to rely upon empirical background information. But this returns us to our guiding question: is it epistemically acceptable to rely upon empirical background information at this juncture?

2.2. Reliability objections and epistemic priority

In any particular course of reasoning or argumentation certain considerations but not others may be relied upon as premises or inference principles, and some may not be so used until others have been established. For instance, suppose that (1) the fact that I am on the graduate faculty of my university is a good indication that I am entitled to serve on doctoral committees, and (2) the fact that I am entitled to serve on doctoral committees is a good indication that I am on the graduate faculty. If you know both these evidential relationships hold, it doesn't follow that you could equally well appeal to either fact to support the other. If you possess some reason to doubt that I am entitled to serve on doctoral committees, then (all else equal) it would be objectionable for you to reason from the claim that I am entitled to serve on doctoral committees to the conclusion that I am on the graduate faculty of my university. If it is certain that I am on the graduate faculty of my university, then you might be able to appeal to this fact to defeat that reason for doubt, arguing from this basis to the conclusion that I am entitled to serve on doctoral committees. But there may also be cases in which the reason for doubt precludes you from making use of *either* consideration in defence of

---

In 'Other Minds' Austin makes one comment that can appear to support an interpretation along Kaplan's lines:

Knowing it's a 'real' goldfinch isn't in question in the ordinary case when I say I know it's a goldfinch: reasonable precautions only are taken. But when it *is* called in question, in *special* cases, then I make sure it's a real goldfinch in ways essentially similar to those in which I made sure it was a goldfinch [. . .]. (1979: 88)

This passage supports the interpretation if we read 'isn't in question in the ordinary case' as meaning that in the ordinary case, asking whether we know or don't know that the goldfinch is real (isn't a dream, hallucination, or stuffed) is the wrong sort of question: we neither know it nor don't it, but we are fully entitled to it. However, this passage is not decisive, since another reason why something might not be in question is because it is obviously the case. Reasonable precautions are those aimed at eliminating those possibilities that have some reason in their favour. Since the possibility that the bird is not real (e.g. is stuffed) has no reason in its favour, it would be unreasonable to call my knowledge into question on the ground that the bird might not be real after all. This interpretation is supported by the contrast between the two sentences in the quoted passage. As the second sentence makes clear, the intended contrast is between cases in which one's possession of knowledge is *called* into question and cases in which it is not. This strongly suggests that in the ordinary case in which I know it's a goldfinch, I know it's a *real* goldfinch as well—my possession of knowledge that it's real isn't called into question because there is no reason to challenge it.

the other: you would first have to defeat the reason for doubt by making use of some other considerations. To put the point generally, how you may acceptably reason or argue will depend upon the reasons that bear on the case.

Austin was aware of this point. Call the relations involved here *epistemic priority relations*, and the requirements and constraints on reasoning and argumentation that involve such relations *priority requirements* and *priority constraints*. Austin adamantly insisted that the epistemic priority relations and requirements that structure acceptable reasoning or argumentation in particular cases do not reflect a context- or circumstance-independent justificatory order amongst the relevant propositions.

[I]n general, *any* kind of statement could state evidence for any other kind, if the circumstances were appropriate. (1962: 116; cf. 111, 140)

[T]here *could* be no *general* answer to the questions what is evidence for what, what is certain, what is doubtful, what needs or does not need evidence, can or can't be verified [because these matters all depend on 'the circumstances']. (1962: 124)

Austin thus held that there are *no substantive fully circumstance-independent priority requirements*—no requirements stating such things as that in order to reasonably believe anything in a certain class, one must have independent reasons in support of some particular proposition p (or in support of some proposition(s) in some other specified class). In these passages Austin doesn't specify what he means by 'the circumstances', and his examples in *Sense and Sensibilia* do not clarify the issue. However, the passages earlier discussed from 'Other Minds' indicate that by 'the circumstances' Austin meant at least in part the reasons to which the particular course of reasoning or argumentation must be responsive. On Austin's view, then, epistemic priority requirements are determined at least in part by the reasons that bear on the case on a particular occasion.

One important type of priority requirement arises from considerations that challenge what Austin calls 'the reliability of our alleged "credentials" ' (1979: 86), that is, considerations that challenge our possession of relevant authority, competence, or reliability. Suppose, for instance, that some consideration suggests that I did not perform a certain mathematical calculation correctly. In that case, I should not be fully convinced of my answer's truth until I have somehow defeated this reason, perhaps by asking someone else or by double-checking my work. And even if I possess the relevant competencies and in fact committed no errors in performance, I cannot use my answer as a defeating consideration: I cannot argue (irrationally making use of the answer yielded by my calculation), 'The correct answer is "7", and that's exactly what I got. So there's no reason to think I made a mistake after all. I performed the calculation correctly.' Under these circumstances, a priority requirement is in place: I am not entitled to be convinced of my answer or to make use of it as a premise in further reasoning unless and until I have independent grounds that defeat the evidence that I made a mistake.

Similar requirements can be imposed regarding entire domains of belief. Suppose that I have believed a certain person regarding a great many things. I now discover evidence that this person is an inveterate liar with a desire to mislead me as much as possible. Under these circumstances, I cannot reasonably believe (on the basis of this person's say-so) any of the things this person tells me unless and until I possess reasons that defeat the evidence that this person is lying to me. Such reasons cannot be provided by things that I believe only on the person's say-so, even if those things are true and their truth decisively indicates that the person wasn't lying. A general priority requirement is thus in place regarding the entire class of things that I have believed on this person's say-so.

What are such priority requirements triggered by: the reasons that are actually present in the case, that the subject takes to be present, that the subject 'possesses', or recognizes as reasons, or what? Austin did not write at a level of detail that would enable us to determine how he would have handled this nest of issues. However, this much is clear: if a person *recognizes* that there are reasons of the relevant sort— thus correctly taking there to be such reasons—then a priority requirement of the relevant sort holds. We can consequently schematize a general priority requirement as follows:

Reliability-related priority requirement: If one recognizes that there is some reason in favour of a possibility *p* that would undermine one's authority, competence, or reliability regarding a certain domain of beliefs, then one cannot reasonably believe anything in that domain unless one has adequate *independent* grounds for believing that *p* is not the case, where an *independent* ground is a ground not itself in that domain.

In what follows, my argument will focus on priority relations and requirements that, like this one, relate to the reasons that we recognize. Such requirements can be rendered intelligible by reflecting on the reasons/situation involved in these cases. A pro tanto reason in favour of a consideration challenging one's authority, competence, or reliability in a given domain is *ipso facto* a pro tanto reason against the truth of each of one's beliefs in the domain. That's why if one recognizes a reason of the former sort, one can't acceptably treat those beliefs as grounds that defeat the pro tanto reason in question: those beliefs are thereby brought into question. Independent reasons are consequently required.

Consider, now, the following principle:

If one recognizes that there is no reason in favour of some possibility that would undermine one's authority, competence, or reliability regarding a certain domain, then (other things equal) one may reasonably believe things in that domain even if one lacks adequate independent grounds for believing that the possibility does not obtain, and one may reasonably dismiss as groundless the suggestion that it does obtain.

This principle says that under certain circumstances, one can reasonably believe things in a certain domain even if one does not have independent grounds for believing that one's beliefs in that domain are reliable. One could accept this principle even while granting the commonsense thought that one can't reasonably believe things in the domain unless one also reasonably believes—for any particular possibility that one recognizes would render one's beliefs unreliable in that domain—that that possibility does not obtain.[25] But a consequence of this principle would be that one could epistemically depend on considerations in the domain in the course of dismissing the suggestion that the possibility obtains.[26]

Would Austin have accepted this principle and its consequence? I think so. Recall that Austin denied that there are any substantive circumstance-independent priority requirements. He consequently would have rejected any principle instantiating the following schema:

If p is a possibility whose obtaining would undermine one's authority, competence, or reliability regarding a certain domain, then in every possible case one cannot reasonably believe anything in the domain unless one has adequate independent grounds for believing that P does not obtain.

On his view, any given principle along these lines will fail to hold in *some* possible circumstances. And as we just saw, a priority requirement of the relevant sort will hold if one recognizes some reason in favour of the possibility in question. So the cases in

---

[25] There is no incompatibility between the commonsensical thought and Austin's view that there are no circumstance-independent priority requirements, because the commonsense thought does not demand that in every case one must have independent reason to believe the relevant propositions. It just says that one must reasonably believe them. This does not generate a circumstance-independent priority requirement. The mistake in thinking otherwise arises from assuming that for a belief to be reasonable because one knows other things that constitute reasons in its favour, one must be able to arrive at it, or establish its truth, via an unproblematic inference from those reasons.

[26] If we combine these elements, here is what we get. The commonsensical thought has the consequence that inference from premises in the relevant class cannot yield reasonable belief that one is not unreliable in the suggested way, because the inference could not do so unless one reasonably believes the premises, which in turn (given the commonsensical thought) would require that one already reasonably believe that the possibility does not obtain. (This consequence is supported by perfectly ordinary examples.) Combining the commonsensical thought with Austin's view of priority requirements yields the following. If one recognizes that p would undercut one's reliability regarding class of beliefs ß, then

(1) one cannot reason from considerations in ß (believed in the relevant way) to the conclusion that p does not obtain and thereby establish or gain knowledge or reasonable belief that *p* does not obtain, but

(2) if there is no reason in favour of *p*, and if one recognizes that this is so, then one can acceptably dismiss the suggestion that *p* on the ground that there is no reason in its favour—even if one has no adequate independent grounds against *p* and so thereby epistemically depends upon considerations in class ß.

This combination of views would seem a non-starter if dismissing an objection that p just amounted to establishing that *p* is not the case by inferring not-*p* from some premises in a way that could enable one thereby to come to know for the first time that not-*p*. But there is reason to draw a distinction here. In the latter case, one is arriving at knowledge that not-*p* for the first time or exhibiting an inference through which one could acquire such knowledge, whereas in dismissing the possibility that p one may be deploying knowledge that not-*p* that one already possesses—not reasoning or arguing to the conclusion that not-*p*, but rather dismissing *p* as something already established or known not to be the case. How, in this instance, would one know that there is no reason in *p*'s favour and that *p* is not the case? One would know it in part in virtue of knowing a bunch of things in class ß. (This answer will be unavailable if one makes the mistake of thinking that if one knows *p* in part in virtue of knowing a bunch of other things, it must be possible in principle to arrive at that knowledge that *p* for the first time by explicit inference from previous knowledge of the other things. For some discussion of issues relevant here, see Leite 2008 and 2011.)

which such a requirement doesn't hold will be cases in which one does not recognize any reason in favour of the possibility in question. Of such cases, one's position will be strongest if there is no such reason and one recognizes as much. So if there are some cases in which such a priority requirement doesn't hold, it would seem to be these. And even if there are other conditions that must be met in these cases, it must be possible for those other conditions to be met, so that there are some possible cases in which the priority requirement does not hold. For this reason, Austin should accept the proposed principle and its consequence.

In fact, it's striking how well this view captures the commitments of our ordinary practice. Consider the following hypothesis.

Children of at least one brunet parent are massively bad at evaluating and responding to evidence, both in conscious deliberation and in non-deliberative belief formation, and they also suffer from widespread and significant deficits and distortions in sensory processing (compensated for by 'infilling' and confabulation).

This hypothesis is clearly false. As we all recognize, there is nothing whatsoever in its favour. We would all quite appropriately dismiss it out of hand. But if you are like me in having a brunet parent, then in dismissing this hypothesis you would be relying upon considerations about which you would lack reliability, competence, or authority if the hypothesis were true: you would have no adequate independent grounds for believing that this hypothesis is incorrect. So our response to this hypothesis indicates our commitment to a principle like the one I've articulated on Austin's behalf.[27]

One might be worried that a principle of the sort under consideration will generate insuperable problems if one's ability to recognize that there are no reasons of the relevant sort depends upon one's having reasonable beliefs in the relevant domain. But this is not so. In the worst case, what would be involved is mutual dependence: one's possession of reasonable beliefs in the relevant domain would require one's recognizing that there is no reason in favour of the relevant possibility, and one's ability to recognize that there is no reason in favour of the possibility would require one's reasonably believing other things in the domain. This sort of mutual epistemic dependence is not inherently problematic. Admittedly, insuperable problems would be generated if one or both of the dependence relations involved a priority relation. But Austin's claim that there are no substantive circumstance-independent epistemic priority relations would lead him to deny that such priority requirements must always be involved. So on his view, there should be no insuperable difficulties along these lines.

To sum up: Consider a proposition p and a set of propositions ß that are related as follows:

1. The truth of certain propositions in ß decisively indicates the falsity of p,
   and

----

[27] I discuss this example at greater length in Leite (2010).

2. If one recognizes some reason in favour of the truth of *p*, then one would possess grounds for a legitimate challenge to one's authority, competence, or reliability regarding propositions in ß.

On Austin's view, the priority relations and requirements that apply when *p* and ß are related in this way will depend upon the actual circumstances—in particular, upon the reasons bearing on whether *p* is the case. If one believes the relevant propositions in ß in a way that would be undercut if one recognizes some reason in favour of the truth of *p*, and if one recognizes some reason in favour of the truth of *p*, then one cannot treat any considerations in ß as evidence for anything else unless one has some reasons that defeat one's evidence that *p*, and such reasons cannot be provided by any of one's beliefs in ß. By contrast, however, if one recognizes that there is no reason in favour of *p*'s being the case, then—assuming all other relevant requirements are met—one can perfectly well rely upon considerations in ß in the course of dismissing the suggestion that *p* is the case.

The proposition *I am dreaming now* and the class of propositions typified by *I am sitting at my desk* are related in the way specified above. Coming to believe something as a result of a dream is not a reliable way of forming beliefs, since most of the beliefs that arise during dreams are false. So if one recognizes some reason in favour of the possibility that one is dreaming, this will ground a reliability-based objection to a wide class of beliefs: one will not be able to acceptably utilize any beliefs in that class to provide evidence that one is not dreaming, and without adequate independent reasons for thinking that one is not dreaming, one would not be entitled to rely upon any of those beliefs for the purposes of further reasoning. By contrast, however, if one recognizes that nothing tells in favour of the possibility that one is dreaming, then on Austin's view one may dismiss that possibility out of hand—even if one could not be in a position to do so without relying upon background beliefs in the relevant class. And in that case there would be no objection in principle to relying upon empirical claims about what dreams are like, so Austin's account of how we can distinguish waking from dreaming would be epistemically unobjectionable.

2.3. *Reducing the worry to rubble*

Here is the only plausible argument I know for the claim that there are ordinarily reasons in favour of the possibility that one is dreaming: 'People including myself sometimes have very lifelike dreams, dreams which at the time seem very much like waking experiences. During such dreams people are often convinced that they are awake and not dreaming. Right now I am in a state very much like a waking experience and am convinced that I am awake, not dreaming. Given these considerations, my situation regarding the question of whether I am dreaming now is analogous to that of a birdwatcher whose neighbour is an ornithological taxidermist with a known penchant for practical jokes. Just as this birdwatcher has some reason in support of the possibility that the thing he observes on the branch might merely be stuffed,

I have some reason in favour of the possibility that I am dreaming right now. It's not a very strong reason, not the sort I would have if I seemed to myself to have awakened in the middle of the night in an extremely unusual, strange, and unexpected situation. But it is some reason nonetheless. Hence, for creatures like us, in the world as it currently is, there is always some pro tanto reason in favour of the possibility that one is asleep and dreaming.'

If this argument fails, then Austin would see no obstacle to relying upon considerations about the world in dismissing the possibility that we are dreaming. Unfortunately, however, he didn't write enough for us to determine whether he would reject this argument. Given his views about human fallibility, he would presumably say that the mere fact that people can on occasion arrive at incorrect convictions while dreaming isn't by itself a reason in favour of the possibility that one is making such an error now. However, this doesn't decide the issue, since he also holds that the fact that other similar-looking, red-headed birds, easily mistaken for goldfinches, frequent the locale is a reason in favour of the possibility that the bird in the garden is not a goldfinch. In principle he could treat the considerations about dreams analogously. Surprisingly enough, however, little turns on the issue. Even if this argument succeeds, Austin's explanation of how we can tell we're not dreaming would still work, as I will argue in the remainder of this section.

Austin would clearly be in trouble if he endorsed all of the following:

1. There is some pro tanto reason in favour of the possibility that one is dreaming.
2. Consequently, in order to establish that one is not dreaming, one may not make use of any considerations in a certain excluded class, where 'making use of' includes treating something as a ground for thinking that a certain consideration is good evidence that one is not dreaming.
3. The claim that dreams have certain features and lack others is a consideration in the excluded class.
4. That dreams have certain features and lack others is a ground for treating the presence of certain features in one's current experience as conclusive evidence that one is not dreaming.

The conjunction of these claims obviously precludes Austin's view. However, he would deny claim (3), and he provides a principled reason for doing so.

As Austin notes, a charge that one's evidence is inadequate must be supported by some specification of the possibility one's evidence putatively fails to rule out.

If you say 'That's not enough,' then you must have in mind some more or less definite lack. [. . .] If there is no definite lack, which you are at least prepared to specify on being pressed, then it's silly (outrageous) just to go on saying 'That's not enough'. (1979: 84)

However, not just any specification will do.

The doubt or question 'But is it a *real* one?' has always (*must* have) a special basis, there must be some 'reason for suggesting' that it isn't real, in the sense of some specific way, or limited number of ways, in which it is suggested that this experience or item may be phoney. Sometimes (usually) the context makes it clear what the suggestion is [. . .]. If the context doesn't make it clear, then I am entitled to ask 'How do you mean? Do you mean it may be stuffed or what? *What are you suggesting*? (1979: 87)

That is, in the right sort of situation, one can quite appropriately respond to an objection by requesting a further specification of the suggested possibility that figures in it. The appropriateness of this response arises from the fact that different subpossibilities contained in the suggestion may require very different forms of rejection. Depending upon the circumstances and the relevant subpossibility, one may be able to respond simply by noting that there is no reason to think that it obtains, or one may be required to offer specific evidence to defeat some reason for thinking that it obtains. Moreover, different defeating considerations may be relevant, depending upon what exactly the possibility in question is. If one's background information makes it appropriate to discriminate subcases within the suggested possibility and to handle different subcases differently, then further clarification or specification of the suggestion is legitimately demanded.

Given this point, here's why Austin would deny claim (3). Suppose that he possesses the relevant empirical background information about people and dreams and grants that there's always some pro tanto reason in favour of the possibility that he's dreaming. What exactly has he granted? He should begin by distinguishing subcases in a way that is appropriately sensitive to his background information, as follows. 'On the one hand, if the suggestion is that I am in a state occurring during sleep that involves lifelike phenomenological states, generates mostly false beliefs including an incorrect conviction that one is awake and perceiving the world, and is *phenomenologically indistinguishable from paradigmatic waking experiences*, then there is no reason to suspect that I am in the suggested state. On the other hand, perhaps the suggestion is that I am in a state occurring during sleep that involves lifelike phenomenological states, generates mostly false beliefs including an incorrect conviction that one is awake and perceiving the world, and *differs phenomenologically from normal waking states in certain specified respects X, Y, and Z*. In that case, there is some reason in favour of the suggestion.'

According to Austin's view, the first subcase can reasonably be dismissed out of hand. What of the second subcase? We've granted that a priority requirement is in place regarding this possibility, so Austin cannot rely upon certain considerations in order to defeat it. Notice, however, that this process of distinguishing subcases in response to background information has the consequence that empirical information is contained in the very specification of the subcase itself: it is characterized as one which phenomenologically differs in certain specified respects from paradigmatic waking experiences. This means that this information is freely available to Austin in his reasoning, and that's the denial of claim (3). So he can reason as follows. 'Can I tell that I am not in a state that phenomenologically differs in respects X, Y, and Z from normal waking experiences? Yes. My current experience has/lacks the relevant features.'

In essence, what we have here is a point about relations amongst reasons. If Austin is attempting to establish that he is not dreaming, he should begin by adducing the total relevant evidence:

A. Fact: People are not infrequently in a state that:

   (i) is lifelike

   (ii) involves a conviction that one is awake and perceiving the world

   (iii) takes place during sleep

   (iv) leads to many incorrect convictions about how things are in the world, including an incorrect conviction that one is awake and perceiving the world.

B. Fact: This state has phenomenological features that differ in respects X, Y, and Z from the phenomenological features characterizing standard cases of waking experience.

C. Fact: I am now in a lifelike phenomenological state, convinced that I am awake and perceiving the world.

D. Fact: There is no relevantly similar state, phenomenologically identical to standard cases of waking experience, that people are not infrequently in.

From this evidence he can appropriately reason as follows.

1. There is no reason in favour of the possibility that I am in a non-waking state that is phenomenologically identical to standard waking experience.

2. There is some reason in favour of the possibility that I am now in a state that has features (i)–(iv) above and differs phenomenologically from standard waking experience in respects X, Y, and Z.

3. So, given this evidence so far, I might be in a state having features (i)–(iv) and differing phenomenologically from standard waking experience in respects X, Y, Z.

4. However, my current state does not differ from standard waking experience in respects X, Y, Z, because it has such and such phenomenological features.

5. So, I am not in a state that has features (i)–(iv) and differs phenomenologically from standard waking experience in respects X, Y, Z.

6. So, since both suggestions have been defeated, I conclude that I am not dreaming now.

Suppose that he now considers the following objection. 'This argument, starting with step 2, depends upon claim (B) above—that is, upon the claim that the relevant state differs from standard waking experience in respects X, Y, Z—but that claim is no longer available once you recognize the reason in favour of the possibility that you are in a state that has features (i)–(iv).' Here's how he should respond. 'If that claim is unavailable at that stage in the reasoning, it will have to be because the evidence that I have calls it into doubt by providing some reason against it. That's why, for instance, the claim that I am standing giving a lecture wouldn't be available to me at this juncture: since I have some reason in favour of the possibility that I am in the described misleading state, if am convinced that I am standing giving a lecture then there is some reason to suspect that I am *not* standing giving a lecture. But my evidence, (A)–(D) above, doesn't support the suggestion that the relevant state—the one that there is some reason to suspect that I am in—is phenomenologically indistinguishable from standard waking experience. It provides reason in favour of the possibility that I am in a state that *does* differ phenomenologically in certain respects from standard waking experience. And so I can determine that I am not in that state by checking whether my current experience has the relevant features.'

Suppose the objector now insists that considerations (A) and (C), taken by themselves, provide some reason in favour of the possibility that he is in a misleading non-waking state *without* specifying it as a state that differs phenomenologically from standard waking experience, and so they preclude him from relying on the fact that the state in question differs phenomenologically from standard waking experience. Austin has a straightforward rejoinder. The objector is simply ignoring some of the relevant facts. To determine what actually has some reason in its favour, you have to look at all of the relevant evidence. The total evidence is such that there is some pro tanto reason in favour of the possibility that one is in a state having features (i)–(iv) and differing in certain phenomenological respects from standard waking experience; moreover, the total evidence is such that this reason is defeated. That is what one sees when one insists on taking all of the relevant evidence into account. Of course, if you deprive yourself of certain background information at the outset, then this response will be unavailable. But we've been given no reason to do that.

It might be thought that while these rejoinders are conversationally or dialectically appropriate, an underlying epistemological problem still arises from the structure of the relevant epistemic priority requirements. In particular, it might be suggested that even if we take all of the relevant reasons into account, and even if we grant that what they support is only the possibility that one is in a state that differs phenomenologically from standard waking experiences, still the resulting epistemic priority requirement will preclude Austin from relying on the empirical claim that the states in question differ phenomenologically. However, this is not so.

A priority requirement tracks underlying rational relations amongst propositions in the circumstances. In the present case, what it captures is the fact that a reason in favour of the possibility that one is in a certain sort of misleading state that frequently gives rise to false convictions about the world also provides reason against each of a wide range of one's convictions. That is why each of these considerations is placed 'out of bounds' by the priority requirement. The crucial question, then, is what the relevant reasons in the circumstances provide reason for or against.

Use 'Ø' as a label for the type of state that there is some reason to suspect one is in. And grant, as this objection does, that the relevant considerations only support the possibility that one is in a misleading state of a type that involves features (i)–(iv) above and differs phenomenologically in certain specified respects from standard waking experiences. Now consider this proposition: *States of type Ø differ phenomenologically from standard waking experiences in the specified ways.* Suppose that you believe this proposition. Conjoin the fact, that you believe this proposition, with the fact, that there is some reason in favour of the possibility that you are in a state of a type Ø that involves features (i)–(iv) and differs phenomenologically in the specified ways. Do these two considerations, taken together, constitute a reason in favour of the possibility that it is *not* the case that states of type Ø differ phenomenologically from standard waking experiences in the specified ways? Obviously not. If what has reason in its favour were in fact the case, it would be *true* that states of type Ø differ phenomenologically from standard waking experiences in the specified respects. So the reasons in favour of the possibility that one is in a state of type Ø do not provide reason against the claim that states of type Ø phenomenologically differ in the specified respects from standard waking states. They do not provide such reason even when conjoined with the fact that one believes that states of type Ø and standard waking experiences so differ.

For this reason, we must reject the overhasty assumption that the priority requirement generated in these circumstances will place Austin's claim about dreams (that is, the claim about 'states of type Ø') out of bounds. Properly formulated, the relevant priority requirement runs as follows, letting 'ß' be the name for the set of propositions that have some pro tanto reason against them because there is pro tanto reason in favour of the possibility that one is in a state of a type that involves features (i)–(iv) and differs phenomenologically in certain specified respects from standard waking experiences:

In order to warrantedly believe any of the propositions in ß, one must have independent evidence (not consisting of considerations in ß) adequate to defeat the reasons in favour of the possibility that one is in a state of a type characterized by features (i)–(iv) and differing phenomenologically in the specified respects from standard waking experience.

This requirement precludes most considerations about the world from constituting the needed defeating reasons, but it allows phenomenological considerations of the sort Austin appeals to. It does not preclude relying on the empirical fact that the state in question differs phenomenologically in certain specified respects from standard waking experiences, because that fact is not in class ß (as defined above). And for this reason, it would be a mistake to think that by placing most of one's beliefs about the world out of play, the reasons for doubt would also remove the claim that dreams differ in certain respects from waking experiences. What there is reason to doubt—and so what is taken out of play—are the claims about which one would be unreliable if the possibility that has some reason in its favour were actual. Those do not include the claim about dreams. That's what the priority requirement, properly formulated, reflects.[28]

We began with the charge that if in ordinary circumstances there is pro tanto reason in favour of the possibility that we are dreaming, then the resulting priority requirement precludes Austin's empirical claim that dreams differ from waking experiences. We saw that Austin can avoid this charge by making obviously acceptable dialectical moves, namely, by demanding appropriately precise specifications of the suggested possibilities and insisting on taking appropriate account of all of the relevant evidence. We can now see that the appropriateness of these responses reflects the underlying facts regarding what has pro tanto reasons in its favour, what doesn't, and what evidential relations obtain in the circumstances. The dialectical moves amount to a demand that the objections and priority demands be formulated in a way that correctly reflects the actual reasons and priority relations that obtain in the circumstances.

It might be worried that Austin's response involves circular reasoning, in the following sense: once he's in doubt about whether he is dreaming, he won't be able to tell whether he is not dreaming unless he already believes that he isn't. But that is not so. At the stage in his deliberation at which he recognizes that there is some pro tanto reason in favour of the possibility that he is dreaming, he can suspend his initial confidence that he is not dreaming. He will still be able to make use of the claim that dreams differ in certain phenomenological respects from waking experiences, for the reasons just described.

---

[28] One structural concern remains. Whenever there is some reason in favour of a possibility characterized as Ø, there will also be some reason in favour of a possibility characterized using a less precise specification, Ø-, that is entailed by Ø. So, consider this specification of the possibility that one is dreaming: 'one is in a state occurring during sleep that involves very lifelike phenomenological states and generates mostly false beliefs about the world as well as an incorrect conviction that one is awake and perceiving the world.' This specification simply leaves out any information about whether the state differs phenomenologically from normal waking states. However, the reasons in favour of the more precisely specified possibility distinguished above are also reasons in favour of the suggestion that one is in this less finely specified state. So even when we include all of the relevant evidence in our description of the circumstances, there is still some reason to suspect that one is in a misleading non-waking state not specified as one that differs phenomenologically from standard waking experience. This would seem to mean that there is also a priority requirement in place regarding *this* possibility so specified, and it would seem that this priority requirement precludes one from relying upon the background empirical information about dreams that licenses treating phenomenological considerations as adequate evidence that one is not dreaming. It consequently still appears that Austin's argument fails.

However, this is not so, as we can see when we take seriously the way in which priority requirements are related to the underlying relations amongst reasons. We are supposing that there is some pro tanto reason to suspect that one is in a misleading non-waking state that differs in certain specified phenomenological respects from standard waking states. There is no reason at all to suspect that one is in a misleading non-waking state that is phenomenologically indistinguishable from standard waking states. In these circumstances, there is reason to suspect that one is in a misleading non-waking state (where the specification simply says nothing at all about whether the state in question differs phenomenologically from standard waking states). But there is reason to suspect this only in virtue of there being reason to suspect that one is in a misleading non-waking state that differs phenomenologically from standard waking states. Consequently, nothing more is needed to defeat the former than is needed to defeat the latter; a more demanding priority requirement is not created.

Suppose, then, that it is asked, 'But how could Austin respond to the suggestion that he is just dreaming that dreams phenomenologically differ in certain specified respects from waking experiences?' The Austinian answer is simply this: 'I'm not just dreaming that dreams differ phenomenologically in those ways from waking experiences; my current experience is nothing like a dream.' That's the right response, on Austin's view, because (a) it does not appeal to any of the considerations that would be placed out of bounds by relevant reasons for doubt, (b) it appeals to something that *is* good evidence that one is not dreaming, and (c) even if there is always some reason in favour of the possibility that one is dreaming, there is no reason in favour of the possibility that one is wrong in thinking that dreams and standard waking experiences differ in those ways.

Here's one final expression of uneasiness: 'This last response is objectionably question-begging because it assumes that dreams and waking experiences differ in certain respects.' But there is no ground for objection here. As we've seen, even if there is always some pro tanto reason in favour of the possibility that one is dreaming, that reason does not call into doubt the claim that dreams and waking experiences differ in certain respects. And if one recognizes that there is no reason in favour of the possibility that one is merely dreaming that dreams and waking experiences differ in certain respects, then on Austin's view one may summarily reject it. This procedure is no more objectionably question-begging than our confident dismissal of the preposterous hypothesis, discussed earlier, regarding the children of brunets.

I conclude that if Austin's larger epistemological framework and empirical assumptions are correct, then so is his account of how we can tell we aren't dreaming.

3. The dream argument for external world scepticism: demolishing the doctrine

Global arguments for external world scepticism appeal to general principles or requirements relating to knowledge, warranted belief, or some other status to show that we cannot have knowledge or possess any beliefs with the relevant status regarding the world around us. One important family of such arguments deploy hypotheses to the effect that one might just be dreaming, a brain in a vat, or the victim of a deceptive evil demon. They maintain that one cannot know or have good reason to believe that such conditions do not obtain, and that because this is so, one cannot know or have good reason to believe anything about the world. Such arguments have garnered a great deal of attention over the last forty years or so. If the epistemological framework developed so far is correct, however, then Austin showed us how to counter them.

To have any hope of succeeding, a global sceptical argument must accomplish at least the following two things:

(1) It must tie (a) *one's ability to have knowledge or good reasons for beliefs in the target class* to (b) *one's possession of adequate evidence that one is not in a certain hypothesized state.*

(2) It must preclude one from deploying considerations in the target class as evidence that one is not in the hypothesized state. That is, it must require *independent* grounds for thinking that one is not in that state.

Requirement (2) is crucial. Requirement (1), taken by itself, could be satisfied by knowledge in the target class, if by knowing certain things in that class one *ipso facto* possesses adequate evidence that one is not in the hypothesized state. So, for example, for all (1) accomplishes, one could (with G. E. Moore) reply to arguments for external world scepticism by pointing out that one is standing giving a lecture (and so not dreaming), that there are no deceptive evil demons, and that technology does not currently exist to create brains in vats. The argument for external world scepticism must preclude one from appealing to empirical considerations about the world in this way. This is what satisfying requirement (2) would accomplish. A key question, then, that any compelling sceptical argument must answer is this: why can't one deploy empirical considerations about the world to dismiss the suggested possibility?

It might be thought that appealing to empirical considerations about the world in this way would simply beg the question, since the sceptic claims that one doesn't know or reasonably believe anything about the world. However, this account of the situation badly underestimates the challenge facing sceptical arguments. We confront sceptical arguments from an initial position in which we take ourselves to know and have excellent reasons for all sorts of claims about the world and so regard ourselves as free to make use of these claims for the purposes of reasoning and inquiry. The sceptical argument must somehow convince us, from that starting point, that we don't actually know or reasonably believe anything about the world. Starting where we do in confronting the argument, we quite reasonably take ourselves to be entitled to make use of empirical considerations about the world. Somehow, the early stages of the argument must *bring us to see* that we can't do that. The crucial question for any sceptical argument, then, is how this is to be accomplished.[29]

---

[29] Standard attempts to delineate a 'sceptical paradox' do not answer this question. Consider, for instance, the influential 'Argument from Ignorance' (DeRose 1995), where 'O' represents an ordinary claim about the world and 'H' a sceptical hypothesis:

1. In order to know O, I must know that not-H.
2. I do not (or cannot) know that not-H.
3. So I do not (or cannot) know that O.

This argument simply asserts in premise (2) that one does not know that one is not dreaming, deceived by an evil demon, or a brain in a vat. But even if premise (1) is true, there is no reason why, if O were adequate evidence that not-H, one couldn't know that not-H in virtue of knowing O. For instance, premise (1), taken by itself, does nothing to preclude a Moore-type response that grants, e.g. that I couldn't know that I am at a computer writing a paper if I didn't also know that I wasn't dreaming, but claims that since I am at a computer writing a paper, I'm manifestly not dreaming. The crucial work in the argument thus takes place off the page; something unmentioned is being assumed to preclude one from satisfying premise (1) *by knowing all sorts of things about the world*. A similar problem plagues reconstructions of sceptical reasoning that deploy the principle that knowledge is closed under known entailments. (For discussion of the relation of closure principles to sceptical argumentation, see my 2004b.)

In one of the most thoughtful and sensitive depictions of scepticism available, Barry Stroud offers an argument for external world scepticism that aims to respond to this concern (1984, chapter 1). His argument is built around the commonsensical claim that 'knowing that one is not dreaming is a condition of knowing something [anything] about the world around us' (1984: 19, *passim*), or as he also puts it, that 'we must know we are not dreaming if we are to know anything about the world around us' (1984: 30). Stroud argues that once we accept this requirement, we are forced to conclude that we cannot know that we are not dreaming: the requirement precludes its own satisfaction (1984: 19–23). His reasoning seems to be as follows. The requirement applies to *every* piece of knowledge 'that goes beyond one's sensory experience' (1984: 22). Since the qualitative features of one's current experience are neutral on the issue (any qualitative feature of waking experience can equally well be dreamed (1984: 18)), any evidence that one is not dreaming will itself have to 'go beyond one's sensory experience' to involve claims about the world around us. Likewise, the very claim that one is not dreaming is something that 'goes beyond one's sensory experience'. The requirement accordingly applies to one's knowledge of all these things as well. Consequently, Stroud concludes, one cannot satisfy the requirement. In order to know the things that enable one to know that one is not dreaming, one will have to know that one is not dreaming. And so to know that one is not dreaming, one will have to know that one is not dreaming. But this is impossible (1984: 22–3).

Taken literally, this argument fails. Stroud's requirement, as he formulates it, only says that a necessary condition of knowing things about the world (things that 'go beyond one's sensory experience') is that one knows that one is not dreaming. If we apply that condition to one's knowledge that one is not dreaming, we get this: A necessary condition of knowing that you are not dreaming is that you know that you are not dreaming. This is a trivial logical truth with no sceptical upshot. More generally, Stroud's requirement—when taken literally—yields at most that if you know anything about the world, you must also know that you are not dreaming. But that requirement doesn't have the consequence that you cannot know that you are not dreaming, since it leaves open the possibility that the dependence relations run both ways and that things one knows about the world come into the story of how one knows one isn't dreaming.

What Stroud's argument needs is a requirement stating a *precondition* or a priority relation, a relation of asymmetric epistemic dependence. To put it formally, the requirement will have to be formulable using an irreflexive relational predicate such that the two demands

aRb and bRa

are not co-satisfiable when a is not identical with b. In what follows I will use the phrase, 'antecedently know', to formulate this logical or structural feature of the requirement. The requirement would then read as follows:

In order to know any proposition about the world, one must antecedently know that one is not dreaming.

Only a requirement with this structure will preclude the possibility that one knows that one is not dreaming wholly or in part by virtue of knowing things about the world.[30]

Now Stroud traces the sceptic's requirement to a more general principle purportedly generated by the concept of knowledge and implicit in our ordinary epistemic practices. According to this more general principle, in order to know any proposition p, one must know the falsity of all propositions q that one knows to be incompatible with one's knowing p (1984: 29–30). To generate a requirement with the right sort of structure, however, this principle likewise must be read as having a priority structure, as follows:

In order to know any proposition p, one must antecedently know the falsity of all propositions q that one knows to be incompatible with one's knowing p.

Given that one knows that dreaming is not a way of coming to know things about the world, this principle generates the requirement needed for the sceptical argument (viz., that to know any p about the world, one must antecedently know that one is not dreaming). And this principle quickly generates the desired result that one cannot know that one is not dreaming. Let p = 'I am not dreaming'. One thing incompatible with knowing that one is not dreaming is that one be dreaming, since one cannot know things that are false. So, substituting 'I am not dreaming' for p and 'I am dreaming' for q, we get:

In order to know that I am not dreaming, I must antecedently know that it is false that I am dreaming.

Or:

In order to know that I am not dreaming, I must antecedently know that I am not dreaming.

This demand is obviously unsatisfiable, giving us the result Stroud sought.

Unfortunately, the general priority principle fuelling this argument generates sceptical results all too easily and without bringing the sceptic's distinctive hypotheses into play. Suppose, for instance, that I am looking at what is plainly a chicken. According to the principle, in order to know that it is a chicken, I must antecedently know that it is not a cow (since its being a cow would be incompatible with my knowing that it is a chicken). So let p = 'It is not a cow'. One thing incompatible with my knowing that it

---

[30] There are interesting issues of detail regarding two possible ways of understanding this requirement. On one reading, the requirement states that for any given p about the world, one cannot know that p unless one antecedently knows—that is, antecedently to knowing that p—that one is not dreaming. On the second reading, it states that in order to know any proposition p about the world at all, one must antecedently know—that is, antecedently to knowing any propositions about the world at all—that one is not dreaming. Assuming that the *know antecedently* relation is transitive, either reading will have the desired consequence in the sceptical argument.

is not a cow is that it *is* a cow, since one cannot know things that are false. So, substituting 'It is not a cow' for *p* and 'It is a cow' for *q*, we get:

In order to know that it is not a cow, I must antecedently know that it is not a cow.

This demand is unsatisfiable. So if this principle is correct, I cannot know that it is not a cow. But the principle demanded that in order to know that it is a chicken, I must antecedently know that it is not a cow. So, I cannot know that it is a chicken, either. An analogous argument can be run for any putative item of knowledge you like. The consequence is an extremely easy argument for a general, sweeping scepticism about anything whatsoever. This sceptical argument is *too* easy, however. The fault lies squarely with the principle.[31]

A convincing sceptical argument wouldn't need a fully general principle, however; a plausible principle applying to the particular sceptical hypothesis would do the trick. So let's consider an argument based simply on a priority version of Stroud's requirement that in order to know what's going on in the world around you, you must know that you are not dreaming.

1. For any proposition that one could come to believe falsely as the result of a dream, one cannot now know or reasonably believe that proposition unless one has adequate independent reasons for believing that one is not now dreaming. (An independent reason for believing that one is not now dreaming would be a consideration which is neither that proposition itself nor the claim that one is not dreaming, and which is not something else that one could come to believe merely as the result of a dream.)
2. Anything that one can do or experience during waking life can also be dreamed about.[32]
3. So (by 2) any consideration that one might appeal to as a reason for believing that one is not now dreaming will either be neutral on the question or will fall under the principle (1). In the latter case, in order to know or reasonably believe it, one will need an adequate independent reason for believing that one is not now dreaming.
4. Consequently (by 3), one cannot have an adequate independent reason for believing that one is not dreaming.
5. So, one cannot now know or even reasonably believe anything that one could come to believe merely as the result of a dream.

---

[31] The implausibility of this principle has also been noted by Pryor (2000) and Byrne (2004). I first articulated the problem in my undergraduate senior honours thesis (UC Berkeley, 1992). Austin may help us understand what is wrong with the principle, since on his view epistemic priority relations depend on the circumstances. So even if something roughly like Stroud's more general principle is right, it will have to be formulated so as to be appropriately sensitive to the factors that determine the actual structure of priority relations in particular cases. Once it is formulated in this way, it won't underwrite the dreaming argument for scepticism in the way Stroud envisages.

[32] Stroud explicitly appeals to a premise along these lines (1984: 18, 22).

This, I believe, is the most plausible version of Stroud's dream argument for external world scepticism. But despite its plausibility, Austin would regard it as a failure.

There are two ways of reading the argument. Either premise (1) is offered as a conceptual truth holding independently of the actual empirical circumstances and premise (2) is treated merely as a claim about conceptual, metaphysical, or 'logical' possibility, or premise (1) is treated as a circumstance-relative priority requirement. On the first reading, the first two premises amount to this. (For clarity, I have reversed their order. The rest of the argument, appropriately modified, will proceed pretty much as before.)

2★. There is a possible state which perfectly mimics standard waking experience and generates convictions about the world which are generally false.
1★. For any proposition that one could come to believe merely as the result of being in that state, one cannot now know or even reasonably believe it unless one has adequate independent reason for believing that one is not now in that state.

Suppose that premise (2★) is true. Even so, Austin would reject premise (1★). Whether an epistemic priority requirement like (1★) holds will depend, he'll say, upon the circumstances; it is not a purely conceptual matter. We won't have reason to accept the requirement unless there is some reason in favour of the suggestion that we might be in such a state. But as things are, there is no reason in favour of that suggestion. So we can reasonably reject requirement (1★), and thus can reasonably reject this argument.

On the alternative reading of the argument, premise (1) is offered as a circumstance-relative priority requirement that happens to hold in circumstances such as ours. Now as we have seen, Austin could grant that there is a circumstance-relative priority requirement in place to the effect (more or less) that in order to know or reasonably believe things about the world, one must have adequate independent reason to believe that one is not dreaming. This is because Austin could grant that even in ordinary circumstances there is some reason in favour of the possibility that one is dreaming. But as we have also seen, an adequate specification of the state in question will involve empirical claims which enable us to satisfy this requirement. So while we should grant there is a way of interpreting or refining premise (1) on which Austin would perhaps find it acceptable, on that understanding of the argument step (3) won't follow. This is because Austin would regard premise (2)—the claim that anything that one can do or experience during waking life can also be dreamed about—as either irrelevant or false. He would regard it as irrelevant if it is interpreted merely as a claim about 'logical', conceptual, or metaphysical possibility, since on Austin's view the mere 'logical', conceptual, or metaphysical possibility of a dream that perfectly mimics waking experience is not a reason in favour of one's being in such a state and consequently has no significance for the question of what constitutes a good reason for believing that one is not dreaming. And he would regard premise (2) as false if it is treated as an empirical claim about what human dream experience is actually like, since on his view standard waking experiences differ in certain phenomenological respects from dreams.

In short, for the argument to be successful by Austin's lights, it would have to be the case that: (A) an appropriate priority relation holds because there is some reason in favour of the possibility that one is dreaming, *and* (B) dreams are phenomenologically indistinguishable from waking experiences. But Austin would deny this conjunction. From his point of view, any plausibility the sceptical argument has is nothing but sleight of hand.

In the epistemological imagination, scepticism is a circumstance-independent problem. The sceptical result is supposed to follow from the mere concepts (or essences) of knowledge or reasonable or justified belief and the mere conceptual, metaphysical, or 'logical' possibility that one is in a state qualitatively indistinguishable from waking experience that generates convictions that generally diverge from how things really are in the world. For scepticism to arise in this way, the concept (or perhaps essence) of knowledge (or of reasonable or justified belief) would have to generate or involve a circumstance-independent priority requirement concerning the possibility in question. For Austin, however, there are no substantive circumstance-independent priority requirements to do the trick.

On Austin's view, then, scepticism is a contingent, ineliminably empirical matter. A successful sceptical argument would have to rest upon empirical background assumptions that both gave us reason to accept an appropriate priority requirement and had the consequence that we cannot satisfy it. The argument would have to appeal to a hypothesis which has some reason in its favour, which generates a priority requirement in relation to our beliefs about the world, and which (given that priority requirement) we cannot determine is not the case. As things are no such sceptical hypothesis arises. The dream argument can be rejected in the ways I have just sketched, and Austin's view allows an even quicker rejection of arguments appealing to the possibilities that we are brains in vats or victims of a deceiving evil demon. To put it succinctly, there are no deceiving evil demons, and at present we have not yet created brains in vats.[33]

This approach to arguments for external world scepticism assumes that only an appropriately structured epistemic priority requirement will preclude Austin's reliance on empirical background information. However, a number of epistemologists have suggested that there is a traditional epistemological project or question that, properly understood, puts all empirical claims about the world out of bounds (McGinn 1989; M. Williams 1996; Stroud 2002; Bonjour 2003).[34] Once that is accomplished, it might be suggested, some requirement such as Stroud's requirement—now understood as *not* involving a priority claim—could do the needed work in generating the sceptical

---

[33] I say 'at present' to emphasize that on Austin's framework we could someday find ourselves facing sceptical problems of our own making, for instance if technologies for creating nonveridical experiences through brain stimulation become sufficiently advanced while being unscrupulously deployed.

[34] There is disagreement among Stroud, McGinn, and Williams about whether the result is properly understood as somehow casting doubt upon the truth of our ordinary claims to knowledge about the external world. Bonjour is less pessimistic than the others, since he holds that the project can be completed completely satisfactorily.

result, because from the perspective generated by the guiding question or project, one lacks any means of determining that one is not dreaming.

Stroud, for instance, suggests that the traditional epistemologist wants to explain how anyone knows or justifiably believes anything about the world at all. The generality of this question, he claims, precludes one from appealing to any empirical background information about the world to provide the explanation (2002: 120). A similar result arguably follows from Laurence Bonjour's question whether I have good reasons—and if so, what they are—for any of my empirical beliefs about the world. If one seriously attempts to answer that question, Bonjour claims, then one must put all empirical background information 'off the table' and show, from that perspective, how one has good grounds for believing anything about the world (2003).

Austin would have reason to refuse to pursue any such project. On his view, the following are all circumstance-dependent matters, determined in part by contingent, empirical facts about the world: (1) what constitutes empirical evidence or reason for what, (2) which possibilities or objections have reason in their favour and which don't, (3) what is required in order to defeat the possibilities that have some reason in their favour, and (4) what priority requirements or constraints obtain regarding a particular claim. The circumstance-dependency of these matters has the consequence that if one is precluded from relying upon any empirical claims about the world, then one simply cannot determine what one has good reason to believe about the world or explain how one knows what one knows about the world: the resources necessary to identify one's epistemic position relative to any particular claim about the world will have been made unavailable. So if Austin is right about the circumstance-dependence of these matters, then he can help himself to a line of thought that I have developed elsewhere on which it looks quite reasonable to reject a project like Stroud's or Bonjour's. He can point out that the project must fail for the purely structural reason just noted, that its failure would reveal nothing about the epistemic status of any of our beliefs about the world, and that there would be another perfectly good way of figuring out what we know or have good reason to believe—namely, by relying on our background information about the world. From this perspective, the project appears to be nothing more than a waste of time.[35]

This perspective sheds light on Austin's over-riding methodological assumption that epistemological reflection must begin from where we are, with the claims to which we are currently committed. On Austin's view, any episode of empirical inquiry, justification, or epistemic assessment must begin with a body of empirical background beliefs in place in order for the episode to proceed at all, since without them one cannot so much as determine what is a reason for what, which objections are to be taken seriously and which aren't, etc. Any of these background materials can come under scrutiny or under fire in the course of the episode. But the objections will have to arise and be rebutted in ways that are appropriately related to that background information.

---

[35] For detailed elaboration and defence of this line of argument, see my (2005).

The response to scepticism explored here depends upon several of Austin's characteristic theses. These are, among others:

1. There are no substantive circumstance-independent epistemic priority requirements.
2. Whether an epistemic priority requirement holds is a function of the reasons in the particular situation. In particular, if a certain suggested possibility would undercut one's reliability regarding a certain class of beliefs, one may nonetheless rely upon beliefs in that class in dismissing the suggestion—provided one recognizes that it has no reason in its favour.
3. The mere fact that a certain state or scenario is a 'logical', conceptual, or metaphysical possibility and is logically, conceptually, or metaphysically compatible with one's current information is not a reason in favour of its obtaining.
4. Dreams differ in certain specifiable ways from waking experiences, so that we can tell on phenomenological grounds that we are not dreaming.

A thorough treatment of scepticism would have to examine and defend each of these claims. If they are right, however, then Austin has shown us how to put the dream argument to rest.[36]

Bibliography

Austin, J. L. (1958), *Lectures at the University of California, Berkeley*. Notes by R. Lawrence and W. Hayes, supplemented by Wallace Matson.

——(1962), *Sense and Sensibilia*, Oxford: Oxford University Press.

Austin, J. L. (1979), *Philosophical Papers*, 3rd ed., Urmson, J. O., Warnock, G. J. (eds.), Oxford: Oxford University Press.

Ayer, A. J. (1940), *The Foundations of Empirical Knowledge*, London: Macmillan.

Blumenfeld, D., Blumenfeld, J. (1978), 'Can I Know that I am not Dreaming?', in Hooker, M. (ed.), *Descartes: Critical and Interpretive Essays*, Baltimore: Johns Hopkins University Press, pp. 234–55.

Bonjour, L., Sosa, E. (2003), *Epistemic Justification: Internalism vs. Externalism, Foundations vs. Virtues*, Oxford: Blackwell Publishers.

Byrne, A. (2004), 'How Hard are the Sceptical Paradoxes?', *Noûs* 38: 299–325.

Collins, J. J., Chow, C. C., Imhoff, T. T. (1995), 'Stochastic Resonance Without Tuning', *Nature* 376: 236–8.

---

[36] I first explored several of this chapter's central lines of thought in my University of California, Berkeley, senior thesis and Harvard University PhD dissertation (2000). At the time, I understood myself to be broadly inspired by Austin, but it was not until Wallace Matson pointed out the relevant passages in the Lawrence and Hayes notes that I realized that the position I had arrived at could be drawn out of Austin's writings. I develop what I regard as the next stage of this work in Leite (2010).

I have profited from extensive conversations with my colleagues Katy Abramson, Gary Ebbs, and Mark Kaplan and comments from Penelope Maddy, Ram Neta, Elizabeth Palmer, Jim Pryor, Fred Schmitt, Kevin Toh, Jonathan Weinberg, and the editors of this volume. Support for this project was provided by the Indiana University Sabbatical Leave Program and the Indiana University College Arts and Humanities Institute.

DeRose, K. (1995), 'Solving the Skeptical Problem', *The Philosophical Review* 104: 1–49.

Descartes, R. (1984), *Meditations on First Philosophy*, in Cottingham, J., Stoothoff, R., Murdoch, D. (eds.), *The Philosophical Writings of Descartes*, vol. II, Cambridge: Cambridge University Press.

Dretske, F. (1970), 'Epistemic Operators', *The Journal of Philosophy* 67: 1007–23.

——(1981), 'The Pragmatic Dimension of Knowledge', *Philosophical Studies* 40: 363–78.

Hobbes, T. (1984), 'Third Set of Objections', in Cottingham, J., Stoothoff, R., Murdoch, D. (eds.), *The Philosophical Writings of Descartes*, vol. II, Cambridge: Cambridge University Press, pp. 121–37.

Hobson, J. A. (1999), *Dreaming as Delirium*, Cambridge, MA: MIT University Press.

——(1988), *The Dreaming Brain*, New York: Basic Books.

——, Stickgold, R., Pace-Schott, E. (1998), 'The Neurophysiology of REM-Sleep Dreaming', *NeuroReport* 9: R1–R14.

Kaplan, M. (Chapter 3, this volume), 'Tales of the Unknown'.

Leite, A. (2004a), 'Is Fallibility an Epistemological Shortcoming?', *The Philosophical Quarterly* 54: 232–51.

——(2004b), 'Skepticism, Closure, and Sensitivity (or Why the Closure Principle is Irrelevant to Skepticism)', *The Croatian Journal of Philosophy* 4: 335–50.

——(2005), 'Epistemological Externalism and the Project of Traditional Epistemology', *Philosophy and Phenomenological Research* 52: 505–33.

——(2008), 'Believing One's Reasons are Good,' *Synthese* 161: 419–41.

——(2010), 'How to Take Skepticism Seriously,' *Philosophical Studies* 148: 39–60.

——(2011), 'Immediate Warrant, Epistemic Responsibility, and Moorean Dogmatism', in Steglich-Peterson, A., Reisner, A. (eds.), *Reasons for Belief*, Cambridge: Cambridge University Press.

McGinn, M. (1989), *Sense and Certainty*, Oxford: Basil Blackwell.

Moore, G. E. (1993), 'Certainty', in Baldwin, T. (ed.), *G. E. Moore: Selected Writings*, London: Routledge, pp. 171–96.

Nozick, R. (1981), *Philosophical Explanations*, Cambridge, MA: Harvard University Press.

Pryor, J. (2000), 'The Skeptic and the Dogmatist', *Noûs* 34: 517–49.

Solms, M. (1997), *The Neuropsychology of Dreams*, Mahwah, NJ: Lawrence Erlbaum Associates.

Stickgold, R., Hobson, J. A., Fosse, R., Fosse, M. (2001), 'Sleep, Learning, and Dreams: Off-line Memory Reprocessing', *Science* 294: 1052–7.

Sosa, E. (2002), 'Tracking, Knowledge, and Competence', in Moser, P. (ed.), *The Oxford Handbook of Epistemology*, Oxford: Oxford University Press, pp. 264–86.

——(2005), 'Dreams and Philosophy', *Proceedings and Addresses of the American Philosophical Association* 79: 7–18.

Stroud, B. (1984), *The Significance of Philosophical Scepticism*, Oxford: Oxford University Press.

——(2002), 'Understanding Human Knowledge in General', in *Understanding Human Knowledge: Philosophical Essays*, Oxford: Oxford University Press.

Williams, B. (1978), *Descartes: The Project of Pure Enquiry*, Harmondsworth: Pelican.

Williams, M. (1996), *Unnatural Doubts*, Princeton, NJ: Princeton University Press.

Williamson, T. (2000), *Knowledge and Its Limits*, Oxford: Oxford University Press.

5

Believing what the Man Says about His Own Feelings

Benjamin McMyler

1. Introduction

J. L. Austin begins the conclusion of his paper 'Other Minds' by linking the 'Predicament' that is the philosophical problem of other minds to an issue concerning human speech.

> I should like to make in conclusion some further remarks about this crucial matter of our believing what the man says about his own feelings. Although I know very well that I do not see my way clearly in this, I cannot help feeling sure that it is fundamental to the whole Predicament, and that it has not been given the attention it deserves, possibly just because it is so obvious. (1979: 114)

He then goes on to quickly discuss and reject a particular view of the epistemology of testimony, after which he concludes,

> It seems, rather, that believing in other persons, in authority and testimony, is an essential part of the act of communicating, an act which we all constantly perform. It is as much an irreducible part of our experience as, say, giving promises, or playing competitive games, or even sensing coloured patches. We can state certain advantages of such performances, and we can elaborate rules of a kind for their 'rational' conduct (as the Law Courts and historians and psychologists work out the rules for accepting testimony). But there is no 'justification' for our doing them as such. (1979: 115)

While 'Other Minds' has long been considered an important if controversial work on the problem of other minds, only recently have philosophers begun to appreciate its importance as a work on the epistemology of testimony.[1] What still hasn't been sufficiently appreciated, however, is the intimate connection that Austin sees between issues concerning the epistemology of testimony and the philosophical problem of

---

[1] Authors who have recognized that 'Other Minds' is concerned with issues regarding the epistemology of testimony include Coady (1992), Welbourne (1993), and most recently Hinchman (2005).

other minds. Austin doesn't do much more than suggest such a connection, but he clearly thinks that 'this crucial matter of our believing what the man says about his own feelings' is 'fundamental to the whole Predicament'. In this paper I want to explore and press further the connection that Austin sees between these issues. I hope to show that one cannot understand Austin's account of our cognitive relation to other minds without appreciating the centrality to this account of issues concerning the epistemology of testimony.

Section 2 examines the place of considerations of the epistemology of testimony in the overall structure of 'Other Minds' leading up to Austin's famous analogy between saying 'I know' and saying 'I promise'. Section 3 offers a rather revisionist reading of this analogy by taking it to be an analogy between the speech act of promising and what epistemologists typically treat as the speech act of testifying. Section 4 argues that the point of the analogy is to begin to give an answer to the question of what constitutes the justification of knowledge based on testimony. The answer Austin gives here is one that draws on the essentially interpersonal character of testimonial knowledge. Knowing that p based on a speaker's testimony that p involves *believing the speaker that p*, where believing the speaker that p cannot be construed as a matter of coming to one's own conclusion about p.[2] Section 5 then turns to Austin's treatment of the problem of other minds. Austin argues that our ordinary cognitive relation to the minds of others doesn't involve inferring conclusions about their psychological states from behavioural evidence (from symptoms). Instead, we can bear a direct, non-inferential cognitive relation to the psychological states of others by simply observing their states in their expressions of those states. Unlike other philosophers who hold that we can bear a kind of 'perceptual' relation to the psychological states of others, however, Austin is explicitly concerned to distinguish our ordinary cognitive relation to other minds from the kind of non-inferential cognitive relation to material objects characteristic of ordinary perception. Section 6 begins to examine the character of this non-inferential and yet non-perceptual cognitive relation we often bear to other minds. Austin first discusses several special worries that he takes to arise with regard to our knowledge of other minds. These special worries all have to do with the way in which many overt expressions of psychological states, unlike the behaviour of ordinary material objects, are intentional acts. Austin then points out that among the intentions with which a psychological state can be expressed are the kind of communicative intentions paradigmatically involved in the case of testimony. Some intentional expressions of psychological states amount to what I call testimonial avowals, and like cases of testimony generally, testimonial avowals call for an audience to believe the

---

[2] More precisely, *testimonially* knowing that p based on a speaker's testimony that p involves believing the speaker rather than coming to one's own conclusion about p. One can certainly treat a speaker's testimony as a consideration on the basis of which one draws one's own conclusion that p. The point is just that this is not a case of acquiring *testimonial* knowledge. Ordinary cases of testimonial knowledge involve believing the speaker that p, and according to Austin, believing the speaker that p is inconsistent with treating what the speaker says as a consideration from which one draws one's own conclusions.

speaker that she is in the particular psychological state that she avows. Finally, section 7 argues that Austin returns at the end of 'Other Minds' to issues concerning the epistemology of testimony, specifically to issues concerning a person's testimony about her own psychological states, in order to draw out what he sees as the second-personal nature of the problem of other minds. As Austin sees it, the problem of other minds is to a large extent an expression of very ordinary worries about the interpersonal relations of authority and responsibility involved in believing others.

My concern in this paper with 'the problem of other minds' will be, like Austin's, a concern with the nature of our cognitive relation to the psychological states of others. My interest in outright *scepticism* about other minds will be only to the extent that it raises the question of what this cognitive relation consists in. In asking whether we can ever have knowledge of the existence and contents of other minds, the sceptic is asking what kind of cognitive relation we do in fact bear towards the minds of others and whether this cognitive relation can ever amount to knowledge. Austin argues that the sceptic offers a picture of our relation to other minds that is inconsistent with our ordinary talk about knowledge and about the psychological states of others, and he suggests an alternative picture that is more consistent with the kinds of things we ordinarily do and say. Obviously this can't amount to a knockdown argument against the sceptic—the sceptic can always insist that our ordinary talk about knowledge and about the psychological states of others is precisely what is in need of justification—but instead of concentrating on the best way of responding to the sceptic, I want to examine in some detail Austin's alternative conception of our cognitive relation to the psychological states of others and what he takes this alternative conception to reveal about some of the motivations behind the philosophical problem of other minds.

Austin is a very suggestive writer, and much of what he says in 'Other Minds' is particularly so. He is often content to point out features of our ordinary epistemic practice without going into any detail with regard to the philosophical conclusions that should be drawn from them. Distinctions are seemingly drawn for their own sake, and arguments often consist of illustrative analogies and examples. In his own contribution to the symposium at which Austin's paper was first delivered, A. J. Ayer says of Austin that while 'he likes his philosophical garden to be neat and tidy', in this case 'he has found so much pruning to do by the way that he has hardly applied his knife to . . . [the] problem' (1946: 188).[3] Though what Ayer says here is clearly meant as a complaint, this is precisely the aspect of Austin's writing that makes it such a fertile source for further inquiry. The reader is left in the position of filling in details and providing further argumentation, and this is what I'll attempt to do here. I'll be offering something like a rational reconstruction of certain regions of Austin's thought in 'Other Minds'. This will involve passing over many of the issues that Austin addresses in the paper, but it will also allow me to piece together and hopefully render coherent a

---

[3]   The text of all three contributions to the symposium entitled 'Other Minds' by Wisdom, Austin, and Ayer were originally published in 1946, the *Aristotelian Society Supplement* 20: 122–97.

central thread of the paper that has gone surprisingly unappreciated. At many points this will require going well beyond anything that Austin says explicitly in the text, but I hope that this will help further an appreciation for their own sake of the issues that interested Austin.

2. The place of testimony in 'Other Minds'

The bulk of 'Other Minds' is taken up by a discussion of knowledge concerning material objects, this pursued by examining the various ways in which we ordinarily respond to the question 'How do you know?' when asked with regard to such statements as 'There is a goldfinch in the garden.' Austin's real target in 'Other Minds' is, nevertheless, knowledge of other minds. The reason Austin spends so much time considering our knowledge of material objects is that he wants to apply the conclusions he gleans from this discussion to what he sees as the more difficult problem of our knowledge of other minds.[4] More specifically, he wants to have a basis upon which to begin to draw out the way in which the problem of other minds is an expression of difficulties importantly *different* in kind from those relevant to our knowledge of material objects.

It is on this further issue of the peculiarity of the problem of other minds that I'd like to focus in this paper, so I will leave to one side most of Austin's more famous discussion of the distinction between knowing and believing and of the philosopher's use and misuse of the notions of reality, sureness, and certainty. Still, it is important to see that Austin's concern with testimony as a mode of access to the minds of others surfaces over and again throughout these discussions. For example, one of the reasons he gives for thinking that knowledge should not be construed as a species of belief is that in saying 'I know' a subject is not self-ascribing a subjective mental state in the same way as she is in saying 'I believe'.

If we like to say that 'I believe', and likewise 'I am sure' and 'I am certain', are descriptions of subjective mental cognitive states or attitudes, or what not, then 'I know' is not that, or at least not merely that: it functions differently in talking. (1979: 78–9)

Of course, as Austin immediately notes, this leaves completely open what exactly the relevant distinction here amounts to. One obvious difference between knowing and believing is that, as Austin puts it, *if I know I can't be wrong*; to show that I am wrong is to show that I did not know, while to show that I am wrong *is not* to show that I did not believe. In contemporary terminology, this is to say that knowledge is factive while belief is not. Nevertheless, Austin thinks there is much more to the way in which

---

[4] It is a point of concern for Austin in *Sense and Sensibilia* that there is no one thing called our 'ordinary knowledge of material objects'. Our cognitive relation to the material world thus is not exhausted by our cognitive relation to middle-sized dry goods. Nevertheless, for my purposes here it is useful to draw a general distinction between knowledge of other minds and knowledge of material objects.

saying 'I know' and saying 'I believe' function differently in talking than this difference with respect to factivity. At this point in 'Other Minds' Austin says that this issue 'must be considered in due course', and he then puts it off until after a long discussion of the various ways in which we ordinarily respond to the question 'How do you know?' Austin's famous discussion of the parallels between saying 'I know' and saying 'I promise', taken up under the heading 'If I know I can't be wrong', is then intended to further cash out the ways in which saying 'I know' differs from saying 'I believe', and, to anticipate, the fundamental issue here concerns the peculiar way in which saying 'I know' functions to communicate information to others. As we will see, the issue Austin is ultimately driving at is one concerning the epistemology of testimony.

Before we turn to Austin's discussion of saying 'I know' and saying 'I promise', however, there is an important section within his discussion of the ways in which we ordinarily respond to the question 'How do you know?' in which Austin foreshadows much of what he goes on to argue in 'Other Minds'. Austin claims that the reasons or justifications we ordinarily give in response to the question 'How do you know?' are different in kind from the reasons or justifications we ordinarily give in response to the question 'Why do you believe?' Giving my reasons for knowing typically involves stating how I come to be in a position to know, while giving my reasons for believing typically involves a recital of symptoms, arguments in support, etc. Austin then claims that one of the most important justifications for knowing typically offered involves the citing of an authority:

Among the cases where we give our reasons for knowing, a special and important class is formed by those where we cite authorities. If asked 'How do you know that the election is today?', I am apt to reply 'I read it in *The Times*', and if asked 'How do you know the Persians were defeated at Marathon?' I am apt to reply 'Herodotus expressly states that they were'. In these cases 'know' is correctly used: we know 'at second hand' when we can cite an authority who was in a position to know (possibly himself also only at second hand). The statement of an authority makes me aware of something, enables me to know something, which I shouldn't otherwise have known. It is a source of knowledge. In many cases, we contrast such reasons for knowing with other reasons for believing the very same thing: 'Even if we didn't know it, even if he hadn't confessed, the evidence against him would be enough to hang him'.

It is evident, of course, that this sort of 'knowledge' is 'liable to be wrong', owing to the unreliability of human testimony (bias, mistake, lying, exaggeration, &c.). Nevertheless, the occurrence of a piece of human testimony radically alters the situation. We say 'We shall never know what Caesar's feelings were on the field of the battle of Philippi', because he did not pen an account of them, *if* he had, then to say 'We shall never know' won't do in the same way, even though we may still perhaps find reason to say 'It doesn't read very plausibly: we shall never *really* know the *truth*' and so on. Naturally, we are judicious: we don't say we know (at second hand) if there is any special reason to doubt the testimony: but there has to be *some* reason. It is fundamental in talking (as in other matters) that we are entitled to trust others, except insofar as there is some concrete reason to distrust them. Believing persons, accepting testimony, is the, or one main, point of talking. We don't play (competitive) games except in the faith that our opponent is trying to win: if he isn't, it isn't a game, but something different. So we don't talk with people (descriptively) except in the faith that they are trying to convey information. (1979: 81–3)

There are several things to note here. First, Austin holds that one of the most common reasons for knowing ordinarily given in response to the question 'How do you know?' involves the citing of an authority. Second, the topic of the statements of authorities, the topic of testimony, here includes such mundane cases as newspaper reports concerning the dates of elections. Importantly, it also includes such things as what people say about their own psychological states, here, what Caesar may have said about his own feelings at the battle of Philippi. Austin is thus working with a very broad conception of testimony, one that encompasses much more than the formal or ritualized instances of what we would term testimony in a court of law or governmental hearing. The topic of testimony is here the topic of ordinary everyday *tellings*. Knowledge based on testimony (or ordinary tellings), encompasses for Austin all those cases of knowledge that are justified by citing an authority.[5] Third, Austin claims that knowing based on testimony is knowing by *believing or trusting others*. And fourth, Austin claims that we often distinguish this particular way of knowing from the process of inferring a conclusion from evidence. The testimony offered in the form of a confession doesn't typically amount to just some more evidence from which we must infer whether the person did what she said (though we can certainly decide to treat it as such).

Of course, this is all very sketchy, but it points to the issues that Austin is ultimately driving towards in 'Other Minds'. Austin goes on to reject a certain conception of the epistemology of testimony according to which testimonial knowledge is just a species of knowledge based on inference from evidence. This mistaken conception of the epistemology of testimony arises from a failure to appreciate the fundamental role that believing or trusting others plays in our cognitive lives. As Austin sees it, this is a failure that is particularly characteristic of the problem of other minds. He thus traces a significant part of the motivation for the problem of other minds to worries about believing and trusting others, worries that are particularly prescient when it comes to the epistemology of testimony.

3. Saying 'I know' and saying 'I promise'

The heart of Austin's treatment of testimony occurs in the section of 'Other Minds' that comes under the heading 'If I know I can't be wrong'. The parallel that Austin draws in this section between saying 'I know' and saying 'I promise' has garnered a great deal of critical attention, and yet I think one would be hard-pressed to find another stretch of Austin's text that has been more wildly misunderstood. In this

---

[5] The distinction between 'formal' and 'informal' testimony is by now a commonplace in the testimony literature. See, for example, Coady (1992).

section and the next I'll be offering what might appear to be a radically revisionist reading of this material, though I'll be doing so by simply attempting to remain faithful to the general point of the text.

As we've already seen, Austin uses the dictum 'If I know I can't be wrong' to attempt to spell out the difference between knowing and believing, and one way of doing this involves taking the dictum to point to the way in which saying 'I know', unlike saying 'I believe', involves self-ascribing a factive state. Still, Austin thinks that the dictum points to much more than this. In particular, it points to the variety of ways in which saying 'I know' is analogous to saying 'I promise'.

'When you know you can't be wrong' is perfectly good sense. You are prohibited from saying 'I know it is so, but I may be wrong', just as you are prohibited from saying 'I promise I will, but I may fail'. If you are aware you may be mistaken, you ought not to say you know, just as, if you are aware you may break your word, you have no business to promise. (1979: 98)

Austin is here making a pragmatic point about the speech acts involved in saying 'I know' and 'I promise'. Unlike his earlier reading of 'If I know I can't be wrong' as pointing to the factivity of *the epistemic state* of knowing as opposed to believing, Austin is here pointing to a feature of *the speech acts performed in saying* 'I know' and 'I promise'. The parallel Austin is drawing is a parallel between two particular speech acts, a speech act involved in saying 'I know' and a speech act involved in saying 'I promise'. Clearly, the speech act paradigmatically involved in saying 'I promise' is the speech act of promising, but what, we must ask, is the parallel speech act that Austin takes to be involved in saying 'I know'?

It is tempting to think that, since the speech act paradigmatically involved in saying 'I promise' is the speech act of promising, Austin must take the parallel speech act involved in saying 'I know' to be the speech act of *knowing*. Some readers have thus attributed to Austin the view that saying 'I know' involves performing some kind of act of knowing.[6] There are two problems with this, however. First, the idea that the parallel speech act involved in saying 'I know' is an act of knowing is just obviously mistaken. Knowing is a state and not an act, and hence there are no conventions according to which saying 'I know', in the appropriate circumstances, is to perform an act of knowing. However, second, there is little textual evidence to support the idea that Austin actually holds such a view. Austin never explicitly speaks of an act of knowing that is analogous to the act of promising. Instead, he continually speaks of the parallel between *saying* 'I know' and *saying* 'I promise', leaving to one side the question of what in the end we should label the particular speech act that he takes to be involved in saying 'I know'.[7] There is thus little reason to think that Austin takes the parallel

---

[6] See, for example, Warnock (1989) and Graham (1977). Danto (1962) also comes close to attributing such a view to Austin.

[7] One possible exception is the first footnote on p. 102 of 'Other Minds'. There Austin says, '"Swear", "guarantee", "give my word", "promise", all these and similar words cover cases both of "knowing" and "promising", thus suggesting that the two are analogous.' Even here, however, the odd quotes around the

speech act involved in saying 'I know' to be an act of knowing. We should therefore look for a more charitable reading of Austin's actual position.

I would like to suggest that we take the parallel speech act involved in saying 'I know', the speech act that Austin claims is in many ways analogous to the speech act of promising, to be the speech act of *testifying*, where testifying is construed broadly so as to encompass ordinary everyday tellings (as we saw Austin construe it earlier). Just as it is clearly true that saying 'I promise' is one way (though only one way) of performing the speech act of promising, it is clearly true that saying 'I know' is one way (though only one way) of performing the speech act of testifying (of telling). If this way of construing the parallel between saying 'I know' and saying 'I promise' is correct, then Austin's interest in the parallel is an interest in the way in which the act of testifying, one of the primary ways in which we communicate information to others, is in many ways analogous to the act of promising.

Note that construing Austin's parallel in this way provides a very straightforward answer to the famous and on many accounts decisive objection that Austin himself raises.

We feel, however, an objection to saying that 'I know' performs the same sort of function as 'I promise'. It is this. Supposing that things turn out badly, then we say, on the one hand 'You're proved wrong, so you *didn't* know', but on the other hand 'You've failed to perform, although you *did* promise.' (1979: 101)

But if the speech act involved in saying 'I know' that Austin is concerned with is the speech act of testifying, then just as you did promise even if you failed to perform, you did testify even if you were proven wrong. Austin's own response to the objection isn't nearly so straightforward.

I believe that this contrast is more apparent than real. The sense in which you 'did promise' is that you did *say* you promised (did say 'I promise'): and you did *say* you knew. That is the gravamen of the charge against you when you let us down, after we have taken your word. But it may well transpire that you never fully intended to do it, or that you had concrete reason to suppose that you wouldn't be able to do it (it might even be manifestly impossible), and in another 'sense' of promise you *can't* then have promised to do it, so that you *didn't* promise. (1979: 101)

terms 'knowing' and 'promising' suggest that Austin means to refer to the expressions 'know' and 'promise' rather than to acts of knowing and promising. Elsewhere in the text when Austin refers to the expressions 'know' and 'promise' he always speaks of an analogy between *the use* of the expressions rather than between the expressions themselves. See, for example, p. 101: 'We feel, however, an objection to saying that "I know" performs the same sort of function as "I promise" '; 'Consider the use of other phrases analogous to "I know" and "I promise".' Here Austin is clearly concerned with the function of these expressions within speech, with how they are used to do things, and so the parallel is one between the acts involved in actually saying 'I know' and 'I promise' rather than between the linguistic expressions themselves. Of course, one can perform many different speech acts in uttering the words 'I know' and 'I promise'. As I have put it, Austin is concerned with the speech act paradigmatically performed in saying 'I promise', namely promising, and a particular parallel speech act often performed in saying 'I know'.

Instead of getting clearer about the specific act involved in saying 'I know', he tries to preserve the parallel by claiming that there is a sense in which, if I say 'I know' or 'I promise' and turn out to be mistaken or not to follow through, then I did know or promise (in the sense that I did *say* 'I know' or 'I promise') and another sense in which, if I say 'I know' or 'I promise' even though I don't believe it or don't intend to follow through, then I didn't really know or promise. Both of these suggestions seem wrong. While it's true that the gravamen of the charge against the person who said 'I know' and was mistaken is not that she knew but that she *said* she knew, the gravamen of the charge against the person who said 'I promise' and failed to perform is not simply that she said she promised but that *she promised*. And while it's true that saying 'I know' without believing is not to know, there is no 'sense' of promising in which saying 'I promise', in the appropriate circumstances, without intending to follow through isn't really to promise. Austin himself takes this back in *How to Do Things with Words* where he develops more sophisticated terms in which to say that a promise can fully 'come off' even if the speaker doesn't intend to follow through. This is a case of what Austin calls an 'abuse' rather than a 'misfire' (1975: 16). I take the fumbling here to be an indication that at the time of writing 'Other Minds' Austin just isn't very clear about the exact terms in which to state the parallel that he is interested in. He is confident that the parallel he has in mind holds up in the face of this challenge—he states flatly, 'I believe that this contrast is more apparent than real'—but he doesn't know exactly how to express the point. I think putting things in terms of a parallel between testifying and promising captures what Austin is trying to say much more perspicuously. Moreover, it renders the parallel completely consistent with Austin's later distinction between abuses and misfires. Just as a promise can 'come off' even though the speaker doesn't intend to follow through, testimony can 'come off' even though the speaker doesn't believe what she testifies. This is just to say that both promises and testimony can be insincere.

One might still wonder, however, whether the act of saying 'I know' can be so neatly identified with the act of testifying construed in this broad sense. Austin is acutely sensitive to the nuances of ordinary language and so would surely hesitate to identify the speech act of saying 'I know' with the act of testifying. In the final class of illocutionary forces Austin offers at the end of *How to Do Things with Words*, the class of expositives, he lists separately the forces of informing, apprising, telling, testifying, reporting, and swearing, even placing the first and second three forces into different groupings (the first three appear in group 3 and the second three appear in group 4).[8] Clearly, this means that Austin thinks there are differences between these various illocutionary forces. But while there certainly *are* differences in the ways in which

---

[8] Notoriously, Austin also includes in group 4 the forces of doubting, knowing, and believing, each preceded by a question mark. This can provide further encouragement for confusing the state of knowing with an illocutionary force or act and can further obscure the way in which Austin's concern with what is involved in saying 'I know' is really a concern with the epistemology of testimony.

we ordinarily use these words (for example, 'testify', 'report', and 'swear' are typically more formal and ceremonial in function than 'inform', 'apprise', and especially 'tell'), Austin gives no principled criterion in terms of which to distinguish them. In fact, Austin is quite vague concerning the issue of individuating speech acts and often simply relies on the existence of different grammatical locutions.[9] As we'll see, this actually introduces a good deal of confusion into his discussion of the analogy between saying 'I know' and saying 'I promise'. As I hope to show, the various parallels that Austin wishes to draw between saying 'I know' and saying 'I promise' can be maintained only by taking the act of saying 'I know' to be one way of performing the speech act of testifying and by construing the speech act of testifying as epistemologists typically construe it, as the general act of giving information from one person to another that is apt to be classed alongside perception, memory, and inference as one of the typical ways in which we acquire knowledge about the world around us.

As we saw in section 2, in the course of 'Other Minds' Austin does use the term 'testimony' in something like this fashion. So why doesn't he use it here? Why doesn't he just say that the relevant analogy he wishes to draw is between the speech act of promising and the speech act of testifying (or telling)? In effect, what Austin does is focus on highly ritualized cases of testimony. Ordinary tellings often serve to communicate information to others through the use of indicative utterances without any explicit force-indicating grammatical markers. I can communicate to an audience the fact that p by very unceremoniously saying that p. Here there is little to grammatically mark out the utterance as an obvious instance of what Austin calls a 'ritual' case, and so it might seem that such a case could have little in common with the much more obviously performative act of saying 'I promise'. Cases of testimony in which we actually come out and say 'I know', on the other hand, can appear more ritualized and thus more likely to involve a performative dimension.

Still, saying 'I know' isn't the only way in which the act of testifying can be explicitly ritualized. Saying 'I hereby testify that p' or 'I must tell you that p' are also ways of highlighting the performative dimension of testifying or telling. Moreover, as Austin later realizes explicitly, there is a performative dimension to all human speech whether it bears an explicitly ritualizing marker or not.[10] In the appropriate circumstances, simply saying 'p' can be one way of performing a speech act with the illocutionary force of testifying, and simply saying 'I'll do A' can be one way of performing the obviously performative act of promising. So while there may be a reason to focus on the more obviously ritualized cases of testimony in order to motivate the analogy between testifying and promising, the analogy should nevertheless obtain between cases of

---

[9] This is no doubt partially the result of Austin's fascination with the explicit performative verb, with the cases in which saying 'I hereby ϕ' is precisely to perform the act of ϕ-ing. Austin is quite clear, however, that not all speech acts are performed by use of an explicit performative verb.

[10] The fact that at the time of writing 'Other Minds' Austin was not as clear as he later became about the way in which the performative/constative distinction breaks down might thus explain some of the confusion here.

telling and promising that do not make use of any obviously ritualizing grammatical markers.

Of course, taking Austin's concern with the speech act involved in saying 'I know' to be a concern with the speech act of testifying broadly construed still leaves open how in fact it is that testimony can serve to transmit knowledge from one person to another; it doesn't yet give any particular answer to the question of how we acquire knowledge and justified belief from the testimony of others. This is just the problem of the epistemology of testimony, but I think that this is precisely the problem that Austin's analogy between saying 'I know' and saying 'I promise' is supposed to go some distance towards solving.

In the above passage, Austin simply notes that there is a normative constraint on saying 'I know' such that I shouldn't say 'I know' if I have some concrete reason to believe that I may be mistaken. Analogously, there is a normative constraint on promising such that I shouldn't say 'I promise' if I have some concrete reason to believe that I may break my word. Of course, I *can* certainly testify or promise even when I know that I am mistaken or that I will break my word. The point is just that there are similar normative constraints present to be violated with regard to both the speech acts of testifying and of promising.

Importantly, Austin's concerns here are very different from those of contemporary epistemologists interested in the normative constraints on assertion. As Austin conceives it, saying 'I know that p' amounts to performing a speech act far more elaborate than the mere act of assertion, and he quickly goes on to contrast saying 'I know that p' with simply asserting 'p' (or 'S is P').[11]

When I say 'S is P', I imply at least that I believe it, and, if I have been strictly brought up, that I am (quite) sure of it: when I say 'I shall do A', I imply at least that I hope to do it, and, if I have been strictly brought up that I (fully) intend to. If I only believe that S is P, I can add 'But of course I may (very well) be wrong:' if I only hope to do A, I can add 'But of course I may (very well) not'. When I only believe or only hope, it is recognized that further evidence or further circumstances are liable to make me change my mind. If I say 'S is P' when I don't even believe it, I am lying: if I say it when I believe it but am not sure of it, I may be misleading but I am not exactly lying. If I say 'I shall do A' when I have not even any hope, not the slightest intention, of doing it, then I am deliberately deceiving: if I say it when I do not fully intend to, I am misleading but I am not deliberately deceiving in the same way.

But now, when I say 'I promise', a new plunge is taken: I have not merely announced my intention, but, by using this formula (performing this ritual), I have bound myself to others, and

---

[11] There is a larger problem with connecting Austin's concerns here with those of philosophers interested in the analysis of assertion, and this has to do with the way in which philosophers often conceive of assertion as the external analogue of judgement. Judgement is not an intrinsically other-directed activity, and conceiving assertion as the external analogue of judgement thus leads philosophers to discuss assertion without much concern for the interpersonal issues that interest Austin. Austin is primarily concerned with how asserting, testifying, promising, declaring beliefs, declaring intentions, etc., serve *to do things with others*. He is interested in the kind of significance that testifying has for others and with how this differs from the kind of significance involved in mere assertion.

staked my reputation, in a new way. Similarly, saying 'I know' is taking a new plunge. But it is *not* saying 'I have performed a specially striking feat of cognition, superior, in the same scale as believing and being sure, even to being quite sure': for there *is* nothing in that scale superior to being quite sure. Just as promising is not something superior, in the same scale as hoping and intending, even to merely fully intending: for there *is* nothing in that scale superior to fully intending. When I say 'I know', I *give others my word*: I *give others my authority for saying* that 'S is P'. (1979: 99)

Austin here contrasts what is involved in saying 'p' or 'I shall do A' with what is involved in saying 'I know that p' or 'I promise to do A'. In saying 'I know' and 'I promise', Austin claims that 'a new plunge' is taken beyond what is involved in saying 'p' or 'I shall do A'. Taking this new plunge involves doing such things as *binding myself to others*, *staking my reputation*, and *giving others my word*, and Austin thinks that these features of what is involved in saying 'I know that p' and 'I promise to do A' make these speech acts different in kind and not merely in degree from the speech acts involved in saying 'p' and 'I shall do A'.

In the above passage, Austin claims that the speech act involved in saying 'I know that p' is to the speech act involved in saying 'p' as the speech act involved in saying 'I promise to do A' is to the speech act involved in saying 'I shall do A'. As we have seen, however, in different contexts I can perform the act of testifying by saying either 'I know that p' or 'p', and in different contexts I can perform the act of promising by saying either 'I promise to do A' or 'I shall do A'. We should thus give up on these particular grammatical locutions and instead take Austin's basic claim to be that the speech act of testifying is to the speech act of something less than testifying (let's call this the speech act of *merely declaring one's belief*) as the speech act of promising is to the speech act of something less than promising (let's call this the speech act of *merely declaring one's intention*). Even here there will surely be intermediate cases between testifying and merely declaring a belief and between promising and merely declaring an intention—it is a common point of contention for us whether and to what extent someone is, for example, promising us to do something or doing something less than this—but focusing on the difference between the clear cases is the only way to understand what is intermediary about the intermediate ones.

4. Testimony and believing a speaker

Austin takes the acts of testifying and promising to involve taking a new plunge beyond the acts of merely declaring a belief or intention, and he takes this new plunge to involve giving my word, binding myself to others, and staking my reputation. The question, then, is how exactly testifying or promising involves giving my word and thereby binding myself to others in a way that merely declaring a belief or intention does not. What exactly is it that I do in testifying or promising that I do not do in merely declaring a belief or intention? Austin attempts to cash this out as follows.

When I have said only that I am sure, and prove to have been mistaken, I am not liable to be rounded on by others in the same way as when I have said 'I know'. I am sure *for my part*, you can take it or leave it: accept it if you think I am an acute and careful person, that's your responsibility. But I don't know 'for my part', and when I say 'I know' I don't mean you can take it or leave it (though of course you *can* take it or leave it). In the same way, when I say I fully intend to, I do so for my part, and, according as you think highly or poorly of my resolution and chances, you will elect to act on it or not to act on it: but if I say I promise, you are *entitled* to act on it, whether or not you choose to do so. If I have said I know or I promise, you insult me in a special way by refusing to accept it. We all *feel* the very great difference between saying even 'I am *absolutely* sure' and saying 'I know': it is like the difference between saying even 'I firmly and irrevocably intend' and 'I promise'. If someone has promised me to do A, then I am entitled to rely on it, and can myself make promises on the strength of it: and so, where someone has said to me 'I know', I am entitled to say *I* know too, at second hand. The right to say 'I know' is transmissible, in the sort of way that other authority is transmissible. Hence, if I say it lightly, I may be *responsible* for getting *you* into trouble. (1979: 100)

It isn't abundantly clear what Austin is saying here, but I would like to offer a general account of the parallel between testifying and promising that I think captures the spirit of what Austin is driving at.

There is a pretty clear intuitive distinction between promising another to do A and merely declaring to another one's intention to do A. When I promise someone to do A, I am doing something different from when I merely declare to her my intention to do A, and this different thing that I am doing when I promise someone to do A involves my assuming a different kind of responsibility with regard to her ability to rely on me to do A. When I promise someone to do A, I am (at least purportedly) trying to make it the case that she can rely on me to do A. I am committing myself to doing A. When I merely declare the intention to do A, on the other hand, I may be trying to make it the case that she knows *that I intend to do A*, but I am not typically trying to make it the case that she can rely on me to do A. And even if I am trying to make it the case that she can rely on me to do A, I seem to be doing so by some kind of indirection—by a detour through my intentions—and thus not in the same way as when I come out and promise her to do A. If this is right, then the relevant difference between promising and merely declaring an intention seems to be a difference with regard to the relationship that I take up towards others in speaking. In promising to do A, I am entering into a different kind of relationship with my audience than when I merely declare the intention to do A, and this different kind of relationship is characterized by my bearing a different kind of responsibility for my audience's ability to rely on me to do A.

There seems to be an analogous difference between testifying that p and merely declaring the belief that p. When I come out and testify to someone that p, I am doing something different from when I merely declare to her my belief that p, and this different thing that I am doing when I testify that p involves my assuming a different kind of responsibility with regard to her epistemic standing with respect to p. When

I testify to someone that p, I am (at least purportedly) trying to make it the case that she knows that p. I am trying to put her epistemically in touch with the fact that p.[12] When I merely declare to her my belief that p, on the other hand, I may be trying to make it the case that she knows *that I believe that* p, but I am not typically trying to make it the case that she knows that p. And even if I am trying to make it the case that she knows that p, I seem to be doing so by some kind of indirection—by a detour through my own beliefs—and thus not in the same way as when I come out and tell her that p. So again, the relevant difference between testifying and merely declaring a belief seems to be a difference with regard to the kind of relationship I take up towards others in speaking. In telling or testifying that p, I am entering into a different kind of relationship with my audience than when I merely declare my belief that p, and this different kind of relationship is characterized by my bearing a different kind of responsibility for my audience's epistemic standing with respect to p.

I think Austin's interest in the parallel between saying 'I know' and saying 'I promise' is an interest in how testifying and promising differ from merely declaring a belief and merely declaring an intention in precisely this respect. According to Austin, just as promising involves entering into a relationship with the audience of one's promise that is different in kind from the relationship one bears to the audience of one's mere declaration of intention, testifying involves entering into a relationship with the audience of one's testimony that is different in kind from the relationship one bears to the audience of one's mere declaration of belief. Austin isn't all that clear about what exactly this difference with respect to the relationship between speaker and audience amounts to, but I think that what he does say is enough to point the way to a sketchy yet nevertheless substantive conception of the epistemology of testimony. In the case of testimony, the difference in the relationship between speaker and audience involved in testifying rather than merely declaring a belief makes it the case that, from an epistemological perspective, an audience's knowing that p based on a speaker's testimony that p is different in kind from its knowing that p based on a speaker's mere declaration of belief that p. *The interpersonal difference* in the kind of relationship I take up towards an audience in testifying that p rather than merely declaring my belief that p makes for *an epistemological difference* in what constitutes the epistemic credentials of the audience's knowledge that p based on my testimony rather than on my mere declaration of belief.

We can begin to spell this out by noting that, when addressed to an audience, the acts of testifying and of merely declaring a belief both call for a particular kind of response from the audience. In general terms, both testifying that p and merely declaring the belief that p call for the audience *to believe the speaker*. Not all assertoric speech acts addressed to an audience call for the audience to believe the speaker. If a

---

[12] One definition of the verb 'tell' is, appropriately, *to make known*, suggesting that in telling another that p I am making it the case that she knows that p, in a sense whether she likes it or not. Consider one common response to unpleasant or disconcerting news: 'Don't tell me that; I don't want to know!'

speaker asserts that *p* as the conclusion of a serious (non-hypothetical) argument, for example, this calls for the audience to believe that *p* but it does not call for the audience to believe the speaker.[13] In arguing that *p,* the speaker intends for the audience to believe that *p* on the basis of the audience's own understanding and assessment of the argument and not on the basis of believing the speaker. The acts of testifying that *p* and declaring the belief that *p*, however, are very different. When a speaker testifies that *p* or declares the belief that *p* to an audience, she intends to communicate information to her audience by way of the audience's believing *her.*[14] Still, only in the case of testifying that *p* does the speaker intend to communicate to the audience the information *that p* by way of its believing her. When a speaker merely declares the belief that *p*, the audience's believing her requires only that the audience believe *that the speaker believes that p.* It is then a further question whether the audience should go on and itself believe that *p*. The audience may go on to believe that *p* on the basis of the speaker's declaration of belief if it thinks that the speaker's belief that *p* is good evidence for the truth of *p*, but here the audience is in the position of coming to its own conclusion about *p*; it is not in the position of believing the speaker that *p*. When an audience believes a speaker's testimony that *p*, however, there is no further question as to whether the audience should itself believe that *p*. In the case of a speaker's testimony that *p*, to believe the speaker is already to believe that *p*, meaning that the audience isn't in the position of coming to its own conclusion about *p* in the same way as when the speaker merely declares the belief that *p*. When an audience believes a speaker's testimony that *p*, the audience *believes the speaker that p*, it *trusts the speaker for the truth.*[15]

This suggests that the epistemic credentials of an audience's knowledge based on a speaker's testimony are different in kind from the epistemic credentials of an audience's knowledge based on a speaker's mere declaration of belief. When an audience comes to know that *p* based on a speaker's mere declaration of belief that *p*, the epistemic credentials of the audience's knowledge are constituted by the audience's coming to its own conclusion about *p*, and as a result, the audience is solely epistemically responsible for the conclusions that it draws. The speaker may be responsible for putting the audience in the position to draw for itself certain conclusions with regard to *p*, but she is not responsible for the epistemic credentials of these conclusions themselves. When an audience comes to know that *p* based on a speaker's testimony that *p*, on the other hand, the epistemic credentials of the audience's knowledge are constituted not by the audience's coming to its own conclusion about *p* but rather by its believing the speaker. The audience must still come to its own conclusion about whether to believe the

---

[13] If the argument isn't serious or genuine, if the speaker asserts that *p* as the conclusion of a hypothetical argument, then the speaker's assertion does not even call for the audience to believe that *p*.

[14] This isn't to deny that a speaker can declare a belief without a communicative intention. A speaker can declare the belief that *p* to herself where she does not intend to communicate anything to anyone. The relevant contrast I will be concerned with is between testimony and cases of mere declaration of belief addressed to an audience with a communicative intention.

[15] See Anscombe (1979).

speaker—whether to take the speaker's word—but when it does decide to believe the speaker, it is not in the position of coming to its own conclusion about the content of the speaker's testimony. As a result, the audience is not solely epistemically responsible for the credentials of its belief that *p*. The speaker is not simply responsible for putting the audience in the position to draw for itself certain conclusions based on what she has said. Rather, the speaker is actually partially responsible for the epistemic credentials of the audience's belief.[16]

The general point of Austin's analogy between testifying and promising is that both testifying and promising are ways in which a speaker gives her word, and a speaker's giving her word involves her entering into a relationship with her audience characterized by the speaker's assuming a particular responsibility towards the audience. There is a sense in which Austin actually understates this point, however. The speech acts of testifying and of promising not only have parallels, they sometimes coincide. There are various uses of the locution 'I promise' that actually do the work of testifying. In speaking to children we often promise them that certain things are the case—'I promise you that there isn't a monster under your bed'—and when the adult practice of giving our word breaks down we often revert to such locutions: 'Did you remember to shut the garage door?' 'Yes.' 'Are you sure?' 'Yes.' 'Really?' 'Look, I promise you that I shut the garage door!' This particular use of 'I promise' certainly expresses exasperation, yet we can see in it an attempt to highlight and insist on features central to the practice of giving and taking testimony, features of interpersonal commitment and responsibility.

5. Symptoms and expressions

It is only after going to such great lengths to elaborate on the parallel between saying 'I know' and saying 'I promise' that Austin finally feels that he is in a position to begin to address the problem of other minds. Austin first notes that we certainly *do* sometimes say that we know of the existence and contents of other minds; we certainly do

---

[16] The epistemologist will likely feel that this position concerning the epistemology of testimony has not been sufficiently established. Even if knowledge based on a speaker's mere declaration of belief that *p* is different from knowledge based on a speaker's testimony that *p*, this does not necessarily mean that the epistemic credentials of testimonial knowledge must be constituted by the kind of interpersonal relations alluded to in the text. Perhaps believing a speaker that *p does* involve the speaker's coming to her own conclusion about *p*, only in a way that is different from knowledge based on a speaker's mere declaration of belief. I haven't here argued against such a view. However, I do think that my construal tracks most straightforwardly what Austin says about this issue. Moreover, I have argued elsewhere that though an audience can treat a speaker's testimony that *p* as evidence from which it can infer the conclusion that *p*, there are good reasons to distinguish such knowledge from knowledge that involves believing the speaker. In particular, it is only when an audience comes to know that *p* by believing the speaker that it is entitled to defer epistemic challenges to its knowledge that *p* back to the original speaker. See McMyler (2007) and (2011). For similar interpersonal conceptions of the epistemology of testimony, see Ross (1986), Moran (2005), and Hinchman (2005).

sometimes say, for example, that we know that another person is angry.[17] Still, we can't always know another's feelings or emotions, especially when it comes to people we have little acquaintance with or little in common with. In order to know what another person is feeling, we generally need to have some experience with the person involved. We also generally need to have some experience with the kind of feeling or emotion in question. We might need to have experienced the feeling or emotion ourselves, and we might need to have experienced the feeling or emotion as manifested by others. One might very well think, then, that our knowledge that some particular person is angry on some particular occasion can only be justified via an inference from the person's behaviour, through independently available considerations concerning our experience with the particular person and with the particular psychological state, to the conclusion that the person is actually experiencing the psychological state.

Austin thinks that such a thought is common to many sceptics and non-sceptics about other minds alike. Taking our cognitive relation to the minds of others to be one that can only consist in an inference from evidence is, as Austin sees it, a fundamental feature of scepticism about other minds. Arguing that the kind of inference thereby available (by analogy or otherwise) is sometimes actually sufficient to yield knowledge, as many non-sceptics attempt to do, is thus only to concede the heart of the sceptic's position. For instance, Austin takes John Wisdom (1952) to make a distinction between the behavioural or physical signs or symptoms of a psychological state and the psychological state itself and to hold that we can only know the psychological state of another on the basis of an inference from the physical symptoms to the conclusion that the person is actually experiencing the psychological state. The person experiencing the psychological state, in contrast, knows it on the basis of the experience of the state itself. Austin thinks that this account of our cognitive relation to the minds of others is mistaken, and he tries to argue that it is mistaken by pointing to the ways in which it is at odds with our ordinary talk about the psychological states of others.

Austin begins by claiming that such a use of the term 'symptom' is confused:

What is important is that we never talk of 'symptoms' or 'signs' except *by way of implied contrast with inspection of the item itself.* No doubt it would often be awkward to have to say exactly where the signs or symptoms end and the item itself begins to appear: but such a division is always implied to exist. And hence the words 'symptom' and 'sign' have no use except in cases where the item, as in the case of disease, is liable to be *hidden,* whether it be in the future, in the past, under the skin, or in some other more or less notorious casket: and when the item is itself before us, we no longer talk of signs and symptoms. When we talk of 'signs of a storm', we mean signs of an impending storm, or of a past storm, or of a storm beyond the horizon: we do *not* mean a storm on top of us. (1979: 105–6)

---

[17] I will follow Austin in limiting my discussion to the cases of feelings and emotions. Nevertheless, I think Austin's conception of our cognitive relation to the psychological states of others can be extended to encompass occurrent thoughts and sensations as well as standing attitudes.

We ordinarily only speak of symptoms or signs of a thing in the absence of the thing itself. To talk about signs or symptoms of another's psychological states is thus already to talk as if the psychological states of another are somehow *hidden* or *suppressed*, and while there certainly are occasions on which we speak of the signs or symptoms of hidden or suppressed psychological states, we typically contrast such cases with cases in which the psychological states *are not* hidden or suppressed.[18]

When the psychological states are no longer suppressed, when they are fully exhibited in another's behaviour, we then talk about *expressions, manifestations,* or *displays* of the psychological states rather than about signs or symptoms.

'Symptoms' or 'signs' of anger tend to mean signs of *rising* or *suppressed* anger. Once the man has exploded, we talk of something different—of an expression or manifestation or display of anger, of an exhibition of temper, and so forth. A twitch of the eyebrow, pallor, a tremor in the voice, all these may be symptoms of anger: but a violent tirade or a blow in the face are not, they are the acts in which the anger is vented. 'Symptoms' of anger are not, at least normally, contrasted with the man's own inner personal feeling of anger, but with the actual display of anger. (1979: 107)

Austin thinks that expressions of psychological states are related in a peculiar way to the psychological states themselves. Rather than being opposed to the actual presence of the state in the manner of signs or symptoms, expressions of psychological states are the natural routes through which, on their natural occasions, the psychological states themselves are exhibited.

It seems fair to say that 'being angry' is in many respects like 'having mumps'. It is a description of a whole pattern of events, including occasion, symptoms, feeling and manifestation, and possibly other factors besides. It is as silly to ask 'What, really, *is* the anger *itself*? as to attempt to fine down 'the disease' to some one chosen item ('the functional disorder'). That the man himself feels something that we don't (in the sense that he feels angry and we don't) is, in the absence of Mr. Wisdom's variety of telepathy, evident enough, and incidentally nothing to complain about as a 'predicament': but there is no call to say that 'that' ('the feeling') *is* the *anger*. The pattern of events whatever its precise form, is, fairly clearly, peculiar to the case of 'feelings' (emotions)—it is not by any means exactly like the case of diseases: and it seems to be this peculiarity which makes us prone to say that, unless we have had experience of a feeling ourselves, we cannot know when someone else is experiencing it. Moreover, it is our confidence in the general pattern that makes us apt to say we 'know' another man is angry when we have only observed parts of the pattern: for the parts of the pattern are related to each other very much more intimately than, for example, newspapermen scurrying in Brighton are related to a fire in Fleet Street. (1979: 109–10)

---

[18] We also talk about signs or symptoms of psychological states when we are not privy to the entirety of the circumstances in which the psychological state is being expressed. If I happen to see a stranger slam a door, I may take this as a sign of anger from which I can infer that the person is angry. Someone present at the meeting from which the stranger just left in a huff, however, may be able to see the person's behaviour as an overt expression of anger rather than as a mere sign or symptom.

According to Austin, expressions of a psychological state are the outwardly observable aspects of the psychological state of a person. To describe a person as angry is to ascribe to the person a property that consists of a whole pattern of things including the person's possible overt manifestation or expression of the state through certain natural routes in certain natural situations. Moreover, the parts of the pattern that makes up the state are so intimately connected that we can know that a person is in the psychological state simply by observing a part of the pattern. We can thus have direct, non-inferential access to the psychological states of others based simply on observing their overt expressions of those states.

In this respect, Austin's conception of our cognitive relation to other minds is similar to Wittgenstein's.[19] In *Zettel* Wittgenstein writes,

'We *see* emotion.'—As opposed to what?—We do not see facial contortions and make inferences from them (like a doctor framing a diagnosis) to joy, grief, boredom. We describe a face immediately as sad, radiant, bored, even when we are unable to give any other description of the features.—Grief, one would like to say, is personified in the face. (1967, §225)

Wittgenstein suggests that it belongs to the concept of emotion that we can perceive another's emotional states directly in her behaviour. To see someone smile just is to see that she's happy (when she is). This is not to say that we can't be mistaken as to whether someone is happy. Smiles can be feigned just as can all behaviour. In the case of a smile that is not genuine, the smiling behaviour has come apart from the emotion that we typically take it to express. But this is not to say that smiling behaviour and happiness *always* stand apart, that there is always a gulf between the behaviour and the psychological state that must be bridged by an act of interpretation.

We say 'The expression in his voice was *genuine*'. If it was spurious we think as it were of another one behind it.—*This* is the face he shews the world, inwardly he has another one.—But this does not mean that when the expression is *genuine* he has two the same. (1997, §606)

In the case of a genuine smile we don't have a dead piece of behaviour that we now have to interpret so as to get at the emotion behind it. A genuine smile is alive with happiness—the behaviour is an expression of the psychological state—which is to say that the emotion can be directly perceived in the behaviour itself.[20]

Austin doesn't explicitly use this kind of perceptual terminology. Unlike Wittgenstein, he doesn't explicitly say that we can *see* the anger in an angry face, that we can *perceive* the psychological states of others in their expressions of those states. He clearly thinks that we can have non-inferential access to the contents of other minds based on observing overt expressions or displays of psychological states, but beyond the use of the notion of

---

[19] For a detailed account of Wittgenstein's conception of expression and its relation to self-knowledge, see Finkelstein (2003).

[20] As Bar-On (2004) puts it, expressive behaviour is 'transparent-to-the-subject's-mental-condition' which in turn allows the consumers of expressive behaviour to perceive the subject's present mental condition.

observation he doesn't explicitly characterize this access in perceptual terms. In fact, Austin quickly goes on to try to distinguish the way in which we know the psychological states of others from the way in which we know ordinary material objects. For Austin, the kind of non-inferential cognitive relation we bear to the contents of other minds is not exhausted by the kind of non-inferential cognitive relation characteristic of ordinary perception.

6. The peculiarity of other minds

The remainder of 'Other Minds' is an attempt to spell out just how our cognitive relation to other minds differs from that characteristic of ordinary perception. Despite the fact that this is clearly the most important part of Austin's treatment of the problem of other minds, what Austin offers in this regard is far sketchier and far more incomplete than anything else in 'Other Minds'. The rest of this paper is an attempt to reconstruct and extend what Austin says in the final five pages of 'Other Minds' in a way that hopefully follows logically from the general trajectory of the paper.

Austin's treatment of the peculiarity of our cognitive relation to other minds consists of two parts. He first discusses several worries that are typically associated with the problem of other minds and which might be taken to distinguish the problem of other minds from the problem of how we know ordinary material objects. While there *is* something important and distinctive about these worries, Austin doesn't do much to make clear what this is. It is only in the second part of Austin's discussion, the part that deals with the issue of 'believing what the man says about his own feelings', that a substantive epistemological distinction between our knowledge of other minds and our knowledge of ordinary material objects emerges. The issue of the epistemology of testimony, in particular, the issue of our knowledge of the psychological states of others based on their testimony about their own psychological states, is thus, for Austin, at the heart of the problem of other minds.

The first part of Austin's discussion focuses on several special ways in which we can be mistaken about the contents of other minds. While there are a whole variety of ways in which we can be mistaken about material objects, when it comes to other minds we are liable to special kinds of mistakes that lead to special kinds of worries. Austin lists three such worries, all of which he thinks commonly arise within our ordinary dealings with others.

We may worry (1) as to whether someone is *deceiving* us, by suppressing his emotions, or by feigning emotions which he does not feel: we may worry (2) as to whether we are *misunderstanding* someone (or he us), in wrongly supposing that he does 'feel like us', that he does share emotions like ours: or we may worry (3) as to whether some action of another person is really deliberate, or perhaps only involuntary or inadvertent in some manner or other. (1979: 112)

Austin thinks none of these kinds of worry are relevant to ordinary material objects.

The goldfinch cannot be assumed, nor the bread suppressed: we may be deceived by the appearance of an oasis, or misinterpret the signs of weather, but the oasis cannot lie to us and we cannot misunderstand the storm in the way we misunderstand the man. (1979: 112)

So what exactly is it that distinguishes these worries from the kinds of worry that can arise with regard to ordinary material objects?

The three worries that Austin lists are all worries concerning the way in which many (though by no means all) expressions of psychological states are *intentional* in nature. By 'intentional' I mean here that many expressions of psychological states are phenomena performed with certain intentions, or for certain reasons, or in the pursuit of certain goals or ends. Many expressions of psychological states are *actions*—they are *things we do* rather than things that simply happen to us—and they are thus subject to our wills. Now, a person's expressions of her psychological states certainly are not *always* subject to her will. People often unintentionally express their psychological states in their behaviour, and here we sometimes speak of the person's expression of an emotion as being the result of the emotion overcoming or getting the better of her. There may also be more 'primitive' expressions of psychological states that aren't so easily treated as actions, for example, a person crying out in pain after being pricked with a pin. The point is just that there are a great many expressions of psychological states that are actions in that they are pieces of behaviour that are apt to be described as intentional.[21] This is not to say that we always have a specific intention or purpose 'in mind' when we intentionally express a psychological state. Even in a situation in which we would not describe an expression of a psychological state as unintentional, the person expressing the state need not have any particular purpose for expressing her state beyond, say, venting it. Nevertheless, many expressions of psychological states are far more like overt actions than like mere twitches or reflexes.

We can now return to Austin's three special worries. Given that many expressions of psychological states are intentional, this means that (1) they can be feigned, (2) understanding them requires understanding the intentions with which they are performed, and (3) there is room for mistaking inadvertent or involuntary behaviour for intentional expressions. None of this is true of ordinary material objects. A goldfinch cannot be feigned; understanding an oasis does not require understanding the intentions behind it; and there is no danger of a pot boiling involuntarily. Our cognitive relation to other minds is thus distinguishable from our cognitive relation to ordinary

---

[21] What about expressions of unconscious psychological states? Finkelstein (2003) argues that unconscious psychological states are characterized by the fact that, though they can be expressed in a person's behaviour, they cannot be expressed by avowing them. If what I say in the text is correct, then perhaps unconscious psychological states are characterized more broadly by the fact that they cannot be expressed intentionally. The fact that one cannot avow an unconscious psychological state would then simply be the result of the fact that avowals are intentional expressions.

material objects by the relevance of the particular kinds of worry associated with the way in which many expressions of psychological states are intentional.

But how exactly does the fact that many expressions are like actions, that they are often intentional, make our knowledge of other minds different from our knowledge of ordinary material objects? It might be the case that there are simply additional possibilities that a subject must be responsive to in order to be credited with knowledge that a person is experiencing a certain psychological state. Knowing that someone is angry might be unlike knowing that there is a goldfinch in the garden simply in the sense that I cannot come to know that someone is angry on the basis of observing her expressive behaviour without being rationally responsive to considerations concerning the person's intentions. Austin sometimes suggests such a view. After laying out the above three worries, he writes,

Though the difficulties are special, the ways of dealing with them are, initially, similar to those employed in the case of the goldfinch. There are (more or less roughly) established procedures for dealing with suspected cases of deception or of misunderstanding or of inadvertence. (1979: 112)

Nevertheless, I think that Austin's considered view is that knowing someone is angry is not simply distinguishable from knowing that there is a goldfinch in the garden by the fact that there are additional special possibilities that must be taken into account. Rather, our non-inferential knowledge of the psychological states of others is often *different in kind* from our non-inferential knowledge of ordinary material objects based on perception, and this is intimately connected to the way in which many expressions of psychological states are intentional. This only becomes clearer, however, when Austin turns to the second part of his discussion of the peculiarity of our knowledge of other minds.

After discussing the above three worries, Austin claims that there is a further feature of other minds that radically distinguishes how we know other minds from how we know ordinary material objects.

The goldfinch, the material object, is, as we insisted above, uninscribed and *mute*: but the man *speaks*. In the complex of occurrences which induces us to say we know another man is angry, the complex of symptoms, occasion, display, and the rest, a peculiar place is occupied by the man's own statement as to what his feelings are. In the usual case we accept this statement without question, and we then say that we know (as it were 'at second-hand') what his feelings are: though of course 'at second-hand' here could not be used to imply that anyone but he could know 'at first-hand', and hence perhaps it is not in fact used. In unusual cases, where his statement conflicts with the description we should otherwise have been inclined to give of the case, we do not feel bound to accept it, though we always feel some uneasiness in rejecting it. (1979: 113–14)

Austin is not claiming, like Descartes, that other minds are to be distinguished from ordinary material objects due to their capacity to employ language. Rather, he is claiming that our knowledge of other minds is peculiarly dependent on what the other tells us about her own psychological states and that this (often) makes our cognitive relation to other minds significantly different from our cognitive relation to ordinary material objects. Austin's concern with a person's own statements about her psychological states is a concern with what nowadays are typically termed *avowals*, psychological state self-ascriptions that exhibit first-person authority. Like Wittgenstein, Austin seems to hold that avowals are to be classed among the natural expressions of a person's psychological states. Austin never explicitly says this, but he does say that a person's own statement about her psychological state 'is not (is not treated primarily as) a sign or symptom, although it can secondarily and artificially be treated as such' (1979: 114). At the very least, Austin holds that avowals are *like* natural expressions of a psychological state in that they are not something from which an audience is in the position of having to make an inference to the conclusion that the speaker is experiencing the psychological state she avows. Unlike Wittgenstein, however, Austin is particularly impressed by the fact that some avowals amount to tellings, to testimony.[22] Among the intentions with which a particular psychological state can be expressed are the kinds of *communicative intentions* paradigmatically involved when a speaker tells an audience that *p*. In this sense, when a person comes out and tells me that she is afraid, not only does her assertion amount to an expression of her fear, it also amounts to testimony. Certainly not all avowals amount to testimony. If a person avows her fear in private simply as a way of venting it, then her expression is not addressed to anyone and does not amount to an instance of testimony. Nevertheless, many avowals are so addressed and do amount to genuine tellings. Let's call such avowals *testimonial avowals*.

An audience's cognitive relation to the psychological states expressed in testimonial avowals appears to be different in kind from an audience's cognitive relation to the psychological states expressed in non-testimonial expressions. When a speaker comes out and tells an audience that she is afraid, it is plausible to think that she is doing something more than simply behaving expressively in front of the audience. There must be some reason why she chooses to express her fear in this particular testimonial way, especially given the fact that the audience could easily come to know that she is afraid simply by observing her non-testimonial expressions of fear. We can imagine a case in which it is clear to everyone concerned that the speaker is visibly afraid. She may be shaking, trembling, etc., and yet we can still imagine her choosing, on top of all this, to tell her audience that she is afraid. It thus seems that the point of a speaker's coming out and telling an audience her mind isn't exhausted by making her psychological states observable to the audience. In telling an audience that she is afraid, as in cases of testimony generally, the speaker is calling for the audience to believe her, to believe her that she is afraid. The point of a speaker's telling an audience her mind is that it draws

---

[22] There are points at which Wittgenstein recognizes that avowals can amount to testimony. See, for example, Wittgenstein (1997: §174).

into play the interpersonal relations of epistemic authority and responsibility involved in the practice of giving and taking testimony.

If this is right, then there are actually three different cognitive relations that we can bear to the psychological states of others.

(1) We can infer the psychological states of others based on (what we treat as) signs or symptoms of those states.[23]

(2) When the psychological states of others are fully exhibited in their behaviour, we can observe their states in their overt expressions of those states.

(3) When the person comes out and tells us her psychological state, we can believe her, accept her testimony.

We commonly adopt all three of these cognitive relations at different points in our ordinary commerce with others; all three are elements of our ordinary epistemic practice with respect to other minds. Nevertheless, Austin is particularly interested in (3). (3) is distinguished from (1) and (2) due to the fact that the nature of the cognitive relation involved in (3) is essentially interpersonal. While the cognitive relations characteristic of (1) and (2) are both genuine ways in which we sometimes come to know the minds of others, the cognitive relation characteristic of (3) is one that puts us essentially in commune with others. (3) draws into play interpersonal relations of authority and responsibility that are absent in the case of (1) and (2), and thus it essentially depends on a particular kind of minded interaction between persons. We might say that (3) involves taking up a *second-personal* cognitive relation to others, one predicated on the other's being in the authoritative position to address claims to us, while (1) and (2) involve taking up a *third-personal* cognitive relation to others.[24] I think it is the second-personal nature of (3) that Austin finds so significant. Austin thinks that there is an important sense in which the problem of other minds is a problem of the second rather than the third-person.

7. Believing a person and the problem of other minds

What impresses Austin about the case of a person's testimony about her own psycho-logical states is that this is a case in which knowing the person's psychological state involves believing her. As I noted at the beginning of this paper, Austin begins the conclusion of 'Other Minds' by saying that he thinks this issue of 'believing what the man says about his own feelings' is 'fundamental to the whole Predicament'

---

[23] Austin sometimes talks as if we can only bear this cognitive relation to signs or symptoms of hidden or suppressed psychological states, but I think his more considered view is that we can often adopt this kind of attitude towards the psychological states of others, though this may be to treat expressions as we would normally treat mere signs or symptoms.

[24] For a recent articulation of the difference between second-personal and third-personal relations to others, though one largely confined to practical relations, see Darwall (2006).

(1979: 114). So how does this issue of believing a person connect to the problem of other minds more generally?

Since believing a person involves entering into a relationship with the person in which we put ourselves in her hands and give up partial responsibility for our knowledge, this clearly makes us dependent on the will of the other in a way that necessarily courts certain kinds of particularly bruising dangers not typically associated with our knowledge of ordinary material objects. Not only does it introduce additional ways in which what we take ourselves to learn may be mistaken, but it also makes room for that particular kind of deliberate abuse that we can only suffer at the hands of another person. Other minds are in a position to call for us to believe them, to draw into play the interpersonal relations of authority and responsibility in virtue of which testimonial knowledge is justified, and then to abuse these relations by failing to live up to them. This kind of second-personal abuse is very different from our making a mistake about the behaviour or characteristics of an ordinary material object, and it is a kind of abuse that has a peculiar kind of significance for us. Other minds are particularly worrying not only because knowing the minds of others often requires understanding their intentions but also because the intentional nature of the actions and expressions of others puts them in a position to be second-personally abusive.

This might very well lead one to question whether believing others can amount to a genuine way of knowing. How can subjecting oneself to the will of another and thereby giving over to the other partial responsibility for one's own belief ever amount to a way of knowing about the world around us? As Austin puts it, the question here is 'Why believe someone?' (1979: 114). What justification is there for taking up the particular cognitive relation to the minds of others characteristic of our ordinary practice of believing others? He writes,

There are answers that we can give to this question, which is here to be taken in the general sense of 'Why believe him ever?' not simply as 'Why believe him this time?' We may say that the man's statements on matters other than his own feelings have constantly been before us in the past, and have been regularly verified by our observations of the facts he reported: so that we have in fact some basis for an induction about his general reliability. Or we may say that his behaviour is most simply 'explained' on the view that he does feel emotions like ours, just as psycho-analysts 'explain' erratic behaviour by analogy with normal behaviour when they use the terminology of 'unconscious desires'.

These answers are, however, dangerous and unhelpful. They are so obvious that they please nobody: while on the other hand they encourage the questioner to push his question to 'profounder' depths, encouraging us, in turn, to exaggerate these answers until they become distortions.

The question, pushed further, becomes a challenge to the very possibility of 'believing another man', in its ordinarily accepted sense, at all. What 'justification' is there for supposing that there is another mind communicating with you at all? How can you know what it would be like for another man to feel anything, and so how can you understand it? It is then that we are tempted to say that we only mean by 'believing him' that we take certain vocal noises as signs for certain impending behaviour, and that 'other minds' are no more really real than unconscious desires. (1979: 114–15)

Austin here considers two possible reasons for believing a person in general, first, that we have good inductive evidence of her general reliability, and second, that her behaviour is best explained by supposing that the person is experiencing the state she avows. Austin claims that these answers are, in a sense, obvious but at the same time dangerous and unhelpful. They are obvious in that we *can* appeal to such things as reasons for believing people. If we are asked why we believe a particular person's avowals, we might state that we know the person to be generally reliable or that it simply wouldn't make sense for her to be dissembling. However, these answers can be dangerous as well. If we are worried about the particular dangers associated with believing others generally, then these answers would alleviate this worry only if they were appealed to as inferential reasons for believing that a person is in the particular state that she avows. This, however, actually eliminates the phenomenon we were seeking to justify.

It will pay to go slowly here. If a person tells me that she is afraid, then I may very well appeal to considerations concerning such things as her general reliability in deciding whether to believe her. Believing a person is a cognitive attitude we adopt on the basis of reasons. However, this kind of rational appeal to considerations of reliability will not yet alleviate any worries about the peculiar dangers associated with believing others generally. These worries are associated with the cognitive attitude itself, with the way in which the cognitive attitude of believing a person involves putting ourselves in her hands and giving up partial responsibility for what we believe. Basing the cognitive attitude on reasons concerning reliability is not yet to eliminate these features of the attitude. This, I think, is why Austin states that the question is 'Why believe him ever?' not simply 'Why believe him this time?' If general considerations about reliability are appealed to as considerations on the basis of which we decide to believe a person on a particular occasion, then they will not alleviate the worries about believing others generally that were the original motivation for the question. In this sense, these answers must be pushed further. These considerations about reliability, or about what best explains a person's action, must be appealed to as considerations on the basis of which we decide whether to believe others generally.

For Austin, to take considerations of a person's reliability to be considerations on the basis of which we decide whether to believe others generally is, I think, to take such considerations to be an inferential basis upon which we believe what the person says on any occasion on which we do believe what the person says. If the person tells me that she is afraid, on any particular occasion, then my believing that she is afraid is justified by an inferential appeal to general considerations about her reliability. This is to construe belief based on testimonial avowals as belief justified by the strength of an inference from considerations about the person's reliability, or from what best explains the person's action, to the conclusion that what the person avows is true.

This amounts to an application of one of the dominant contemporary views about the epistemology of testimony to the particular case of testimonial avowals. Reductionism about testimony is the view that the epistemic credentials of knowledge and belief based on testimony can be reduced to the epistemic credentials of other sources of knowledge and belief, typically to those of perception, memory, and inference.[25] Reductionists about testimony are also committed to the more specific claim that the justification of testimonial knowledge consists in the strength of an inference from the speaker's saying that p, through independently available considerations of such things as the speaker's reliability, competence, and sincerity, to the conclusion that p. Details aside, the upshot of such an account is that testimonial knowledge is simply a species of inferential knowledge. Austin can be read as here envisioning a kind of reductionism about testimony applied to the specific case of testimonial avowals. On such an account, an audience's knowledge that a speaker is experiencing the particular psychological state she avows is simply a species of knowledge based on either inductive or abductive inference.

Pushed to this point, the two answers that Austin considers *do* begin to answer to the worries about believing others that motivated the initial question. If our knowledge of the psychological states of another based on her testimonial avowals is simply a species of knowledge based on inference, then such knowledge doesn't necessarily incur any particularly noteworthy kinds of risk. Of course, any knowledge based on broadly inductive inference is liable to be mistaken, and due to the frequency of experienced instances of incompetence and insincerity, it may be the case that what others say is a particularly flimsy inferential basis upon which to draw conclusions. But none of this supports the idea that there is anything particularly problematic about our knowledge of other minds as such. If our knowledge of other minds based on their testimonial avowals is simply a species of non-deductive inferential knowledge, then it should be just as problematic (or unproblematic) as non-deductive inferential knowledge generally.

In meeting our initial worry about the dangers associated with believing others, however, reductionism about testimonial avowals actually eliminates the phenomenon it was seeking to justify. Austin claims that construing the epistemic credentials of an audience's knowledge based on testimonial avowals in terms of the strength of an inference is a distortion of our ordinary epistemic practice. This particular distortion is, as he puts it, a challenge to the very possibility of 'believing another man' in its ordinarily accepted sense.[26] Reductionism about testimonial avowals distorts our

---

[25] Reductionists about testimony include Fricker (1987, 1994, and 1995), and Lyons (1997). Anti-reductionists about testimony hold that the epistemic credentials of knowledge and belief based on testimony *cannot* be reduced to the credentials of other sources of knowledge and hence that testimony is a 'basic', 'autonomous', or *sui generis* source of knowledge. Anti-reductionists include Coady (1992), Burge (1993), and McDowell (1998).

[26] I am here taking Austin's concern with 'believing what the man says about his own feelings' to be a concern with *believing someone that p*. Given what I have said about believing a person that *p*, the way in which Austin frames this issue in the conclusion of 'Other Minds' is somewhat sloppy. Though he sometimes simply speaks of what is involved in 'believing what the man says', I think that, given what he goes on to say about

ordinary epistemic practice by taking our believing a speaker's avowal to be justified by the strength an inference from the avowal, through independently available considerations concerning such things as our past experience with her general reliability, to the conclusion that the speaker is actually in the state she avows. But if the justification of the audience's knowledge of the speaker's psychological state is constituted by the strength of an inference, then the audience must be in the position of coming to its own conclusion about what the speaker avows. Inferring that p from a body of inductive evidence involves a subject's coming to her own conclusion about p, and hence the subject is completely epistemically responsible for the credentials of the conclusions that she draws from within her own epistemic position.[27] In this sense, reductionism about testimonial avowals eliminates the interpersonal relations of authority and responsibility that Austin has claimed characterize our ordinary practice of believing others. Reductionism about testimonial avowals renders our knowledge of other minds less worrisome only at the price of eliminating our ordinary practice of believing others.

Austin is quite clear that we often do not treat the testimonial avowals of others as signs or symptoms from which we can only draw inferences. Crucially, however, merely treating testimonial avowals as genuine expressions of a person's psychological states that allow an audience to directly observe the states expressed in the avowal is not any help here. If testimonial avowals allow us to simply observe the psychological states of others, then our knowledge of other minds based on such observation should be just as problematic (or unproblematic) as any other knowledge based on observation. It may be the case that the observation of the psychological states of others is often more difficult than the observation of the behaviour and characteristics of ordinary material objects, particularly due to the way in which many expressions of psychological states are intentional, but it shouldn't be the case that there are any worries about our knowledge of other minds that are different in kind from those associated with observational knowledge generally. Again, just as perceiving that there is a goldfinch in the garden involves coming to one's own conclusion about the presence of the bird,

---

this, his real concern is best understood as a concern with believing a person that p. Austin often does speak in this way. He says the question is 'Why believe him?', in the sense of 'Why believe him ever?', where this can lead us to question the very possibility of 'believing another man' in its ordinarily accepted sense. He goes on to say, 'It seems, rather, that believing in other persons, in authority and testimony, is an essential part of the act of communicating, an act which we all perform.' This is also unfortunate. Speaking of 'believing in other persons' can lead one to think that Austin is making a claim about believing *in the existence* of other persons. Austin is sometimes read in this way. But again, I think his real concern is with believing a person that p. Note that he also speaks of believing 'in authority and testimony'. It seems quite implausible that this could be a claim about believing *in the existence* of authority and testimony. It is much more plausible to think that his concern with 'believing in other persons, in authority and testimony' is a concern with believing others, believing authorities, and believing their testimony.

[27] A speaker may very well be responsible for putting an audience in a position to draw for itself certain conclusions, but I don't take this to be a genuinely epistemic responsibility. The speaker may be held to account for this morally or socially, but she cannot be held epistemically responsible for the credentials of the conclusions that the audience draws for itself.

observing the psychological states of others in their expressions of those states involves coming to one's own conclusion about the nature of their states. In this sense, I think that Austin would take such a construal of our knowledge of other minds to be just as eliminative of our ordinary practice of believing others as the reductionist account discussed above. If we are always only in the position of simply observing the psychological states expressed in another's avowals, then this too leaves no room for the interpersonal relations of authority and responsibility characteristic of our ordinary practice of believing others.

By now one might be thinking that this is just so much the worse for our ordinary practice of believing others. If construing our knowledge of other minds as either inferential or perceptual avoids the peculiar worries we have about the ordinary practice of believing others, then perhaps this is good reason to think that this practice, or at least our essentially interpersonal account of it, is mistaken. Perhaps we should simply rest content with the possibility of inferential and/or observational knowledge of other minds. Austin seems to think that resting content here is not a viable option. To do so would leave us in a position where, granted, we are perfectly able to acquire knowledge of the psychological states of others but where, nevertheless, we are not cognitively in commune with them. It would leave us in a position where we are able to cognitively relate to others third-personally but not second-personally. In this sense, we would still be left with something that Austin thinks deserves to be called a problem of other minds.

Austin is unwilling to rest content with the possibility of inferential and/or observational knowledge of other minds. This doesn't mean that he offers another way to avoid the kinds of worries about believing others that can drive one to those accounts. Rather, he seems to think that we must simply learn to get over these worries, to give up looking for a justification for believing people in general. Since believing a person involves entering into a relationship with the person in which we put ourselves in her hands and give up partial responsibility for our knowledge, this makes us dependent on the will of the other in a way that necessarily courts certain kinds of particularly bruising dangers not typically associated with our knowledge of ordinary material objects. We can try to eliminate these risks from our cognitive lives by construing our cognitive relation to the psychological states of others in such a way as to make ourselves completely responsible for the epistemic credentials of any knowledge gained thereby. In this sense, we might construe our cognitive relation to other minds as inferential or simply perceptual. However, this would be to distort our ordinary epistemic practice. Our knowledge of the psychological states of others is often based on believing the person, and it is often important to us that this is so. The kind of second-personal cognitive relation to other minds involved in believing a person is in this sense non-optional. We couldn't simply give this up and still be the kind of minded creatures that we are. Knowledge based on believing others is a fundamental and irreducible feature of our lives as social beings.

8. Conclusion

Austin's 'Other Minds' was originally delivered to a symposium of the same title at a joint session of The Aristotelian Society and The Mind Association. John Wisdom's contribution to the symposium concludes with a long quotation from Virginia Woolf describing the loneliness characteristic of a life lived through letters, telephones, and conversations.

Let us consider letters—how they come at breakfast, and at night, with their yellow stamps and their green stamps, immortalized by the postmark—for to see one's own letter on another's table is to realize how soon deeds sever and become alien. Then at last the power of the mind to quit the body is manifest, and perhaps we fear or hate or wish annihilated this phantom of ourselves, lying on the table. Still, there are letters that merely say how dinner's at seven; others ordering coal; making appointments. The hand in them is scarcely perceptible, let alone the voice or the scowl. Ah, but when the post knocks and the letter comes always the miracle seems repeated—speech attempted. Venerable are letters, infinitely brave, forlorn, and lost.

Life would split asunder without them. 'Come to tea, come to dinner, what's the truth of the story? have you heard the news? life in the capital is gay; the Russian dancers . . . .' These are our stays and props. These lace our days together and make of life a perfect globe. And yet, and yet . . . when we go to dinner, when pressing finger-tips we hope to meet somewhere soon, a doubt insinuates itself; is this the way to spend our days? the rare, the limited, so soon dealt out to us—drinking tea? dining out? And the notes accumulate. And the telephones ring. And everywhere we go wires and tubes surround us to carry the voices that try to penetrate before the last card is dealt and the days are over. 'Try to penetrate,' for as we lift the cup, shake the hand, express the hope, something whispers, Is this all? Can I never know, share, be certain? Am I doomed all my days to write letters, send voices, which fall upon the tea-table, fade upon the passage, make appointments, while life dwindles, to come and dine? Yet letters are venerable; and the telephone valiant, for the journey is a lonely one, and if bound together by notes and telephones we went in company, perhaps—who knows?—we might talk by the way. (1922: 92–3)[28]

Wisdom ends his paper by asking,

This isolation which we may defeat but cannot vanquish, does it find voice in the old puzzle as to whether we really know what is in the minds of others? Does the contradiction in the philosopher's request for perfect knowledge of others reflect a conflict in the human heart which dreads and yet demands the otherness of others? (1952: 229)

I think Austin's answer to these questions is clearly 'Yes', and as un-Austinian as it may sound, these questions about loneliness and isolation are precisely what drives Austin's discussion in 'Other Minds'. Austin thinks that the way in which we know the minds of others is often a way of knowing that is necessarily dependent on the otherness of the other. Insofar as knowing the psychological states of others often involves believing the person, such knowledge is necessarily dependent on the will of the other. And yet

---

[28] I have here cited a bit more of the passage than does Wisdom (1952).

the philosophical problem of other minds can be motivated by an unwillingness to countenance such dependence on others as a genuine way of knowing. About the three worries that arise from the way in which many expressions of psychological states are intentional, Austin states, 'Any or all of them may be at the bottom of the passage from Mrs. Woolf: all work together in the feeling of loneliness which affects everybody at times' (1979: 112). As I have tried to show here, Austin's ultimate concern is with how the problem of other minds is a kind of expression of such loneliness. The problem of other minds is to a significant extent motivated by ordinary human worries about believing others, worries concerning the ways in which the interpersonal relations involved in believing others can break down and concerning the peculiar kind of significance that such breakdown has for us.[29]

Bibliography

Austin, J. L. (1962), *Sense and Sensibilia*, Oxford: Oxford University Press.

——(1975), *How to Do Things with Words*, Oxford: Oxford University Press.

——(1979), *Philosophical Papers*, 3rd ed., Urmson, J. O., Warnock, G. J. (eds.), Oxford: Oxford University Press.

Anscombe, G. E. M. (1979), 'What Is It to Believe Someone?', in C. F. Delaney (ed.), *Rationality and Religious Belief*, Notre Dame: Notre Dame University Press, pp. 141–51.

Ayer, A. J. (1946), 'Other Minds', *Aristotelian Society Supplement* 20: 188–97.

Bar-On, D. (2004), *Speaking My Mind*, Oxford: Clarendon Press.

Burge, T. (1993), 'Content Preservation', *The Philosophical Review* 102: 457–88.

Coady, C. A. J. (1992), *Testimony*, Oxford: Clarendon Press.

Danto, A. (1962), 'Seven Objections against Austin's Analysis of "I Know"', *Philosophical Studies* 13: 84–91.

Darwall, S. (2006), *The Second-Person Standpoint*, Cambridge, MA: Harvard University Press.

Finkelstein, D. (2003), *Expression and the Inner*, Cambridge, MA: Harvard University Press.

Fricker, E. (1987), 'The Epistemology of Testimony', *Aristotelian Society Supplement* 61, 57–83.

——(1994), 'Against Gullibility', in Matilal, B. K., Chakrabarti, A. (eds.), *Knowing From Words*, Dordrecht: Kluwer Publishing, pp. 125–61.

——(1995), 'Telling and Trusting: Reductionism and Anti-Reductionism in the Epistemology of Testimony', *Mind* 104: 393–411.

Graham, K. (1977), *J. L. Austin: A Critique of Ordinary Language Philosophy*, Atlantic Highlands, NJ: Humanities Press.

Hinchman, E. (2005), 'Telling as Inviting to Trust', *Philosophy and Phenomenological Research* 70: 562–87.

Lyons, J. (1997), 'Testimony, Induction, and Folk Psychology', *Australasian Journal of Philosophy* 75: 163–77.

[29] I would like to thank Jim Conant, Jay Elliott, David Finkelstein, Erica Holberg, participants of the University of Chicago Philosophy of Mind Workshop, the editors of this volume, and two anonymous referees for Oxford University Press for helpful comments and stimulating discussion of this material.

McDowell, J. (1998), 'Knowledge by Hearsay', in *Meaning, Knowledge, and Reality*, Cambridge, MA: Harvard University Press, pp. 414–43.

McMyler, B. (2007), 'Knowing at Second Hand', *Inquiry* 50: 511–40.

——(2011), *Testimony, Trust, and Authority*, Oxford: Oxford University Press.

Moran, R. (2005), 'Getting Told, Being Believed', *Philosopher's Imprint* 5: 1–29.

Ross, A. (1986), 'Why Do We Believe What We Are Told?'. *Ratio* 27: 69–88.

Warnock, G. J. (1989), *J. L. Austin*, London: Routledge.

Welbourne, M. (1993), *The Community of Knowledge*, Hampshire: Gregg Revivals.

Wisdom, J. (1952), 'Symposium: Other Minds', in *Other Minds*, Oxford: Basil Blackwell, pp. 192–217.

Wittgenstein, L. (1967), *Zettel*, Berkeley: University of California Press.

——(1997), *Philosophical Investigations*, Oxford: Blackwell.

Woolf, V. (1922), *Jacob's Room*, New York: Harcourt Press.

6

Knowing Knowing (that Such and Such)

Avner Baz

It is widely assumed nowadays that J. L. Austin's broaching of the topic of the different things we do with words has no significant bearing on the philosophical quest for an understanding of our concepts. More specifically, it is assumed that the things we ordinarily and normally illocutionarily do with 'x', where 'x' is a word or an expression in our language, are not essential to what 'x' means, or to our concept of x. This assumption is intimately connected with the idea that our words are first and foremost instruments of *representation*, and only *as such* are usable for doing things other than, or beyond mere, representing.

Focusing on our concept of 'propositional knowledge'—'*knowing that* such and such'—I mean in this paper to question the above assumption. And I shall question it by way of questioning another prevalent assumption—the assumption, namely, that the position known in contemporary analytic philosophy as 'contextualism' constitutes some sort of a clear and straightforward continuation of Austin's work.[1] I do not lay claim to be interpreting Austin in what follows, exactly, but really only to be pursuing questions he has helped opening, making use of materials that he has provided.

1. Stage setting I: questions and materials

I shall be questioning the idea that our words are first and foremost instruments of representation, and that what they mean, or what concepts they 'express', or what phenomena they pick out or refer to, may therefore be discovered apart from a

---

[1] The only philosopher I know of for whom the idea of a link between contextualism on the one hand and Austin on the other proceeds from a serious and sustained interpretation of Austin's texts—an interpretation, as will emerge, that I ultimately find unsatisfying—is Charles Travis. His most detailed argument for the link to Austin, in the case of knowledge, is presented in Travis (2005, but see also 1997). Others who have proposed that Austin, with or without Wittgenstein, either just was a contextualist or at any rate was the forefather of contextualism are DeRose (2002: 196), Recanati (2004: 84 and 141ff.), Brady and Pritchard (2005: 162), and Cappelen and Lepore (2005: 5).

consideration of the various things we do, or might do, with them. Some think that this idea was more or less endorsed by Austin himself. After all, he distinguishes between the 'locutionary act' and the 'illocutionary act'; he essentially cashes the locutionary act in the Fregean (and Kantian) terms of uttering words 'with a certain sense and with a certain reference' (1975: 94); and he seems to allow that we could sometimes at least know the locution without knowing the illocution. He says, for example, that 'it may be perfectly clear what I mean by "It is going to charge" . . . , but not clear whether it is meant as a statement or a warning' (1975: 98 and 1979: 251), or that 'we may entirely clear up the "use of a sentence" on a particular occasion, in the sense of the locutionary act, without yet touching upon its use in the sense of an *illocutionary* act' (1975: 101). At other times, however, Austin refers to the idea that the locution has 'primacy as against the illocution' as a 'temptation', and reminds his audience that it may also sometimes be clear to us what illocution has been performed, but unclear what the exact locution is (1975: 115–16, fn. 1).

These are commonplaces, hardly contestable; and Austin certainly believed that in philosophy we should try to mostly stick to those. I believe, however, that there *are* issues here that Austin never quite came to resolve, or even to articulate clearly enough. He openly admits as much when he says, in the final lecture of *How to Do Things with Words*:

> We may well suspect that the theory of 'meaning' as equivalent to 'sense and reference' will certainly require some weeding-out and reformulating in terms of the distinction between locutionary and illocutionary acts (*if these notions are sound*: they are only adumbrated here). I admit that not enough has been done here: I have taken the old 'sense and reference' on the strength of current view. (1975: 149)

Then there is also Austin's 'playing Old Harry with the true/false fetish' (1975: 151). It is not clear what exactly it was meant to come to. If it mostly consists in urging that 'True' and 'False' are just 'general labels for a whole dimension of different appraisals which have something or other to do with the relation between what we say and the facts' (1979: 250–1; see also 1975: 149), then it is not yet clear why the philosopher who takes the meaning of our words to be essentially a matter of their representational power, and therefore to be capturable in terms of 'truth conditions'—I shall be calling this philosopher 'the traditionalist'—should feel much threatened by it. Granted that there are typically finer, more precise, and more useful terms that may be used in appraising the (presumably) essentially representational relation between our words and the world, he would say, what's wrong with focusing on the most general form of appraisal? If, on the other hand, playing Old Harry with the true/false fetish consists in reminding philosophers that our statements 'fit the facts always more or less loosely, in different ways on different occasions for different intents and purposes' (1979: 130) then again traditionalists are likely to protest that this may well be true, but that, as theorizers, they are wholly justified in setting aside this type of 'friction' in their inquiry after the truth conditions of utterances.[2]

More potentially troubling to the traditionalist, but also more enigmatic, is a famous, some would surely say infamous, footnote to 'A Plea for Excuses'. In that footnote, Austin, having said that ordinary language—as it reveals itself in an examination of 'what we should say when, and so why and what we should mean by it' (1979: 181)— should provide 'the first word' for philosophy, implores his readers to 'forget, for once and for a while, that other curious question "Is it true?"' (1979: 185). Here Austin seems to urge the traditionalist not to ask, in his investigation of our concepts, precisely the question that the traditionalist has taken to be absolutely essential to such an investigation. But an urging is not yet an argument; and Austin never quite tells us what is wrong with pressing the question of truth and falsity as somehow fundamental to conceptual inquiry.

There is also, however, Austin's *practice*. In a recent article, Keith DeRose, one of the leading proponents of contextualism with respect to 'knowing that', cites the footnote from 'A Plea for Excuses' and says that he finds it 'troubling'. It is clear why DeRose should find this footnote troubling: Current 'contextualism' is *essentially* a theory about the truth conditions of 'assertoric' ('indicative') sentences. But DeRose also notes that the footnote is consistent with Austin's writings on epistemology, in which Austin 'avoid[s] issues of whether our epistemological claims (especially claims about what is and is not known) are true or false' (De Rose 2002: 196).[3] And this is true. In 'Other Minds' Austin says things like the following:

If you say 'That's not enough' [as a way of challenging a knowledge claim and the basis given as its support], then you must have in mind some more or less definite lack. [...] If there is no definite lack, which you are at least prepared to specify on being pressed, then it's silly (outrageous) just to go on saying 'That's not enough'. (1979: 84)

He also says that what's enough will be a matter of what is 'within reason', and will depend on '*present* intents and purposes' (1979: 84). One could see in these passages of Austin's all of the main ingredients of contemporary contextualism about 'knowing that'—except that he seems content to speak in terms of when we would be 'right' to say we know (1979: 98), or 'justified' in saying this (1979: 101), and, as in the above quotation, in terms of what would or would not be 'silly' or 'outrageous' or 'within reason' to say. He never asks when it would be *true* to say of someone, who has claimed to know that there is a goldfinch in the garden, that he knows there's a goldfinch in the

---

[2] Strawson, by the way, believed that Austin's talk of statements always fitting the facts more or less loosely was fundamentally misguided (Strawson 1950). If it's raining and I state that it is raining, how, or in what sense, does my statement fit the facts only more or less loosely? For Strawson, Austin has here succumbed to metaphysics. But that's another story.

[3] Grice also complains about Austin's footnote (1989: 13). Famously, and rather fatefully, Grice maintained that Austin had never made very clear, let alone justified, his objection to raising the question of truth and falsity.

garden. He never says that if the knowledge claimer has said enough for all intents and purposes to support his claim, then he just *knows*, or at any rate has claimed something *true*. Why doesn't he? The traditionalist is bound to find this feature of Austin's practice unjustified and unmotivated, if not sheerly perverse; and, once again, Austin does preciously little to disarm such a response.

One thing he does do is to bring into 'Other Minds' materials from his work on 'performative utterances'. And he even argues, quite extensively, that 'I know' is more akin, in its functioning and force, to 'I promise'—a clear performative—than we tend to realize, and that, therefore, to suppose that it is a 'descriptive phrase' is to have fallen prey to 'the descriptive fallacy' (1979: 98–103). This is an interesting and potentially important claim, and I shall pursue a *version* of it in what follows. Contemporary theorizers about 'know that' and cognates, within the mainstream of analytic philosophy, have proceeded as if it did not matter to the assessment in terms of truth and falsity, and to its very applicability, what illocutionarily speaking was done with the words under assessment. Relatedly, they have proceeded as if, semantically, there was no significant difference between one's saying 'I know that such and such', and having someone say to one 'You know that such and such' or having someone say of one 'He knows that such and such'. The same proposition or Fregean thought, with the same truth conditions, may be expressed by all three utterances, most philosophers in the mainstream would maintain.

But again, the things that Austin says of how 'I know' 'functions [. . .] in talking' (1979: 79) are not of the sort that can be expected to make the traditionalist feel much threatened. To begin with, 'I know', however akin it might be to 'I promise', is surely not a performative: you can say 'I know' fully felicitously and, for all that, not know, it would seem. In addition, many in the mainstream would even contest Austin's claim that pure performative utterances 'couldn't possibly be true or false' (1975: 6; 1979: 235), and would rather say, as against Austin, that these utterances, when felicitously performed, *make themselves true.*[4] And finally, 'I know' is but one inflection of the verb, however central its role might be in everyday practice, and Austin is focusing on just one, and not even the most common, type of use of this particular inflection.[5]

I conclude that for all we have found in Austin, we still have not seen an argument for why the philosopher who wishes to become clearer with respect to our concept of propositional knowledge, or wishes to discover the meaning, or 'semantics', of 'know that' and cognates, should not primarily do so by asking when 'assertoric' utterances featuring these expressions would be true. Nor have we been told why this philosopher ought to attend to the different things we illocutionarily do with these expressions.

---

[4] For a strong expression of this idea, see Lewis (1983: 247–8). For a more recent reassertion of it, see Soames (2003: 128).

[5] I elaborate on this limitation of Austin's account of 'I know' in Baz (forthcoming).

2. Stage setting II: the traditionalist and the contextualist

Setting aside the question of what exactly, if anything, Austin had against the assumption that it ought to be possible for us to become clearer with respect to what our words mean, or what concepts they embody or 'express', without attending to the different things we do, or might do, with them, I think the following can safely be said: In the wake of Paul Grice's 'Logic and Conversation' (1989),[6] and encouraged by John Searle's influential interpretation-cum-'improvement' of Austin's thoughts (1968, 1999), the mainstream of analytic philosophy has felt itself entitled to inquire after the meaning of our words, or the concepts they express, mostly just by way of looking for their 'truth conditions', while disregarding the different things we do with them.

Thus Searle (1968, 1999) has maintained that in every (felicitous) utterance, at least of a whole sentence, there will be a moment of 'reference' and a moment of 'predication', and he accordingly has maintained that we could identify, in every utterance, and regardless of its illocutionary force, the 'proposition', or 'content', that it, or its utterer, 'expresses'—some fundamental component that is in principle truth evaluable. Searle also accused ordinary language philosophers such as Austin of committing various fallacies, all stemming from their failure properly to distinguish 'use' from 'meaning'—where the former involves the question of illocutionary force, but the latter is to be cashed out entirely in terms of reference and truth conditions (1999: 131–56).[7] Grice, whose primary concern was to secure what he called 'conceptual analysis' from the threat to it that he detected in Austin's writings and in the writings of other so called 'ordinary language philosophers', maintained that the truth evaluable component of the utterance was essentially determined (barring indexicality, ambiguity, etc.) by 'the conventional meaning of the words (the sentence)' uttered (1989: 25). The contextualist then comes onto the scene, and argues, as against views such as Grice's, that what 'So and so knows that such and such' requires of the world, in order to be true of so and so and such and such, is a function, not alone of what the words mean but also of features of the context in which 'knows that' is predicated of that pair. The contextualist still presupposes, however, with the traditional philosopher and with Searle and Grice, that it ought to be possible for us to tell what our words speak of and what they, and therefore we, say about it, apart from a consideration of what is being, or might be, done with the words. And he still takes it, with the traditionalist, that our words are essentially instruments of representation and that therefore their essential powers will be known to us when, and only when, we know when and under what conditions they would be true.

As against the traditionalist ('invariantist', 'anti-contextualist') philosopher's assumption that our concept of 'knowing that such and such' is such that one could simply and

---

[6] Originally given as the William James Lectures at Harvard, in 1967.

[7] Barring, of course, indexicality, ambiguity, etc., and perhaps also relative to certain very general 'background assumptions' (Searle 1978). For a good critique of Searle and Grice on these issues, see Glock (1996).

directly ask, about any pair of person N and fact (or proposition) referable to by 'such and such',[8] whether or not S knows that such and such (at t), and that the correct answer to that question would be so for everybody and at all times, the contextualist has insisted that the correct answer to the traditionalist's question is going to depend on the context in which it is being asked or answered. The traditionalist's question thus receives a 'semantic ascent' in the hands of the contextualist and becomes 'Would it be true for so and so, situated as he or she is, to say of N, "She knows that such and such"?'[9]

The contextualist question does not constitute a rejection of the traditionalist's question, only an amendment to it. In particular, the contextualist shares with the anti-contextualist the following idea: The basic thing we do with 'know that' and its cognates is to *apply* (the concept of) 'knowing that'—in the sense of performing an act of Kantian 'judgement' with it—to pairs of person and fact (or proposition).[10] The idea, put otherwise, is that the basic role of 'know that' and cognates is to enable us to *represent*, 'describe', people as knowing this or that. *In thus representing* we could of course also be performing any of many illocutionary acts, but what illocutionary act we perform does not affect the identity of our representation *qua representation*; and it certainly cannot make it philosophically unwise or misleading for us to take what we've produced *as a representation* and raise the question of truth and falsity about it. To find out what 'knowing that' means, or names, or refers to, we should look for the conditions under which people may truly be represented as knowing that such and such—the conditions under which 'know that' or one of its cognates may truly be applied to them.

The contextualist's invitation to ask ourselves of everyday 'assertoric' utterances featuring 'know that' or one of its cognates whether what is said in them is true or false, is therefore nothing but an invitation to perform a secondary, parasitic, act of Kantian judgement—to see whether (the concept of) 'knowing that', with its 'truth conditions' presumably fixed or determined by the 'knowledge ascriber's' context, truly or falsely applies to the person and fact in question. And of course, *we* are not expected to do anything, in thus applying the ascriber's 'know that', other than to perform this pure act of judgement. *Our* application of 'know that' or one of its cognates is essentially done *outside of ordinary and normal practice*; and both the traditionalist and the contextualist assume that there is no problem with *that*.[11] The aim of this chapter is to question this assumption, from what is arguably an Austinian perspective.

---

[8] I shall use throughout 'knowing that such and such' as opposed to 'knowing that P' or 'knowing that F' so as to avoid the question of whether what is known is a proposition or a fact. On this, see Williamson (2000: 43).

[9] For the idea of 'semantic ascent', see Lewis (1996: 566).

[10] By 'Kantian judgement' I mean the fitting of a particular with a universal, or vice versa, and doing nothing else besides.

[11] Cavell has most aptly described the underlying assumption here—i.e. that it ought to be possible for us to perform such pure acts of judgement—as the assumption, or fantasy, that it ought to be possible for us 'to speak without the commitments speech exacts' (Cavell 1979: 215).

3. Travis' 'milk in the refrigerator' example and knowledge as a liability

I begin with one of the examples that Charles Travis employs for supporting his claim that the semantics of knowledge ascriptions and denials is 'context (or occasion) sensitive'.[12] More specifically, Travis contends that for an utterance of the form 'N (I, you, she, etc.) know(s) that such and such' to be true, only the 'real doubts' as to such and such's obtaining need to be 'discharged' for N, where what counts as real (as opposed to 'mere') doubt is going to depend on the circumstances in which the utterance is made and be, in this sense, context sensitive.[13] Replace Travis' 'real' with 'relevant', his 'doubts' with 'alternatives' or 'possibilities', and his 'being discharged for N' with something like 'eliminated by N's evidence (or experience)', and you essentially get what is known as the 'relevant alternatives' version of contextualism with respect to knowledge, as advocated, for example, by David Lewis (1996), Michael Williams (2001), and, more recently, by Jonathan Schaffer (2004, 2005, 2006) and Michael Blome-Tillmann (2009).[14] With Timothy Williamson, I take the 'relevant alternatives' form of contextualism with respect to propositional knowledge to be the most plausible and compelling, as well as the most prevalent form of that position.[15] Indeed, for reasons that will emerge in the next section, I think it has an important grain of truth in it (but regrettably also too much 'truth').

[12] As I said, Travis' contextualism is unique in that it takes its bearing from a serious and thorough interpretation of Austin and Wittgenstein. While I find Travis' interpretation too representationalist or descriptivist to capture the radicality of Austin's and Wittgenstein's break with the tradition, there are many other moments in which I find his thoughts very congenial. I focus in much more detail on Travis' contextualism as an interpretation of Wittgenstein and Austin in Baz (2008); but for the purposes of the present chapter I mostly ignore Travis' differences from other contextualists.

[13] This is a brief summary of Travis' account of the semantics of knowledge ascriptions in Travis (1989: 151–87). I set aside the thorny question of what exactly it means for a doubt (or alternative) to be discharged (or eliminated) for one. In Travis 2005 we get an account that, so far as I can tell, is formally the same. It's just that this time Travis does not speak in terms of conceivable doubts that should be divided into mere doubts, on the one hand, and real doubts, on the other; rather, he talks in terms of a distinction between ways for P to be false that count as things that *might (or may) be* and ways for P to be false that do not count. Again the claim is that the determination of what might be is occasion sensitive. I should note that, as seen from the perspective of current debates, Travis is not always sufficiently careful in distinguishing between contextualism proper (the view that the semantics of knowledge ascriptions depend on the context in which the *ascribing* is being done) and what is known as 'subject sensitive invariantism' (as advocated by Hawthorne 2004 and Stanley 2005). This complaint against Travis is brought by Millar (2005: 340).

[14] Williams, I should note, mostly focuses on justification, rather than on knowledge. This, I think, has to do with his 'epistemological anti-realism', which bears a certain affinity to the Austinian perspective that I develop in this paper. But of course, 'know' and cognates, and hence the concept of knowledge, do play important roles in human discourse; and Williams, unlike Austin, does little to bring them to light. Focusing as he does on the question of the importance of *knowledge* (cf. Williams 2001: 2 and 5), Williams is insufficiently attentive to the question of the importance of 'know' and cognates.

[15] '[Although] different contextualists offer different context shifting mechanisms [. . .] most of them make some play with the idea of change in the contextual relevance of various possibilities of error'

The example reads:

Hugo, engrossed in the paper, says, 'I need some milk for my coffee.' Odile replies, 'You know where the milk is.' Suddenly defensive, Hugo replies: 'Well, I don't really *know* that, do I? Perhaps the cat broke into the refrigerator, or there was just now a very stealthy milk thief, or it evaporated or suddenly congealed.' (Travis 1989: 156)

Upon considering this little story, we are expected to find that Hugo's reply 'fails to count against Odile's words'. Under these circumstances, Travis says, Hugo's reply 'does not even tend to show that Hugo does not know where the milk is' (1989: 156). This and similar examples are supposed to support Travis' contention that 'N know(s) that such and such' only requires, in order to be true, that N will have discharged all of the real doubts as to such and such's obtaining, and not the merely conceivable doubts, where the distinction between real and mere doubts is context sensitive. This is what we are supposed to realize about 'the cognitive achievement' that is required for knowledge (1989: 173). Hugo's response fails to count against Odile's ascription of knowledge to him, because the doubts of which he supposedly speaks happen to be mere doubts on that occasion, and therefore incapable of undermining Odile's ascription of knowledge to him (on the most natural way of imagining the circumstances, of course; we could imagine them to be real, if we stretched our imagination a bit).

But how exactly are we to imagine Odile's meaning of her words? What is she doing when she says 'You know where the milk is'? And what could Hugo possibly be doing in responding to her as he does? For the traditionalist, this is altogether beside the point. His question is just this: Does Hugo, as he stands (or sits), *know* that the milk is in the refrigerator? That Odile said what she said, and how she meant, or could possibly have meant, her words, is just irrelevant as far as the traditionalist is concerned, and neither is it relevant what Hugo is imagined to have done, and said, with his words in responding to her. But for the reasons presented in the previous section I want to suggest that the contextualist too has no real use for the particular way in which Odile meant her words, and for how, if at all, Hugo meant his response. For the contextualist the question is just this: Would it be *true* to say in reference to Hugo, as he stands, 'He knows that the milk is in the refrigerator'?—a question that the traditionalist will find unnecessarily cumbersome, but otherwise perfectly in order. The basic difference is that for the contextualist, as opposed to the traditional philosopher, it matters who is imagined to do the saying, and under what circumstances. I will argue, however, that it does matter how Odile and Hugo are imagined to mean, or fail to mean, their words; and that it even matters for the very thing that both the contextualist and the traditionalist are interested in: the question of what 'knowing (that such and such)' means, and when, or under what conditions, someone counts, or ought to count, as knowing that such and such.

(Williamson 2005a: 97). Schaffer (2005) raises serious objections to other forms of contextualism with respect to propositional knowledge.

The most natural way of imagining Travis' example, it seems to me, is to hear Odile as *rebuking* Hugo for his laziness, or chauvinism, or both.[16] If this is how we hear her words, then it matters very little that she chose words of the form 'N know(s) that such and such' to make her point. What she says to him is, in effect, that if he wants milk, he should go and get some himself. The problem with Hugo's 'response' would then seem to be, not that the 'doubts' he 'raises' are irrelevant, or mere doubts, but rather that the occasion is not one for 'raising doubts'. He has missed altogether the point of her words, or else has attempted a very lame joke.

Of course, this is likely to impress neither the traditional philosopher nor the contextualist; for both of them, it would seem to only touch upon the '*merely pragmatic*' dimension of the exchange. Both the traditional philosopher and the contextualist would say: 'Look, Odile said of Hugo—whatever else she said or meant to be saying—that he knew where the milk was, or that it was in the refrigerator (perhaps, as you just said, as a way of saying that he has no epistemic excuse for not getting the milk himself, and thereby implying that he has no other excuse either). Hugo denies her ascription of knowledge to him, and supports his denial by citing various conceivable doubts, or alternatives to the milk's being in the refrigerator. And now the question is just this: Given that the doubts he raises, and many conceivable others, are ones that he has not actually ruled out, and is not in a position to rule out, does he or doesn't he know what Odile says he knows?'

As I said, for both the traditional philosopher and the contextualist, this last question would always make perfect sense, and would always have a correct answer. The difference is just this: The traditional philosopher takes it that there is essentially only one correct answer to this question[17]—either 'Yes' or 'No'—and that this one answer could in principle be given by anyone, and would be correct regardless of the circumstances under which it is given; for the contextualist, by contrast, the correct answer to this question would be sometimes 'Yes', sometimes 'No', and sometimes 'The question is not determinate enough to be answered either correctly or incorrectly', depending on the circumstances under which the question has been raised, and the circumstances under which we attend to the question. The traditional philosopher, Travis argues, will then owe us a story about how we are to tell, occasion *in*sensitively, which of the countlessly many conceivable doubts that are clearly undischarged for Hugo must be discharged, and which ones needn't be discharged, if he is to know what Odile claims he knows. And according to Travis, there is just no principled and

---

[16] Or we could imagine her to be encouraging Hugo to regain his trust in his faculties, say after a serious head injury. For lack of space, I cannot pursue this interpretation of Travis' example. I will only say that this way of imagining the example, thought through, would also show the limitations of the contextualist's account.

[17] Assuming, of course, that we ask about Hugo as he is *at some particular moment in time*. I disregard here the possibility of 'borderline' cases, since it seems to me to weigh neither here nor there when it comes to the disagreement between contextualists and anti-contextualists. So far as I can see, both positions can easily accommodate borderline cases.

plausible way of drawing the distinction context insensitively: Requiring that *all* conceivable doubts as to such and such's obtaining be discharged, if it is to be known that such and such, would lead to scepticism (as Travis thinks of it); requiring none of those doubts to be discharged would make knowledge uninterestingly easy to attain. Both ways would make the concept of propositional knowledge useless and hence empty, according to Travis (1989: 168; 1991: 245).[18]

Go back to Odile's words, however, and to the idea that she means them as a rebuke. Imagining her words in this way points to a much neglected region of our concept of knowledge,[19] one in which knowledge is some sort of a liability, sometimes even a burden, and is the basis not for deference and respect, but for reproach, accusation, and blame. Whereas philosophers have almost invariably thought of knowledge as some sort of an achievement that *entitles* us to certain things,[20] and therefore have almost invariably spoken of utterances of the form 'I know that such and such' as knowledge *claims*, knowledge thought of in this second way is not something to be claimed, but rather is something to admit, confess, or acknowledge; and in second and third person it is something more aptly said to be imputed, rather than, say, attributed. This region of our concept of propositional knowledge is, arguably, at least as central to it as the region that has predominated in the tradition, and it is quite thought-provoking, I think, to find that it has virtually been ignored by contextualists and anti-contextualists, sceptics and anti-sceptics, alike.[21] Imagine what the history of the philosophical treatment of scepticism would have looked like, if scepticism was

---

[18] 'Subject sensitive invariantists' such as Fantl and McGrath (2002), Hawthorne (2004), and Stanley (2005), would argue against Travis that he has missed their anti-contextualist way of drawing the distinction between relevant and irrelevant alternatives.

[19] I say 'points to', because, as I said, it's not even clear that Odile, in Travis' example, may plausibly be thought to be concerned with Hugo's *knowledge* of where the milk is. In considering what I go on to argue in the text, the reader is invited to substitute a clearer example, such as charging someone with having known that the company was in trouble, or that he wouldn't be able to keep his promise. I chose to stick with Travis' example.

[20] Thus, for example, Williamson has argued that only knowing that such and such entitles us to assert that such and such (2000: 238–69); see also DeRose (2002). Fantl and McGrath (2002) argue that knowing that such and such rationally entitles us to 'act as if such and such'. And Hawthorne and Stanley (2008) argue—less plausibly, to my mind—that *only* knowing that such and such entitles us to use the proposition *that such and such* as a reason for action.

[21] I know of only two exceptions. The first is Warnock (1983). Warnock, however, takes the fact that assertoric sentences featuring 'know' and cognates are used in the performance of a great variety of speech acts—including those of charging someone with having known something and of admitting or confessing to have known something—as reason for thinking that we should distinguish the question of 'what to know something is, what "knowing" means' from the question of 'whether possession of a given item of putative knowledge is, on this or that occasion, claimed or disclosed, admitted or avowed, presupposed or advertised [...]' (1983: 49). He is relying, together with Searle, Grice, and many others, on the very notion of word (and sentence) meaning that this paper is questioning. The other exception is Hanfling (2000), who notes, in the context of arguing for a form of 'relevant alternatives' account of knowledge, that 'In some cases [...] the possession of knowledge is a matter of *admission* rather than claim or entitlement' (2000: 122). What Hanfling fails to note is that these cases actually belong to what he calls 'commenting situations' (2000: 96–7)—situations in which the obtaining of such and such is not in question. In such cases, I am about to argue, the relevant alternatives machinery is actually altogether beside the point, and therefore semantically inert.

thought of, not as denying us something that we would ordinarily claim, or wish to claim, for ourselves, but rather as aiming to disburden us of something that it is difficult, or shameful, or painful to possess. Even Austin, for all of his sensitivity to the nuances of human speech, writes of knowledge in 'Other Minds' as the sort of thing that one would naturally claim, or wish to claim for oneself, and that others would naturally *challenge*. His comparison of 'I know' and 'I promise' would not work, if the former was taken to be meant as, for example, an acknowledgement. ('I know he is angry with me; I just haven't had the time to speak with him about what happened.') It might be said, in Austin's defense, that he was responding to the tradition and therefore was justified in focusing on the tradition's favored use of 'I know'.

Now why is any of this relevant to an understanding of our concept of propositional knowledge? After all, anything that we possess, or might possess, could, conceivably, become a liability, or a burden. Why should knowledge be any different? And why should any of this be of interest to someone who wishes to find out what knowledge, or the possession of knowledge, *is*? The answer to this is that a piece of knowledge, unlike, perhaps, a piece of furniture, is not something whose nature, and whose possession by someone, can philosophically safely be determined regardless of the specific point of the determination. When, for example, you *charge* me with knowing (or having known) that such and such, then, normally, what conceivable doubts (or alternatives) there are with respect to such and such's obtaining, and which of them is real (or relevant), and whether I have discharged (or eliminated) all of the real ones, would be altogether beside the point. If you charge me, for example, with having known that the milk was in the refrigerator, and you complain that I therefore had no excuse for not getting up and getting some by myself, then it would be uncomprehending ('outrageous') for me to say, for example, that for all I knew the milk might have been on the counter; unless I *actually believed* that it might be on the counter, and unless *this* is at least part of the reason why I did not get up to get some.

It might be replied, on behalf of Travis and other relevant alternatives contextualists, that the milk's being on the counter, for example, is clearly an alternative to its being in the refrigerator; that, in the situation envisioned above, that alternative was made real, or relevant to my knowledge (or lack thereof) that it was in the refrigerator, by my actually believing that it might be on the counter; and that it was clearly (we can suppose) an alternative to the milk's being in the refrigerator that was un-discharged for me at the time. The problem with this way of trying to defend the contextualist's account is that there is no reason to think that *this* way of making alternatives to such and such's obtaining real, or relevant, has anything to do with the occasion sensitivity of knowledge ascriptions as he thinks of it. If I really did believe that the milk might be on the counter, then I did not know that it was in the refrigerator, and this has nothing to do with the relevance or irrelevance of alternatives to its being in the refrigerator and with the question of which of the relevant ones was eliminated or discharged for me at the time. If you find my belief unjustified, then you can charge me with *that*, and say, perhaps, that I *should have known* that it was in the refrigerator; but you cannot—no one can—rightfully charge me with having known that it was.

It might further be argued on behalf of the contextualist: 'But of course none of the above is relevant to the contextualist account of the context sensitivity of knowledge, or to anyone's account of the context sensitivity or insensitivity of knowledge, for that matter. Everybody agrees that for anyone to be a candidate for knowing that such and such, that person has got, first of all, to take it ('believe', in philosophers' jargon) that such and such. If she takes it that not such and such, or is unsure whether such and such, or at any rate is just not taking it that such and such, then she cannot know that such and such; and this has nothing to do with the alternatives to such and such that may or may not be discharged for her. The occasion sensitivity of knowing that such and such, as contextualists think of it, only comes into play when we consider people who take it that such and such.'

But now, where does this leave us? You say, *charge*, that I knew the milk was in the refrigerator. Now either I did not take it that it was, or I did.[22] If I did not (because, say, I actually thought that it might be on the counter), then—in any context of assessment—I did not know (though perhaps I *should have* known) that it was in the refrigerator. If, on the other hand, I took it that it was in the refrigerator, and you charge me with having known this, then the philosopher's question of whether all 'real' or 'relevant' doubts as to our being out of milk have been discharged or eliminated—that question is beside the point, *as far as you and I are concerned*. And if I were to try to defend myself by 'raising' *any* conceivable doubt, as Hugo does in Travis' example, then my words would fail to count against yours because I would not be in a position to mean them as raising doubts, and therefore would not *be* raising a doubt by means of them, not because I would be raising a doubt that was not real, or relevant.[23] It is, in any case, still knowledge that you and I are talking about—my (alleged) knowledge that the milk is in the refrigerator. But the question of which doubts or alternatives to its being there are relevant, and which of the relevant ones have been discharged or eliminated, as Travis and other contextualists think of it, is out of place in our context, and is therefore irrelevant to an understanding of your knowledge ascription to me. Nor would a third party witness to our exchange need to attend to this question in order to understand your accusation, and to be able to assess the appropriateness of my response to it.

---

[22] I should say that I actually believe that this is a false dichotomy. I am using the dichotomy between taking it that such and such and not taking it that such and such heuristically here. As with many of our concepts—as for example with 'knowing that', or 'acting voluntarily' (Austin 1979: 190)—the concept of 'taking it that such and such' only felicitously applies, *either* positively *or* negatively, to a person and a fact, under certain conditions and when the application has some point.

[23] Now, of course I could try lying to you: I could falsely deny having taken it that the milk was in the refrigerator. But then, and supposing that you believe my lie, we are, insofar as our 'conversational score' is concerned, back with our first disjunct.

That the question on which the relevant alternatives contextualist account is supposed to bear does not normally arise in situations in which someone is charged with knowing, or having known, that such and such, is not a linguistic accident. It is, on the contrary, a function of our interest in what goes by the name of 'knowledge' in situations of this sort. Situations of this sort are a subset of a wider set of situations in which, while it does matter to the conversants that, or whether, someone actually knows, or knew, that such and such, they themselves *already* take it that such and such—there is no doubt in their mind as to *its* obtaining and they therefore are not looking for anyone's assurance of it.[24] In asking whether the other knows, or in taking it that she does, they therefore are not normally concerned with whether 'her assurances are good enough' (Travis 1989: 177), or with whether 'her evidence is [or was] good enough to know' (Fantl and McGrath 2002: 67; see also Stanley 2005: 88) or with whether her belief that such and such (or her otherwise taking it that such and such) 'rises to the level of knowledge' (Bach 2005: 63). And this means that the question to which both contextualists and anti-contextualists have proposed competing answers is just not a question to which competent employers of 'know that' and its cognates would (need to) attend in situations of this sort.

It might be objected: 'But does not all this just show that we need to distinguish between knowledge ("knowledge") as it concerns us in the everyday and knowledge (*knowledge*) as philosophers think of it?[25] Why should it matter for a *philosophical* reflection on what knowledge is, and requires, that for the imputer of knowledge and the person charged with knowing some particular fact, the question of which doubts as to the obtaining of that fact are relevant, and whether all of the relevant doubts have been discharged, is beside the point? This question may still be raised. Indeed, this is precisely the question that philosophers ought to raise, and think about, if they wish to find out whether (it would be true to say that) Hugo, for example, *knows* that the milk was in the refrigerator. That the question is not one that people in contexts such as that of Odile and Hugo would need to attend to and, indeed, that it would make no sense for people in such contexts to attend to this question—all this is beside the point as far as the truth conditions (and truth value) of utterances featuring "know" and its cognates are concerned.'

This moment of conflict is one to which we were bound all along to come. I am hoping, though, that some of what we saw on the way has put us in a position for beginning to look at the conflict with fresh eyes. So far we have seen this: The contextualist 'relevant alternatives' account of our concept of 'knowing that', which essentially just adds context sensitivity to the tradition's understanding of knowing that such and such as a cognitive achievement that places one in a position to legitimately dismiss alternatives to such and such—this account is unfaithful to at least one central region of our everyday employment of 'know that' and cognates. It presents as essential

---

[24] These are the sorts of situations that Hanfling calls 'commenting situations' (2000: 96ff).

[25] The latter being what Wittgenstein would call 'knowledge with a metaphysical emphasis' (1969: §482).

to the applicability of the concept a question that, in 'applying' the concept in this region, we simply do not ask.[26] It thereby encourages a distorted picture of what is at issue when knowing that such and such is at issue, in this region.

Had Lewis considered the possibility that knowledge might be a liability with which we might be charged, as opposed to some sort of an achievement that we would naturally wish to claim for ourselves, I cannot imagine that he would have maintained that it is enough just to mention or consider an alternative to p to make it relevant, and hence one that must be eliminated if p is to be known (Lewis 1996: 559). He would have seen right away that if this were generally true, then it would have been way too easy to disown a painful, or shameful, or otherwise unwanted piece of knowledge.[27] Nor would Schaffer have said, had he attended more carefully to ordinary and normal practice, that 'the social role of knowledge ascriptions is to identify people who can help us answer our questions' (Schaffer 2006: 100).[28] If 'knowledge ascription' means anything (clear), then Odile can surely be said to be ascribing knowledge to Hugo, in Travis' example. But she does not need him to answer any question (except perhaps for the question of why it does not occur to him that he should get the milk himself). She takes it for granted that the milk is in the refrigerator, and does not need Hugo to assure, let alone inform, her of that. She therefore has no need to attend to the question of whether he has what Travis calls 'good enough assurances' as to the milk's being in the refrigerator. The mechanism of context sensitive relevant alternatives—just like any other metaphysical account of knowledge—may still somehow be applied to their exchange from the outside; but it plays no role within it.

4. DeRose's 'Bank' example, and knowing as a matter of being in a position to give assurance

In 'A Plea for Excuses', Austin says something that seems to me very pertinent to what we have seen thus far, and to what we shall be seeing next. He speaks of our words as 'invoking models', and then he cautions:

It must be remembered that there is no necessity whatsoever that the various models used in creating our vocabulary, primitive or recent, should all fit together neatly as parts into one single,

---

[26] It should be noted that the notion of 'applying a word (or a concept)', which features centrally in contemporary analytic philosophy, has no straightforward connection with anything that we might naturally describe, outside of philosophy, as 'applying a word (or a concept)'. It is a philosophical term of art that's meant to capture that element of pure judgement—somehow fitting a word to an object, or case, and doing nothing else besides—that is presupposed to underlie human discourse.

[27] Of course, I am not the only one who finds this part of Lewis's account objectionable. But it is telling, again, that the routine objection to this part of Lewis's account has been that it makes it all too easy for *someone else* ('the sceptic') to *rob us* of knowledge that we supposedly possess.

[28] See also Craig (1990) who, while claiming to be breaking away from the confines of the traditional analysis of knowledge, has from the perspective of the present paper stayed very much within those confines.

total model or scheme of, for example, the doing of actions [substitute here 'knowing that such and such', AB]. It is possible, and indeed highly likely, that our assortment of models will include some, or many, that are overlapping, conflicting, or more generally simply *disparate*. (1979: 203)[29]

This suggests one serious problem with the invitation to competent speakers to 'intuit', upon being presented with an 'example' of some purportedly human situation, whether or not (it would be true for so and so to say that) one of the protagonists knows that such and such—a procedure that is absolutely central to theorizing about knowledge within the mainstream of analytic philosophy. What the philosopher in effect does is to invite us to apply a word whose competent application requires different things when guided or informed by different models, and he invites us to do so *apart from any particular model*. One reason why our intuitive answers to the philosopher's questions tend to be 'unsystematic' (see Gendler and Hawthorne 2005) may therefore be that in answering the philosopher's question we are pulled by disparate and possibly conflicting models.

The philosopher who thinks of knowing that such and such as essentially requiring the eliminations of doubts or alternatives, or as a matter of 'having proof' (see Travis 2005: 313) has been focusing on only one of the models that guide us in our everyday employment of 'know that' and cognates. This might be taken to mean that the philosopher's account is not so much wrong, or distorted, as partial. And why can't the philosopher, in theorizing about knowledge, focus on just one of the models that underlie our employment of these words? Surely, it might be protested, knowing that such and such *does* sometimes, and perhaps centrally, matter to us because the knower that such and such is in a position to assure us that such and such. Isn't it only natural that the philosopher, whose business, presumably, is to look for things of which he can assure himself and others, would be primarily interested in this region or aspect of our concept of knowing that?

However, has the philosopher given us a faithful account even just of that region of our concept of propositional knowledge that seems closest to his pre-occupations? Let us think more closely about knowing as being in the position to give assurance, taking as our stalking horse a simplified version of DeRose's well known 'Bank' example (DeRose 1992: 913): A couple is standing in front of the bank on a Friday afternoon. They have checks they need to deposit. It is late, and they wonder whether they should get in line or go home and come back the next morning. The wife raises the worry that the bank may not be open on Saturday. Her husband then tells her that he knows it is open on Saturday, for he was there two weeks earlier on a Saturday and it was open. The wife then challenges his basis by raising the worry that the bank might have

---

[29] It is not clear that Austin means to suggest here that our different uses of *the same word or expression* may be guided by different models. This, anyway, is what I am suggesting.

changed its hours since his visit. I leave out complications having to do with how urgent or important it is for the couple to deposit their checks.

In such situations, there might indeed be utterances of sentences of the form 'I know that such and such' which are claims, or are at least somewhat akin to claims,[30] and which may plausibly be said to be in the business of assuring someone else that such and such obtains. I note, however, that we don't very often use 'I know that such and such' in situations in which the other looks for an *assurance* that such and such. Normally, we simply assert 'Such and such', and then give our basis if asked, 'How do you know?' And the reason for this is quite straightforward, it seems to me: if the other is not satisfied that you are in a position to give her assurance as to the obtaining of such and such, then your *claiming* to be in that position is unlikely to help. There is normally no work at the level of communicated *content* that 'I know that such and such' can do in such situations, which cannot equally well be done by 'Such and such' together with a basis that shows that, or how, one is in a position to give assurance as to the obtaining of such and such. Pace DeRose (2002: 185), the 'new plunge' one normally takes in saying 'I know' in such contexts is therefore not epistemological, but *personal* (see Austin 1979: 99–100). 'I know', in such situations, is likely to mean something like 'I swear' or 'Trust me' or 'Why don't you trust me?' or 'Stop worrying so much', and therefore not to be functioning as 'a descriptive phrase' (1979: 103). There is therefore good reason to think that its utterance in such a situation would more felicitously be assessed in terms of whether the speaker was justified (reasonable, responsible, sincere . . .) in doing what he did with the words than in terms of whether she said something true.

Setting that issue aside for a moment, it seems undeniable that something at least very much like a distinction between relevant and irrelevant doubts or alternatives is typically in play in such situations: Normally, to claim to know that the bank is open on Saturday, on the basis of having been there two weeks earlier on a Saturday, is not to have claimed to know that, for example, they have not changed their hours since then, *unless* that possibility has somehow been made relevant or salient prior to the claiming. It would normally be incompetent (silly, outrageous . . .) to complain against the claimer that he hasn't ruled out that possibility; for (we are here assuming) he did not claim to have ruled it out.[31] In order to know this about the claimer's utterance of 'I know that the bank is open on Saturday', it is not enough to know what words he

---

[30] To say, for example, of someone who, upon being asked if he knows whether some flight has a layover in Chicago, looks at his itinerary and says 'Yes I know—it does stop in Chicago', that he *claims* to know that the flight has a layover in Chicago, as Stewart Cohen does (1999: 58), is to stretch our concept of 'claiming' very thin: that person, on the most natural reading of Cohen's own story, is not so much *claiming to know* that the flight has a layover in Chicago as simply *letting the other know that he knows* (in the sense of having got the desired information). He might just as well have shown the other person his itinerary and pointed out the desired information on it. I owe this last way of pressing the point to Dan Dennett.

[31] This is why it is quite odd, or philosophically forced, for the wife, in DeRose's example, to raise the worry that the bank might have changed its hours since her husband's visit, and then to ask him 'Do you know that the bank will be open tomorrow?' (1992: 913). Every competent speaker would know that having

used; we need to also know certain pertinent features of the context in which the claim was made, such as what doubt or worry the claimer meant, or could reasonably have been expected to mean, to alleviate or dismiss.

So far so good for the relevant alternatives contextualist. But so far we have also not gone beyond Austin's discussion in 'Other Minds'. Specifically, we have not asked whether the envisioned knowledge claim is true, or under what conditions it would be. If we look closely at the sort of situations broached in DeRose's example, however, we find that the question of whether or not 'know(s) that' truly applies to the claimer and what he claims to know, as both the traditionalist and the contextualist are thinking about it, is not a question that competent employers of 'know that' and its cognates would normally (need to) attend to, let alone answer, in such situations. Here I must be briefer, but the point is in fact quite simple: Competent speakers know that, conceptually speaking, a (knowledge) claim will normally not be more solid than the basis upon which it is made can make it.[32] Sometimes the basis would be obvious (as when, in Cohen's 1999 'Airport' example, we see the person checking his itinerary and finding the desired flight information on it); sometimes the claimer would offer it without being prompted (as in DeRose's original 'Bank' example). And quite often, the person would be prompted to provide his audience with his basis, typically by being asked 'How do you know?'—the question on which Austin focuses in 'Other Minds'. In any case, once it is clear to all participants on what basis the claim (or so-called 'claim') was made—and competent knowledge claims would normally have a basis that the claimer would be able to provide—the theorist's question of whether the claimer *knows* that such and such, or whether he can *truly* be said to know, normally becomes moot in the sort of situations that we are here discussing: It is not a question that the participants would normally (need to) attend to in such situations. Once the basis is known—that is, once it is clear to the participants what information they possess *in common* (for if the basis is not itself in doubt, as usually it is not, there is no longer reason to think of it as *the claimer's*)—the question normally becomes whether *it* (the basis, as opposed to anything about the claimer) provides the participants with sufficient assurance as to the obtaining of such and such. The answer to *that* question would typically depend, among other things, on the participants' sensibilities, basic attitudes, past experiences, risk aversion, etc., and would not normally be felicitously assessable in terms of 'truth and falsity'.[33] If, on the other hand, the people in need of information

been to the bank two weeks earlier on a Saturday is not a basis for claiming to know that it hasn't changed its hours since then.

[32] I argue this point in much more detail in Baz (2009).

[33] In Baz (2009) I press this point by inviting the reader to imagine a disagreement arising between two people in a situation such as that of DeRose and his wife in front of the bank, about what they ought to do next: the one says that they ought to go home and come back the next morning, for example, and the other says that they ought first to inquire further. Here, presumably, the disagreement occurs *within one context*, so no contextualist resolution of the disagreement—'both sides are speaking truth'—could plausibly be offered. If we nonetheless insist on thinking of the disagreement as about what the correct answer ought to be to the philosopher's question of whether they *know* that such and such, we find ourselves in the, to my mind,

either do not know on what basis the knowledge claim was made, or know the basis but for some reason are unable to assess it, then they most definitely are not in a position to answer the philosopher's question of whether the knowledge claim was true or false.

In inviting us to intuit, in the face of examples of the sort we are here discussing, whether his protagonists know that such and such, or whether and under what conditions it would be true to say that they know that such and such, the philosopher is placing *us* in a rather artificial and peculiar context—one that is crucially different from the sorts of contexts that people in the sorts of situations he depicts in his examples would be in. For, wishing to isolate what is needed for knowing that such and such *beyond* the obtaining of such and such (knowledge is 'factive'),[34] *the philosopher assures us, his readers, that such and such.*[35] Coming from the author of the example, this assurance is as good as, in our world, an assurance from God would be. It is not the sort of assurance that anyone in situations of the sort we are here discussing can reasonably expect, or be expected, to have.

There is therefore no doubt in *our* mind that such and such, as we turn to consider whether one of the protagonists knows, or may truly be said to know, that such and such. This makes our context similar to the sorts of contexts we discussed in the *previous* section. But as we saw, in *those* sorts of contexts people who wonder whether someone else knows, or may truly be said to know, that such and such, do not normally ask whether that person has good enough assurances as to such and such, or whether he has discharged or eliminated all (of the relevant) doubts as to such and such. *This* question would normally arise in the sorts of contexts that we are discussing in *this* section. But people in *these* sorts of contexts do not and cannot have the kind of assurance as to such and such that *we* have, as the readers of the example. *They* can do no more, and therefore *need* do no more, than be reasonable (responsible, thoughtful, careful, not silly or outrageous . . .) enough for all intents and purposes, in giving others assurances, and in responding to (accepting, challenging, rejecting, assessing, criticizing . . .) assurances given by others. The competent employment of 'know that' and its cognates can come, and therefore need come, to no more than this in such situations.

---

manifestly undesirable situation of being committed to saying that one of the two disputants is answering the question incorrectly, and is saying something false. If this is how philosophy is to weigh in on everyday practical disputes, it should not expect everyday disputants to take what it has to say as of any relevance to them.

[34] And beyond the putative knower's taking it ('outright believing') that such and such.

[35] It is an essential feature of the whole appeal to examples in contemporary theorizing about knowing that such and such that the reader is told by the author that such and such (that the bank will be open the next morning, that the animal that looks like a zebra happens to be a real zebra and not a painted mule, that what appears to be a barn happens to really be a barn, and so on).

5. Scepticism and the dialectic of (semantically pure) 'knowledge'

The discussion of the previous two sections was not meant to provide anything like an exhaustive survey, or even a representative sample, of the different uses of 'know that' and its cognates. Unlike Austin (1975: 123), I do not believe in the prophylactic usefulness of such surveys, or lists. Like Wittgenstein, I believe that our employment of our words is complex and open-ended, that there is no telling in advance where philosophical difficulties might arise, and that reminders of 'what we should say when' and what the significance would be of saying this or that under various circumstances are therefore most effectively assembled when assembled for 'a particular purpose' (Wittgenstein 1963: §127)—in response to some particular philosophical difficulty. I therefore took my cues from the very examples that contextualists have used in arguing for their position.

Both the contextualist and the traditionalist (anti-contextualist) have been pressing in their inquiry a particular form of question—'Does N *know* that such and such?', or, alternatively, 'Would it be true for so and so (who may be N himself) to say of N, "He *knows* that such and such"?' This form of question, I've argued, *as either the traditionalist or the contextualist thinks of it*, does not naturally belong in the very situations on which the two parties have tended to focus. More precisely, in the first sort of contexts that we discussed, the question of truth and falsity does arise naturally, but what it comes to— what competently answering it and assessing answers to it involve and require—is importantly different from what both the traditionalist and the contextualist would have us expect; in the second sort of contexts the question of truth and falsity normally does not arise at all.

It might be objected, 'But surely you can't deny that we do at least sometimes wish to know whether someone who assures us that such and such *knows* that such and such, in the philosopher's sense of having proper assurances as to such and such. For example, the president tells us that a foreign country has weapons of mass destruction, and we wish to know whether this is something he really does *know*. For if it is, then, *perhaps*, he is justified in taking the country to war, and perhaps would be wrong not to; but if he does not know this, then he would not be justified in starting a war before more decisive information has been gathered.'

I have not denied that questions that might look or sound just like the philosopher's question could naturally arise in everyday contexts. My underlying point has rather been this: When competently raised, everyday questions concerning someone's knowledge of this or that *have a point*—they are expressive in one way or another of some particular interest in that person and his epistemic (or other) relation to such and such. Austin's way of putting this point is to say that everyday questions are expressive of and answerable to the participants' 'intents and purposes'. In competently going about answering everyday questions, or trying to, and in assessing answers to them, we are beholden to their point and are guided by it. And no such point is present when we are invited by the philosopher to intuit whether the protagonist of his example knows, or whether it would be true for so and so to say of her that she knows. All that ordinarily and normally guides us in answering everyday questions has methodologically been removed, and we are left with nothing but the depicted case and some familiar words to which we are invited to respond ('Does he or doesn't he know?', 'Did he say something true or something false in saying he knew?'). It is no wonder that a *seemingly* everyday question that would ordinarily and normally not puzzle us at all, comes to seem so mysterious and intractable when we do philosophy. It is no wonder that it has seemed to philosophers that they have nothing but *intuition* to go on in answering the philosophical question. I do not suppose that anyone would find nearly as compelling the idea that she goes on nothing but intuition when, in the everyday, she says or finds that someone does or does not know something.[36]

What is it exactly that we wish to know about the president? (I initially assume that the war has not yet taken place and that it has not yet been established beyond any reasonable doubt that the other country did not have weapons of mass destruction.) Do we wish to know whether he has been lying to us, or to the people, or at any rate has grossly misrepresented the information he's got in his eagerness to go to war? These are good questions; and we know, at least in principle, how one might go about trying to answer them. But they are not the philosopher's question. Do we wish to know whether the president has credible and strong enough indications—a good enough basis for his claim—that the other country has weapons of mass destruction, whether he is justified in telling us (he knows) this? These are the sorts of questions on which Austin would have us focus; and they can fully be answered at the level of what competence and reasonableness (responsibility, etc.) require, without invoking the assessment in terms of true and false applications of 'know that'.

For many years now, however, the philosophical investigation of our concepts has proceeded precisely from the idea that what competently (reasonably, responsibly . . .) going on with our words ordinarily and normally involves and requires is too unclear, and unsystematic, to reliably reveal the contours of our concepts. In particular, it has widely been maintained that an appeal to ordinary and normal practice that is not informed by a *theory* is bound to lead us to confuse 'semantics' and 'pragmatics'.[37] That in the case of philosophically treacherous words or concepts such as 'knowing that' what philosophers have tended to think of as belonging to semantics *can* philosophically fruitfully and safely be separated from what they have tended to think of as belonging to pragmatics, is something that has often been insisted on by the critics of Austin and other ordinary language philosophers, but to the best of my knowledge never shown. For all we know, we may have nothing better to go by in attempting to

---

[36] In Baz (forthcoming a) and Baz (forthcoming b) I discuss in much more detail the recent debate about the appeal to 'intuitions' in philosophy.

[37] This was Searle's contention (1999: 131). It has since been repeated by many. See, for example, Burge (1992: 13), and Soames (2003: 30, 123, 146).

become clearer with respect to these concepts than Austinian appeals to normal and competent practice.

Following Austin's procedures does not mean being barred from drawing in our conceptual investigations any number of useful distinctions among the various things we know in knowing how to go on competently with the words in question—for example between saying something and merely implicating it, or between speaking nonsense and merely saying something inappropriate. One does not have to rely on the traditional categories of semantics and pragmatics in order to usefully draw such distinctions. But the distinctions we draw ought to really be useful, as opposed to obstructive, and this may not be something that we could know about them in advance and independently of the particular matter at hand. Our knowledge of how to go on competently with the words, as opposed to theoretical commitments and presuppositions, should in any case be the last court of appeal.[38] For remember that at least very many philosophical difficulties owe whatever sense and appeal they have to theoretical presuppositions—for example, to the presupposition that what philosophers have commonly thought of as belonging to semantics and what they have commonly thought of as belonging to pragmatics may in every case philosophically fruitfully and safely be separated, theoretically speaking.

Contemporary contextualism, in questioning the presumed clear-cut separation of semantics from pragmatics, constitutes an important step toward an acknowledgement of the truth of ordinary language philosophy as exemplified by Austin's procedures. But it is not enough just to question the separation of semantics and pragmatics, as these two categories have traditionally been understood. The traditional categories themselves need to be questioned.

Go back one last time to the president. If his basis is inadequate (or non-existent), then he definitely should not have told us that (he knew) the other country had weapons of mass destruction. He would also not be justified in going to war, if the only or main reason for doing so is the alleged possession by the other country of such weapons. An Austinian assessment can tell us this much. Imagine, however, that it turns out that the president does actually have credible indications that the other country has weapons of mass destruction: a top secret letter has been intercepted that details quantities and locations, one of our spies has managed to get into one of the facilities and saw the weapons with his own eyes, one of their top scientists defected and told us, the leader of the other country was shown on national TV visiting a facility and examining the weapons, etc. It would seem that we do, and that the president does, have all of the information anyone could reasonably ask for under the circumstances

---

[38]   When I speak of our knowledge of how to go on competently with the words I mean to include in this not only our ability to carry on in everyday discourse, but also our ability to expand the reaches of our words when the need (poetic, philosophical, scientific, or other) and proper occasion arise. For this reason, I do not take what I say in the text to be in tension with Austin's saying that ordinary language, while it ought to be 'the first word' in philosophy, is 'not the last word' (1979: 185).

and given present intents and purposes. The Austinian assessment has run its course, let us assume. There is still the question of whether the president would be justified (responsible, wise) in going to war, or perhaps even wrong (irresponsible, cowardly, foolish) not to do this; but surely, we shouldn't expect a philosophical account of knowledge to answer *these* questions for us. What more could we philosophically usefully ask about the case, and in particular about the president's epistemic relation to the (alleged) presence of weapons of mass destruction in the other country?

The envisaged answer here, coming respectively from the traditionalist and the contextualist, is that we may, and should, still ask this: Does the president *know*? Has he been saying something *true* in saying he '*knows*'? It is in pressing these questions from a purely theoretical perspective that we open the door to all of the seemingly intractable problems with which contemporary theorizing about knowledge has been plagued. For mightn't the seemingly solid evidence have been misinterpreted? Can we, or the president, trust the experts on this? Mightn't the evidence have been fabricated or misrepresented by people in the military who are eager to go to war, or alternatively by enemies of the current regime in the other country? (See Lewis 1996: 549.) In the case of more mundane claims to know that such and such, one does not have to stretch one's imagination nearly as far in order to come up with 'un-discharged' ways in which such and such might fail to obtain, despite all that we know or reasonably take for granted. This seemingly undeniable fact—that the world may sometimes outstrip our wildest imagination, not to mention our reasonable expectations—has forced the traditionalist to opt either for fallibilism, which seems wrong of our concept of knowing that, coupled with anti-scepticism, which often seems merely dogmatic, or else for infallibilism and its attendant scepticism (Lewis 1996: 550).

Austin's way of handling such seemingly weighty matters will again seem to both the traditionalist and the contextualist to be fudging over important distinctions. For, once again, he seems to suppose that these sorts of issues can fully be disposed of at the level of what competently going on with the words involves and requires—the level of what we ought and ought not to *say*:

'When you know you can't be wrong' is perfectly good sense. You are prohibited from saying 'I know it is so, but I may be wrong', just as you are prohibited from saying 'I promise I will, but I may fail'. If you are aware you may be mistaken, you ought not to say you know, just as, if you are aware you may break your word, you have no business to promise. But of course, being aware that you may be mistaken doesn't mean merely being aware that you are a fallible human being: it means that you have some concrete reason to suppose that you may be mistaken in this case. (1979: 98)

'But', both the traditionalist and the contextualist are likely to protest, 'isn't there more that needs to be said here? Beyond the question of what we ought and ought not to *say*, which may lead us to run together "semantic" and "pragmatic" considerations that ought to be carefully kept apart, isn't there the fundamental question of truth and falsity? Indeed, isn't it the case that we ought not to say we know if we are aware we may be mistaken, *because* if we said it we would be saying something *false*?'

The contextualist wants not to evade these questions, as Austin would seem to him to do, but rather to address them head on. So he says: 'Better fallibilism than scepticism; but it would be better if we could dodge the choice' (Lewis, 1996: 550). And he tells us how we can do this: Supposing that the other country does have weapons of mass destruction, we could infallibly know this, if only we could have a way of somehow *semantically legitimately* (as opposed to merely pragmatically legitimately) disregarding the above seemingly farfetched scenarios. And he offers us the liberating formula: It may be that in the president's (or our) context, the above scenarios do not constitute *real* doubts, or *relevant* alternatives, and therefore need not be discharged or eliminated by the president in order for him to truly say he knows. Not only reasonableness, but *truth* itself, does not require these possibilities' discharge or elimination.

But what sort of infallibilism is this? For all we know, and however seemingly farfetched, couldn't one of the above scenarios turn out to be actual, and couldn't it further turn out that the president could not reasonably or justly be faulted for having failed to suspect that things might so turn out? Simply to insist that this couldn't happen would seem merely dogmatic. If you agree with Austin's general approach, you could respond to this by saying something like 'We would then not know what to say', or 'What would you have said [if you were in our place, or if you were the president and had the (purported) information he had]?', or 'Who would have thought?!', or 'How could he, or we, have known?!' (see 1979: 88).[39] After all, we ourselves had presumably found the president's basis satisfying and his claim justified.

For the contextualist, however, this sort of response would not be good enough. For surely, semantically (or metaphysically) speaking, if one of those scenarios turned out to be actual, it would show that the president had not known, wouldn't it? However *justified* the president would still be in having *said* he knew, however *unjustified* anyone would be who faulted him for having said it, he still would have said something false. The contextualist is looking for a theoretically more satisfying response to the challenge from 'farfetched' possibilities—a response that would account for the seemingly undeniable semantic fact that, if such a possibility turned out to be actual, it would reveal that the president had said something false in saying he knew.

The first part of the contextualist response to the invocation of 'sceptical scenarios' would be put by Lewis roughly as follows: 'Now that *you* have raised the possibility of such outlandish scenarios, they have become relevant in *this* context, and so, in the context that you have now enacted, they must have been eliminated by the president, if, in *this* context, he is to truly be said to have known' (see 1996: 559). This, according to Lewis, is what makes knowledge elusive: do some epistemology (or be paranoiac), consider incredible scenarios, and you'll thereby make it so that there'll be very little

---

[39] The Austin quotations are taken from a context that's not exactly like our present one. But I do not think I am unfaithful to their spirit in the use that I make of them here.

you or others could truly be said to know; but only in those contexts that are sufficiently affected or shaped by *your* worries and concerns. Travis and most other contextualists would not be happy with this part of Lewis' response. Most contextualists would want to allow that alternatives may legitimately count as irrelevant, or mere, even if they *are* attended to—perhaps on the ground that there is no good reason to attend to them (other than sheer philosophical playfulness, or thick-headedness), or on the ground that their negation is 'pragmatically presupposed' in the context of assessment (Blome-Tillman 2009). For Travis, scepticism just is 'incorrect', and remains so even in the study (1989: 187).[40] For most other contextualists, scepticism is true in the study, but, pace Lewis, not because the mere 'attending' to a possibility automatically makes it relevant; rather, the epistemologist's traditional concerns and the nature of his inquiry are supposed to somehow turn possibilities that outside the study would normally be irrelevant into relevant possibilities.

But now, what if no one raised (or considered, or unreasonably failed to consider) the possibility of any sceptical scenario in the original context in which the president's words were assessed, but it *now* turns out that the documents *were in fact* fabricated and that there were no weapons of mass destruction? Here Lewis and Travis give essentially the same answer. Lewis simply says that 'the possibility that actually obtains is never properly ignored' (1996: 554), and then adds that a possibility that 'saliently resembles actuality' may not properly be ignored either (1996: 557). Travis puts the idea this way: 'If there are facts to make this a case of F's not obtaining, then for any claim that A knows that F (or, equivalently, any occasion for judging whether A knows that F), there are some facts which show some doubt to be real for that claim or on that occasion which A has not discharged' (1989: 162). In this way, Lewis and Travis build the so called 'factivity' of knowledge (If you know that such and such, then such and such) and its infallibility (If you know, you (somehow epistemically) can't be wrong) into their account of what makes alternatives (or doubts) relevant (or real). If you turn out to have been wrong in taking it (and asserting) that such and such, or, as in Gettier cases, if you turn out to have been right only by some sort of luck (the documents were fabricated, but there were nonetheless weapons of mass destruction), then you simply did not know—in whichever context of evaluation—and it would therefore have been false, in *any* context, to say of you that you knew. For all that, we may still 'know a lot' (Lewis 1996: 549), and in many ordinary contexts may truly be said to know many things.

It is not at all clear that this account would, or indeed should, satisfy the sceptic. For it seems to amount to the claim that, on the assumption that the 'relevant alternatives'

---

[40] Travis' considered position is actually not that scepticism is incorrect, but that it is nonsensical—that the sceptic, in saying that we don't, or can't, know this or that, does not so much as succeed in saying something that may either be correct or incorrect (see Travis 1991). In this, as well as in other respects, Travis is closer to the perspective developed in this paper than other so-called contextualists. For reasons that should be clear by now, however, I find Travis' account of the sceptic's failure to make sense in attempting to state his position ultimately unsatisfying. I discuss Travis' treatment of scepticism in detail in Baz (2008).

theorist of knowledge—be he a contextualist or a non-contextualist—is right about the semantics of 'know' and cognates, many of our everyday 'knowledge ascriptions' *may* be true; but we do not and cannot (truly be said to) *know* them to be true. Only God could (truly be said to) *know* that some finite and fallible creature knows that such and such. For *we* do not and cannot (truly be said to) know that none of the sceptical alternatives that have not been ruled out by the putative knower (or her evidence, or experience, or what have you) either is actual or resembles actuality too closely. We therefore do not and cannot (truly be said to) know that none of those un-eliminated sceptical alternatives to such and such's obtaining would be relevant, in every context, for deciding whether someone knows that such and such. But *that*, presumably, is something we must know in order to know that someone knows that such and such. The actual ruling out or elimination of all sceptical alternatives may not, perhaps, be needed for knowledge; but it seems still to be needed for the knowledge of knowledge. The 'relevant alternatives' account of knowledge—in either its contextualist or non-contextualist version—is therefore bound to seem to the sceptic as, at best, a roundabout way of acknowledging the truth of his position, an attempt to dispose of a genuine and serious difficulty by playing with words (this point is made by Sosa 2000).

At the other end of the field, anti-sceptical anti-contextualists also have not found the contextualist account satisfying. Once you allow that over and above the question of what commitments we take upon ourselves, or may reasonably be taken to have taken upon ourselves, in 'assertorically' saying this or that in this or that context, there is *always* the further question of truth and falsity,[41] you open the door for people to dismiss all of the contextualist's data on the grounds that they pertain to the level of 'speaker's meaning', as opposed to 'sentence (or word) meaning'. Once it is allowed that the speech act of raising, or answering, the question of truth and falsity is itself beholden to nothing but, well, *THE TRUTH*, and carries no commitments other than theoretical ones, it becomes hard to say what's wrong with a theory that tells us when 'know(s) that' truly applies, context *in*sensitively, and then explains away seemingly recalcitrant intuitions by appealing to complex extra-semantic factors. The anti-contextualist will argue that contextualism too is not free of counter-intuitive implications.[42]

---

[41] Again, I do not say that assessment of utterances in terms of truth and falsity is never in place. Of course it sometimes is in place—otherwise we would not have these words, and concepts. My point is just that we should keep this form of assessment to its natural, proper, places.

[42] The literature is full of examples that purport to establish the counter-intuitive commitments of either side to the debate. Witness here Hawthorne (2004), who says, in the course of arguing for his 'subject sensitive invariantist' (anti-contextualist) theory of knowledge, as the most plausible account of the so called 'lottery paradox': 'This is not to say, of course, that there are no counterintuitive consequences to this version of sensitive invariantism. As far as I can see, every candidate story about our puzzle has counterintuitive results' (162). On the contextualist side, Cohen (2005) similarly acknowledges: 'Inevitably the conflict between contextualism and [Subject Sensitive Invariantism] will come down to which view has greater intuitive costs. And no doubt contextualism does have intuitive costs, despite my best attempts to mitigate them' (207).

6. A concluding remark

It is hard to see how the current state of affairs in the debate between contextualists and anti-contextualists with respect to knowledge can be described as anything but a stalemate—a stalemate that seems to me to bespeak a crisis of philosophical paradigm. The former have relied heavily on examples of supposedly everyday situations and utterances that were designed to elicit certain intuitions from us concerning whether it would be true for someone to say of someone, N, 'N knows that such and such'. The latter have either questioned or outright denied the intuitions, or their robustness (see Bach 2005: 62); or accepted them but then tried to explain them away by attributing them to various pragmatic or psychological—and so presumably semantically irrelevant—factors;[43] or accepted them but then tried to show that they (can) support a theory other than contextualism;[44] or else have altogether denied the relevance of those intuitions, and indeed of anything having to do with how we (ought to) use our words, to the age-old philosophical quest for an understanding of *knowledge*.[45] Various other kinds of moves, on both sides, such as appeals to the theoretical advantages or disadvantages of either position,[46] or to ways in which 'know' and its cognates compare in their functioning to other words,[47] have been, at best, indecisive. I do not say that all of the arguments on both sides have been equally compelling, and it should be clear by now that, on the whole, I take the contextualist to be closer to the truth than the anti-contextualist. I also think, however, that it is not clear what *could* possibly bring this ongoing dispute, in its present terms, to an end.

---

[43] For a trenchant 'invariantist' criticism of contextualism, one which questions the contextualist's general reliance on intuitions, and discounts the intuitions on which contextualists centrally rely as revelatory not of the truth value of 'knowledge attributions', but rather of nothing more than 'our willingness to make [a knowledge attribution] and the audience's willingness to accept it', see Bach (2005). Similar objections to the contextualist argument can be found in Feldman (1999), Rysiew (2001) and (2007), Williamson (2005b), and Brown (2005).

[44] Showing that the intuitions on which contextualists rely can be accounted for by a sophisticated invariantist, who appeals to the difference between knowing a fact and knowing that you know it, and knowing that you know that you know it, and so on, and to the different types of utterance (and action) each of those warrants, is one of the aims of Williamson (2005b). For a different kind of sophisticated invariantist counter-interpretation of the contextualist's data, one that appeals to varying extra-epistemic features of the *putative knower's* context, see Hawthorne (2004) and Stanley (2005).

[45] Sosa (2000) charges the contextualist position in epistemology with committing the fallacy of inferring an answer to a philosophical question from information about the correct use of the words in its formulation. Hazlett similarly argues—by appealing to examples that are supposed to show the 'non-factivity' of our ordinary concept of 'knowing that such and such'—that 'traditional epistemology and ordinary language epistemology [. . .] would both be best served by going their separate ways' (2010: 522).

[46] In particular, there has been quite a lot of controversy about how satisfying the contextualist's understanding and handling of scepticism—which contextualists have often presented as an attractive feature of their theory (cf. DeRose 1995 and Cohen 1998, 1999)—really is. See, for example, Feldman (1999, 2001) and Wright (2005).

[47] See Stanley (2004) and Ludlow's (2005) cautious and subtle response on behalf of contextualism to criticisms such as Stanley's. I must say that I cannot see why 'know' and cognates cannot be, to a significant extent, *sui generis* in their properties and behavior, even if not in their superficial grammar.

The way out of the dispute, I have argued, is to give up the assumption that it ought to be possible for us just to apply our words to cases even without doing any work with them in doing that, and that the application should then always be assessable in terms of truth and falsity. Philosophical problems about knowledge, Travis argues following Wittgenstein, arise when 'language goes on a holiday' (1991: 246). Travis is thinking primarily about scepticism here. I basically agree. Getting us to suppose that it ought to be possible for us just to apply 'know that' or one of its cognates to any pair of person and fact apart from any context of significant use has been the crucial move in the sceptic's, but not just the sceptic's, conjuring trick. I have tried to show, however, that at least in the case of 'know that' and cognates the contextualist's semantic ascent, as found for example in Travis, is not enough for bringing the words of our philosophizing all the way back to the language-games that are their natural, 'original home' (Wittgenstein 1963: §116). It is therefore not enough for saving us from difficulties for which not the meaning of the word (or concept) under investigation is responsible, but a conception of language that encourages ill-founded expectations of what the meaning of a word *must* be, and do. If we are to find our way out of those difficulties, 'true' and 'false' will also need to be brought back to the language-games that are their original home.[48]

Bibliography

Austin, J. L. (1975), *How to Do Things with Words*, 2nd ed., Urmson, J. O., Sbisà, M. (eds.), Oxford: Clarendon Press.
—— (1979), *Philosophical Papers*, 3rd ed., Urmson, J. O., Warnock, G. J. (eds.), Oxford: Oxford University Press.
Bach, K. (2005), 'The Emperor New "Knows"', in Preyer and Peter, pp. 51–90.
Baz, A. (2008), 'The Reaches of Words', *International Journal of Philosophical Studies* 16: 31–56.
—— (2009), 'Who Knows?', *European Journal of Philosophy* 17: 201–23.
—— (forthcoming a), 'Must Philosophers Rely on Intuitions?', *Journal of Philosophy*.
—— (forthcoming b), *When Words are Called for*, Cambridge, MA: Harvard University Press.
Blome-Tillmann, M. (2009), 'Knowledge and Presuppositions', *Mind* 118: 241–94.
Brady, M., Pritchard D. (2005), 'Epistemological Contextualism: Problems and Prospects', *Philosophical Quarterly* 55: 161–71.
Brown, J. (2005), 'Adapt or Die: The Death of Invariantism?', *Philosophical Quarterly* 55: 264–85.
Burge, T. (1992), 'Philosophy of Language and Mind: 1950–1990', *Philosophical Review* 101: 3–51.
Cappelen, H., Lepore, E. (2005), *Insensitive Semantics*, Malden, MA: Blackwell Publishing.
Cavell, S. (1979), *The Claim of Reason*, Oxford: Oxford University Press.

---

[48] I wish to thank Jody Azzouni, Nancy Bauer, James Conant, Juliet Floyd, Warren Goldfarb, Kelly Jolley, Gary Kemp, Michael Kremer, Jean-Philippe Narboux, Mark Richard, Thomas Ricketts, Peter Sullivan, Charles Travis, and the Editors, for helpful responses—critical, encouraging, or both—to earlier versions of this chapter. This chapter owes a great deal to Stanley Cavell's work.

Cohen, S. (1998), 'Contextualist Solutions to Epistemological Problems: Scepticism, Gettier, and the Lottery', *Australasian Journal of Philosophy* 76: 289–306.

—— (1999), 'Contextualism, Skepticism, and the Structure of Reasons', *Philosophical Perspectives* 13: 57–89.

—— (2005), 'Knowledge, Speaker, and Subject', *Philosophical Quarterly* 55: 199–212.

Craig, E. (1990), *Knowledge and the State of Nature: An Essay in Conceptual Synthesis*, Oxford: Oxford University Press.

DeRose, K. (1992), 'Contextualism and Knowledge Attributions', *Philosophy and Phenomenological Research* 52: 913–29.

—— (1995), 'Solving the Skeptical Problem', *Philosophical Review* 104: 1–52.

—— (2002), 'Assertion, Knowledge, and Context', *Philosophical Review* 111: 167–203.

Fantl, J., McGrath, M. (2002), 'Evidence, Pragmatics, and Justification', *Philosophical Review* 111: 67–94.

Feldman, R. (1999), 'Contextualism and Skepticism', *Philosophical Perspectives* 33: 91–114.

—— (2001), 'Skeptical Problems, Contextualist Solutions', *Philosophical Studies* 103: 61–85.

Gendler T., Hawthorne, J. (2005), 'The Real Guide to Fake Barns', *Philosophical Studies* 124: 331–52.

Glock, H. J. (1996), 'Abusing Use', *Dialectica* 50: 205–23.

Grice, P. (1989), 'Logic and Conversation', in *Studies in the Way of Words*, Cambridge, MA: Harvard University Press.

Hanfling, O. (2000), *Philosophy and Ordinary Language: The Bent and Genius of our Tongue*, London: Routledge.

Hawthorne, J. (2004), *Knowledge and Lotteries*, Oxford: Oxford University Press.

—— Stanley, J. (2008), 'Knowledge and Action', *Journal of Philosophy* 105: 571–90.

Hazlett, A. (2010), ' The Myth of Factive Verbs', *Philosophy and Phenomenological Research* 80: 497–522.

Kant, I. (1998), *Critique of Pure Reason*, Guyer, P., Wood, A. (eds. and trans.), Cambridge: Cambridge University Press.

—— (2000), *Critique of the Power of Judgment*, Guyer, P. (ed.), Guyer, P., Mathews, E. (trans.), Cambridge: Cambridge University Press.

Lewis, D. (1983), 'Scorekeeping in a Language Game', *Philosophical Papers*, vol. 1, Oxford: Oxford University Press, pp. 33–49.

—— (1996), 'Elusive Knowledge', *Australasian Journal of Philosophy* 74: 549–67.

Ludlow, P. (2005), 'Contextualism and the New Linguistic Turn in Epistemology', in Preyer and Peter, pp. 11–50.

Millar, A. (2005), 'Travis' Sense of Occasion', *Philosophical Quarterly* 55: 337–42.

Preyer, G., Peter, G. (eds.) (2005), *Contextualism in Philosophy. Knowledge, Meaning, Truth*, Oxford: Oxford University Press.

Recanati, F. (2004), *Literal Meaning*, Cambridge: Cambridge University Press.

Rysiew, P. (2001), 'The Context-Sensitivity of Knowledge Attributions', *Noûs* 35: 477–514.

—— (2007), 'Speaking of Knowing', *Noûs*, 41: 627–62.

Schaffer, J. (2004), 'From Contextualism to Contrastivism', *Philosophical Studies* 119: 73–103.

—— (2005), 'What Shifts? Thresholds, Standards, or Alternatives?', in Preyer and Peter, pp. 115–30.

Schaffer, J. (2006), 'The Irrelevance of the Subject: Against Subject Sensitive Invariantism', *Philosophical Studies* 127: 87–107.

Searle, J. (1968), 'Austin on Locutionary and Illocutionary Acts', *Philosophical Review* 77: 405–24.

—— (1978), 'Literal Meaning', *Erkenntnis* 13: 207–24.

—— (1999), *Speech Acts*, Cambridge: Cambridge University Press.

Soames, S. (2003), *Philosophical Analysis in the 20th Century, Volume 2: The Age of Meaning*, Princeton: Princeton University Press.

Sosa, E. (2000), 'Skepticism and Contextualism', *Philosophical Issues* 10: 1–18.

Stanley, J. (2004), 'On the Linguistic Basis for Contextualism', *Philosophical Studies* 119: 119–46.

—— (2005), *Knowledge and Practical Interests*, Oxford: Oxford University Press.

Strawson, P. (1950), 'Truth', *Proceedings of the Aristotelian Society,* Supplementary Volume 24: 129–30.

Travis, C. (1989), *The Uses of Sense*, Oxford: Oxford University Press.

—— (1991), 'Annals of Analysis', *Mind*, 100: 237–64.

—— (1997), 'Pragmatics', in Hale, B., Wright, C. (eds.), *A Companion to the Philosophy of Language*. Oxford: Blackwell.

—— (2005), 'A Sense of Occasion', *Philosophical Quarterly* 55: 286–314.

Warnock, G. J. (1983), 'Claims to Knowledge', in *Morality and Language*, Totowa, NJ: Barnes and Noble.

Williamson, T. (2000), *Knowledge and its Limits*, Oxford: Oxford University Press.

—— (2005a), 'Knowledge, Context, and the Agent's Point of View', in Preyer and Peter, pp. 91–114.

—— (2005b), 'Contextualism, Subject-Sensitive Invariantism and Knowledge of Knowledge', *Philosophical Quarterly* 55: 213–35.

Wittgenstein, L. (1963), *Philosophical Investigations*, G. E. M. Anscombe (trans.), Oxford: Basil Blackwell.

—— (1969), *On Certainty*, Anscombe, G. E. M., Wright, G. H. von (eds.), Paul, Denis, Anscombe, G. E. M. (trans.), New York: Harper and Row.

Wright, C. (2005), 'Contextualism and Scepticism: Even-Handedness, Factivity, and Surreptitiously Raising Standards', *Philosophical Quarterly* 55: 236–62.

7

Truth and Merit

Charles Travis

The traditional 'statement' is an abstraction, an ideal, and so is its traditional truth or falsity.   (Austin 1975: 148)

The thought which we express in the Pythagorean theorem is timelessly true, independent of whether anyone held it true. Like a planet which already interacted with other planets before anyone had seen it, it is not true for the first time after its discovery.   (Frege 1918: 69)

Frege and Austin present two deep and compelling, but starkly contrasting, pictures of truth. One must, it may seem, choose. *Perhaps* it would so seem to the authors. But there is no choosing between *insights*. We need to see how to fit together what each has right. I aim to say how. I will first set out three elements in Frege's picture, then three elements in Austin's. I will then look for the context in which truth is to be treated in Frege's way, and that in which it calls for Austin's treatment. We can then see both as true pictures of one phenomenon.

1.1. Invisibility

'Invisible' is here shorthand for invisible, intangible, inaudible, etc. It refers to what is not, even in an instance, as geometrically, or acoustically, or physically, some certain way; moreover, what need not be—and in the cases at hand is not—so much as apt for having instances. The letter A is, geometrically, a certain way. So is an instance of it—*this* letter A on the billboard. The thought that time is now short is not geometrically any way. Nor does it have instances—even if there are instances of someone thinking it.

The invisible, on present use, is thus opposed to what we might call, still on a slightly stretched use, 'the perceivable'. Frege starts on his point about the perceivable as follows:

One finds truth predicated of pictures, presentations (ideas), sentences and thoughts. It is striking that here visible and audible things occur together with items which cannot be perceived by the senses. This indicates that shifts have occurred in its sense. Indeed! So is a picture, as pure visible, tangible, thing really true? And a stone, a leaf, not true? Clearly one wouldn't call the picture true if an intention did not attach to it. The picture is *meant* to represent something. (1918: 59)

Imagine Monet painting Rouen Cathedral. Consider the canvas he produced: one covered in a certain way with paint. If it is to be true or false, there must be a way things are according to it. For sake of argument, suppose that there needs to be a way Rouen Cathedral is according to it. What way? There is a region of the canvas which is rather like an image of a stone wall with flying buttress attached. Positioned within that region is a patch of blue paint. Such a canvas *could* be an image of a stone wall with a patch of blue stone in it, or of a stone wall defaced by a crude graffito. Or an image of a stone wall with shadow cast on it in late morning light. *If* the canvas further represents Rouen Cathedral as being as thus depicted, then there would be different things it would be for Rouen Cathedral to be as represented, depending on what it is that blue patch depicts: on how it does its representing, thus how it represents the cathedral to be. Paint patterns cannot teach us how a canvas represents things. If they needed to fix that, there would be no way a canvas depicted things. Thus it is that the painting, considered as mere painted canvas, represents nothing as so. Hence no question as to the truth yet arises.

What, to begin, must we add to a painting to make it depict something as so—e.g. Rouen Cathedral as looking thus and so (or thus and so on a certain occasion, or at a certain time of day, or after a planned remodelling). Frege's answer is: an intention. The painting is meant to depict *in* a certain way, thereby what it depicts (Rouen Cathedral) *as* a certain way. 'Intention' can stand in for whatever exactly plays the role an intention thus might. What matters is that the painting is to be taken in a certain way. This may be because the artist meant it so to be taken. Or there may be a more complex story to tell.

Intentions are always liable to leave issues undecided. In the painting, a saint's effigy above the entrance is depicted as blue. The effigy has blue projected on it by lasers at certain times of day. There is an understanding of it being as thus depicted on which, thanks to the lasers, it is that, and another on which the lasers merely make it look that way. If that is how things are, then how the painting is to be taken is liable to leave it undecided whether things are as thus depicted. The intention was to depict the effigy as blue. Whether it is as *thus* depicted depends on what you count as an effigy being blue. There may be no further intention towards the depicting which decides what one *ought* to count for purposes of being as thus intended to depict.

One attitude towards raising a question of truth would be that one has not done this if truth is liable to depend on whether things were represented as this way or that, and nothing about the would-be representation decides in which way it in fact represented things. But one need not take such an attitude. If I represented an effigy as blue, whether it is as represented *could* depend on what you count as an effigy being blue. But then again, it may not. There *may* be a question of truth which is decided by just that much as to how I represented things. We *could* thus think of me as having raised a question of truth. If it so happens that truth is not decided by this much (an odd effigy, as in the case of the laser), then the question I raised happens to have no answer. So, as it happens, my representation is neither true nor false.

One *might* resist the idea that a representation of something as so could be in that position. Perhaps Frege wanted to. But one need not. And he need not have. There is a difference between a canvas with no intention attaching to it, and one with an intention attaching to represent things in such-and-such way, where that intention *may* prove inadequate to decide whether things are as represented. There is a difference between a Delvaux fantasy, say, and a painting of a flying buttress where there turns out to be just a clever fake. Still, one *could* insist that truth has not come into question unless the representation is such that the world could not but make it either true, or, at worst, false. To ask whether Frege insisted on this is to adumbrate the topic of the last section of this essay.

So it is by an intention attaching to it—or what does the work an intention would— that a picture represents in a certain way, and thus things as a certain way. It is thus at least by means of an intention (or its like) that a representation raises a question of truth, namely, whether representing in *that* way is representing truly. An intention—that things be represented thus and so—is, in some sense invisible, even if someone's holding an intention need not be. That things be represented thus and so is not a visible, tangible, thing. What matters about this? For Frege, it is the intention itself— thus, an invisible thing—which raises the question of truth. This is not to say that the intention need be intelligible, or need determine the question of truth it does, independent of visible things. An intention attaching to a painting may be that it should represent the colour of the wall in this way: the colour of the paint in the image of the wall should *be* the colour of the wall (this being an idea which, of course, admits of understandings). Or, again, it should be the colour a photo would have if made with such-and-such film and such-and-such colour filter, at such-and-such hour. Then how the painting represents the wall, given that it is so to be taken, depends on how the artist mixed his paints when making that image. If he chose pigment badly, then, with that intention attaching to the picture, he misrepresented it, even if the colour of the image is not what he meant it to be.

On Frege's view, though, only the invisible *can* raise a question of truth. What he has in mind here emerges in a further discussion of invisibility. Considering an objection to the view that it is the invisible which raises questions of truth, he says,

But don't we see that the sun has set? And don't we thus also see that this is true? That the sun has set is no object which emits rays which arrive in my eyes, is no visible thing like the sun itself. We *recognize* it as true that the sun has set on the basis of sense impressions. (1918: 61, italics mine. See also 2001/1897: 53)

That the sun has set is a circumstance which now obtains. It does not represent anything as so. *A fortiori* it requires neither an intention nor anything else to fix a *way* it represents things. But that the sun has set bears on representing: if it has, then there is a particular way to represent things which will be representing truly. Such is the fact one captures in saying that it is true that the sun has set. Frege insists that, in a sense in which the sun itself (or its afterglow) is visible, that it has set is not.

A distinction can help us understand this point. I begin with a related one, crucial for Frege. He speaks of an *object* falling under what *he* calls 'a concept' as the fundamental logical relation. (See 2001/1892–5: 25.) As he speaks of it, a concept is a function from (sequences of) objects to truth-values. Fundamental as this relation is for logic, another underlies it which is fundamental for our cognitive engagement with the world, notably, in judging. Suppose we so speak that the function *being empty* is the one which maps precisely the empty things into the value true. If a function is what a function does—is known by what it maps into what—which function holds this title? That depends on how things are. If the way my cup is—its being as it is—is a cup being empty, then it is a function which maps my cup into the true; if not, not.

Judging is engaging with the world precisely so as to be right or wrong about it according to how it is. A thought is the content of a judgement. It is, that is, a particular way of making one's fate—being right or wrong—depend on how the world is. It decides how the way things are *matters* to thus being right or wrong; how the world is to speak to that. It does that in fixing when things being as they are would be one's being right. The thought is that things are such that *p*; one is right just where things being as they are *is* things being such that *p*. The role of the thought is to fix when this would be.

Departing from Frege, we might think of a concept as intrinsically of a way for an object, or sequence of them, to be—of being wooden, or square, or an iguana, say. For a given concept to be the one it is, on this way of thinking, would be for it to be *of* the way it is. So any concept is the concept of being an iguana just in case it is of being an iguana. There is, then, that way which a given concept is of. What this way is fixes when something (or some sequence of things) would count as being that way—when, say, something would count as an iguana, or as wooden. The way some things are— their being as they are—is, *inter alia*, something being an iguana, or wooden. The way other things are is not something being that. What is that way might still be if it were different in some ways. If Sid gives Pia an iguana for Christmas, it is still an iguana after it comes to belong to her. It would still be if she dyed it puce. Anything different from it in other ways—as that orange is, say—would not be an iguana. So what way for a thing to be being an iguana is fixes that range of cases of something being as it is which would be something being an iguana, and that range which would be something not being one. So, in particular, it fixes which actual cases of things being as they are are ones of those things being iguanas. So it fixes which concept in Frege's sense—which function from objects to truth-values—is, in fact, the concept *iguana* (in Frege's sense). Had things been other than they are, it would still fix which concept in Frege's sense would be the concept of an iguana. But that might turn out to be a different concept. For different things might turn out to be the iguanas were the world different enough.

A concept in our present sense thus, as Frege says of a thought, 'always contains something which reaches out beyond the particular case, by which this is presented to consciousness as falling under something general' (2001/1882: 23, *Kernsatz* 4). The particular case is presented as belonging to a *range* of possible cases. The concept in this sense thus has a particular sort of generality which concepts in Frege's sense lack (though they are general in other senses). By this particular sort of generality that attaches to it, it does what concepts in Frege's sense cannot. It imposes that demand on title, satisfaction of which qualifies some one of Frege's concepts as the concept *iguana*, say, and satisfaction of which would have qualified other Fregean concepts for that title had the world been suitably different.

It is time to note two uses, or senses, of 'thing'. It may be a count noun. Or it may bear, as I will call it, a catholic reading. If there are, on the first use, ways for a thing to be, there is, on the second, ways for things to be, where it is inept to ask 'Which ones?'—as it would be if I said, 'Things have been slow around here lately.' If being wooden is a way for a box to be, then that box being wooden is a way for things (catholic use) to be. If we speak so that, for every way for things to be, there is its concept, then in addition to the concept of something being an iguana—a way for an object to be, so a one-place concept—there is also the concept of that iguana sunning itself. It is satisfied, as what it is of is instanced, not by some object or other being as it is, but rather by *things* (catholic use) being as they are. So we might call it a zero-place concept. So speaking underlines its having *just* that particular sort of generality that marks positive place concepts. So it is apt for the same roles in identifying the way a given judging is hostage to the world—with the obvious difference that the lot of positive-place concepts is to play sub-roles in the role which, so speaking, a zero-place concept plays. The generality in question belongs, for Frege, to a thought. If we think of a thought as, for example, the thought of that iguana sunning itself, then a zero-place concept just is a thought. If we think of the thought as *that* the iguana is sunning itself, then the thought is of a zero-place concept as satisfied.

Another feature goes with the above sort of generality. A way for things to be, as we are now conceiving this, is, for anything that is that way, a way there would still be, and which would still be identifiable, even if that things were not just the way it is. Had that sunning iguana, startled, hidden under the rock, there would remain, for all that, such a thing as something being an iguana sunning, and nothing would change in what mattered to being one; in when something's being as it was *was* its being an iguana. One could still have thoughts as to one thing or another being precisely *that*. *Mutatis mutandis* for zero-place concepts, once recognized. I will take these two features, to identify what I will call the conceptual.

What contrasts with the conceptual is that which instances what concepts, on present use, are concepts of. That iguana's being as it is just *is* something sunning itself. Things being as they are just is that iguana sunning. Things being as they are admits no range of instances. It fixes no distinction between what matters, or would, and what does (would) not, in how things are, or were (subjunctively, or in the past) to being *it*.

If we were to speak of mattering at all here, *everything* matters to being it—as everything matters, too, to some object, or sequence of them, being just as it is. So, too, one could not have thought of things as precisely what they in fact are had things not been precisely as they in fact are. No way one could then think things would qualify as that: there would then have been no such thing as qualifying. Something being as an object (that iguana, say) is, is not, on present understanding, a way *for* a thing to be; things being as they are not a way for *things* to be. Such things lack the marks of the conceptual, in present sense. I will call them *non-conceptual*.

One might, perhaps, speak of recognizing how things are, perhaps even of recognizing things being as they are. One may also recognize that an iguana is sunning on that rock. But there is a great gulf between these two sorts of recognition. Recognizing how things are is, if anything, just being aware (well enough) of how things are. It is such things as awareness of the iguana, sunning. Recognizing that there is an iguana sunning on that rock is, as Frege insists, recognizing things being as they are as an iguana sunning on that rock; recognizing the way things are as instancing a certain generality, of that particular sort that marks the conceptual. It is recognizing the place of actual circumstances in that range of cases which would be ones of an iguana sunning. This was the point of Frege's remark about the setting sun. It is the distinction he had in mind when, in a similar remark, he says that if we speak of seeing 'that this flower has five petals [...] we mean by that something connected with thought and judging' (2001/1897: 53). We recognize the way that flower is as a flower having five petals. We can factor that generality out of its being as it is. We recognize the flower, being as it is, as connecting to the conceptual in a particular way; as what would (so does) satisfy a certain concept. Frege goes on to suggest a non-perceptual understanding of 'see that' in such cases; the same sort of non-perceptual understanding it bears in 'I see that the banks have decided to undermine the pound'.

The main point, for *present* purposes, of speaking of concepts as per above, and thus stressing the distinction between the non-conceptual and the conceptual as this does, is that very much of Frege's and Austin's concerns with truth are about how the non-conceptual relates to the conceptual. Where they do differ, it is precisely here that the difference lies. The above is not only a good way of framing Frege's concerns, but an even better way of framing a comparison between these two.

Frege concludes his case for the invisibility of what 'brings truth into question at all' with this:

Without meaning to give a definition, I call thoughts something for which truth can come in question at all. [...] The thought, non-perceivable in itself, clothes itself in the vestments of a sentence and is thus graspable. We say, the sentence expresses a thought.

The thought is something non-perceivable, and all perceptually observable things are excluded from the domain of that for which truth can come into question at all. (1918: 60–61)

A thought, as he also tells us, is marked by that special sort of generality which is the mark of the conceptual. So it is the conceptual which 'brings truth into question at all'.

And it is what is invisible, in the present sense, which does this: a sort of generality; a demand on membership in a range by which certain ranges of cases belong to it—recognizably so, but not in a sense of recognition, if there is one, in which it is a *perceptual* accomplishment—mere awareness of what is, visibly, there.

The generality of the conceptual might *attach* to visible, tangible things. I pass a sign which reads, 'Vous n'avez pas la priorité.' In French this says: you do not have right of way. I feel accordingly belittled. That French sentence is a visible thing. There is a certain way it is written. It is the, or an, expression in French of a certain concept: that of one not having right of way. That instance of it I just passed surely expresses the concept of one who then passes it not then (or at the impending roundabout) having the right of way. I am sure that the French traffic code makes more explicit the understanding on which I do not have this.

The generality attaching to the sign is not a visible thing. Frege also tells us that the sign, being visible, is 'excluded from the domain of things for which truth can come into question at all'. I do not think Frege means to tell us that signs (*panneaux*) are not the sorts of things which can state truth or falsehood. Rather, the idea would be: a *panneau* does so only in attaching to (expressing) something *invisible* which raises the question it raises. Knowing which question of truth is raised is knowing which invisible bearer of truth raises it. There is thus a certain priority attaching to the invisible in matters of truth.

There is this much reason. A visible truth-bearer, such as the *panneau*, is identifiable as the truth-bearer, it is independent of identifying the question of truth it raises; that is, independent of identifying just that generality of the conceptual which belongs to what the sign expresses, so *what* question of truth is raised. Which means that, in principle, just what generality attaches to the question the sign raises is negotiable. One may ask just how the sign ought to be taken, in particular, whether this or that instance of things being as they are belongs to the range of cases which would be ones of things being as the sign says. The answer to the question one thus raises is liable to depend on all sorts of factors—e.g. on what the reasonable French driver would be prepared to recognize as instancing the generality properly taken to attach to that sign. Whereas an invisible bit of the conceptual is identified as the bit it is by nothing other than that generality which in fact is its (and, perhaps, its relations to other bits of the conceptual, also so identified). So, it may seem, what generality *it* has can depend on nothing. Which one *could* take to mean: for any candidate for instancing it (for bearing the fundamental logical relation to it), whether that candidate does instance it can depend on nothing other than the candidate being the candidate it is, and that bit of the conceptual being the bit it is. So whether a *thought* is true can depend on none of those factors which *may* bear on whether something visible or audible expressed what is, in fact, truth.

Monet's canvas is meant to show how Rouen Cathedral looks. Neither the canvas nor its looking as it does shows how to go from it to instances of things (or of the Cathedral) so looking. That depends on how the canvas is to be taken as representing—not itself something visible. This banal point models a more general one about the non-conceptual. If the sun has just set, then things being as they now are, a bit of the non-conceptual, instances the sun just having set, a bit of the conceptual. That bit of the non-conceptual, things being as they are, does not show us how to get to those bits of the conceptual it instances—to, for example, the sun just having set. It does not decide anything as to what else would be an instance, even given the fact that *it* is one. For that we need, so to speak, a technique for classifying things as instances or not, a way in which things being as they were would matter to their instancing, or not, the sun just having set. To see that the sun has just set is to recognize in things being as they are what matters to this; so to be sensitive to what thus does matter. A technique of classifying, what *matters* to classifying in one way or another—that certain way of looking beyond the particular case which belongs to this bit of the conceptual, *the sun just having set*, is not something visible. It is what is thus invisible that raises questions of truth. The first part of Frege's discourse ends here.

1.2. Identity under predication

The second point of Frege's I will consider here is that predicating truth of a thought does not yield a thought with a different content, hence does not yield a new thought. I express this, somewhat picturesquely, as: truth is identity under predication. Frege expresses the idea this way:

> One can anyway observe that we cannot recognize a property of a thing without at the same time finding the thought that this thing has that property true. So for each property of a thing there is a connected property of a thought, namely, that of truth. It is also noteworthy that the sentence, 'I smell the scent of violets', has, clearly, the same content as the sentence 'It is true that I smell the scent of violets.' So it seems that nothing is added to the thought by attaching the property of truth to it. (1918: 61)

Nothing is added to a thought by predicating truth of it. This is not because truth is somehow an insubstantial notion, or not a condition for a thought to be in (though Frege flirts with that idea). Rather, the stated reason for it here is that to recognize a property of a thing is already to be thinking of truth—of the thought that that thing has that property as *true*. Truth enters the picture, so to speak, at the ground level. We think of it in thinking of anything as so—for example, in thinking that the sun has set. If I now try to inject it anew into the picture by mentioning its being true that the sun has set, I assign truth no role that it did not play already. So I add nothing new to the thought in question. This is to say nothing as to how rich the role was which truth played already.

The underlying point here is about judging (though one can think of things as a certain way without taking them to be so). Judging is, as Frege tells us, exposing oneself to risk of error. (In 'Der Gedanke', this is in two stages: first, 'by the step with which I win myself an environment I expose myself to risk of error' (1918: 73.) Second, to judge is to judge of an environment.) In judgement, what *one* may think of—what one may think to instance such-and-such—is the limit of what there is for anyone to judge of (where there is no one one must be to do what *one* might do). This, and this alone, holds sway over whether one has succumbed to, or escaped, any error risked in judging. One *judges* only what others might. The ways one may judge things to be are only those others can. Which is so just where others, too, can take that which in fact instances those ways, or which instances things being otherwise, to do so. Only against this background can it be a mark of the sway of *things* that someone judges correctly only where anyone who so judged would.

Truth is that particular correctness for which judging is eligible. This eligibility is the mark of judgement. To judge, Frege tells us, is to pursue the goal truth. Pursuit here takes a special form. If I play poker, I play to win. To do that, I play the odds: raise or fold, depending on what I think my chances are. Whatever I do, I thus reckon with the possibility that it was not, in fact, the winning move. If I judge that the sun has set then, of course, as a rational person, I recognize that there is such a thing as my turning out to be wrong about this. It is just in that sense that in judging I inevitably expose myself to risk of error. But suppose that, as with the poker, I see myself as perhaps holding, perhaps not, the winning hand: it might turn out that the sun has set, or, again, it might not. To see myself in that way is *per se* not to judge—to take it to be so—that the sun has set. It is to take it to be so that the sun might have set, or might not have. So to judge that the sun has set is to see myself as with the winning hand, in a way that I need not see myself in seeing and raising you in poker. It is to see *so* judging as the only thing which, as to what I judge of, would be, for me, pursuing the goal truth. So to judge that the sun has set is *ipso facto* to see my so judging (myself in doing so) as judging truly. So to judge that the sun has set, and further, that this is true, would be redundant. This is Frege's underlying point.

That truth is thus an identity under predication can be formulated in seductive, and possibly misleading, ways. One *can* capture the idea in saying things of the form, 'It is true that the sun has set iff the sun has set.' One thus exploits a feature of normal discourse. Those two instances of 'the sun has set' demand to be read as saying the same thing of the sun, or, more generally, to speak of the same way for things to be. Where I say how things must be for it to be true that the sun has set, I speak of that very way for things to be which I judge them in judging that the sun has set, so which I mention in speaking of its being true so to judge. Formulas of this form, read as thus mentioning twice just one way for things to be, express truisms. This speaks in favour of no form of insubstantiality of truth. This shows up in one way where we speak of the truth of what someone said on some occasion in speaking of the sun having set where what he said is not what *we* would in speaking in those terms. When my friend in Sydney texts me, 'The sun has set', I would be unlikely to express truth in saying, 'What he said is true iff the sun has set.' One might ask when, in *such* a case, I should take him to have expressed truth. But this adumbrates Austin.

1.3. Definability

The third element I will note in Frege's picture is the (supposed) indefinability of truth. The main part of the argument is as follows:

Truth admits no more or less. Or perhaps it does? Can one not establish that truth consists in the occurrence of a correspondence in a certain respect? But in which? What would we then need to do to decide if something was true? We would need to investigate whether it was true that—say, an idea and something real—corresponded in the relevant respect. And with that we would face a question of the same kind, and the game could begin anew. This attempt to explain truth as a correspondence thus fails. And so too would any other attempt to define truth. For in a definition one presents certain characteristics of truth. And in applying them to a particular case it would always be a matter of whether it was true that these characteristics occurred. So one would turn in circles. (1918: 60)

I take this point out of order. Frege argues for it in the midst of his case for invisibility, before broaching the idea of truth as identity under predication. But I think one cannot see the point of Frege's argument (if argument it is) without first having on board the idea of truth as identity under predication. For the point is: definability of truth (as Frege conceives this) clashes with this feature.

There are two notable oddities in Frege's argument. First, if Frege wants to make a case that truth is indefinable, one would expect him to do it for things which bring truth into question, hence might be true—so, for him, invisible things. Instead, Frege considers defining the truth of a picture, or an idea (something which presents things as thus and so). These are precisely things he thinks do not bring truth into question, so cannot be true or false—unless their truth is just that of some invisible item attaching to them. One might, for example, call a statement (an *Aussage*) true iff it expresses a true thought. But then one *has* defined a statement's truth in terms of a thought's. What one needs to see is why one cannot say, in other terms, what it is for something to be true, where its truth is *not* a matter of the truth of something else. One *might* best do this by reference to something whose truth is not that.

The second oddity is the way Frege concludes this argument. He says: 'From this it is probable that the content of the word "true" is entirely singular and indefinable' (1918: 60). It could only be sarcasm if I produced for you a standard proof of the Pythagorean theorem and concluded it with, 'This makes it highly probable that the square of the hypotenuse is the sum of the square of the other sides.' For Frege, of all people, this is a strange way to conclude a *proof*. One can only conclude that he did not think he had one.

In any event, the definability of truth seems to clash with its status as identity under predication. Conversely, that truth *is* such an identity, is a case against *some* forms of definition. Consider this maxim: Whatever you hear three times is true★. Take that as a definition. Now consider the thought that the sun has set. This thought is hostage to a particular aspect of the way the world is: whether the sun has set. Now consider the thought that it is true★ that the sun has set. This thought is also hostage to a particular aspect of how things are: by the definition, to whether you have heard three times that the sun has set. But then this can hardly be the same thought as the thought that the sun has set. So truth★ is not an identity under predication.

One might generalize: suppose that for something (of the right sort) to be true is for it to be F. The thought that the sun has set remains hostage to the world in the way described above. The thought that it is true that the sun has set, by contrast, is hostage to whether the thought that the sun has set is F. As above, these being two different things for one's fate to turn on, these must be two different thoughts.

The thought that the sun has set and the thought that it is true that it has are one for this reason. To be a thought is to be the content of some judgement. To be a given thought is to fix how one is exposed to error in some given judgement there is for one to make. To be the thought that the sun has set is to fix that particular way of thus exposing oneself. But to judge *anything* is to see oneself as, so to speak, holding the winning hand in a game of being hostage to the world; as judging what one *must* to achieve the goal *truth* in the matter at hand. Things not being as one *thus* sees them is already part of the risk one runs in standing towards the sun's having set as one does in judging it to have. So the thought that one holds the winning hand—that one achieves truth in so judging—fixes no new way of exposing oneself to error; no way one was not exposed already merely in judging the sun to have set. So it is no new content for a judgement to have. So it is no new thought.

So the above argument breaks down wherever one substitutes for 'F' something which is part of what it *is* for something to be true; which is, accordingly, such that, whatever thought one judges, one *ipso facto* exposes oneself to the risk of error if that thought is not that way. The laws of truth (logic), Frege tells us (1918: 59), unfold the content of the concept truth. For a thought to be true is for it to be what it must to fall under a concept with that content. It is, for example, to have a negation, and for all of its negations to be false. But to judge it is already to treat it as fitting that bill.

Truth *is* indefinable in this sense. It could not be defined in terms of what one did not need to grasp already to be judging at all. It could not be defined in a way that might inform one who did not already grasp what truth was. Judging truly is holding a winning hand in a certain kind of game. But one cannot know what this comes to except in knowing what truth is. Truth could not be reduced to something else. What could? In truth's case, given its special role in judging, one could not get so far as an attempt.

Frege ends his discussion of identity under predication as follows:

The meaning of the word 'true' appears to be entirely singular. Might we here have to do with something which cannot be called a property in the usual sense at all? Despite this doubt I will for the present, following usual usage, express myself as though truth were a property, until something more suitable is found. (1918: 61–2)

One cannot, Frege tells us, take any thing to have any property without thereby taking a certain thought to be true. So truth, if a property, is an unusual one. Being an identity under predication is unusual. Still, in taking the sun to have set I must *take* a certain thought to *be* true—a definite way for a thought to be, or not; a definite sort of success for a thought to enjoy. What more need a property be?

2.1. History

The starkest contrast between Frege and Austin on truth is their choice of what 'brings truth into question at all'. For Frege this is something invisible. It is that generality of the conceptual embodied in some particular identifiable bit of it—a thought, in his terms, or a zero-place concept in mine. For Austin it is an historical event, or something produced in one; an exemplary case of something visible and tangible in our present sense. For Austin, it is a statement so conceived, as for Frege it is a thought, which brings truth into question:

A statement is made and its making is an historic event, the utterance by a certain speaker or writer of certain words (a sentence) to an audience with reference to an historic situation, event or what not. (1979: 119–20)

What truth is is then seen in what it would be to state truly; or, again, for what one said in speaking to be what is true. Truth is brought into question by someone stating something.

Now it need not be that what was said is identifiable independent of what it would be for its sayer thus to have spoken truth. It need not be that, anyway, the speaker said things to be such-and-such way; now the question is whether *that* is true—whether things *are* that way. *What* way things were said to be may depend on what speaking truly in speaking as, and when, this speaker spoke would be. This locates an *apparent* stark contrast with Frege. For Frege, if words are (an *Aussage* is) true, that is because they (it) expressed such-and-such thought, where that thought is true. If, as Frege suggests, truth reduces to the truth of a thought, then which thought the *Aussage* expressed does not depend on what truth is. It is not as if expressing one thought rather than another is part of the *Aussage*'s satisfying *truth*'s demands. Austin's shifted perspective thus leaves room at the outset for an interesting new idea.

In the central case, Austin means, in speaking of a 'statement', to speak of 'the historic use of a sentence by an utterer'. But, as he himself recognizes, 'statement' has other good uses too. To avoid ambiguity, I will use the inelegant nominalization 'stating' when I mean to speak of what Austin thus takes as this central case.

For Frege, truth comes in a package with a kind of attitude: what he calls *judging*. It is that success to which judging is uniquely liable. Some linguistic activity is also liable to such success. But it is the attitude which is fundamental to understanding what truth is. For Austin there is *something* fundamental about communication; or at least something fundamental about what truth is which it takes that case to make perspicuous.

In judging something so I represent things to myself as thus and so. This does not require, as communication does, something identifiable anyway, other than by its representing—say, by a geometric, or acoustic, form—which *is to be taken* in one way or another. (Nor *could* it be thus effected.) One might call representing to myself *autorepresenting*, and communicating *allorepresenting*. For Frege autorepresenting has a central role in truth in way that allorepresenting does not. It is the reverse for Austin. One might expect this to be a very fundamental difference between them as to what truth is. But, as I will argue, the difference can be considerably slighter than it first seems.

Frege and Austin differ in their choice of central case. Neither denies that there are others. Austin lists some others as follows:

I suggest that the following are the primary forms of expression:
It is true (to say) that the cat is on the mat.
That statement (of his, etc.) is true.
The statement that the cat is on the mat is true. (1979: 118)

If it is true to say that the cat is on the mat, this is not just about what it is true for so-and-so to do on such-and-such occasion. (Further, what it is true to say it is also true to judge.) That the cat is on the mat may be stated by different people on different occasions. (A sentence 'may be used on two occasions or by two persons in making the *same* statement' (1979: 120).) But for Austin, such uses of 'true' are to be understood in terms of what he chooses as the central case, just as for Frege other uses of 'true' are to be understood in terms of his candidate for centrality. The next section will be dedicated to seeing just how such less central cases look given Austin's choice for centrality.

The contrast between Frege and Austin must lie in the *point* of each one's choice of central case. Austin states the point of his choice most clearly as follows:

If you just take a bunch of sentences [...] impeccably formulated in some language or other, there can be no question of sorting them out into those that are true and those that are false; for [...] the question of truth and falsehood does not turn only on what a sentence *is*, nor yet on what it *means*, but on, speaking very broadly, the circumstances in which it is uttered. (1962: 110)

How do questions of truth depend on circumstance? What someone said on an occasion is true just in case things are as he thus said them to be. Suppose he said, 'There is red meat on the white rug', speaking of the rug in Pia's salon, at a given time, using all words to mean (speak of) what they do speak of in English. He thus spoke of there then being red meat on that rug, and of that as the way things were. Which *might* make one think that whether he thus spoke truth turns precisely on whether there was then red meat on that rug.

So let us set about so settling it. Returning from marketing, Sid crosses the white rug, heading for the kitchen. As he does so, the bottom of his recycled-paper bag breaks, and the kidneys he has bought for the mixed grill fall in their butcher paper to the rug. Is there, now, red meat on the white rug? One question is whether kidneys count as meat. Though one would not offer them to vegetarians, their usual rubric (at any rate, in Sid's parts) is *offal*. Meat, on one understanding of the term, is flesh. And flesh, as one typically would understand that, is muscle. Thinking in this way, one should say that, however unenviable the condition of the rug, it does not, at any rate, have meat on it. On the other hand, what Sid dropped is, in fact, the meat course for Sunday brunch. So meat *can* be understood to be something which those kidneys are. Then there is the matter of being on the rug. The meat is still wrapped in its butcher paper. So, on one way of understanding things, it is (so far) only the paper that is on the rug. On the other hand, if Sid, now missing the kidneys, asks where they are, telling him, 'On the rug', *may* be saying no less than *where they are*.

How, then, *should* we settle the question whether there is meat on the rug? There *could* be an answer to that question. But there need not be. As I now speak (in this essay) nothing dictates counting kidneys as meat, nor counting their place in the surroundings as being on the rug. What it is to be meat, and to be on a rug, does not as such determine any one right answer. So if there is an answer, the circumstances in which to give it must play some role in fixing what that answer is. The present circumstances of this essay highlight that fact precisely by failing to do so.

But, if there is no unique right answer to the question whether the situation at hand counts as there being meat on the rug, there *can* be a unique right answer to the question whether things are as Pia said in so describing it. *That* is the point of historicism. Pia, noticing the ruined eco-bag, says, 'Sid, there's meat on the rug.' What now matters is not how *we* should settle the question whether there is meat on the rug, but rather how that question ought to be settled in the circumstances of Pia's speaking to it. Pia does so in particular circumstances which, unlike those of this essay, may call for an answer. Pia is, say, chiding Sid for being oblivious to the quotidian. In which case, kidneys may well do for meat, being wrapped in paper will do for being on the rug. That is how to answer the question in her circumstances. It is *that* fact, rather than how the question is to be answered in ours, which determines whether she spoke truth.

What our words speak of—being meat, being on a rug—admits of understandings. There are different things being on a rug may, sometimes rightly, be taken to be; each with its own results for when things would be that way. Thus for *all* the ways for things to be our words speak of. Do I speak truth in saying that the cat is on the mat if its paws are off it? For a start, what would be the point (if any) of my saying so now, in these circumstances? With no answers to such questions, there is no answer to this one. What it is as such to be on a mat provides none. Circumstances must matter if there is to be either truth or falsehood to tell in so speaking. So history matters. The historical event of my saying such-and-such to be such-and-such way may be my saying what is true, or it may be my saying what is false. But we must refer to history—to what I was doing in speaking as I did—to see whether it is the one or the other (or neither).

We begin to get at that deeper possibility which Austin's shift in perspective makes room for. I described the cat as on the mat. What did I thus say to be so? Something so if its paws hang off? Or something not so in that case? Well, for what ought *I*, in so speaking, be held responsible? What treatment of the world is licensed if *my* words are true? I am held responsible for what *ought* to be demanded for speaking truly, in my circumstances, in describing things in the terms I did. What I said to be so is thus fixed (in part) by what speaking truly (then) would be. Just what Austin foresees.

The point's present linguistic cast *could* make one underestimate it. Frege suggests, in passing, that some things which appear as closed sentences may really be open ones:

Often [...] the mere form of words which can be fixed by writing or the phonograph is insufficient for the expression of the thought. [...] If the present tense is used to indicate a time, one needs to know when the sentence was uttered in order to grasp the thought correctly. [...] In all such cases, the mere string of words, as is fixed in writing, is not the complete expression of the thought, but to grasp it correctly one still needs knowledge of certain circumstances accompanying its speaking. (1918: 64)

The English string of words, 'The cat is on the mat', say, might be an open sentence, closed by reference to time: one made by the speaking of it, and *to* that speaking's time. So the English predicate, '__ is on the mat' is really a two-place predicate, true or false of an object such as a cat, and a time. Other predicates, on their surface, mere one, or two (or etc.) ones, may actually have many more places to be filled by times, places, speakers, indicated objects, and so on. Frege's suggestion shows that Austin's underlying point should really be understood as about open sentences. Let an English open sentence—say, '__ is on the rug'—have n places to be filled, for any n you like. So it is true, or false, of n-tuples of given sorts—an object, a time, a place, what have you. It thus speaks of a way for such an n-tuple to be. Then Austin's point is: the way it thus speaks of admits of understandings. There are various things it may be understood to be for an object to be on a rug at a time, for it to be on a rug at a time at a place, if that is relevant, for it to be on a rug at a time relative to any other set of parameters you think relevant. It is ways for n-tuples to be, or those our words speak of, which, intrinsically, admit of understandings.

The underlying point can take non-linguistic form. Frege tells us (in my terms) that a zero-place concept, and equally for any n, has a generality which looks out in a particular way beyond the particular case: for any concept there is a *range* of cases which would be ones of being that which the concept is a concept of. This is just to say: if it is a concept that is in question at all, then there is a determinate way things being as they are (or a thing being as it is) is to *matter* to the concept's being satisfied. For it to be a concept of a way *for* things to be, not *everything* can matter. Things need not be *just* as they are to be that way. What Frege calls a 'concept' is a function from (n-tuples of) objects to truth-values. But seeing such a function as what captures a particular generality of (an element of) a thought can mislead.

Suppose, on different usage, we take a concept to be identifiable by that which it is a concept of—some determinate way for things to be. Then Austin's point takes this form. A concept does, as Frege tells us, look beyond the particular case in some particular, determinate, way. But that way of looking outward leaves it negotiable which particular cases are to be classified within the range of cases of satisfying that concept (instancing the relevant way for things to be). The proper outcome of such negotiation is fixed by circumstances for engaging in it, or for treating one or another outcome as proper. Whether the cat's being as it is is its being on the mat may depend on the circumstances in which, or the point for which, one is to treat it as that or not. If the generality of a thought-element (say, of something being on a mat) were captured by some function from objects to truth-values, then the cat, being as it is, must map onto the value true, or not, full stop. (Though such a function could no more capture it than it could that of a whole thought (say, that the cat is on the mat).) Whereas for Austin, it may *count*, or be to be counted, as a case of something being on the mat for some purposes, on some occasions, but not so count on others. If a concept is intrinsically one *of* being thus and so, then the link between concepts and what satisfies them is, Austin holds, *via* such a notion of counting, in given circumstances, as such-and-such, rather than just being *tout court*. Concepts, if they look beyond the particular case as Austin says they do in the zero-place case (a thought, or what *it* is of— the cat being on the mat), cannot be identified by any function from objects to truth-values (even if, for particular purposes, they may be treated as so identifiable).

This last point brings out the deep sense in which, for Austin, truth is an historical matter, and the deep change which Austin's change of perspective brings with it. Frege's argument for the invisibility of what raises questions of truth was, as I have read it, primarily a case for bringing the conceptual into the picture: no truth except of the conceptual (by its standing, I have argued, towards the non-conceptual)—an abstraction from the simple idea: no truth without representation. Nothing in Austin challenges *that* idea. For Frege, though, that idea appears to go with an ahistorical view of what being true is. For Austin, such ahistoricism obscures crucial aspects of what truth is. The difference comes out neatly in the above contrast between the views of each towards the way in which the conceptual looks out beyond the particular case. Austin's departure from Frege, such as it is, is elaborated within the framework Frege himself provides.

2.2. Ahistorical truth

We have now dealt with Austin's central case. In my saying something to be so, the words I use invoke a particular bit of the conceptual. To just what cases—what bits of the non-conceptual—this bit of the conceptual reaches *so used* depends on the circumstances of its invocation. These decide for what work, in them, that bit of the conceptual ought to be held responsible; what is to be expected if it has *here* been deployed *truly*. They thereby decided (where it is decided) whether *this* (things being as they are) is any other than things are according to the invocation; any other than for what was invoked to do the work expected of it. What of other cases of truth-bearing?

What, for a start, would it be true to say? Perhaps that the cat is on the mat. This may just mean: it would be true for me, now, to say that cat to be on that mat. What it would now be true to say is what, if now said, would be said truly. Historicism for the central case already tells us when this would be. But if I tell you it is, or would be, true to say that the cat is on the mat, what I say need not be confined to saying something now. I may tell you something it would be true to say *wherever* it might be said, no particular occasion required for the saying. How should that idea be understood?

To identify something it would be true to say, I must invoke some bit of the conceptual, some zero-place concept. If occasions matter as they do on Austin's historicism, one would not always say the same thing to be so in invoking that bit of the conceptual to state something. Nor, more generally, would one always speak of the same thing being so in invoking it—here in mentioning something it would be true to say. I may mention something it would be true to say in invoking the concept of the cat being on the mat. I thus speak of a way which, according to me, it would be true to say things. Things would be the way I say it would be true to say things are just where they would be as said, where I speak, in saying the cat to be on the mat. Historicism has already said where that would be. A zero-place concept need not be deployed assertively in order for the occasion of its deployment to do its work. (A caveat: saying that such-and-such need not always be saying such-and-such to be so. I am concerned here only with understandings on which it is that.)

When, in general, would one say what I thus said it would be true to say? When, in general, would one say things to be the way I thus spoke of? The point of historicism is that one would not always say the same thing to be so in invoking a given bit of the conceptual. In particular, one would not always speak of the way I mentioned in, or by, invoking the concept of the cat being on the mat. Paws off the mat may matter to whether things are the way I so spoke of, but not to whether they are the way you now thus would, or vice-versa. Where one would not speak of the right thing in invoking the concept I did, one would have to say what I said it would be true to say in another way, by invoking some other concept—if this could be said at all. What *other* concept might then do this job?

Austin tells us: 'a state of affairs which makes [a statement] true' can only be specified '*in words* (either the same, or, with luck, others)' (1979: 123). Sometimes the words *must* be others. When may they be? On occasion I may say what I want to say, or at least say to be so what I want to, equally well in different ways. I might say, 'There is meat on the rug', or, archly, 'There are edible animal parts on the carpet.' I can tell you what I think Frege's argument for *Sinn* is in any of several ways. My being right in this conspicuously does not depend on stating it in precisely the way Frege did. Kidneys instance the concept *meat* on some invocations of it, but not on others—on some, but not other, understandings of what being meat might be. So, normally, I could do this only where invoking the concept meat would be invoking it on an understanding on which kidneys would do. Even so, I could not reasonably expect that just *any* (sometimes) conceivable thing which would instance that one zero-place concept (there being meat on the rug) would, *ipso facto*, instance the other (there being edible animal parts on the carpet). Had beasts grown edible fur, things might have instanced the second of these without instancing the first. (That edible fur need not be meat on any plausible understanding of being meat.) So *this* cannot be a condition on there being different ways for me to say the thing I want to, or to say the same thing to be so—on that perfectly good notion of this on which the above may be doing it.

Not everything which would satisfy the concept *rug* (e.g. *moquette*) would satisfy the concept *carpet* (as opposed to *carpeting*). Yet invoking either may be speaking of the same thing—that carpet. Similarly, not everything which satisfied *there being edible animal parts on the carpet* would satisfy *there being meat on the rug*. Yet invoking either may be speaking of the same way things are or not, on that good understanding of speaking of a way things are or not just canvassed. How so?

The conceivability of edible fur, or that just mentioned, need not bear on whether the above two ways of saying something are ways, on an occasion, for me to say the same thing—the thing I wanted to—or the same thing to be so. Why not? To start with, there is a good sense (if it is not more than that) in which, in the circumstances, there being edible fur does not count, is not to be treated, as a way things might be. (The world would belie this if there in fact were edible fur in reasonable proximity.) Edible fur—something on the order of cotton candy—is, I think, conceivable. Genetic engineers may envisage it already for all I know. But it need not, for all that, count as possible.

That thought expands here along these lines. In the circumstances, treating edible fur as what there might be is not the way to guide one's treatment of things. It is not, at least, when it comes to engaging in those projects, or pursuing those aims to which, in the circumstances, I would speak—for whose guidance I am to be held responsible—in saying what I wanted to. This last remark condenses historicism's story of what it is for things being as they are to make for my having spoken truly—said what is true—in invoking, in my circumstances, some particular bit of the conceptual. So if edible fur is not, in the circumstances, to be treated as what there might be, then it does not bear on whether I would then have spoken truly in invoking the one of those above two zero-place concepts just where I would have done so in invoking the other—on that understanding of *just where* relevant to whether I would then count as having spoken of the same thing each time.

Stating something is, as said, offering a guide to treating things. Against this background, stating something in either of the two ways just mentioned may, in the circumstances, be offering the same guide. Against that background, each may say the same—may be to be held responsible for just the same—as to how to treat things. This can just be what it is for these to be two ways for me to say just what I wanted to, and to say the *same* thing to be so.

Suppose, now, that on one occasion I mention something it would be true to say to be so, and on another you are to say just *that* to be so. When would you count as having done so? I mention what I do in invoking the concept *there being meat on the rug*. You say what you do in invoking the concept *there being edible animal parts on the carpet*. Under what conditions would that be a success? The short answer is: just where invoking the first of these concepts on my occasion, and the second on yours, each time in saying something so, would be offering the same guide to treating things: the difference the guide you give makes, on yours, to how things are to be treated matches (nearly enough) the difference the guide given in invoking the concept I did would make to this. If there is meat on the rug, on the understanding on which I spoke of this, then there is urgent call for stain remover. Equally so if there are edible animal parts on the carpet, on the understanding on which you spoke of that. And so on. Along these lines, Austinian historicism makes sense of a notion of saying the same thing, so, too, of the same thing being so, which is both crucial to our cognitive economy and, without historicism, deeply mysterious.

There is one more notable case: that of (thinking) something it would be true to think. Here we deal in things necessarily ahistorical. For, as Frege showed, what *I* may think is what there is for *one* to think: there is no one one must be to think it (nor occasion which is *the* one on which it must be thought). What there is for *one* to think, is, on his view, that *available* for thinkers to agree on, or dispute—though where there would be a case of *such* agreement or disagreement need not be decided independent of some particular occasion for saying so.

To see what truth comes to in this case, we might ask what I say of someone in saying him to believe that such-and-such. In doing this, I mention a thing there is to think. I do so by invoking some zero-place concept—say, that of meat being on the rug. In my invoking of it, I identify a way for things to be, where the circumstances of my invocation contribute to fixing just what way this would be. And I say the person to judge that things are—to take them to be—*that* way. The way I thus identify is the way things would be where there was meat on the rug on the understanding on which, in the circumstances, I spoke of this. It is a way things could be said to be, on my occasion, in speaking of there being meat on the rug, and a way things could be said to be on others—perhaps on mine too—by thus invoking different zero-place concepts. It is not (in general) tied specifically to any given one. As we have just seen, the 'where' in the above 'would be where there was meat on the rug' must be understood accordingly. Historicism, in what has already been said about it, thus tells us what it is that I might say someone to think, and by what its features are fixed.

There is then the matter of someone thinking such a thing. Here we can follow Frege. Judging something, he tells us, is exposing oneself to risk of error. Something there is to think is a particular way of doing this; a particular way for the world to matter to whether one succumbs or escapes. What the thing is is fixed by when, if so exposed, one would succumb, when escape. Any thinker at a time exposes himself to risk of error. He is exposed to the error he is. He sets his course, or is prepared to, as he

does, or is; there are countless ways for him to go awry. He arrives at the lecture hall at
4pm to discover that the lecture was at 3pm, or is in the basement, or is not the lecture
he expected—had he but known, he would have stayed in bed. Such are among the
myriad disappointments a given thinker, at a time, exposes himself to suffering.

For a thinker to think a particular thing there is to think—that things are such-
and-such way—is for his exposure to error to articulate in a particular way; for there to
be a certain discernible pattern in the way he is liable to disappointment, or to escaping
it. (Something there is to think is thus a way for *a thinker's* exposure to error to
articulate, not merely for this or that thinker's exposure to do so.) That a thing to
think (a thought, in Frege's terms) is so identifiable is part of what it is for whole
thoughts, as Frege puts it, to enjoy pride of place (relative to anything that might be an
element in one). (See 1919: 253.) The thought is that things are such-and-such way;
there is a discernible way in which the thinker succumbing to or escaping error turns,
or may turn, on whether things are that way. There is more to the story. One thinks
what is a guide to conducting one's life; to treating things. So for one to think that
such-and-such is for one to be suitably sensitive, in the way one is prepared to conduct
his life, to the distinction between things being the way in question and their not;
sensitive to it in a way such that that distinction can enter rationally into what one is
prepared to do, and how one arrives at such preparedness.

So to credit someone with thinking such-and-such is to credit him with thinking
things such-and-such way, which is to credit him with suitable sensitivity to whether
things are that way. There are many things any of which suitable sensitivity might
sometimes come to. It need not involve, nor is generally confined to, sensitivity to the
instancing of some particular zero-place concept which, on one occasion or another,
might be invoked in *saying* things to be this way. So much is part of the ahistorical
nature of objects of thought. Someone suitably sensitive to the instancing of meat
being on the rug may or may not *thereby* be suitably sensitive to the instancing of edible
animal parts being there, partly depending on how he is, but partly depending on what
would count, for the purpose, as *suitable* sensitivity to this. So if I credit someone with
thinking such-and-such—say, that there is meat on the rug—I credit him with some
such suitable sensitivity; but what exactly I thus say of him depends on the circumstances of my saying it in just the way that what I say of the rug in saying there to be
meat on it does. Historicism speaks here as it speaks throughout.

That meat is on the rug on one understanding of this being so, and that meat is on
the rug on another are, or may be, two different ways for things to be. There are,
accordingly, or may be, two different things for one to think. Sensitivity, moreover
suitable sensitivity, to whether things are the one way *need* not be sensitivity to whether
they are the other. Thinking the one thing and thinking the other are, thus, two
different ways for a thinker to be. This *can* suggest a picture on which what someone
'really' thinks is fixed uniquely, and precisely, just by how *he* is. So a given thinker may
think one, or the other, or both, of the above things according to the precise nature of
his sensitivity to things. Where it may be tempting to apply this picture, historicism has

a reminder for us. What would be thinking such-and-such on some invocations of that concept would not be on others. Thinking such-and-such is something one may count as doing on some occasions for the counting, but not on others. Before looking for that precise understanding of meat being on a rug on which *that* is the way Pia thinks things, one should recall that whether she thinks this on any given such understanding is liable to depend on what one understands by her so doing. Austinian historicism contributes in this way, among others, to our understanding of the mind.

Someone *could* say, 'It is true that there is meat on the rug just in case there is meat on the rug.' If he thus said anything at all, it seems, whatever it was would be true. What could make that right? Just this (if it is so). *One* way for things to be, there being meat on the rug, is mentioned twice, the first time in identifying a way for it would be true to say things to be, the second in identifying the way things would be if it *were* true to say so. Such a double-mention, in the context of *one* statement, will speak of that way for things to be, both times, on the same understanding of things being that way. Where this is so, the upshot is a truism. All of which, we now see, says nothing as to just *what* truism one would express in these words on a given occasion. Such depends on how one ought to understand, on that occasion, meat being on a rug. Which points to why it is that the existence of such truisms has *no* implications as to the richness, or not, the concept truth is.

Is truth identity under predication? The core of that idea was: to judge that there is meat on the rug is already to judge that this is true—that so judging is a winning way of exposing oneself to risk of error. That idea survives historicism. To set out historicism, one needs to say quite a bit as to what it would be to be speaking, or thinking, truly, for something to be true to say, and so on. To say this is just to elaborate what one sees oneself as doing in taking something to be true, or true to say. As I have urged, that idea of identity under predication cuts against saying what it is for something to be true, or done truly, only where what one thus says is *not* part of what this is.

2.3. Merit

Austin's final word on truth is the set of lectures *How To Do Things With Words*. These aim for the demise of two closely related dichotomies (or 'fetishes'): one between that which is either true or false and that which is not; and one between fact and value. The procedure, in both cases, is to exhibit what is in common between evaluations as to truth or falsity and evaluations as to the particular sorts of success or failure, goodness or badness, to which other sorts of things we say—e.g. commendations—are liable. Truth, Austin stresses, calls for the same sorts of virtues as does, say, fitting advice or a just verdict. It, like them, is the sort of thing which is *merited* or not.

The lectures are meant to bring us to see that:

Truth and falsity are [. . .] names for [. . .] a dimension of assessment—how the words stand in respect of satisfactoriness to the facts, events, situations, etc., to which they refer. (1975: 148)

But adequacy to what words represent as so 'depends not merely on [their] meanings [. . .] but on what act you were performing in what circumstances' (1975: 144). Which makes truth and falsity 'a general dimension of being a right or proper thing to say as opposed to a wrong thing, in these circumstances, to this audience, for these purposes, and with these intentions' (1975: 144).

Stating truly may thus prove not a (very) 'different *class* of assessment from arguing soundly, advising well, judging fairly, and blaming justifiably', 'the good reasons [. . .] for stating' not 'so very different from the good reasons [. . .] for [. . .] arguing, warning, and judging' (1975: 141).

When a constative is confronted with the facts, we in fact appraise it in ways involving the employment of a vast array of terms which overlap with those that we use in the appraisal of performatives. (1975: 142)

Thinking of the rug as having meat on it may be a good, or adequate, way to think for the purposes of an occasion. *This* may be the rug being truly so describable. It being true so to describe the rug thus assimilates to it being right to call Sid mean for tipping as he did, or boorish for offering one at all to whom he did.

A fact-value dichotomy collapses because questions of truth do not *contrast* with questions of value as they would have to for the dichotomy in question. Whether it was true for Pia to say there was meat on the rug depends on whether the way the rug was *ought* to be so counted. Such is liable to depend on the value, to us, of counting this as meat being on the rug or not—recognizing it as instancing that way for things to be, where this is *Anerkennung*, and not the pure cognitive achievement which 'Erkennung' speaks of. Frege's fundamental relation is not one that either holds, or fails to hold, *per se*, between the rug in that condition and something having meat on it. Meat being on a rug admits of understandings. One speaks truth in meeting one's responsibilities; those one incurs in purporting to do so (purporting to say how things are). Things must be as one is to be held responsible for their being, given the description one gave of things—is to be held responsible, that is, so far as *truth* is concerned. Truth is, in part, a matter of for what, in the circumstances, one ought to be held responsible.

What speaking truth would be on an occasion is fixed in part by what images are then apt for treating current matters; which, thus, *ought* to be employed. This *ought* resembles that in 'Ought Sid to be deemed rude or merely gauche?' Should I put things by saying that there is meat on the rug? One *could* put it that way if one counted Mary's lamb, for whom we have certain weekend plans, or Sid standing there, his belly full of sirloin, as meat on the rug. There *could* be occasions for so speaking. Is this one? Suppose that, eyeing the doomed lamb, I so speak. Do I thus commit myself to more than is so? I do if counting the lamb as meat is not a sufficiently good way of thinking of meat in the circumstances in which I speak—if, say, all attention is focused on what happened to Sid's steak. Truth—things being as I said—depends both on how the world is *and* on how, in what terms, it is *then* well thought of. The question is which bits of the non-conceptual are to be counted, for this purpose, as instancing this bit of the conceptual. It is a question of *Anerkennung*, where there is *no* question of pure *Erkennung*.

Sid is standing on the rug, belly full of sirloin. Should that count as meat being on the rug? It is, in ways, *like* things which surely would so count. Sid's belly surrounds the sirloin topologically speaking as butcher paper would. We can see how we would have to think of meat being on a rug to think of this as an instance of it. So one sometimes might. Here is a discernible way one *might* fit the non-conceptual to the conceptual— discern ranges of instances. But is this a way to do it in the kitchen, as we begin to search for what has fallen from the broken bag? Are the similarities here helpful, useful? Or is the better course here to exploit the dissimilarities? The concept of meat on a rug does not decide this. This occasion for exploitation must tell us if anything can. It can do so only given what the goal *truth* here demands.

To hold words *satisfactory* for a given situation is not just to hold a view as to how the things described are, but also one as to the right way of thinking of that which the concepts thus expressed are concepts of—e.g. of meat being on a rug. Austin's point is: the right way of thinking of being such-and-such is always the right way for, or on, given occasions for so thinking. Truth is *thus* the name of a general dimension of assessment of the suitability of words both for the specific situations they are used to speak of, *and* for agents who, in the circumstances of their speaking, are to take them in one way or another.

In speaking of there being meat on the rug I commit myself to the *suitability* of a way of thinking of the rug in its current condition. We are all staring at Sid's ruined eco-bag, wondering what happened to the meat. There is nothing on the rug but Mary's lamb. 'There is meat on the rug' is hardly suitable for that. The way the rug is *might* be described, for *some* purposes, as there being meat on it. But not for these. Meat on the rug should not *so* be understood here. It is thanks to such facts that I can speak truth, or falsehood, at all in using this description. If I take myself to be speaking truth in giving it, there are thus two ways I might be wrong. The world might be other than I think. I may be shocked to find no sirloin on the rug. Or I may be wrong as to the sort of rug which, here, is aptly so described. If the first is failure to appreciate the world's condition, the second is failure to appreciate the circumstances in which I speak. Those two different things to be wrong about correspond to two different things to say in using the words in question: that *this* is meat being on a rug; or, given what meat on it would be, that such is the way the rug is.

Which descriptions it would be true to give of things depends on the occasion for the giving. Whether a given instance of saying something is truly describable as speaking truly also so depends. Pia said there to be meat on the rug. Did *she* speak truth? Only if she met the responsibilities she ought to have in so speaking on that occasion; only if she ought to be held responsible for no more than things as they are. What responsibilities were these? The answer to that question, as to any other, is liable to depend on the occasion for giving it. On the rug, Sid has displayed his new work of art: a ribeye in a block of perspex. There may be two ways of viewing the circumstances of Pia's speaking, neither incorrect as such. On one the circumstances demanded more of Pia's speaking truth than the world delivered. On the other they did not. There may then be occasions for viewing things in the first way, while there can be others for viewing things in the second. In the first sort, Pia may truly be said not to have spoken truth; in the second to have done so.

On Austin's view, representing in, or by, descriptions articulates into identifiable sub-tasks: suiting one's way of representing to the work it ought to do on its occasion, and then suiting it to the world it represents as a certain way. Applied to what we say, can truth then be an identity under predication? In judging, truth is at work at ground level. To judge that there is meat on the rug is to see this as what judging *truly* would be. It is, *ipso facto*, to see oneself as doing all that judging truly would be. It is for that reason and no other that judging it to be true that there is meat on the rug is judging no more than what one does in judging there to be meat on the rug. A similar point holds of stating. This, too, is aiming at truth, or so representing oneself. So if to arrive at that goal is to do such-and-such—fit words, say, to the work expected of them—then in stating, say, that there is meat on the rug, one represents oneself as doing that. If one were to *say* oneself to be doing precisely what one thus represents oneself as doing—in, say, saying it now to be true to say that there is meat on the rug—one would thus thereby represent nothing as so that one had not already represented as so in simply saying there to be meat on the rug. So, for the same reason as in judging, if one were to say oneself to be saying *truly* that there was meat on the rug just in case there was meat on the rug, one would state a truism. Which is no sign that there is any less to being true than Austin points to.

Frege tells us,

We express recognition (Anerkennung) of truth in a statement's form. We do not use the word 'true' for this. And even if we do use it, the true assertive force does not lie there, but in the form of the statement, and where this loses its assertive force, the word 'true' cannot restore it. (1918: 63)

We represent ourselves as recognizing *truth* in stating what we do merely in stating what we do. Truth need not be mentioned. If we substitute 'act' for 'form', the point holds on Austin's view. To say there to be meat on the rug, or just to speak of there so being, is to speak of the condition of the rug. Whereas to speak of it being true to describe the rug as having meat on it is to speak of the fate of a particular description. On its face, there are two different topics here. But one says there to be meat on the rug in using a particular description—either of the rug as having meat on it, or some other which would suffer the same fate. In using this description in the act of stating, one represents it as a way of telling truth. Whereas in so representing it by *mentioning* it as a way of speaking truth, one represents what it would thus speak of—the condition of the rug—as what it needs to be for this to *be*, to instance, speaking truly. So one speaks truth in the first of these ways just in case one does in the second—just so long as in both cases one speaks of there being meat on the rug on the same understanding of there so being. For all of which, speaking truth may depend on all those factors Austin calls to our attention.

If I describe the rug as having meat on it, I am right just in case counting the rug's being as it is as its having meat on it is a right way of fitting the non-conceptual to the conceptual on the occasion of my so describing things. If I describe *that there is meat on the rug* as something it would be true to say, I am, again, right on that same condition. If I did both things at once—e.g. in the context of one statement—I would be right in both, or in neither. But suppose I do each thing on a different occasion. I say, 'There is meat on the rug', say, where so counting things is a *wrong* way of fitting the non-conceptual to the conceptual. So I speak falsely. I say, 'It would be true to say that there is meat on the rug', or 'Describing the rug as having meat on it would be speaking truly' on an occasion on which so counting the condition of the rug would be a right way of fitting the non-conceptual to the conceptual. So I speak truly. Does this truth not entail that I spoke truly on that occasion where, as we have said already, I in fact spoke falsely? No. For what I say it would be true to say where I speak of this is not what I did say on the first: what is so according to the one thing is not that which is so according to the other.

I may, on an occasion, say what counts, on some further one as having spoken truly, and on some yet further one as not having done so. But I cannot, on any occasion, count as having done what would have counted as speaking truly on the occasion on which I did it, but which, on this further occasion, does not. For that would be for me to count as having fitted the non-conceptual to the conceptual, on my occasion, in what was then a right way—as it then did count as fitting—while, simultaneously, counting as not having done so. There is no occasion for counting me as having done all that.

Austin's view of truth takes this form. The conceptual—the general—does not alone decide how it relates to the non-conceptual—the particular case. It alone does not decide which pairs, to which it contributes but one member, belong to the extension of that fundamental relation, *instancing*. More positively put, it allows for different ways of allocating particular cases to the ranges of generality it marks out, so as to be flexible as to the work done by assigning a case to a given range—the sort of guide such an assignment may be to one's dealings with the world. So it is the work that would be done by a given assignment, the kind of guidance this would be, that must decide how the conceptual is to be taken as relating to the particular for the purposes of given representing. In general, such can give no determinate results apart from a particular occasion on which such an allocation is to be put to work.

As he tells this story, Austin places great stress on a feature I have so far suppressed: a statement is not always true or false. But *so* much was in the cards as soon as our starting point was in view. What meat being on a rug is does not, as such, decide what does and does not instance this. There are, after all, Mary's lamb, and Sid's belly. There are various ways of thinking about such things. The *point*, on an occasion, of classifying Mary's lamb as meat on the rug, or as not, may decide how we should then speak of things. It *may*; but it need not. If (the concept of) meat being on a rug does not as such do the needed work, nothing else is *guaranteed* to do it either. Is France a hexagon? Just what are you prepared to call a hexagon? Tell me what is to follow, on an occasion, from my calling France one and I *might* have an answer for you. But I might not. It might still be all the same whether you so call France or not.

Austin's view of truth is, he tells us, meant as an attack on a dichotomy between fact and value: what to do in saying how things are is just a particular question as to what to do, continuous with others in the relation of its answer to what matters, or ought to matter to us. There seems room here for conflict with Frege, who is most concerned to stress that questions of truth arise for stances as to how things *are*, their truth settled (if at all) solely by things being as they are, no matter how that matters to us. But we must here recall the difference, on Austin's view, between the question whether things are such-and-such way and, where someone spoke of things as being that way, the question whether things are as he thus said (or spoke of their being). To settle the question what to do, on an occasion, to say how things are, and to settle it in favour of speaking of things as being such-and-such way is to settle for what one is held responsible in then so speaking—e.g. whether for more than the presence of Mary's lamb on the carpet would make so. It is for that that what matters (or ought to matter) to us matters. As to whether the world is as one is thus responsible for it being, that is as much purely a question of how things are as it is on Frege's view. The difference is just that, on Austin's view, how what matters for us in our dealings with the world matters for what one makes oneself responsible in speaking of things as some given way is, as much as anything else, part of what being true is. This idea can fit with Frege's conception of the objectivity of judgement. The demise of a fact-value distinction is not the demise of fact.

3.1. Reconciliation

A question of truth arises just where something is *represented* as so: that things are a certain way. For such a question to arise, there must be, on the one hand, how things *were* thus represented, so what they need to be to be that way, and, on the other, how things, or the things so represented, in fact are. There is truth just where things being as they are is their being as represented. So one raises a question of truth in representing only where one's representing makes for such a thing as how things must be to be as represented; so only where it distinguishes what matters to things so being from what does not.

Frege stresses this. Austinian historicism acknowledges it. So far, Frege and Austin are one. Each, though, develops this idea differently. Frege thinks in terms of identifiable questions of truth—ones there are for *one* to raise. Representing, so speaking, truly or falsely is raising some specific one of these. One speaks truly just where *that* question has a positive answer. For Austin, speaking truly is satisfying the demands of an occasion. To speak truth is, to be sure, to say things to be as they are and not otherwise.

But for any question of truth there is for *one* to raise, what would be doing this in raising any *given* such question on an occasion is liable to vary not just with what the question is, but also with the occasion of its raising. An occasion may add to, or modify, what a given question anyway demands. If whether there is meat on the rug is such a question, then whether the meat may be unwrapped will depend on the occasion of its raising. And so it would be for any other such question we know to ask. When things would be as I represented them is not settled by the mere fact of my having raised such-and-such question, though, depending on what the question is, and how the world is, such may—or may not—decide whether I in fact spoke truth.

Truth is a point at which the conceptual and the non-conceptual meet. What questions arise at that point as to *when* something would be true depend on how things are. I may ask of the way the rug in fact is whether just this is things being as represented on some occasion in speaking of there being meat on it; I can think that just this *is* that. I could not have had that thought—thought just *that* to be things being as represented—were the rug not just as it is. Such would not change how things were represented in what raised that question, on any reasonable understanding of this. Which points to a way in which a way for *one* to represent things cannot foresee all such questions which *may* arise, so how reference, after the fact, to the circumstances of a representing of things as that way is always liable to be called for. Such lies at the core of Austin's view.

On the other hand, it is absolutely central to the notions of truth, and of judgement, that to think, or speak, truly or falsely is to represent things as a way there is for *one* to think them. Any one of us may judge, or say, only what there is for *one*—no particular one—to represent (to himself, or to others) as so. As Frege stresses, thoughts—the contents of a truth-evaluable stance—are *essentially* shareable. They must be so to be thoughts at all. So if on one occasion I say something to be so, others may say, or think, just that to be so on others. Austin's account of truth-telling must be true to this idea. It is so on the right (the needed) understanding of same-saying. It was the burden of section 2.2 to set out just what this understanding is.

Frege and Austin stress different strands in the notion truth. But there is not much on which they need divide. Each of their ways of portraying truth is a correct way, and, each, the right one for the purposes each philosopher envisages. For each spoke to different questions about truth's role. Seeing the concerns of just one thinker as the only ones in which truth figures can make them seem at odds where they need not be. Frege's central concern was, in his own picturesque terms, for truth to be something whose content would be unfolded in laws of logic. Truth was to be that by which logic got a grip on thought. Which leads him to say—rightly for his purpose:

A concept that is not sharply defined is wrongly termed a concept. Such quasi-conceptual constructions cannot be recognized as concepts by logic; it is impossible to lay down precise laws for them. The law of excluded middle is really just another form of the requirement that the concept should have a sharp boundary. Any object Δ that you choose to take either falls under the concept Φ or does not fall under it, *tertium non datur*. (Frege 1903, §56)

Suppose there is on the rug one rack of ribs and one clump of *ris d'agneau*. Suppose that the concept *meat* is undefined for the case of *ris d'agneau*, or the concept *piece*, in the context *piece of meat*, for the case of *racks* of ribs, or *clumps* of *ris d'agneau*. Then the thought that there are two pieces of meat on the rug lacks a truth-value. And the rot spreads. For now what of the concept *equinumerous with the concept either zero or one*? Is the concept *piece of meat on the rug* in its extension? There is no saying. Arithmetic is in trouble. Which might seem to exclude Austin's role for occasions: specify an object and a (genuine) concept; then of what conditions of things it could be said truly that that object falls under that concept cannot depend on the occasion of saying this.

Frege's problem, given his concern, is that, as he says, logic does not apply to what he calls 'quasi-conceptual constructions'. Nor, he adds, could any precise laws do so. Logic, though, is concerned, *au fond*, with what is so or not: with what follows from something's being so, and what entails that it is. If we think of thoughts as identified by what is so according to them, then logic describes the most general ways the truth of some thoughts may depend on that of others—the most general structure of dependencies that would be found in any, or any large enough, system of thoughts. There is no place in such a system for what would behave as a quasi-conceptual construction would. That such is excluded is, as Frege notes, reflected, in classical logic, in the law of excluded middle. A zero-place quasi-conceptual construction is liable to be neither true nor false, a possibility excluded by this law—and excluded equally by intuitionist logic, even without generating this law.

Logic does not describe the behaviour of quasi-conceptual constructions. Its concern is with what is *so*, and what not; with what else would be so or not if such-and-such. It is concerned with that in whose obtaining a judgement is correct or not. So to see logic as speaking to a thought is already, *ipso facto*, to see that thought as of what is so, or what it not, that *that* is so or not. So, it may seem, a thought must be of what would be so or not no matter how things were. Which may seem at odds with Austin's view of what it is to represent as so.

But if logic does not apply to quasi-conceptual constructions, this just means that we must apply logic only to what is *treatable* as a conceptual construction in Frege's sense— so treatable, that is, for purposes of the application we want to make. Pia said there to be meat on the rug. If it turned out that the rug was empty but for a ribeye encased in perspex, nothing to be understood as to how things were according to her might then decide whether things were as she thus said. In which case, she would have spoken neither truth nor falsehood. Which is compatible with there being no problem as to whether what she said *is* true or false, or would be under those circumstances which matter, for present purposes, in considering what follows from what. In which case, we can treat Pia as having expressed a thought by Frege's standards; something treatable as a zero-place *concept*, and no mere quasi-conceptual construction. To count Pia as having said something true (or false), we must count things as flatly being as she said (or not), independent of how one thinks of this. So we count her as having expressed a thought—one we can then mention as *the thought that there is meat on the rug*—which, just in being the thought it is, decides wherever need be what makes it true and what makes it false. It can be correct, on occasion, so to view her. What she did may then count as doing that.

At the same time, it may be considerations of the merit, in the circumstances, of describing the condition of the rug in those terms, where there *are* two ways of viewing this, which make it right so to view her. Truth enters at this point, too, in pointing to how we may rightly regard one another. Both Frege's and Austin's views of truth thus find their place.

One applies logic to quasi-conceptual constructions on a premise: so far as it matters for our current inferential ends, those constructions will behave like concepts in Frege's sense. The world *may* always let us down in this. In which case we may discover that logic does not quite have the import it seemed to. That ribeye encased in perspex may show this. But that the world *may* let us down does not mean it *will*. Logic can have just the import it would on our application. Such is something we can sometimes know. Austin's view of truth makes room for logic's application. Where it applies, it applies just as Frege's view of truth requires.

Bibliography

Austin, J. L. (1950), 'Truth', *Proceedings of the Aristotelian Society*, suppl. vol. 24: 111–28. Reprinted in Austin (1979), pp. 117–33.

—— (1962), *Sense and Sensibilia*, Oxford: Oxford University Press.

—— (1975), *How To Do Things with Words*, Oxford: Oxford University Press.

—— (1979), *Philosophical Papers*, 3rd ed., Urmson, J. O., Sbisà, M. (eds.), Oxford: Oxford University Press.

Frege, G. (2001), *Schriften zur Logik und Sprachphilosophie*, Gabriel, G. (ed.), Hamburg: Felix Meiner.

—— (2001/1882), '17 Kernsätze zur Logik', in Frege (2001), pp. 23–4.

—— (2001/1892–5), 'Ausführungen über Sinn und Bedeutung', in Frege (2001), pp. 25–34.

—— (2001/1897), 'Logik', in Frege (2001), pp. 35–73.

—— (1903), *Grundgesetze der Arithmetik*. Jena: H. Pohle. Selections in translation in *Translations from the Philosophical Writings of Gottlob Frege*, Geach, P., Black, M. (eds.), Oxford: Basil Blackwell, 1960. Translations from and page references to this volume.

—— (1918), 'Der Gedanke', *Beiträge zur Philosophie des deutschen Idealismus* 1: 58–77.

—— (1919), 'Notes for Ludwig Darmstaedter', in *Posthumous Writings*, Hermes, H., Kambartel, F., Kaulbach, F. (eds.), Oxford: Basil Blackwell, 1979, pp. 253–7.

8

'There's many a Slip between Cup and Lip': Dimension and Negation in Austin[1]

Jean-Philippe Narboux

Happy families are all alike; every unhappy family is unhappy after its own fashion.

Leo Tolstoy, *Anna Karenina*

Austin has secularized the notion of human fallibility, restored it to the worldly prose of our lives. In his hands, the fact of our inherent fallibility is cashed out in terms of our being ordinarily fallible in a vast miscellany of distinct ways, rather than in terms of some single, deeply ingrained and corrupt disposition (Austin 1979: 98). He takes philosophy to have concurred with theology in the sort of 'onomatolatry' that results in *ranking* the many sorts of 'breakdowns' to which human 'machinery' is liable, by measuring them against *a few substantives erected into standards*: *Unum, verum, bonum,* 'the old favourites', as Austin calls them (1979: 128, 180).[2] The many distinctions marked by ordinary language, hence the very distinctions we ordinarily value, were deprecated in favour of a few transcendent standards, sacrificed to 'the deeply ingrained

[1] I would like to thank Avner Baz, Juliet Floyd, and Martin Gustafsson for very helpful comments and suggestions.
[2] This is of course reminiscent of Nietzsche, and some of my formulations are meant to echo that connection. In drawing a parallel between Nietzsche's genealogy of metaphysics and (what I take to be) Austin's own genealogy of metaphysics, however, I certainly do not mean to suggest that their respective understandings of the genealogical task are the same. In fact, I will point to some important divergences between them. Nor do I mean to imply, for example, that Austin assimilates truth to force. Cavell is right, I think, to object to Derrida's reading of *How to Do Things with Words* on the score that it mistakes the theory of infelicities for an attempt to reduce truth to force (see Cavell 1994: 80–1; 1995: 50–1; Cavell's objection can be further substantiated by the observation that Austin emphatically rejects both performative theories of truth and performative theories of negation). I think, however, that it is anything but clear that truth boils down to force in Nietzsche (thus Derrida's suspicion may well be equally misguided as far as Nietzsche is concerned). And I want to insist that in arguing that truth is a dimension of assessment among others, Austin both questions the very value of truth as traditionally conceived and traces it to a moralization of the issue of truth.

worship of tidy-looking dichotomies'(1962: 3). Austin's fundamental insight is this: attention to areas that neighbour notorious centres of philosophy typically reveals that there is 'many a slip between cup and lip', that is, many a way in which things may go amiss, with no hope of reducing that variety to some hierarchy of dichotomies except by doing violence to it (1979: 183; 1975: 147). The false problems in which philosophy gets bogged down arise from such violence. Hence Austin's ironic reminder: 'There are more deadly sins than one; nor does the way to salvation lie through any hierarchy' (1979: 129).

For Austin, the metaphysical ranking of all ills in the light of a few transcendent standards is still at play in the transcendental line of thinking initiated by Kant. To launch a critique of the legitimacy of the conditions of all assessability is not yet to inquire into the value of those conditions themselves.[3] The transcendental problematic takes the question of how language and thought so much as engage at all with the world to lie at a deeper level than the question whether their encounter with the world (should they engage with it at all) takes the shape of success or failure. The kind of scepticism it has to address does not invoke the possibility of systematic error, but what might be called the possibility of systematic disharmony: the possibility that language fails in its purport to give any picture of the world at all, true *or false*. Transcendental philosophy of the best sort does not attempt to overcome the possibility of such a systematic disharmony, but shows how the very notion of such disharmony collapses into 'mere nonsense'.[4] The very alternative between harmony and disharmony (indeed, the very idea of harmony) is shown to be misguided, in that it construes the ability of language to engage with the world as a teleological achievement (typically to be backed up by some theological guarantee), as if the world could somehow desert us by ceasing to align with language.[5] Versions of the transcendental approach differ in how deeply ingrained in our thinking they take that teleological illusion to be. The notion of the transcendental harmony between language and world is thus taken to refer, now to a 'transcendental fact', now to a set of 'ineffable features', now (in the

---

[3] Nietzsche reproaches Kant for having taken standards of assessment at face value, resting content with a mere 'inventory' of them (see Deleuze 1962: 2,102–8).

[4] This characterization of the transcendental problematic is borrowed from Conant (2004); see also Brandom (2002: 23).

[5] See Deleuze (1963: 22–3): 'In the framework of dogmatic rationalism, the theory of knowledge rested upon the idea of a *correspondence* between subject and object, of an *agreement* between the order of ideas and the order of things. Such an agreement possessed two features: it involved some finality, and it required a theological principle as a source and guarantee of this guarantee, of this finality. [...] The fundamental insight of what Kant calls his "Copernican Revolution" consists in this: to substitute to the idea of a harmony between subject and object (*teleological* agreement) the principle of a necessary submission of the object to the subject.'
To that extent, Wittgenstein's use of the term 'harmony' as a synonym for the transcendental agreement that is constitutive of *sense* and prior to *truth* (see, for example, Wittgenstein 1953: §429) is slippery. In what follows, I shall nevertheless expand on that use of the term 'harmony', if only as a means to formulate both Austin's suspicion that transcendental agreement remains (covertly) teleological and his vindication of an ordinary notion of harmony or fit that admits of a variety of degrees and dimensions (among which are truth and felicity).

most consistent versions of the transcendental approach) to the ultimate expression of the illusion. But all concur in the verdict that the semantic standpoint from which the relation between words and world is allegedly assessable is but the illusion of a standpoint.[6]

However, the spectre dispelled by the transcendental approach is still likely to leave its *trace* upon transcendental philosophy. The genuine question as to whether our words, as used in a given ordinary situation, satisfactorily engage with that situation, have some intelligible grip on it, is likely to be construed as a *yes-no* question. You might say that the very structure of the illusion of sense explored by transcendental philosophy leaves a trace upon its frame. The main contention of this paper is that Austin launches an attack on this remnant of hierarchic thinking, this idea that the harmony between words and world is an all-or-nothing matter that conditions, and therefore falls outside of the scope of, assessment. I shall try to show that this fallacy, which I shall call the *harmony fallacy*, is one that the transcendental problematic is likely to fuel. The modern concept of the *intentionality* of language and thought, insofar as it construes *aboutness* as a relation that *either obtains or not*—as if (in Austin's invaluable phrase) it was only 'straight ahead' that we could 'shoot words at the world' (1962: 74)—has its roots in that fallacy.

In this essay, I propose to look at Austin's work from a wide angle, bringing out the often downplayed *systematic* aspect of its conceptual apparatus and its method (rather than trying to emulate him in implementing that method—the true Austinian task, no doubt, but one beyond my skills). I will do so in order to suggest that Austin's accomplishments, far from belonging to the margins of mainstream philosophy (whether traditional or contemporary), not only contest its method but shake some of its foundations. That Austin often seems to leave it to his readers fully to appraise the *philosophical* relevance of his findings does not betray uncertainties as to such relevance, but rather has to do with the enormity and multi-faceted character of the task. Thus it may be necessary, in order to appraise the philosophical originality of Austin, to read him as a classic.

This essay has three parts. In the first, I try to show the significance of Austin's thesis that falsity and infelicity (hence nonsense of the kind which infelicities partake in) stand on a par as independent dimensions of unsatisfactoriness in terms of which utterances are assessable. In the second part, I trace the denial of that Austinian thesis to the traditional supremacy conferred on contradictory negation over other modes of negation. Finally, in the third part, I try to show that this supremacy serves as a principle of closure that turns dimensions of assessment into logical spaces of possibilities. Austin dismantles this principle of closure by undermining the postulate according to which

---

[6] As James Conant has shown, the works of Kant and Frege at once acknowledge their commitment to that latter (stronger) diagnosis and fail (fully) to honour it. Wittgenstein was to draw the lessons of such failure in his early work (Conant 1991, 2002).

negations divide neatly into internal (relevant) negations and external (irrelevant) negations.

1. Falsity and nonsense; or, that 'there is many a slip between cup and lip'[7]

1.1.

Austin's challenge to what I have called the *harmony fallacy* is best read as a reaction against the universalist picture of the essence of thought and language that reaches its high peak in the works of Frege and early Wittgenstein.

Frege identified the content of a judgement with the sense of the question to which that judgement can be seen as a positive or negative answer. (Frege 1977: 31–2). He thus tied the concept of a thought to the concept of a *yes–no question*. (Ricketts 1986: 71–2). In so doing, Frege at once availed himself of a distinction between grasping a thought and recognizing its truth-value,[8] and secured a direct link between falsity and negation. For if one cannot grasp what a yes–no question puts forward for consideration without being in a position to settle the issue, that yes–no question would be indistinguishable from its correct answer. Indeed, a question that cannot so much as be raised before it is correctly answered fails to be a genuine question. To the extent that a judgement is an answer to a yes–no question, its content is internally related to the content of that yes–no question. One can therefore grasp the content of a judgement, or a thought, without knowing whether it is true or false. To grasp a thought is to be faced with the question whether it is to be affirmed or denied.[9]

If a thought is the sense of a yes–no question, then something is a thought only if grasping it involves seeing that it cannot be both true and false (that is, it cannot be both affirmed and denied) and that it is either true or false (that is, either it can be correctly affirmed or it can be correctly denied). But to grasp a thought is not merely to realize that it may not be both true and false and that it is either true or false. It is also to realize which other thoughts it patently entails and which other thoughts it is patently inconsistent with (Ricketts 1985: 6; 1986a: 73). Thus one's understanding of a given judgment displays conformity to the standards to which any judgement whatsoever must conform in order to be a judgement at all. These maximally general standards are

---

[7] Austin's allusion to this proverb is a good example of his predilection for 'allusions which are at once literary and commonplace [. . .] simultaneously the highest reaches and the widest reaches of the language' (Ricks 1998: 266–7).

[8] In fact, Frege took the assimilation of a thought to the sense of a yes–no question to entitle him to a stronger thesis, namely the thesis that one can grasp a thought without either taking it to be true or taking it to be false.

[9] Moreover, to the extent that a judgement (affirmative or negative) is an answer (positive or negative) to a yes–no question, for an affirmative judgement to assent to what that yes–no question offers for consideration and to assert it, on the one hand, and for a negative judgment to reject as false what that yes–no question offers for consideration and to deny it (to assert its negation), on the other hand, are one and the same thing.

standards of consistency, for they are the standards to which any judgement whatsoever must conform on pain of contradiction. And they are standards of *truth* insofar as they are the standards governing the assessment of any judgement whatsoever as true or false. What we mean by the word 'true' shows forth in the assertoric use of language rather than in our use of the word 'true' as a predicate (Ricketts 1985: 8; Diamond 2003: 28–9). Being made in conformity with these maximally general standards, judgements have objective purport; and the laws that encapsulate the standards display or unfold the meaning of the word 'true'.

One corollary of Frege's view of logic as the maximally general science, insofar as it is tied to his view of variables as intrinsically unrestricted, is that concepts must have sharp boundaries (Ricketts 1985: 6; 1986b: 180). For any given concept, it must be determinate, for any object whatsoever, whether that object falls under the concept or not. Frege's law of the excluded middle, 'Either Fx or not Fx', denounces as inconsistent the use of any partially defined concept, that is, the use of any concept whose relevance is restricted to a certain domain.

Being assessable as true or false, then, is not an extrinsic feature of a thought. On the contrary, only what is assessable as true or false counts as a thought. So a thought cannot fail to have an intelligible grip on the world. The very possibility of a gap between it and the world is unintelligible (Ricketts 1986a: 66). The only gap there can be between a given thought and the world is the benign gap of falsity. But for a thought to be false is not for it to be in disharmony with the world; on the contrary, it is only insofar as it is intrinsically assessable as true or false, and in that sense in *harmony* with the world, that a thought is subject to falsity.[10]

This picture of thought and language may seem to be undermined by Frege's concession that some assertions (most notably assertions of sentences containing a definite description that fails to satisfy either the existence condition or the uniqueness condition associated with it) are truth-valueless. Frege claims that the assertion of a sentence containing a definite description *presupposes*, rather than implies, the truth of the associated existence and uniqueness claim, so that neither it nor its negation may be asserted in case that truth is not secured. Readers of Frege notoriously disagree over how to appraise that claim (see McDowell 1998). But this much seems clear: unless Frege's claim can be construed as the claim that such an assertion simply fails to be what it purports to be, namely the expression of a thought, rather than as the claim that there are truth-valueless thoughts—in other words, unless it can be cast as the claim that some utterances masquerading as assertions elicit the illusion of grasping a sense, rather than as the claim that there are truth-value gaps—it does not cohere well with Frege's overall picture of thought and language as presuppositionless (Dummett 1978: 4–5,

---

[10] Wittgenstein says that 'the agreement [*Übereinstimmung*], the harmony [*Harmonie*], of thought and reality consists in this: if I say falsely that something is *red*, then, for all that, it isn't *red*. And when I want to explain the word "red" to someone, in the sentence "That is not red", I do it by point to something red' (Wittgenstein 1953, §429). On that use of the term 'harmony', see Travis (2003: 204).

Ricketts 1986b: 185). It conflicts directly with the view that a proposition's having sense (its being true or false) does not depend on the truth of some other proposition or, equivalently, with the view that the laws of logic are at once universally applicable to reasoning on any topic whatsoever and immediately applicable without presupposition.[11]

In sum, among the fundamental tenets of Frege's picture of the relation between thought (or language) and world are the following:

(A) A (genuine) thought is the content of a *yes-no* question.

(B) An utterance expresses a (genuine) thought if and only if it is assessable as true or false.

(C) The determination of whether an utterance expresses a (genuine) thought or not *precedes* its critical assessment as true or false.

(D) The critical assessment of a (genuine) thought as true or false *neither permits nor requires a semantic perspective.*

(E) A (genuine) thought *does not presuppose* the truth of any other thought.

(F) For *any given pair* comprised of an object and a meaningful predicate, there is a thought to the effect that the latter applies to the former.

(G) The *benign gap of falsity is the only gap* there may be between a (genuine) thought and the world.

From the perspective of Frege's work, each of these tenets may be read as a mere truism, drawing solely upon the clarification of our practice of making assertions (Diamond 2003).

1.2.

I am suggesting that Austin dismantles Frege's overall picture of thought insofar as he rejects each and every one of the above tenets (which is not to say that he challenges every element of Frege's picture). As we shall see, his groundbreaking rejection of (A) is fundamental. But it will suffice at this stage, in order to make palpable the scope of the challenge mounted by Austin against the above picture, to consider (in this subsection and the next) some evidence that he rejects (B), (C), and (G).

The rejection of (C) shows forth, symptomatically, in Austin's twofold characterization of the various ways in which performative utterances such as 'I name this ship the *Queen Elizabeth*' or 'I bet you sixpence it will rain tomorrow' (1975: 5) may go wrong,

---

[11] Frege's claim that everyday language contains meaningless conceptual expressions creates an even more vivid conflict with the picture of thought and language as presuppositionless. That '[ ] + [ ] = 1', notwithstanding its appearance, in fact fails to express a concept in everyday language, since otherwise the question whether 'the Sun + the Sun = 1' or 'not (the Sun + the Sun = 1)' would make sense, presupposes the truth of the judgement that '"the Sun" has a meaning' (Ricketts 1986b: 187). Either the principle that each object must fall or fail to fall under the concept meant by a predicate applies unconditionally to all conceptual expressions and it makes sense to ask whether 'the Sun + the Sun = 1' or not, or some questions of that form in everyday language may turn out to be pseudo-questions—but then that principle fails to apply unconditionally.

as utterances that purport to *do* something—that is, of (what he calls) 'infelicities'. In effect, contrary to current orthodoxy, Austin characterizes infelicities both as modalities of a dimension of unsatisfactoriness that *stands on a par with falsity* (itself construed as a dimension) and as *types of nonsense*. That is to say, infelicities are at once ways of being 'incorrect' and ways of being 'nonsensical'.

On the one hand, infelicities are defined as the 'things that can be and go wrong' on uttering a performative or as ways in which a performative may be 'at least to some extent a failure' (1975: 14). They thus *add to* the false, or rather they belong to a dimension that adds to the dimension of falsity and lies upon the same level as falsity, namely that of (negative) assessment or criticism. In effect, far from *superseding* the idea of truth, construed as the general theme of the amenability of (some of) our utterances to objective assessment, the doctrine of felicities is a step towards its *generalization* to all utterances. In that sense, it does not so much preside over a demise as over an extension of the theme of truth (Austin 1979: 131; Cavell 1994: 80–1, 1995: 50–1). On the other hand, Austin traces the various infelicities that a performative utterance may be affected by to the various *misuses* that can be made of the utterance, and equates them with those 'rather special varieties of nonsense' that the misuses engender (1975: 4).[12] Although infelicitous performative utterances are certainly not nonsensical in any of the ways in which pseudo-statements that set out but fail to be statements are so—if only because performative utterances merely 'masquerade' as (merely have 'the grammatical make-up' of) statements, without so much as setting out to *be* statements— they nonetheless are nonsensical *in some other ways*. Austin's characterization of infelicities as types of nonsense is of a piece with his insistence that 'there are more ways of outraging speech than contradiction merely' (1975: 48; see also 1975: 20, 47–8 and 1979: 62–3). Being no less irreducible to ungrammaticality or contradiction than the new types of nonsense pinpointed by the logical positivists, the types of nonsense to which infelicities amount are equally new (Austin says 'fresh') in character (1975: 2, 51). There are therefore more (benign) gaps between language and reality than one (this negates tenet (G) above). Infelicities constitute such gaps insofar as they constitute (some of the) logically distinct kinds of nonsense to which our utterances are exposed.[13]

---

[12] Austin declares later in the book that all three aspects of an utterance (that is, the locutionary, the illocutionary, and the perlocutionary) may be delineated 'by means of the possible slips between cup and lip, that is, in this case, the different types of nonsense which may be engendered in performing them' (Austin 1975: 147), which implies that the dimension of nonsense along which *illocutions* are assessable stands on a par with the dimension of nonsense along which *locutions* are. But this is perfectly compatible with that dimension of nonsense *also* standing on a par with the dimension of *falsity* along which locutions are assessable.

[13] That Austin countenances the existence of a variety of logically distinct kinds of nonsense and of a variety of degrees of nonsense, as against the early Wittgenstein, does not mean that he embraces the so-called 'substantial' view of nonsense which is both explored and dispelled as an illusion in the *Tractatus* (far from being advocated by it, as some readings have implied). The core assumption of the substantial view is that there is room, over and above 'mere nonsense', for a sort of nonsense that somehow still partakes (to some degree) of sense, if only because it presupposes it (for a defence of the reading of the *Tractatus* which I am

The implication of the above dual characterization is that those 'fresh types of nonsense' to which Austin alludes right at the beginning of *How to Do Things with Words* (1975: 2) and which he later goes on to call 'infelicities' are ways of assessing an utterance. They constitute distinct ways of criticizing an utterance, not mere variations over one single way of excluding a sequence of (spoken or written) signs from the sphere of language altogether by disqualifying it from being so much as a candidate for assessment. In a word, there is room for nonsense being a 'dimension of assessment', rather than the (negative) status of whatever fails to be assessable.

To say that nonsense (as infelicity) is a dimension standing on a par with falsity is to say that it is in a certain sense *independent* from it. In effect, its being assessable as true or false does not require that an utterance should fail to be nonsensical in any of the ways designated by the various terms for 'infelicities' (you may give a bad advice to a donkey); and an utterance may fail to be nonsensical in any of those ways (that is, it may be felicitous) and still not be assessable as true or false (the performative 'I name this ship the *Queen Elizabeth*', even if felicitous, can neither be said to be true nor be said to be false).[14] Thus Austin rejects (B) above. The independence between dimensions, hence the very relevance of the concept of dimension, is even clearer in Austin's second theory of performativity, which equates the constative and the performative with aspects of every utterance (which Austin famously calls the 'locutionary' and the 'illocutionary' aspects) rather than with disjoint classes of utterances. Falsity and infelicity then turn out to be dimensions of unsatisfactoriness to which every utterance is subject.

Now it may seem that infelicities of the sort Austin calls 'misfires' are more plausibly described as 'types of nonsense' than the infelicities he calls 'abuses' (1975: 16). For whereas the former stop the purported speech act from being achieved at all, as in the case when 'I appoint you consul' is said of a horse, the latter only make it 'hollow' as when I say 'I promise that I shall come' without intending to fulfil the promise thus made (1975: 40). Conversely, it may seem that abuses are more apt to warrant the parallel between falsity and infelicity that Austin is at pain to draw. However, as an objection to Austin's scheme of infelicities, this merely begs the question. For it assumes that one and the same dimension may not encompass both conditions for succeeding *to be* a speech act and conditions for succeeding *as* a speech act, on the ground that the former are conditions for being assess*able* whereas the latter are conditions that are themselves being assessed.

assuming here, see Conant 2002). In particular, and contrary to what is suggested in Searle 1969, Austin nowhere makes room for an assertion failing (fully) to make sense because it breaks a rule legislating on the circumstances in which it is 'appropriate' to make it, i.e. the circumstances with which *it* is compatible. Whether the early Wittgenstein should be read as Austin implicitly reads him is yet another issue. Juliet Floyd has cogently argued that Wittgenstein's *Tractatus* is equally to be read as impugning the very dichotomy between sense and nonsense (Floyd 2002: 340).

[14] This is not to say that it can be said to be neither true nor false.

1.3.

According to Austin, it is one and the same metaphysical move that (i) consigns sense and nonsense below the threshold of assessment, (ii) promotes the true—false standard as the primary (if not the unique) dimension of assessment, and (iii) ends up distorting the very fact that the true–false standard is indeed a *dimension* (which means that the true–false standard is neither a *non*-standard, like a property or a relation, nor a *simple* standard that do not admit of a variety of forms). Conversely, Austin's core insight into the 'constative fallacy'—the assumption that 'the business of a "statement" can only be to "describe" some state of affairs, or [more generally] to "state some fact", which it must do either truly or falsely' (1975: 1) (given his contention that to 'state' is not necessarily to 'describe' (in the strict sense), Austin's use of the phrase 'the descriptive fallacy' is a lose way of referring to what, strictly speaking, needs to be called 'the constative fallacy')—is that the hierarchy *between* dimensions of assessment, epitomized by the subordination of sense to truth, cannot be dismantled unless the hierarchy *inside* each dimension is also dismantled. His deepest genealogical insight into the constative fallacy is that it *acts twice as a principle for assessing standards of assessment themselves*, insofar as it imposes a hierarchical order both upon dimensions of assessment and upon the modalities which each dimension of assessment comprises.

Thus, the 'dimension of the false', less misleadingly designated as the 'dimension of *misfit*', is subordinated (if not merely reduced) to a single dichotomy in between the 'false' and the 'not false' (i.e. the 'true'), to the detriment of a whole array of equally important terms of criticism that partake of that dimension (terms of 'misfit' such as 'exaggerated', 'vague', 'bald', 'rough', 'misleading' (1979: 129)) and of a whole array of terms of positive assessment (terms of 'fit' such as 'precise', 'exact', 'rough', 'accurate' (1979: 161–2)). Similarly, the 'dimension of nonsense' constituted by infelicities, better designated as the 'dimension of *infelicity*' (or perhaps as '*a* dimension of the *outrageous* in speech'), is subordinated (if not merely reduced) to a single dichotomy between the 'meaningful' and the 'meaningless', to the detriment of a whole array of equally important terms of criticism that partake of that dimension (such as 'void', 'disallowed', 'vitiated, 'hollow' (1975: 18)). Again, the 'dimension of freedom', less misleadingly designated as the 'dimension of *responsibility*', is subordinated (if not merely reduced) to a single dichotomy between the 'free' and the 'not free' (or between the 'intentional' and the 'not intentional'), to the detriment both of a whole array of equally important terms of criticism (terms of 'attenuation', e.g. 'accidentally', 'unwittingly', 'spontaneously', 'impulsively', 'involuntarily', 'inadvertently', 'tactlessly', 'carelessly', 'clumsily' (1979: 175–204)) and of a whole array of equally important terms of positive assessment (terms of 'aggravation', e.g. 'intentionally', 'deliberately', 'on purpose' (1979: 272–87)). Again the 'dimension of reality' is subordinated (if not merely reduced) to a single dichotomy between the 'real' and the 'not real', to the detriment of a whole array of equally important terms of assessment, both negative and positive.[15]

The subordination of the whole dimension of felicity to a single dichotomy between 'sense' and 'nonsense' duplicates the subordination of the whole dimension of fit to the sole dichotomy of the 'true' and the 'false'. Paradoxically, it also fuels the subordination of sense to truth by aligning both dichotomies with one another, unwittingly turning the dichotomy of the true and the false into a dichotomy of sense. On the face of it, the issue of sense appears to precede the issue of truth, and may even be said to lie at a deeper level than it. It only does so, however, to the extent that it is already subordinated, as a yes-no issue (i.e. 'is it meaningful or *not* meaningful?'), to the yes-no issue of truth. Austin takes the opposite course. He shows at once infelicity to be a dimension standing on a par with falsity and falsity itself to be one dimension among others (1975: 149). And he does so by showing at once that the harmony between words and world, far from being the transcendental condition of all assessment, is ordinarily subject to multidimensional assessment (for example, to assess an utterance along the dimension of felicity is to assess it along *a* dimension of harmony) and that to assess an utterance as true or false is to invoke a whole dimension that *is* indeed a dimension of harmony.[16] In a nutshell, harmony (sense) may be subject to assessment (rather than rendering assessment along the dimension of truth possible in the first place), while the assessment of truth may bear on harmony (fit). Disabilities (like being 'void' or 'hollow') do not disqualify from being assessable, while conversely assessment may bear on disabilities (like being 'rough' or 'misleading').[17] It may be retorted that this is to play fast and loose with the term 'harmony'. What is correct here is that 'truth' and 'felicity' constitute two distinct dimensions of assessment, and are as such independent from, and not to be conflated with, one another. They are indeed two distinct dimensions of harmony. But if what is implied is that harmony of the first kind, should it hold between words and worlds, merely makes words eligible for harmony of the second kind, then the objection is ill-conceived.

Each of the various dimensions of unsatisfactoriness delineated by Austin evinces a unity that both warrants the delineation and undermines the assumption that *being unsatisfactory* (or *going wrong*) neatly and naturally divides (exclusively and exhaustively) into *not qualifying for being satisfied (or not)* and *not being satisfied*, or again into *failing to have any intelligible grip on the world* and *failing to have a worldly counterpart*. Each dimension of unsatisfactoriness, as a dimension of assessment, cuts across that dichotomy and unmasks it as the mere product of a transcendental argument to the effect that, if our

---

[15] See Austin (1962: 71): 'Other members of this group, on the affirmative side, are, for example, "proper", "genuine", "live", "true", "authentic", "natural"; and on the negative side, "artificial", "fake", "false", "bogus", "makeshift", "dummy", "synthetic", "toy", "dream", "illusion", "mirage", "hallucination" belong here as well.'

[16] Namely, that of 'fitting the facts' (1979: 130, 161). That 'truth' refers to a (convention-saturated) dimension of harmony rather than to a (simple natural) property or relation constitutes perhaps the main thesis of 'Truth'.

[17] In some passages, Austin presents the term 'disabilities' as interchangeable with the term 'infelicities' (see, for example, 1975: 136).

practice of assessment is to be accountable, there must be conditions for being assessable that are not themselves assessable in any ordinary sense of the word.

Some standards of assessment *are* standards of being. Thus, 'it is sometimes said of a bad poem, for instance, that it isn't really a poem at all; a certain standard must be reached, as it were, even to *qualify*' (1962: 73).[18] Conversely, some standards of being are standards of assessment rather than standards of existence. Thus, it is to be noticed 'that something which is not a real duck is not a *non-existent* duck, or indeed a non-existent anything; and that something existent, e.g. a toy, may perfectly well not be real, e.g. not a real duck' (1962: 68). Austin's scrutiny of the various extenuating or aggravating terms that may serve to qualify the ascription of an action to an agent directly undermines the assumption that for an action to make sense, or for it not to be unfree, is for that action to count as a positive answer to the *yes-no* question set by an *intention*, i.e. by something that is a *candidate* for being carried out *or not* (or for being realized *or not*).[19] If you want to insist that all human action, insofar as it is not unfree, can be called 'intentional', then you might say that Austin's reflections on the subject of excuses elucidate many other ways of going wrong, for an intention, than not being carried out, and many other ways of failing to make full sense than failing to be an intention altogether.

Thus, Austin's work not only undercuts the widely shared assumption that for an utterance to make sense is for it to be a *candidate* for truth or falsehood, or for it to exert a *normative* constraint upon its appraisal in the light of facts. Austin attempts to follow through the consequences of dismantling the whole collusion of the two 'fetishes' that are jointly at work in this assumption, namely the true-false dichotomy and the value-fact dichotomy (1975: 151). It is the joint work of these two fetishes which, in particular, leads one to disregard our ordinary use of terms of nonsense as terms of criticism and to regard such terms as mere terms of exclusion, designating the negative upshot of a preliminary stage that merely *clears the ground*, in the positive case, for the stage of assessment proper. In saying that '[t]he principle of Logic, that "Every proposition must be true or false", has too long operated as the simplest, most persuasive and most pervasive form of the descriptive fallacy' (1979: 131), Austin is tracing the constative fallacy to the assumption that assessability is declined along a *dichotomy* of *success* and *failure*. Thus the fallacy fundamentally lies in the logical constant '*or*', or in the exclusive and exhaustive character it takes on when coupled with the contradictory negation that is folded into the term 'false' ('false' = '*not*-true'): the impugned principle is better cast as the principle that 'every proposition must be true-*or-not*-true'. Now the dichotomy between succeeding as an *X* and not succeeding as an *X* is itself a reflection of, and in turn reinvigorates, the prior dichotomy between

---

[18]   Stanley Cavell and Michael Fried have argued in the same vein that the fact that counting as an instance of a certain art *at all* is, for a given object, a matter of its being able *significantly* to engage with the potentialities of the medium defining that art, has become inescapable with the advent of modernism.

[19]   For a formulation of that second assumption as a version of the first, see Brandom (1994: 13).

succeeding to be an *X* and not succeeding to be an *X*, which treats not succeeding *as* an *X* in terms of succeeding to *be* an *X* and induces an apparently principled and necessary gap between not succeeding as an *X* and not succeeding to be an *X*. This is consequently a reflection of the prior dichotomy of the *assessable* and the *nonsensical*.

What this suggests is that the obsession with the true-or-false dichotomy when discussing statements (1975: 145; 1979: 129, 161), or with the free-or-not-free dichotomy when discussing action (1975: 145; 1979: 130, 161), or with the beautiful-or-ugly dichotomy when discussing art (1979: 183), or with the good-or-bad dichotomy when discussing morality (1962: 73), or with the 'real' when discussing reality (1962: 71), are all expressions of the fundamental obsession with 'self-contradiction' (or 'inconsistency') when discussing nonsense, or of the fundamental dichotomy erroneously drawn between inconsistency and sense (1979: 66), coupled with the assumption that inconsistency debars an utterance (an action, etc.) from assessability. (Austin also denies that latter assumption. He even comes very close to assimilating inconsistency to a certain type of abuse, that of 'non-fulfilment' or 'breach' (1975: 51–4).)

To the extent that the generalized notion of a 'condition of satisfaction' (see for example Dummett 1973; Searle 1983) revolves around a generalization of the dichotomy between *not qualifying for being satisfied (or not)* and *not being satisfied*, or of the dichotomy between *not being endowed with aboutness (intentionality)* and being *incorrect*, it is not in line but directly at odds with Austin's generalized notion of 'unsatisfactoriness' or 'unhappiness'. The constative fallacy is not that of giving primacy to the 'direction of fit' that is peculiar to the constative dimension (from words to world),[20] but that of holding all fit and misfit between words and world (from whichever direction) to owe their possibility to conditions that are not themselves assessable. To the extent that 'intentionalism' can be defined by the thesis that all meeting of thought and reality answers some antecedent yes-no question whose content normatively governs it,[21] the generalized notion of a 'condition of satisfaction' may be held to be the hallmark of intentionalism. To construe the concept of speech act along the lines of intentionalism is to commit the very fallacy that this concept was meant to undercut in the first place.

2. Dimension and negation; or, that 'there are more deadly sins than one'[22]

2.1.

So far I have argued that the constative fallacy partakes of a more fundamental fallacy, the harmony fallacy. The latter was shown to consist in deducing harmony as that

---

[20] On the contrast between constative utterances and performative utterances in terms of *direction of fit*, see Austin (1975: 46–7). A few pages later, Austin expresses reservations about the ultimate validity of that contrast (54–5).

[21] Wittgenstein (1975; i.e. middle Wittgenstein) and Searle (1983) are two *loci classici* of that doctrine.

[22] Austin (1979: 129).

without which success and failure are unintelligible (for lack of any norm constraining their appraisal in the light of facts) and that which as such falls out of the scope of appraisal. I have also argued that the fallacy turns, ultimately, upon the assumptions (i) that only what (fully) succeeds in being an X may be assessed not to succeed *as* an X, and (ii) that being infected by some self-contradiction is the privileged manner in which some candidate X does not (fully) succeed in being an X. Finally, I have suggested that the harmony fallacy induces both an (outer) hierarchy between dimensions of assessment and an (inner) hierarchy inside each dimension of assessment, so that the two sorts of hierarchies can only be dismantled together. Now, to achieve such dismantling, it is necessary to undo a third hierarchy, which is equally constitutive of the harmony fallacy: the hierarchy between kinds of opposites. The obsession with self-contradiction, in effect, translates into an inclination to subordinate all kinds of opposites to contradictory negation. Hence we need to ask what becomes of the relation between going wrong and contradictory negation, once falsity is deemed a dimension of unsatisfactoriness among others and no longer privileged as the only philosophically relevant way of going wrong.

The concept of a 'dimension of assessment' is the pillar upon which rests Austin's longstanding project of reassessing the very standards which are operative in the philosophical 'assessment' of standards themselves. Austin's own, less pompous way of hinting at that project is to express doubts as to the importance of importance: 'I'm not sure importance is important', he says in the concluding paragraph of 'Pretending' (1979: 272; see also 1962: 62). Austin defines a 'dimension-word' as 'the most general and comprehensive term in a whole group of terms of the same kind, terms that fulfil the same function' (1962: 71; see also 73). In other words, the 'dimension of assessment' designated by a 'dimension-word' is named after the most general and comprehensive term fulfilling the function around which it revolves. Examples of dimension-words are 'felicitous', 'real', 'good', 'true', 'beautiful', 'free', and 'serious'. A dimension is a complex standard, or a complex of standards. Seen from its negative side, a dimension of assessment is what Austin calls a 'dimension of unsatisfactoriness' or a 'dimension of criticism' (or again a 'dimension of unhappiness'). Seen from its positive side, it is what Austin calls a 'dimension of success' (or a 'dimension of happiness'). The choice of the term 'happiness' as the most general term for any positive assessment whatsoever (i.e. as a term for any positive assessment along any dimension) is motivated by the need to use a term more encompassing and less philosophically overloaded than 'true'. More significantly, it refers to what Austin regards as a major insight of Aristotle in opposition to (what he regards as) Plato's predilection for dichotomies, namely the thesis that the semantic unity of some words—most notably the word 'εὐδαιμονία', which Austin proposes to translate either by 'happiness' or by 'success' (1979: 18–19)[23]—defeats 'the rigid dichotomy "same

---

[23] That the term '*success*' lacks any moral overtone is perhaps 'no great disadvantage', remarks Austin, given that 'εὐδαιμονία is certainly quite an unchristian ideal' (1979: 19).

meaning, different meaning"' (1979: 28).[24] Aristotle's doctrine of παρώνυμα, whose core thesis according to Austin is that 'παρώνυμα are words which have meanings partly the same and partly different' (1979: 28), is thus the ancestor of the doctrine of dimensions.[25] In other words, the various more or less specific terms that fall under the head of a dimension-word, designating the various 'types' or 'forms' that comprise the dimension, may be said to 'have meanings partly the same and partly different'. The dimension-word is neither univocal (the less general terms that fulfil the same function do not designate things that are 'similar' to each other) nor equivocal or ambiguous (1962: 64; 1979: 26–7, 71, 73–4).

Like its Aristotelian precursor, Austin's theory of dimensions of assessment is meant to counter the inclination to think that 'all things called by some one name are similar to some one pattern, or are all more similar to each other than any of them is to anything else' (1979: 74; see also 1979: 69). In providing a genealogical account of the obliteration of the semantic unity peculiar to dimension-words, it affords a genealogical insight into the principle subtending the hierarchy that was forced upon dimensions. As I read him, Austin implicitly draws upon that complex genealogical insight when he maintains that 'It is essential to realize that "true" and "false", like "free" and "unfree", do not stand for anything *simple* at all; but only for a general dimension of being a right or proper thing to say as opposed to a wrong thing' (1962: 145); or, again, that just 'as "truth" is not a name for a characteristic of assertions, so "freedom" is not a name for a *characteristic* of actions, but the name of a *dimension* in which actions are assessed' (1979: 180, italics added).

It is the all-or-nothing alternative imposed on the issue of semantic unity that directly leads one to the positing of a single simple supra-sensible character C (say, *the false*) as the *meaning* of the opposite of a dimension-word (say, the dimension-word 'true'), and to taking the distinction between C and not-C (e.g. between *the false* and *the not-false*) to *exhaust* the dimension which it designates. Thus the distinction between C and its opposite is held to be a dichotomy (but, that dichotomy really is a merely contrived dichotomy, in which the two terms 'live by taking each other's washing' (1962: 4)). Invoking the example of a word which is not a dimension-word but whose semantic unity also defeats the 'rigid dichotomy' mentioned above, Austin retraces the process of hypostasizing its meaning:

Consider the expressions 'cricket ball', 'cricket bat', 'cricket pavilion', 'cricket weather'. If someone did not know about cricket and were obsessed with the use of such normal words as 'yellow', he might gaze at the ball, the bat, the building, the weather, trying to detect the 'common quality' which (he assumes) is attributed to these things by the prefix 'cricket'. But no such quality meets his eyes; and so perhaps he concludes that 'cricket' must designate a *non-natural*

---

[24] On that 'rigid dichotomy', see also (1979: 74). Austin invokes Aristotle's thesis about the semantic unity of 'happiness' in his (1962: 64), and (1979: 74).

[25] Austin puts forward that exegesis of Aristotle's theory of παρώνυμα, in reaction to a study by Prichard, in his 'ΑΓΑΘΟΝ and ΕΥΔΑΙΜΟΝΙΑ' (1979: 20–31); he explicitly invokes it in his (1979: 71, 74).

quality, a quality to be detected not in any ordinary way but by *intuition*. (1962: 64; see also 1979: 73–4, where Austin takes the same example in order to illustrate Aristotle's insight)

The structure of that move just is the structure of the 'transcendental argument' for the 'existence of universals' as Austin reconstructs it in 'Are there *A Priori* Concepts?' (1979: 337). Arguments of that sort, Austin points out in introducing the notion, deserve to be called 'transcendental' in two respects: they deduce a condition *sine qua non* as that to which a certain fact owes its possibility (here, the fact that we call various sorts of things by the same name), and they posit the existence of an entity which is 'emphatically *not* anything we stumble across' (1979: 34), or which is 'different in kind from sensa' (1979: 34, n. 1) (here, the universal).

The specific form taken by that move, when applied to the various types of failures or breakdowns that a dimension-word (e.g. 'free', or 'real') may serve to rule out, is as follows. For lack of any detectable simple character common to all the ways of going wrong which the dimension-word may be invoked to rule out, the (alleged) use of a single most specific term of criticism (a negative-looking term like 'involuntary' (or perhaps 'not-intentional') or 'hallucination' (or perhaps the fabricated term 'sense-datum')) is erected as the unique standard against which the uses of all the other specific terms grouped under the dimension-word are to be measured. As the specific term of criticism used as the prominent standard is turned into a maximally general term of criticism and is equated with the (alleged) opposite of the dimension-word (unfree = involuntary (or: unfree = not-intentional); unreal = hallucination (or: unreal = sense-datum)), all the other (equally specific) terms of criticism ordinarily used with the same function, including the very term that comes into prominence (i.e. 'accidentally', 'inadvertently', 'impulsively', 'clumsily', . . . , *and* 'involuntarily'; 'artificial', 'fake', 'toy', 'illusion', . . . , and 'hallucination'), are dismissed as unimportant (see, for example, 1962: 63). Exclusive regard for one single use involves massive disregard for all the others. To use the Platonic contrast studied by Austin in his 'The Line and the Cave in Plato's *Republic*', the various specific ways of going wrong referred to by these terms of assessment are all levelled down as mere copies of the original way of going wrong, as if all these other terms were equivalent (1979: 197).[26] The various standards of assessment that constitute their meanings are devalued in the face of one single standard being posited as the meaning of the dimension-word to the very extent that it already covertly acts as a standard for assessing all standards of the dimension. It is in this manner that a variety of ways of going wrong come to be reduced to a single way of going wrong, and a dimension of assessment comes to be miscast as a dichotomy (that between going wrong in that way and *not* going wrong in that way). Hence the assumption that each and every statement either is false or not, that each and every conduct either is involuntary or not, that each and every perception either is a

---

[26] As Austin observes, philosophers are apt to 'equate even "inadvertently" with "automatically": as though to say I trod on your toe inadvertently means to say I trod on it automatically. Or we collapse succumbing to temptation into losing control of ourselves—a bad patch, this, for telescoping' (1979: 198).

hallucination or not, and so on. Ever since Plato, the method of dichotomies has been the supreme fetish of metaphysics, for metaphysics only ever elevates to the rank of a standard what can be arrived at by dichotomizing. It has often been noticed that Plato's dichotomies are *biased*. They are biased towards their expected result, namely the selection, among a variety of contestants, of the single contestant that truly deserves the term under definition (on Plato's method of division as a method to sort genuine contestants from impersonators, see Deleuze 1969: 293). Austin holds the assimilation of all differences to contradictions to issue in (if not in fact to derive from) the undue *moralization* of each and every philosophical topic.

2.2.

The hierarchy of standards to which traditional philosophy has committed itself undergoes in Austin's hands a reversal or, better, a revaluation (i.e. a reversal of the very *way* in which standards are assessed).[27] According to Austin, traditional philosophy (including Kant's criticism) is to be criticized not so much for its failure to go beyond a mere inventory of standards (as Nietzsche mistakenly thought—see note 3 above) as for its failure ever to have really proceeded to work through that inventory. Austin urges his reader to scrutinize those terms of assessment that were always deemed *minor*, and those subjects which were always overshadowed (if not altogether eclipsed) by the philosophical controversies reckoned as the most important ones (1979: 183). In laying out maps of such areas, one may come across entire dimensions of assessment awaiting delineation, like the dimension of the infelicitous, or that of the excusable. The terms of assessment which were always ranked as the least important (because the most *ordinary*) and consequently dismissed, are in fact, he argues, the *most* important (because the most *specific*). Terms of assessment are more valuable the more specific, and equally specific terms of assessment are equally valuable.[28] Their equal value is a function of their heterogeneity and mutual independence. More than one term of a given dimension may apply and not all terms of a given dimension may apply. Austin observes that 'possible ways of being *not* real [...] are both numerous for particular kinds of things, and liable to be quite different for things of different kinds' (1962: 70), while a performative utterance (and more generally a conventional action) 'can go wrong in two ways at once (we can insincerely promise a donkey to give it a carrot)' (1975: 23; see also 15). On the other hand not every performative

---

[27] For Austin, as already for Nietzsche, really to question a hierarchy is not so much to turn it upside down as to question its underlying *principle*. On Nietzsche's concept of *Umwertung*, see Deleuze (1969: 302).

[28] In Austin's scheme of 'infelicities' in his (1975: 18), for example, the term (AB) 'void' ('misfire') is less specific, hence less valuable as a term of assessment, than the terms (A) 'disallowed' ('misinvocation') and (B) 'vitiated' ('misexecution'). 'Void' and the term (Γ) 'hollow' are equally specific, hence equally valuable. The same is true of the term 'disallowed' compared to the term 'vitiated', and of the term (Γ1) 'insincerity' compared to the term (Γ2) 'breach'. In a similar scheme of 'excuses', the term 'involuntarily', *pace* traditional philosophy, would not be *more* valuable as a term of assessment than the terms 'inadvertently' and 'carelessly'. And in a scheme of 'unreality', the term 'illusory', *pace* traditional philosophy, would not be *more* valuable than the terms 'artificial' and 'fake'.

utterance (conventional action) 'is liable to every form of infelicity' (1975: 19). The dimension-word itself, insofar as it is a mere place-holder for specific terms of assessment (call it a 'variable of assessment'), is the least important (since the least specific) of all. It only acquires a special importance from a special ability to rule out a variety of specific ways of going wrong on a variety of specific occasions and for a variety of specific purposes. It does so in virtue of the abovementioned feature (shared by dimension-words) of being a 'trouser-word', that is, a word whose positive use is parasitic upon its negative use.[29] For example, 'the function of "real" is not to contribute positively to the characterization of anything, but to exclude possible ways of being *not* real' (1962: 70). Similarly, 'there is little doubt that to say we acted "freely" (in the philosopher's use, which is only faintly related to the everyday use) is to say only that we acted *not* un-freely, in one or another of the many heterogeneous ways of so acting (under duress, or what not)' (1979: 180). The crucial point is that it is only as a variable of assessment that the dimension-word is maximally general within that dimension. It is only to the extent that it wears its polymorphic use on its sleeves that a dimension-word may be said to be more fundamental than the word traditionally elected. Thus, it is only to the extent that the concept of 'responsibility in general' itself bears witness to the fact 'that there isn't much point in discussing it in general terms', that it is true to say 'that questions of whether a person was responsible for this or that are prior to questions of freedom' (1979: 273) or that 'philosophical tradition apart, Responsibility would be a better candidate for the role here assigned to Freedom' (1979: 181). In the same manner, 'fit' seems to fare better than 'true' as a dimension-word for the dimension of 'truth', and 'infelicity' (or 'outrage to speech') to fare better than 'nonsense' as a dimension-word for a dimension of pragmatic nonsense.

Austin rehabilitates the distinctions marked by ordinary language on the ground of their specificity. These distinctions, which are none other than the distinctions that *we* value, were sacrificed by philosophers in their worship of 'tidy-looking dichotomies' (1962: 3). Austin thinks an utterance (action, perception, work of art) is not assessable unless there is a genuine question as to whether it goes wrong or not. He also thinks no question can be genuine that lacks specificity, and that a specific question as to whether an utterance (action, perception, work of art) goes wrong or not asks whether it does so or not *in some specific way*. But he argues that things may go wrong in a variety of specific ways according to a variety of specific circumstances, that only a question that actually *arises* may qualify as a genuine question, and that for a way of going wrong to be specific is for it to occupy a definite place in a series of heterogeneous ways of going wrong. Thus, although Austin agrees with Frege that terms of assessment are relevant when and only when 'what it is that is in question' is specified, and that 'what it is that is in question' is specified when and only when 'what it is that is being excluded' by the

---

[29] Note that the word 'intentionally' is not a trouser-word (see 1979: 285) to the extent that it is not uniquely or even primarily used as a dimension-word.

term of assessment is specified (1962: 71), he is led to reject as utterly ungrounded the three following assumptions: (i) that a specific question arises when and only when the candidate to assessment is not self-contradictory; (ii) that the relevant specific question may be extractable from something less than the total situation in which what is being assessed is to be situated; and, (iii) that the relevant specific opposition may always be equated with that of contradictory negation—that is, that the relevant specific question is necessarily and primarily to be construed as a yes-no question (thus he rejects, respectively, tenets (F), (E), and (A) of the Fregean picture). The refutation of that last assumption lies at the heart of Austin's philosophical enterprise. In showing that the contrasts on which *we* ordinarily rely do not align with the contradictory oppositions imposed by metaphysics in its flight from the ordinary, Austin shows such oppositions to be oppositions which we simply cannot lay hold of, that are too out of measure to matter to us: 'A distinction which we are not in fact able to draw is—to put it politely—not worth making' (1962: 77).

Unhappiness along a certain dimension, not to speak of unhappiness in general (if there is indeed such a thing) cannot be equated with the truth of the unique statement that contradicts the statement expressive of happiness, as (it has been held) the falsity of a statement *can* be equated with the truth of the unique statement that contradicts it (in fact, as we shall soon see, Austin criticizes that assumption too). To express unhappiness along a given dimension, the operation of sentential negation will typically have to be applied to more than one statement at once and not to be always applied to the same statements. Moreover, no unhappiness is ever best or primarily captured by means of a *formal* device of negation (like the syntactical device of sentential negation).

For example, consider an action that is unhappy, in the sense that 'I did it but only *in a way*, not just flatly like that' (1979: 187). To say that this action is unhappy, or excusable, is to say that it is excusable in at least one of an indefinite variety of specific ways, each of which is expressible through a single application of the device of sentential negation: it may be true that I 'couldn't help', or that I 'didn't mean to', or that I 'didn't realize', and so on (1979: 187). It follows that for my action not to be excusable is not for it not to be done impulsively. Nor is it for it not to be done accidentally, or not to be done inadvertently, or not to be done under duress (and so on) either. Thus, the statement 'I did it' admits of many contraries, but it is anything but clear that it admits of a contradictory. In particular, 'I did not do it' does not contradict 'I did it', since both are wrong when the action is unhappy or excusable. Or, take a performative utterance that is infelicitous. According to Austin's scheme, a performative utterance is infelicitous if (and, if we regard Austin's scheme as a model, complete by definition, only if) it is infelicitous in at least one of six distinct senses, in that it does *not* comply with at least one in a list of six conditions (1975: 14–15). The assessment of the performative utterance as infelicitous in a certain sense amounts to the application of a counterpart term of criticism (a term of negative assessment) that is (or is equivalent to) a negative-looking term.[30] The application of that term of criticism is underwritten by a true negative general statement to the effect that the corresponding condition does not obtain (1975: 46, 53). That statement rests in turn, through existential generalization, upon some true particular statement that instantiates it (thus: 'I divorce you' / (A1) 'we do *not* admit any procedure at all for effecting divorce' (1975: 27); 'I pick George' / (A2) 'George in the circumstances is an inappropriate [i.e. is *not* an appropriate] object for the procedure of picking' (1975: 28)).[31] Alternatively, it may rest indirectly upon some happy negative utterance (not necessarily a statement) that grounds an instance of it (thus: 'I challenge you' / 'we merely shrug it off [i.e. we do *not* take account of it]' (1975: 27); 'Go and pick up wood' / (A1) (or (A2) or (B2)) 'I do*n't* take orders from you' (1975: 28); '"I do", said when / (A2) you are in the prohibited [i.e. *not* in the permitted] degrees of relationship, or / (A2) before a ship's captain *not* at sea' (1975: 34).)[32] Thus, the first-person past constative 'I *V*ed' (or the third-person present constative 'He *V*s'), where *V* is an empty-place for a performative verb admits of many contraries, and it is anything but clear that it admits of a contradictory. In particular, 'I did not *V*' (or 'He does not *V*') does not contradict 'I *V*ed' (or 'He *V*s') since both are wrong when the performative is infelicitous.[33] Again, there is no simple contrast between the case where *all* is well with one's perception and the case where *something* is amiss (1962: 9). I may have some reason to believe that I do not see a material thing and not have any reason to believe that I am being deceived by my senses, and *vice versa* (1962: 8–9). And, again, it is anything but clear that the statement that 'I perceive so-and-so' admits of a contradictory. In particular, 'I do not perceive so-and-so' does not contradict 'I perceive so-and-so' since both may be wrong when I am the victim of a hallucination.

---

[30] Thus the terms of infelicities (Γ) 'abuse', (B1) 'flaw', or (B2) 'hitch' are held by Austin to be equivalent (respectively) to the negative-looking (that is to say, *morphologically* negative) terms (Γ) 'disrespect', (B1) 'misexecution', (B2) 'non-execution'. Restricting ourselves to morphologically negative terms of criticism, we obtain the following list of terms for infelicities: (AB) 'misfire', (A) 'misinvocation', (B) 'miscarriage' (or 'misexecution'), (Γ) 'disrespect', (A1) 'non-play', (A2) misapplication (or misplay), (B1) misexecution, (B2) non-executions, (Γ1) insincerity, (Γ2) non-fulfilment (or 'disloyalty' or 'infraction' or 'indiscipline') (Austin 1975: 18).

[31] Other examples are: '"I appoint you", said when . . . / (A2) I'm *not* entitled to appoint' (1975: 34); '"I condole with you", said when / (Γ1) I did *not* really sympathize with you'; '"I promise", said when / (Γ1) I do *not* intend to do what I promise' (1975: 40).

[32] Other examples are: '"I give", said when / (A2) it is *not* mine to give or when / (A2) it is *non*-detached flesh' (1975: 34); '"I bet you the race won't be run today" when / (B1) more than [i.e. *not* just] one race was arranged' (1975: 36); 'my attempt to marry by saying "I will"' / 'the woman says (B2) "I will *not*"' (1975: 37); 'I challenge you' / (B2) 'I fail to send [i.e. I do *not* send] my seconds' (1975: 40).

[33] As for the result of applying sentential negation to the performative itself, to the extent that it yields anything, it does not yield a performative that contradicts the first (such that both cannot be felicitous and both cannot be infelicitous) but a constative which is negative in the meta-linguistic sense (thus 'I am not ordering you to leave' which, in 'I am not ordering you to leave, I am praying you to leave', is equivalent to 'I am not "*ordering*" you to leave . . .' or 'It is not correct to say that "I am ordering you to leave"' (just as 'She is not pretty', in 'She is not pretty, she is gorgeous', is equivalent to 'She is not "*pretty* . . ."' or 'It won't do to say "She is pretty"').

Again, it will not pay to assume that whenever someone's action is unsatisfactory in the sense that he is *pretending* to do or to be doing something, the statement to the effect that he is *not* doing what he is pretending to do or to be doing will be true. (What of the man who is pretending to be cleaning the windows but who *really* is doing something different, namely noting the valuables? That he is *really* doing something else does not mean that he is not cleaning the windows (1979: 259, 262).)[34]

The possibility of capturing, by a particular true negative statement, the particular breakdown that makes for things being unhappy owes more to the particular *content* of that statement than to the prefix *not*. Being of universal range, that device cannot capture, by itself, so much as the *kind* of breakdown instantiated. By contrast, many ordinary negative-looking terms, especially adverbs, can be used to capture kinds of breakdowns that were delineated through them in the first place. Such terms belong to *semantics* rather than to syntax and constitute genuine terms of (negative) assessment. Thus, the specific kind of breakdown instantiated can often be captured through the negative *qualification* conveyed by a (often negative-looking) term. Thus, 'X involuntarily did A' does not only specify the sense in which it is not fair to say baldly that 'X did A', namely that it is not fair to say baldly that he *did A* (rather than that it is not fair to say baldly that X did it, or that it is not fair to say baldly he did simply *A*), but it specifies the sense in which it is not fair to say baldly he *did* A, namely, precisely, that he did it all right (he made that small gesture), but only *involuntarily*. Austin is thus led to rehabilitate all kinds of oppositions as equally, if not more, important than the opposition between contradictories (1979: 191). Even morphological features of negative-looking terms may crucially point to distinctions between kinds of breakdowns (1979: 280–1).

Only if *all* the oppositions that compose a given dimension could be turned into dichotomies, so as to all find a place in one single tree of dichotomies, could the opposition between happiness and unhappiness be equated with one fundamental contradictory opposition or dichotomy. Austin removes all hope for such a reduction by showing that the assumption that 'a word must have an opposite or one opposite' is unwarranted (1979: 192). Even the hierarchies among opposites that we are most likely to take for granted rest on sand. According to Austin it is not even true that something cannot be done both deliberately and not intentionally (see, for example, 1979: 278). A fair amount of 'Three Ways of Spilling Ink' is dedicated to showing that the three terms of aggravation 'intentionally', 'on purpose', and 'deliberately' are too heterogeneous not to stand on a par, by showing that there is always 'some "opposite" of one of the three expressions which is *not* an "opposite" of the other two' (1979: 276).

---

[34] This much, then, is right in the British Idealists' contention that accounts of falsity and negation cannot dispense with *contrary* negation. But they spoilt that insight by invoking contradiction as a principle of closure securing the completeness of each disjunctive sphere of contraries and finally the completeness of reality itself (thereby turned into a system). Austin alludes to a consequence of that move: the assimilation of *degrees* of fit to *segments* of truth (1979: 130, n. 1). For a detailed criticism of that move, see Narboux (2005, 2009).

Austin's argument that dimensions of assessment do not admit of an *outer* hierarchy either proceeds along the same lines. For example, that an utterance is assessable along distinct independent dimensions of unhappiness is shown by the fact that it may not be unsatisfactory along one or more dimensions and still be unsatisfactory. For example, it may not be infelicitous in any of the ways in which an utterance may be infelicitous, and still be unsatisfactory in the sense that it is excusable, or that it does not secure uptake, or that it is pretended, or that it does not fit the facts (1975: 21–2, 104–7, 133–47). Austin's work reduces to pieces the assumption that all conceivable dimensions of assessment can be ordered in a single tree of dichotomies, with one fundamental contradictory opposition or dichotomy (say, that between being satisfied and not being satisfied) holding across all conceivable dimensions—hence standing above them all. That there are no *original* dimensions of assessment does not mean, on the other hand, that dimensions cannot be modelled through the conscious elaboration of what Austin calls 'working-models'.[35]

2.3.

Clearly, it is not so much an obsession with sentential negation as such as a restrictive conception of its scope (that is to say, of *which* sentence it is supposed to attach to when things go wrong in a certain way) that obstructs access to the multiplicity and complexity of dimensions. Or you might say that the obsession that is operative, at bottom, is more an obsession with *self*-contradiction than an obsession with contradiction merely (though that latter obsession too is operative). This is best illustrated by the fact that the liability of assertions (that is, constative utterances) to infelicities cannot so much as come into view unless it is realized 'that in order to explain what can go wrong with statements we cannot just concentrate on the proposition involved (whatever that is) as has been done traditionally' (1975: 52). For, while the falsity of an assertion is

---

[35] The demise of the hierarchy of copy and original, in Austin, does not lead to a rehabilitation of the notion of a *simulacrum* (i.e. of a copy that does not even resemble), as in Nietzsche, but to a new vindication of the notion of a *model* (thus, from Austin's standpoint, Nietzsche failed to distinguish between the two notions of an original and of a model). Austin most systematically puts to work the method of working-models in 'How to Talk: some simple ways' (1979: 134, 146–7, 150–1). A model which is not acknowledged to be at work prejudges of the distinctions which we are to make and constricts our imagination (1979: 66). A consciously elaborated working-model, by contrast, is not meant to mirror actual linguistic use (if only because 'its careful separation of syntactics from semantics, its list if explicitly formulated rules and conventions, and its careful delimitation of their spheres of application—all are misleading' (1979: 67)) but only to embody *some* dimensions against the standards of which actual linguistic use may be assessed. Austin's method of working-models bears certain affinities with Wittgenstein's so-called 'method of language-games'. One fundamental affinity lies in the fact that both Austinian working-models and Wittgensteinian language-games are tracts of ordinary usage that are turned into complete wholes by being used as *models* or *objects of comparison* (which are complete by definition). Austin stresses that models (by contrast with fragments of actual language) are by construction 'prepared linguistically for the worst' (1979: 68). Wittgenstein stresses that language-games, when used as paradigms, are complete (see 1953, §2), so that they are not to be expanded by filling antecedent lacunas with *additional elements* but rather by *adjoining* new *dimensions* (on Wittgenstein's method of language-games, see Narboux (2008b); on Wittgenstein's evolution with respect to the notion of dimension, see Narboux (2004)). Thus, like Wittgenstein, Austin takes the very definition of a model or scheme (as a mere standard of comparison) to exclude the possibility of 'a single, total model' (1979: 203).

equivalent to the truth of the assertion of its sentential negation, the infelicity affecting an assertion is tied to the truth of the sentential negation of *another* assertion (that is, of another element of the 'total speech act situation' in which the infelicitous assertion is made). The constative utterance 'John's children are all bald' 'misfires' (more precisely, 'misplays') if 'not (John has some children)' is true, just as the performative formula 'I do' 'does not succeed in being a contract when the reference fails (or even when it is ambiguous)' (1975: 51). My constative utterance 'the cat is on the mat' is an 'abuse' (more precisely, an 'insincerity') if it is true that 'not (I believe that the cat is on the mat)', just as my performative utterance 'I promise' is an 'insincerity' if it is true that 'not (I intend to keep it)' (1975: 50). On the one hand, the felicity of an assertion may be incompatible with the truth of the sentential negation of *another* assertion without their conjunction being a *contradiction*. On the other hand, the felicity of a performative utterance may well *contradict* the truth of the sentential negation of *another* element in the total speech act situation ('I promise' seems flatly to contradict 'not (I ought to keep my promise)', just as 'the cat is on the mat' contradicts 'not (the cat is on the mat)' (1975: 51)). The crucial point, again, is that self-contradiction is not the only outrage to sense there is (1979: 48, 50–1) and that not all logical paradoxes have to do with the syntactical concept of self-contradiction. The above logical paradoxes, like all para-doxes that rest upon the invocation of terms of assessment, are irreducibly semantic in character (1979: 128–9, n. 2). Thus the very *sense* of an assertion may be incompatible (in a variety of distinct ways) with the truths of the sentential negations of (a variety of distinct) assertions unfolding circumstances of its making. This directly undercuts elements (*E*) and (*G*) of Frege's picture. In arguing that the contextual unit that is relevant for the assessment of the sense of an assertion includes (what he calls) 'the total speech act situation' in which the assertion is made, Austin is arguing that Frege's own understanding and defence of the 'Context Principle' do not go far enough.[36]

Austin resorts to the device of meta-linguistic negation—the sort of negation exemplified by 'This horse is not *good*, it is *excellent*'—in order to characterize dimen-sions of unsatisfactoriness. (For an account of meta-linguistic negation, see Horn 1989.) For lack of a unique sentential negation, corresponding to a unique way of going wrong, the semantic ascent afforded by meta-linguistic negation makes it actually possible to capture in a single move a whole array of ways of going wrong. Thus the dimension of unsatisfactoriness along which actions in general are assessable—the dimension of excuses—can be said to encompass 'all the ways in which each action may not be "free", i.e. the cases in which it will not do to say simply "X did A"', or all the cases in which one may legitimately 'argue that it is not quite fair or correct to say *baldly* "X did A"', 'the tenor of so many excuses [being] that I did it but only *in a way*, not just flatly like that' (1979: 180, 176, 187). Again, pretending may be said to belong with 'acting or rehearsing, or merely imitating or mimicking' in a dimension of

---

[36] I explore this topic at length in Narboux (2009).

unsatisfactoriness encompassing 'all the possible ways and varieties of *not exactly doing things*' (1979: 267, 271). Presumably, where it is not quite fair or correct to say baldly 'X did A', neither is it quite fair or correct to say baldly 'X did not do A' (or to say baldly 'it is not X who did A' or to say baldly 'it is not A that X did'). Meta-linguistic negation serves to repudiate the relevance of a term. For example, 'we can say "I did *not* sit in it 'intentionally'" as a way of repudiating the suggestion that I sat in it intentionally' (1979: 190). Notice that the adverbs 'simply', 'quite', 'baldly', 'exactly', are not dispensable in these formulations. They are at work to ensure that these formulations *do* characterize dimensions (if only *negatively*). We should not conflate the meta-linguistic negation to the effect that performative utterances [like 'I bet you sixpence it will rain tomorrow'] 'are not "true or false"' (1975: 5)—which should be para-phrased as the claim that they can neither be said to be 'true' nor be said to be 'false', *not* as the claim that they can be said to be neither true nor false—with the meta-linguistic negation to the effect that it is not exactly incorrect to say that 'France is hexagonal' (only 'it is a rough description' (1975: 143)). If it is not incorrect to say P, then it is correct to say P, but that it is not exactly incorrect to say P does not mean that it is correct to say P. Apart from the specialized use which he makes of meta-linguistic negation to characterize a dimension of happiness at a stroke, Austin makes massive methodological use of meta-linguistic negation, whether to repudiate the relevance of a certain term of assessment or to repudiate the relevance of an entire dimension of assessment. This is only expected given that his method consists in examining 'what we should say when' (1979: 182) and that, as he points out in a footnote to 'A Plea for Excuses', although 'we are sometimes not so good at observing what we *can't* say as what we can, yet the first is pretty regularly the more revealing' (1979: 190).

Although he criticizes the assumption that the device of sentential negation is the unique and primary means of capturing breakdowns, paradoxically Austin does not criticize but vindicates the assumption that such negation allows us to express (if not capture) *any* breakdown. There is a sense in which he shows the relevance of sentential negation to be even more universal than has been customarily assumed. This seems to have to do with the fact that sentential negation, as its name indicates, is a syntactical device. And it would seem that sentential negation derives its expressive power from the systematic manner in which it combines with truth and falsity. It is striking that Austin never questions Frege's thesis that sentential negation is not to be construed as a pragmatic force with which the sentence is uttered. And he emphatically denies, in Frege's spirit (see Dummett 1973, ch. 10), that truth and falsity can be assimilated to forces (for example, to acceptance and rejection) along the lines of so-called performative theories of truth. (See his criticism of Strawson's tendencies toward a performative theory of truth in 1979: 132–3.)

This may lead one to wonder whether the Fregean picture is not in order so long as it is explicitly confined to an account of assertions *as assertions*, or to an account of the sole *assertive aspect* of utterances (what Austin calls their 'locutionary' aspect). We need to consider next what Austin has to say about the relation between falsity and sentential negation. Austin considers that relation in his essay 'Truth', in the course of refuting the view according to which 'To say that an assertion is true is not to make any further assertion at all. In all sentences of the form 'p is true' the phrase 'is true' is logically superfluous. To say that a proposition is true is just to assert it, and to say that it is false is just to assert its contradictory' (1979: 126). Although it is anything but clear that this view can be safely ascribed to Frege, it does embody the very blurring of the distinction between syntax and semantics which, from the perspective occupied by Austin, would seem to account for Frege's inability to recognize truth as a dimension of assessment, that is to say, as a complex unified array of *irreducibly semantic standards* of assessment. Not that semantics, in Frege, is reduced to syntax. Rather, to the extent that there is no room for a genuinely semantic standpoint in Frege (point (*D*) above), this is due to the impossibility of such reduction (whether this means that semantic features are reckoned 'ineffable' by Frege is a hotly debated issue, which falls outside the scope of this essay). Accordingly, one might even go so far as to say that Austin's entire doctrine of dimensions is heir to Frege's rejection of all attempts to *define* truth as a *property* possessed by propositions on account of their *relation* to the world. But it is as if Frege had failed to distinguish between the rejection of the attempt to define truth as correspondence-based *property* and the rejection of the claim that truth is an array of *standards*.

In 'Truth', Austin criticizes both the reduction of semantics to syntax that leads to the faulty reduction of falsity to sentential negation and the reduction of syntax to semantics that leads to the faulty reduction of sentential negation to falsity. The reduction of sentential negation to falsity, congenial to coherentism (British Idealism, for example, evinces at least a tendency toward such reduction), proceeds through the reduction of contradiction to contrariety and the reduction of negation to affirmation. Negation is held to be 'just a second order affirmation (to the effect that a certain first order affirmation is false)' (1979: 128). And negation is conceived as a merely elimina-tive device (see Bosanquet 1885, 1888; Bradley 1897, 1922; Mabbott 1929; Ryle 1929) by equating that second order affirmation itself with a second order affirmation to the effect that the disjunctive set of all the statements that are contrary to the first order affirmation under consideration contains one true disjunct. For example, the negative statement 'This car is not blue' is equated with the second order affirmative statement to the effect that the first order statement 'Either this car is green or this car is red or . . . or this car is white' is true. Against that first version of the conflation between the syntactical concept of sentential negation and the semantic concept of falsity, Austin maintains that affirmation and negation stand on a par: 'Affirmation and negation are exactly on a level, in this sense, that no language can exist which does not contain conventions for both and that both refer to the world equally directly, not to statements about the world: whereas a language can quite well exist without any device to do the work of "true" and "false"' (1979: 128–9). The reduction of falsity to sentential negation, congenial to correspondence views (Logical Positivism, for exam-ple, is at least inclined to it), proceeds through the reduction of contrariety to contradiction. The phrase 'is false' is held to be *redundant*. Against that second version of the conflation between the syntactical concept of sentential negation and the semantic concept of falsity, Austin puts forward the three following objections. First, the statement that *it is false that S* does not refer to something to which the statement that *not-S* can refer, for the latter refers to the world or any part of it *exclusive* of itself (namely of the statement that *not-S*, while the former refers to the world or any part of it *inclusive* of the statement that *not-S*, though once again exclusive of itself (namely of the statement that it is false that *S*) (I adapt here Austin's first argument to the effect that 'is *true*' is not logically superfluous (1979: 126–7)). Second, the statement that *not-S* and the statement that it is false that *S* do *not* behave so as to be assessable in parallel ways. It may be, for example, that both the statement that 'He is at home' and the statement that 'He is not at home' are false[37] (he is lying upstairs dead), so that they fail to be contradictory statements, and that 'He is not at home' (which is false) does not have the same truth-value as 'It is false that he is at home' (which is true). Or again, it may be that both the statement that 'It is a real cat' and the statement that 'It is not a real cat' are false (that good acquaintance of mine has just delivered a philippic), so that they fail to be contradictory statements, and that 'It is not a real cat' (which is false) does not have the same truth-value as 'It is false that it is a real cat' (which is true) (1979: 67). So Austin agrees with intuitionists that truth and negation do not commute (it is not true that $S \neq$ it is true that not-S), although on a quite distinct, non-epistemic, basis.

Finally, the statement, 'It is false that he is at home' suggests that the question has come up whether he is at home (or even that someone has asserted that he his). By contrast, this is not true of the statement, 'He is at home' (1979: 128). Note that this does not mean that 'It is false that' here *amounts to* the performative 'I reject your statement to the effect that'. For to say that 'it is false that' is in many cases *also* and crucially to make an *assertion* (see again Austin's criticism of Strawson at 1979: 133).[38] Nor does it mean that there is no use of 'not' in which it has the force of rejection. Rather, the point is that the negation to which 'It is false that he is at home' does amount is the *meta*-linguistic (or *semantic*) negation 'He is not "*at home*"' (that is, 'It is incorrect to say baldly that "He is at home"'). So Frege's contention that negation is not a force is confirmed rather than undermined by this (apparent) exception.

But, now, is it the case *at least* that those assertions that are true or false are to be construed as answers to yes-no questions or, at any rate, that the aspect of an utterance that is assessable as true or false is to be so construed? Can it be granted that contradictory negation is tied to assertoric sense insofar as it is tied to the structure of the yes-no question corresponding to a given assertion? Both queries

---

[37] Hence *not true*. Austin does not question the assumption that *if* a statement is not true, *then* it is false (or, equivalently, that *if* a statement is not false, *then* it is true).

[38] Austin doesn't deny that 'It is true that...' and 'It it false that...' may mark, on *some* occasions, endorsement and rejection respectively—he objects to the generalization and its alleged philosophical grounds.

are addressed by Austin in the concluding part of 'How to Talk: some simple ways'. Both are answered in the negative. Austin shows, in effect, that assertoric sense cannot *in general* be construed as the content of a yes-no question. Precisely because (sentential) negation *is* indeed tied to the structure peculiar to a yes-no question, only those types of assertions whose content can be construed as the content of a yes-no question (that is to say, types of assertions whose force is not identificatory) do admit of a counterpart negative form. This is not to say that assertions of others types than those (that is to say, assertions with identificatory force) do not themselves admit of meaningful (sentential) negations. But their negations are not of the same type as them. In other words, their illocutionary force changes as they undergo the opertion of negation.

The major part of 'How to Talk' is dedicated to laying out the differences between four distinct types of speech acts which one may be performing in making an assertion of the form 'I is a T'. In asserting, say, that 'this car is red', I may be *stating* that this car is red (rather than not red), or I may be *placing* this car as red (rather than blue, or yellow, or green, and so on), or I may be *instancing* this car as being red (rather than as not being one of the red things), or I may be *casting* this car, (rather than this other car or that other car, and so on) as red (1979: 142–3). In the concluding pages of the essay, Austin argues that only those types of assertions which are not types of *identification* (namely, stating and instancing) admit of sentential negation. This argument rests on the observation that 'there is no such thing as a negative or counter identification' (1979: 152). I can neither identify the colour of this car nor identify this car as a red thing, in other words I can neither answer the question '*which* is the colour of this car?' nor answer the question '*which* of these cars is red?', by asserting that 'this car is not red'. As Austin puts it: 'to identify as not is nonsense for not to identify' (1979: 153). Conversely, the contents of those types of assertions which *are* types of identification (namely placing and casting) cannot be the contents of yes-no questions even should they fit exactly a name to an item (as in placing) or fit exactly an item to a name (as in casting) and therefore be strictly assessable as true or false.

3. Negation and the bounds of sense; or, 'there are other ways of killing a cat than drowning it in butter'[39]

3.1.

I have argued that Austin shows the hierarchy imposed by metaphysics upon dimensions of assessment to rest upon a prior postulate, according to which all pairs of opposite terms of assessment ultimately reduce to pairs of contradictory opposites. The hierarchy imposed upon forms of opposition provides the necessary framework to assign to the harmony between words and world the same all-or-nothing character that is also assigned to the upshot of such confrontation, and, moreover, to exempt

---

[39] Austin (1975: 48). In a footnote to 'Performative/Constative', Austin adds: 'English proverb. I am told that this rather refined way of disposing of cats is not found in France'.

harmony from assessment. However, Austin also shows that that whole framework itself rests upon a prior, possibly even more unconscious, postulate: the postulate that negations divide neatly into *internal* (or relevant) negations and *external* (or irrelevant) negations. Or, to put it differently, that the framework rests upon the prior postulate that each dimension of assessment lays out a *logical space of relevant possibilities*. It is to Austin's attack on that further postulate that we must now turn.

It was Kant who first devised the concept of a logical space of real possibilities, in the 'Ideal of Pure Reason' (see Kant 2003: 487ff.).[40] Kant challenges Spinoza's contention that all negations are equally meaningless, because all equally irrelevant (Deleuze 1981: 123–6). Spinoza holds, in effect, that it is no less gratuitous or irrelevant to deny of a car that it has wheels or of a bird that it has wings, than to deny of a rock that it is a horse or to deny of the soul that it is a fire-shovel. By contrast, Kant holds that the predicates which can be truly denied of a given subject from a formal standpoint further divide into the predicates which belong to the *disjunctive* sphere constituted by all the *contrary* predicates which might have held of that subject, and the predicates which do not belong to that sphere and can be denied of that subject from a purely *formal* standpoint only. The assertions that deny a predicate belonging to the disjunctive sphere of the possibilities that really bear on the subject constitute *real* or *internal* negations. The assertions that deny a predicate regardless of whether it belongs to such a sphere constitute *formal* or *external* negations. Thus, the two notions of a *logical space* of real possibilities and of an *internal negation* go strictly together. According to Kant, Spinoza was therefore right to deem the contradictory negation of a statement meaningless as such. For the contradictory negation of a statement may only acquire a meaning in virtue of that statement being embedded in a space of contrary statements. However, Spinoza failed to appreciate the real function of contradiction, which is to secure the closure of that space.[41]

As I read him, Austin rejects the assumption that being assessable in the light of a standard of assessment consists in being assigned coordinates in a logical space. In order to appreciate that point, we need to find our way into the system constituted by the following five Austinian theses:

(1) Norms and conventions do not have sharply delimitated ranges of application (1975: 31–2; 1979: 67).

(2) Those ranges of application never extend beyond the range of ordinary cases (1975: 38; 1979: 67).

(3) Terms of assessment are typically 'adjuster-words' (1962: 74).

(4) Terms of assessment (whether they are 'trouser-words' or not) can only be brought to bear on a situation if that situation is in some way not standard or not

---

[40] This concept was taken over by the British Idealists. On the 'Ideal of Pure Reason', see Lebrun (1970: 287–325), and Deleuze (1969: 343).

[41] On Bosanquet's illuminating argument to this effect, see Narboux (2005).

orthodox (which is not to say that it is not ordinary): 'No modification without aberration' (1979: 189).

(5) Dimension-words are typically 'trouser-words', that is to say, words whose negative use 'wears the trousers' in the sense that their affirmative use is entirely parasitic on it (1962: 71; 1979: 192).

One caveat may be in place before we embark on this. The suggestion that Austin shows that our words are apt to have what might be called a more *oblique grip* on the world than we may assume may seem to go against the grain of his method. For it may seem to be in tension with the phenomenological claim which he makes on behalf of 'ordinary language', to the effect that 'when we examine what we should say when, what words we should use in what situations, we are looking again not *merely* at words (or "meanings", whatever they may be) but also at the realities we use the words to talk about: we are using a sharpened awareness of words to sharpen our perception of, though not as the final arbiter of, the phenomena' (1979: 182). It might even seem that his accepting the term 'linguistic phenomenology' as a characterization of his method is in tension with the assumption as to the adequacy of ordinary language considered as a universal medium. The truth, however, is that Austin maintains *both* that language 'embodies all the distinctions men have found worth drawing, and the connexions they have found worth marking' between phenomena *and* that it is necessary for us 'to prise [words] off the world, to hold them apart from and against it, so that we can realize their inadequacies and arbitrariness, and can re-look at the world without blinkers' (1979: 182).[42] As we shall see, his theory that words evolve in accordance with the principle of the survival of the fittest is meant to account for both facts at once, that is, both for the fact that linguistic distinctions provide access to the very phenomenal distinctions which they were meant to capture in the first place, *and* for the fact that no *living* system of linguistic distinctions can be protected against all conceivable risks of losing its grip on the phenomena (1979: 68).[43]

3.2.

Let us first concentrate on Austin's thesis that a single breakdown may fall in the range of more than one term of assessment.[44] As we have seen, under the head of 'infelicities',

---

[42] See also (1979: 124), where he says that 'in philosophy—above all in discussing truth [. . .] it is precisely our business to prise the words off the world and keep them off it.'

[43] What is at stake is not whether diction is *coarser* than experience (so that experience is bound to be non-conceptual in character). The issue, in particular, is not whether some shades to be experienced are too fine-grained not to elude our conceptual repertoire *or*, on the contrary, every shade is such that an experience of it always already actualizes a concept, if only the paradigmatic concept which this experience itself makes available and which is capturable by the demonstrative phrase 'coloured thus' (as John McDowell argues against Gareth Evans in *Mind and World* (1994: 56–60). Both parties to the issue whether facts are more fine-grained than language take language to be a kind of net cast upon the world, whose meshes *either* let things slip through *or not*).

[44] This thesis should not be conflated with the thesis (considered above in section 2.3) that what is affected by a given breakdown may be simultaneously affected by other breakdowns along the same dimension as well as by breakdowns along other dimensions.

Austin groups cases where the purported act fails altogether to be an act with cases where it fails to be fully an act or to be a full act. But in fact Austin goes so far as to maintain that 'these distinctions are not hard and fast, and more specially that such words as "purported" and "professed" will not bear very much stressing' (1975: 16–17). We have also seen that, under the head of 'excuses', he includes both break-downs that affect the stage of 'decision and resolve' together with breakdowns which affect the 'executive stage' of action (1979: 193–4). Again, Austin goes so far as to claim that the various ways in which it may be argued 'that it is not quite fair or correct to say *baldly* "X did A" [...] can be combined or *overlap* or *run into each other*' (1979: 176, italics added).

I have argued that the fact that Austin's schemes are apt to look confused, if not inconsistent, when measured by the standards of intentionalism, only pleads against the latter. In order to take the full measure of the challenge which Austin mounts against the harmony fallacy, we need to appraise the significance of his recurring remarks as to (not only the essentially incomplete character but) the essentially non-exclusive char-acter of the classifications of breakdowns which he puts forward (that is to say, as to the overlapping of the classes which they comprehend). Far from being mere asides, such remarks lie at the very heart of his project. Consider the three 'universal rules of logical division' listed by Kant in his *Lectures on Logic*: 'that the members of the division exclude or are opposed to one another, that furthermore they belong under one higher concept (*conceptus communis*), and finally that taken together they constitute the sphere of the divided concept or are equal to it'—in a word, that 'the members of the division must be separated from one another through *contradictory* opposition, not through mere contrariety (*contrarium*)' (Kant 1992: 637). Austin thinks all three rules fail to hold when it comes to the logical division of unhappiness into dimensions or to the logical division of a given dimension of unhappiness into forms or types. He would also say that only a *model* or *scheme* of the logical division of a given dimension (like the model of infelicities) can be said to conform to the *third* rule.[45]

While the official theme of Lectures 2–4 of *How To Do Things With Words* is the justification of the division of the concept of Infelicity, their *leitmotiv* (and even, I am ready to argue, their true theme) is the latitude that is allowed in placing a breakdown in the scheme of infelicities. The scenario in which 'I see a vessel on the stocks, walk up and smash the bottle hung at the stem, proclaim "I name this ship the *Mr. Stalin*" and for good measure kick away the chocks: but the trouble is, I was not the person chosen to name it' (1975: 23) may be seen either as a case of 'misfire' due to 'misapplication' of the accepted conventional procedure (I did not have the 'capacity' to perform the act) or as a case of 'misfire' due to 'non-play' (either in the sense that there is no conventional procedure to be invoked or in the sense that the conventional procedure

[45] When Austin denies that a classification of breakdowns is possible (for example, in 1975: 13), he means to deny the possibility of a classification conforming to the three Kantian rules; he does not mean to exclude the possibility of putting forward a classificatory *scheme* or *model*.

I invoke (part of which is getting oneself appointed) is bound to be rejected) (1975: 24). Austin mentions another case that seems to evince the same sort of indeterminacy: 'When the saint baptized the penguins, was this void because the procedure of baptizing is inappropriate to be applied to penguins, or because there is no accepted procedure of baptizing anything except human?' (1975: 24). And he concludes on that basis, at the end of Lecture 2, that cases of infelicity are not exclusive. It is not only that 'we can go wrong in two ways at once (we can insincerely promise a donkey to give it a carrot)' but 'more importantly, [...] the ways of going wrong "shade into one another" and "overlap", and the decision between them is "arbitrary" in various ways' (1975: 23). Austin declares in the next lecture that it is 'more or less an optional matter how we classify some given particular example' (1975: 26).

It may happen that a case of 'misapplication' admits of two distinct readings *as* a case of 'misapplication', that is, as an instance of the infringement of a single rule—like in cases where either persons or circumstances can be reckoned inappropriate (1975: 34–5). It may also happen that a case of 'misinvocation' can be construed either as a case of 'misapplication' or as a case of 'non-play', which would be an instance of the infringement of either of two distinct rules that specify a type of misfire. Moreover, in cases such as those of giving an order to somebody on a desert island, marrying a monkey, baptizing a penguin, and appointing a horse consul, it may even turn out that a case of 'misfire' can be construed either as a case of 'misinvocation' or as a case of 'misexecution', which would be an instance of the infringement of either of two distinct rules that lie across the fundamental divide between 'misfires'. Thus, if 'at a party, you say, when picking sides, "I pick George"', only to be rebuked by 'George's grunt "I'm not playing"', the act may be taken to 'misfire' 'because there is no convention that you can pick people who aren't playing, or because George in the circumstances is an inappropriate object for the procedure of picking', *or again* because 'the procedure has not been completely executed' (1975: 28). Thus, 'I'm not playing' may be read as 'There is not any procedure to which I am subject', or as 'I am not an appropriate object for the procedure', or again as 'I have not been subjected to the whole of the procedure'. The same holds true of the words 'I don't take orders from you' (that is, 'You're not entitled to give me orders') uttered as a rebuke to someone who says to me 'Go and pick up wood' on a desert island (1975: 28). Austin even goes so far as to suggest that one and the same speech act scenario may afford both a reading under which the act is *not* accomplished (it 'misfires') and a reading under which it *is* (it is merely 'abused') (1975: 37, n. 1). Failure to hand a gift over, he remarks, might equally be seen as a failure to execute the procedure completely (i.e. as a 'hitch' or 'non-execution' causing the act to 'miscarry'), hence as a failure of the purported speech act to *be* an act at all, *or* as a failure to display the subsequent conduct which the speech act has made in order (i.e. as a 'disloyalty' or 'non-fulfilment'), hence as an 'abuse' of the speech act that *was* accomplished. The crucial point is that 'it does not matter in principle at all how we decide in particular cases, though we may agree,

234 THE PHILOSOPHY OF J. L. AUSTIN

either on the facts or by introducing further definitions, to prefer one solution rather than another' (1975: 29).

This means that the negation underlying the infelicity of a performative may be held to have a more or less external scope (or equivalently a more or less internal scope). Perhaps the most important point made by Austin in the course of his examination of 'misfires' in Lecture 3 is that the two obvious ways of countering that indeterminacy of scope are equally barred. Neither can the negation underlying the infelicity be completely internalized nor can it be completely externalized *in principle*. For, on the one hand, no convention can encompass or anticipate any conceivable manner in which it may be come to be rejected, or turn any conceivable rejection *of* it into a mere inappropriateness *to* it. On the other hand, no set of facts can account for the normative status of a convention (1975: 29).

The relative indeterminacy of the scope of the negation underlying the infelicity of a performative is rooted in the relative indeterminacy of the limits of the range of application of any norm, convention, or procedure (this is thesis 1 above). Thus, I may wonder whether I may baptize a dog, should it prove to be rational, or whether such a speech act is bound to be non-played (1975: 31). Neither the conventions governing the concept of baptism nor the circumstances of its candidate application can settle that issue.

Thus, the range of application of a norm, convention, or procedure is not only limited in the sense that *not all* ordinary situations fall under it: it is bound to prove to be limited in the face of recalcitrant cases that are either too novel or too far-fetched (in a word, too *non*-ordinary) to be assessed in its light (this is thesis 2 above). Austin formulates that point by saying that 'language breaks down in extraordinary cases' (1979: 68), that 'the most *adroit* of languages may fail to 'work' in an abnormal situation or to cope, or cope reasonably simply, with novel discoveries' (1979: 130), or again that 'however well-equipped our language, it can never be forearmed against all possible cases that may arise and call for description: fact is richer than diction' (1979: 195). We have come across such cases already, in section 2.3: The case where it is true neither that 'he is at home' nor that 'he is not at home' (he is lying dead upstairs), or again the case where it is true neither that 'it is a cat' nor that 'it is not a cat' (it has just delivered a philippic).[46]

This point is bound up with Austin's theory that words evolve in accordance with the principle of the survival of the fittest. This evolutionary theory offers a non-teleological prospect on the harmony between words and world, thereby making otiose the postulation of some design as a condition *sine qua non* of that harmony, just as the theory of dimensions provided a non-teleological account of the 'extraordinary' status that befalls words like 'true', 'good' or 'real', one that counters the urge to hypostasize their meanings (1979: 128). Those words and forms of words are apt to

---

[46] For an illuminating discussion of the decisive job done by this move in Austin's attempt to defuse the 'sceptical trap', see Mark Kaplan's 'Tales of the Unknown' (Chapter 3, this volume).

survive which best accommodate ordinary situations (1979: 185, 281). Being bound by precedent, ordinary language 'blinkers the already feeble imagination' and is bound both to overlook extraordinary situations and to break down when it has to cope with them (1979: 68–9). Words and world are meant for each other only in the trivial sense that words are designed in the first place to articulate the world (or, at any rate, our demeanours in and toward the world). And when the world *seems* to display *counter-finalities*, it is only because it *then* seems *as if* we had hitherto assumed, in designing our language, that the world was designed so as *not* to display such abnormalities as it now displays. The behaviour of the world is then at odds, not with some design of its own, but with the standards of linguistic use set by us in response to its standard behaviour.

Terms of assessment typically serve to keep norms, conventions, or procedures at work in situations which are so out of the ordinary that they threaten to render them otiose. In other words (this is point (3) above), terms of assessment typically function as flexibility devices, adjuster words, allowing us to compromise with the world so as to maintain some grip of our words upon it (1962: 73). Suppose that

one day we come across a new kind of animal, which looks and behaves very much as pigs do, but not *quite* as pigs do; it is somehow different. Well, we might just keep silent, not knowing what to say; we don't want to say positively it *is* a pig, or that it is *not*. Or we might, if for instance we expected to want to refer to these new creatures pretty often, invent a quite new word for them. But what we could do, and probably would do first of all, is to say, 'It's *like* a pig.' (1962: 74)

Not only does the dimension of assessment constituted by the distinction of the real and the unreal fail to coincide with a dichotomy (either to be real or not), but those terms of assessment which that dimension comprises may all enable a conceptual norm to *keep* a grip on the world along that dimension *even* in situations where, because of an apparent lack of cooperativeness on the world's part, that conceptual norm can no longer function in conformity with a yes-no regime (that is, with a simple alternative between applying and not applying). Likewise, not only does the dimension of assessment constituted by the free and the unfree fail to coincide with a dichotomy (either to be free or not), but those terms of assessment which that dimension comprises may all be invoked in order to maintain the assessability of an action *as an action* in situations where it is threatened, because it will no longer do either to say baldly 'X did A' or to say baldly 'X did not do A'. Again, it is not just that an utterance does not need to 'depict' a fact whose 'logical multiplicity' (i.e. logical dimensions) it shares in order to be assessable as true or false, as if dimensions could be read into the world (1979: 125). For an utterance may well be assessable along the dimension of the true and the false just to the extent that it is brought under terms of assessment that enable its predicate to retain its grip upon the world, in a situation where such grip could not be so retained were it to be construed as a yes-no issue. Thus, even though it will not do either to say simply that '"France is hexagonal" is true' or simply that '"France is hexagonal" is false', it can still be said that the statement is 'rough'.

As for terms of infelicities, they enable us still to speak of an utterance and still to assess it (still to have something to assess) in situations where the utterance has failed altogether to perform the action that it was meant to perform. Thus to say that the utterance has 'misfired' exempts us from saying that the utterance turned out to be no utterance at all. Even talk of 'displacement behaviour' allows us still to discern a conduct awaiting assessment in situations where we might be tempted no longer to discern any conduct (1979: 204).

Far from being a yes–no question that first needs to be settled in order for the yes–no question whether a given conceptual norm *does* apply or *not* so much as to be raised, harmony is typically achieved by first renouncing the construal of the latter question as a yes–no question. The ability of our words to engage with the world presupposes their ability to negotiate their engagement with it.[47] To allow for a certain amount of looseness in their grip on the world, should the need arise, is the surest way for our words to keep their grip on it. As Austin notes, 'the more precise a vocabulary is, the less easily adaptable it is to the demands of novel situations' (1962: 130).[48] For the arrow of intentionality (for the normative character of a concept) still to be directed onto the world may be for it to be directed onto it along modalities that had not— indeed, that *could* not have—been anticipated. If this destroys the logic of the concept of intentionality, then so much the worse for that concept. As Austin puts it,

if we think of words as being shot like arrows at the world, the function of these adjuster-words is to free us from the disability of being able to shoot only straight ahead; by their use on occasion, such words as 'pig' can be, so to speak, brought into connexion with targets lying slightly off the simple, straightforward line on which they are ordinarily aimed. And in this way we gain, besides flexibility, precision; for if I can say, 'Not a real pig, but like a pig', I don't have to tamper with the meaning of 'pig' itself. (1962: 74–5)

It is one and the same fallacy that debars harmony from being genuinely assessable and that debars it from being negotiable.

3.3.

How can the relative indeterminacy of the scope of the negation whose obtaining captures a given breakdown fails to cancel or undermine retroactively the very assessability of what is being assessed? How can that assessability not be cancelled or undermined retroactively by the relative arbitrariness of the decision whether a norm is still relevant to a situation that, as it were, puts its elasticity to trial? The simple answer is

---

[47] I have argued elsewhere that in the *Philosophical Investigations* Wittgenstein does not rest content with confining the *internal* relation of intentionality to language, as he is often supposed to, but dismantles the whole dichotomy between internal relations and external relations, which he finds to subtend the very notion of intentional 'directedness'. See Narboux (2006b).

[48] The need to accommodate 'items of types which do not exactly match any of the patterns in our stock (the sense of any of our name)' is the *rationale* behind moving from model S_0 to model S_1 in 'How to Talk' (1979: 146–50).

that such assessability would indeed be found retrospectively to disintegrate *if* for something to be assessable in the light of a certain dimension (more generally: of a certain standard) was for it to be embedded in a logical space. And since it does *not*, it follows that for something to be assessable in the light of a certain dimension (more generally: of a certain standard) is *not* for it to be embedded in a logical space. Since a given breakdown in given circumstances can be equated with more than one negation (or with a negation with more than one scope), it will not even do to say that the logical space in which what is assessed needs to be embedded if it is to be determinately assessable varies with the circumstances. All that can be said is that no assessment is possible that does not proceed in the light of some model or other, which model embodies some dimensions or others.

Only if any negation that may prove to underwrite a given breakdown *had* first to be presumed not to obtain, and if any breakdown that may prove to occur *had* first to be presumed not to occur, would the relative indeterminacy over which norm or convention exactly breaks down, and the relative indeterminacy over whether a given norm or convention altogether breaks down or can still compromise with the world, constitute threats to assessability. It is only through a retrospective teleological illusion that any conceivable way for things to go wrong is read back into smoothness as an internal negation that is to be overcome if things are to go smoothly. The assumption that any standard of assessment in the light of which an utterance, perception, or action may turn to be assessable was always constitutive of it (always constituted an ingredient of it) is precisely the assumption which Austin's fourth thesis, 'No modification without aberration', is meant to block. To take our standards always already to presume some cooperativeness from the world, or to reify all the conceivable ways in which our words may lose their grip on the world into as many background assumptions (as in Searle 1969, 1983), is to fall prey to that teleological illusion. In fact, teleological talk here only makes sense retrospectively (Narboux 2006a, 2008a).

Happiness along a given dimension, let alone happiness in general, is not a property that befalls an utterance, perception, or action in virtue of its overcoming all conceivable ways in which it might have gone amiss. Rather, it is something that is positively assigned to it and whose assignment is in order only when it is meant to rule out some specific breakdown—that is, where it negates an internal negation. This in turn does not mean that to assign happiness along a given dimension is to assign more than a default status (this is thesis 5 above: dimensions-words are typically trouser-words).[49] Likewise, familiarity does not simply pertain to an atmosphere but rather is something that is positively assigned to it and whose assignment is in place only when it is meant to rule out some specific feeling of unfamiliarity, does not mean that familiarity is more

---

[49] Thus, the point which Michael Dummett makes concerning the correctness of an assertion—that there is no *positive reward* for it (see, for example, Dummett 1978)—is generalized by Austin to all dimensions of correctness (that is, of satisfactoriness).

than a default status.[50] For things to go happily just is for them to go 'smoothly', for them not (external negation) to go wrong. An affirmation of happiness is not the internal negation of an infinite conjunction of internal negations, even less the internal negation of an indefinite negation (as the metaphysician, whose 'wile consists [. . .] in not specifying or limiting what may go wrong' (1979: 87) is only too prone to assume), but the merely external negation (that is, the mere want) of those negations whose relevance (that is, internality) has actually arisen. Or rather, since those negations are in fact positive abnormalities that wear the trousers, happiness along a given dimension is mere want of those ills whose relevance has actually arisen. That is why there is typically only one way for things to be happy, while many a way for them to be unhappy.

Bibliography

Austin, J. L. (1962), *Sense and Sensibilia*, Warnock, G. J. (ed.), Oxford: Oxford University Press.

—— (1975), *How to Do Things with Words*, 2nd ed., Urmson, J. O., Sbisà, M. (eds.), Oxford: Oxford University Press.

—— (1979), *Philosophical Papers*, 3rd ed., Urmson, J. O, Warnock, G. J. (eds.), Oxford: Oxford University Press.

Arendt, H. (1978), *The Life of the Mind*, New York, NY: Harcourt.

Bosanquet, B. (1885), *Knowledge and Reality*, London: Kegan Paul.

—— (1888), *Logic or the Morphology of Knowledge*, Oxford: Clarendon Press.

Bradley, F. H. (1897), *Appearance and Reality*, 2nd ed., Oxford: Clarendon Press.

—— (1922), *The Principles of Logic*, 2nd ed., London: Oxford University Press.

Brandom, R. (1994), *Making it Explicit*, Cambridge, MA: Harvard University Press.

—— (2002), *Tales of the Mighty Dead: Historical Essays in the Metaphysics of Intentionality*, Cambridge, MA: Harvard University Press.

Cavell, S. (1994), *A Pitch of Philosophy: Autobiographical Exercises*, Cambridge, MA: Harvard University Press.

—— (1995), *Philosophical Passages: Wittgenstein, Emerson, Austin, Derrida*, Oxford: Basil Blackwell.

Conant, J. (1991), 'The Search for Logically Alien Thought: Descartes, Kant, Frege and the *Tractatus*', *Philosophical Topics* 20: 115–80.

—— (2002), 'The Method of the *Tractatus*', in Reck, E. (ed.), *From Frege to Wittgenstein*, Oxford: Oxford University Press, pp. 374–462.

—— (2004), 'Varieties of Scepticism', in McManus, D. (ed.), *Wittgenstein and Scepticism*, London: Routledge, pp. 97–136.

Deleuze, G. (1962), *Nietzsche et la philosophie*, Paris: Presses Universitaires de France.

—— (1963), *La philosophie critique de Kant*, Paris: Presses Universitaires de France.

—— (1969), *Logique du sens*, Paris: Minuit.

—— (1981), *Spinoza, philosophie pratique*, Paris: Minuit.

---

[50] That is how I read what Wittgenstein says about feelings of familiarity (see Narboux 2006a, 2008a).

Diamond, C. (2003), 'Unfolding Truth and Reading Wittgenstein', *SATS—Nordic Journal of Philosophy* 4: 24–58.

Dummett, M. (1973), *Frege: Philosophy of Language*, London: Duckworth.

——(1978), 'Truth', in *Truth and Other Enigmas*, London: Duckworth, pp. 1–24.

Floyd, J. (2002), 'Number and Ascriptions of Number in Wittgenstein's *Tractatus*', in Reck, E. (ed.), *From Frege to Wittgenstein*, Oxford: Oxford University Press, pp. 308–52.

Frege, G. (1977), 'Negation', in Geach, P. (ed.), *Logical Investigations*, New Haven: Yale University Press, pp. 31–53.

Horn, L. (1989), *A Natural History of Negation*, Chicago, IL: Chicago University Press.

Kant, I. (1992), *Lectures on Logic*, Young, J. M. (ed. and trans.), Cambridge: Cambridge University Press.

——(2003), *Critique of Pure Reason*, trans. N. Kemp Smith, New York: Palgrave Macmillan.

Lebrun, G. (1970), *Kant et la fin de la métaphysique*, Paris: Armand Colin.

Mabbott, J. D. (1929), 'Symposium: Negation', in *Proceedings of the Aristotelian Society, Supplementary Volumes*, vol. 9, Knowledge, Experience and Realism, pp. 67–79.

McDowell, J. (1994), *Mind and World*, Cambridge, MA: Harvard University Press.

——(1998), 'Truth–Value Gaps', in *Mind, Knowledge and Reality*, Cambridge, MA: Harvard University Press, pp. 199–213.

Narboux, J.-P. (2004), 'Diagramme, dimension, et synopsis', in Batt, N. (ed.), *Penser par le diagramme*, Saint-Denis: Presses de l'Université de Vincennes, pp. 115–41.

——(2005), 'Négation, contrariété et contradiction: sur la théorie éliminativiste dans l'idéalisme anglais', *Archives de philosophie* 68: 419–46.

——(2006a), 'L'obvie en négatif', *Critique* 708: 400–15.

——(2006b), 'L'intentionnalité: un parcours fléché', in Chauviré, C., Laugier, S. (eds.), *Lire les Recherches Philosophiques de Wittgenstein*, Paris: Vrin, pp. 189–206.

——(2008a), 'Logique et téléologie chez Kant et Wittgenstein', in Bouton C. (ed.), *La troisième Critique de Kant*, Paris: Vrin, pp. 283–96.

——(2008b), 'Introduction à "La philosophie telle que je la vois" de F. Waismann', in Narboux, J.-P. and Soulez, A. (eds.), *Textures logiques*, Paris: L'Harmattan, pp. 65–70.

——(2008c), 'Négation et dimension chez Waismann', in Narboux, J.-P., Soulez, A. (eds.), *Textures logiques*, Paris: L'Harmattan, pp. 261–90.

——(2009), 'The Logical Fabric of Assertions: Some Lessons from Austin's "How to Talk: Some Simple Ways"', in Ambroise, B. and Laugier, S. (eds.), *La philosophie du langage ordinaire: histoire et actualité de la philosophie d'Oxford (1925–2000)*, Hildesheim: Olms.

Ricketts, T. (1985), 'Frege, the *Tractatus*, and the Logocentric Predicament', *Noûs* 19: 3–15.

——(1986a), 'Objectivity and Objecthood: Frege's Metaphysics of Judgment', in Haaparanta, L., Hintikka, J. (eds.), *Frege Synthesized*, Dordrecht: Riedel, pp. 65–95.

——(1986b), 'Generality, Meaning, and Sense in Frege', *Pacific Philosophical Quarterly* 67: 172–95.

Ricks, C. (1998), 'Austin's Swink', in *Essays in Appreciation*, Oxford: Oxford University Press, pp. 260–79.

Ryle, G. (1929), 'Symposium: Negation', *Proceedings of the Aristotelian Society, Supplementary Volumes*, vol. 9, Knowledge, Experience and Realism, pp. 80–96.

Sahlins, M. (2008), *The Western Illusion of Human Nature*, Chicago, IL: Prickly Paradigm Press.

Searle, J. (1969), 'Assertions and Aberrations, in Fann, K. T. (ed.), *Symposium on J. L. Austin*, London: Routledge and Kegan Paul, pp. 205–18.

—— (1983), *Intentionality: An Essay in the Philosophy of Mind*, Cambridge: Cambridge University Press.

Spinoza, B. (1954), *Spinoza: Œuvres complètes*, Paris: Gallimard.

Travis, C. (2003), *Les liaisons ordinaires: Wittgenstein sur la pensée et le monde*, Paris: Vrin.

Wittgenstein, L. (1953), *Philosophical Investigations*, trans. Anscombe, G. E. M., Oxford: Basil Blackwell.

—— (1975), *Philosophical Remarks*, ed. Rhees, R. and trans. Hargreaves, R., White, R., Oxford: Basil Blackwell.

Index

'*ΑΓΑΘΟΝ* and *ΕΥΔΑΙΜΟΝΙΑ* in the *Ethics* of Aristotle' (Austin's essay, mentioned and/or quoted) 216, 217
Alston, W. 17
antiquarianism in the history of philosophy 5, 7
Apel, K-O. 17n14
'A Plea for Excuses' (Austin's essay, mentioned and/or quoted) 1, 3, 10, 14, 15, 33, 36, 43, 44, 48, 49, 75, 78n1, 148, 159, 160, 166n38, 204, 205, 212, 215, 218, 219, 220, 221, 223, 224n35, 225, 226, 231, 232, 234, 235, 236
appearance 37, 38, 40, 46, 48, 53
'Are There A Priori Concepts?' (Austin's essay, mentioned and/or quoted) 43n11, 218, 225
argument from ignorance 22, 51–76, 105n29
argument from illusion 81n6
    disjunctivist responses to 21
Aristotelian Society 59n8, 143
Aristotle 44, 216
assertion (assertive force) 43, 73, 91n24, 124, 198, 208–9, 211n13, 217, 224–30, 237n49
avowal 115, 134n21, 136, 139–42
Ayer, A. J. 10, 17n14, 41–2, 81–2, 116

Bach, K. 171n43
background information (*see also* knowledge, background) 79, 90–2, 99, 101, 110–11
Bar-On, D. 132n20
Baz, A. 21, 24–5
Bennett, J. 22, 41, 43–8
Bergmann, G. 17n14
Berkeley, G. 91n24
Berlin, I. 5n4, 10
Blome-Tillmann, M. 152
BonJour, L. 23, 110–11
Bosanquet, B. 9, 227
Bradley, F. H. 8n7, 9, 11
Broad, C. D. 9
Burnyeat, M. 36n3, 37n6
Butler, J. 16–17

Caesar, J. 118–19
Caird, E. 9
Cassam, Q. 20, 37n6
Cavell, S. 18–20, 22, 32–5, 37n6, 44, 48, 49, 73, 151n11, 204n2, 214n18
Chisholm, R. 19, 66, 73
circumstance 14, 23, 24, 26, 54, 60–1, 63–8, 70–3, 75, 80, 89–103, 108–9, 120–4,

131n18, 164, 166, 180, 188–90, 192–4, 196–8, 201–3, 211n13, 220, 222, 225, 233, 234, 237
    circumstance dependent (circumstance relative; *see also* context-sensitive) 109, 111, 152–4
    circumstance independent 93, 95–6, 110, 112
Cohen, S. 161n50, 170n42
Collingwood, R. G. 10n10
Conant, J. 205n4, 206n6
concept (conceptual; *see also* Frege; generality; possibility) 12, 25, 39, 43n11, 49, 74, 109, 110, 112, 146, 148, 150, 159n26, 162, 165–6, 172, 178–82, 185–6, 189–203
    conceptual vs. non-conceptual 25, 26, 180–2, 190, 196–7, 199, 201
    zero-place concept 179, 186, 189–94, 202
constative 43, 123n10, 211, 215, 222, 224, 225
    fallacy 212, 215
context-sensitivity (*see also* circumstance; occasion) 19, 20, 24, 125, 152, 153, 159
contextualism (contextualist) 2, 17, 19, 20, 24–5, 146, 148, 150–8, 162–4, 166–72
Craig, E. 159n28
Crary, A. 20
criteria 37, 38, 39, 40, 46

Deleuze, G. 205n5
delirium tremens 84n11
DeRose, K. 24, 51, 148, 159–62
Descartes, R. 42, 79n3, 85, 135
Derrida, J. 15–16, 43n10, 43n11, 204n2
dichotomies (*see also* fact-value dichotomy) 14, 15, 157n22, 211n13, 212–18, 223–4, 235–6
dimension 26, 147, 195–6, 204–6, 210–27, 229–35, 237–8
disengagement 36–8, 41, 43–9
dream (dreaming; *see also* waking experience) 23, 51–2, 55, 58, 71, 79–87, 89–92, 97–112
    dream argument 23, 79, 104, 108–12
    dream hypothesis 52
    neurophysiology of dreaming 83n10
    phenomenology of dreaming 23, 80–7, 99–104, 109–12
Dreben, B. 20n16
Dretske, F. 53, 91n24
Dummett, M. 237n49
Dworkin, A. 18

epistemology (*see also* knowledge, theory of) 19, 20, 23, 36n3, 37–8, 45, 60n8, 68–9, 75–6, 87, 148, 168, 171n45
epistemological (epistemic) 21, 24–5, 42, 46, 70n15, 73–6, 78–9, 84, 85, 87, 91, 92, 101, 104, 110, 111, 148, 152n14, 154, 161, 164, 167, 171n44, 228
    obligation 91n24
    priority 23, 92–7, 99, 101–3, 106–12
    reason 89–90
everyday (*see also* ordinary) 62, 80, 151, 158, 163–5, 170, 171
    language (use, usage, discourse) 1, 9, 14, 21, 158, 160, 166
    practice 19, 149
evidence 64n10, 68, 74, 84–106, 111, 152, 158, 167, 170
excuses 44, 154, 156, 214, 219, 225, 232
experimental philosophy 21

fact-value dichotomy 26, 195–6, 200, 214
fallacy:
    constative fallacy 212, 215
    descriptive fallacy 149, 212, 214
    harmony fallacy 206, 207, 215–16, 232, 236
    rate fallacy 70n15
fallibilism (fallibilist) 84, 167–8
fallibility 54–5, 84, 89, 98, 167, 170, 204
Fann, K. T. 3
felicity (*see also* infelicity) 205n5, 213, 225
Felman, S. 16–17
Finkelstein, D. 134n21
Fischer, E. 20
Fish, S. 16
Flew, A. 12–13
Floyd, J. 12, 211n13
force (*see also* illocution; assertion; pragmatic) 149, 204n2, 226, 228
Foucault, M. 16
free speech 18
Frege, G. 21, 27, 175, 206n6, 220–1, 226, 227
    on assertion 191, 198, 207–9
    on concepts 25–6, 178–82, 185, 186, 189–203, 207–9
    on judgement 178–80, 182–7, 193–8, 200–2, 207–9
    on logic 178, 181–5, 201–3, 208–9
    on objects 178, 189–90, 202
    on thought 175–87, 190, 193–4, 201–3, 207–9
    on truth 25–6, 175–87, 190, 196, 198, 200–3, 207–9, 227
Fried, M. 214n18

Gellner, E. 17n14
generality (*see also* concept) 35, 111, 179–81, 186, 189–91, 199, 207–8, 216, 220, 222

Glendinning, S. 12, 15, 21–2, 26
Glyph (journal) 15
Grice, H. P. 11n11, 16–17, 19, 73, 75, 79n2, 148n3, 150
Green, T. H. 8–9, 11

Habermas, J. 16n14
Hampshire, S. 10n9, 11
Hanfling, O. 155n21
Hare, R. M. 11n11
Hart, H. L. A. 11n11, 11n12, 17
Hawthorn, J. 155n20, 170n42
Hazlett, A. 171n45
Hegel, G. W. F. 8n7
Heidegger, M. 42n8, 47
Herodotus 118
historicism 188, 191–5, 200
Hitler, A. 47
Hobbes, T. 85–6
Hobson, J. A. 83n10
Horn, L. 225
Hornsby, J. 18
'How to Talk – Some Simple Ways' (Austin's essay, mentioned and/or quoted) 2, 26, 175, 224n35, 229, 236n48
How to Do Things with Words (Austin's lecture series, mentioned and/or quoted) 1, 2, 3, 4, 35n2, 43, 44, 49, 122, 147, 195, 196, 204, 205, 210, 211, 212, 213, 214, 215, 219, 220, 221, 222, 224, 225, 226, 229, 230, 232, 233, 234
Husserl, E. 42n8, 48, 49

idealism 12
    British 227
'Ifs and Cans' (Austin's essay, mentioned and/or quoted) 10, 14
illocution 146–7, 210n12, 211
    illocutionary act 18, 25, 122n8, 147, 149, 151
    illocutionary force 65, 122, 123, 150, 229
infelicity 206, 211–13, 220, 225, 232–4
invariantism (invariantist; *see also* contextualism) 150, 152n13, 155n18, 170n42, 171n43, 171n44
intuition 21, 24, 39, 160, 165, 170–1, 218

Jacob's Room (novel by Virginia Woolf) 143
Joachim, H. H. 9
Joseph, H. W. B. 11n12
judgement 124n11, 151, 159n26, 178–80, 182–7, 193–8, 200–2

Kant, I. 44, 205, 206n6, 219, 230, 232
Kaplan, M. 19–20, 22, 23, 25, 37n6, 91n24, 234n46

knowledge 19, 22, 24, 25, 42–3, 46, 51–76,
    79–95, 104–10, 118–19, 123, 140–2, 146,
    149, 152–3, 155–72
  as a liability 152–9
  attribution (ascription) 63, 67–9, 73, 152–9,
    170–2
  background knowledge 79, 87
  challenge 60, 156, 160, 168
  claim 52, 54–5, 59n8, 60, 64–5, 68–9, 71n16,
    148, 155, 162–9
  closure 72n17, 105n29
  factivity of 117, 163, 169
  of material objects 117–18, 133, 135, 138,
    142
  of other minds 53, 115–19, 130, 133, 135–6,
    138, 140–3
  perceptual 52
  role of authority in 93–7, 118–19, 125–6,
    137–8, 141–2
  self- 132n19
  theory of (see also epistemology) 74, 76,
    170n42, 205n5
  testimonial 23, 115, 124, 127–9, 138, 140–3
  vs. belief 117
  vs. promising 6–7, 23–4, 115, 118, 119–29

Lacey, N. 11
Langton, R. 18
Lawrence, R. 82n7
Leite, A. 22–3
Lewis, D. 159, 167–9
locution (locutionary) 147, 210n12, 211, 226
logic (see also possibility) 42n9, 44, 45, 63,
    208–9, 214, 225, 230, 232, 235, 236
  intuitionist 202, 228
  logical positivism 12, 227
loneliness 143–4

MacAdam, J. 9
McDowell, J. 39n7
McGinn, C. 7
McGinn, M. 23, 74, 110
MacKinnon, C. 18
MacKinnon, D. 10n9
McMyler, B. 6–7, 23–4
MacNabb, D. 10n9
McTaggart, J. M. E. 9, 11
Martin, M. G. F. 20
meaning (see also concept; meaningfulness;
    semantic; sense) 25, 39, 80, 147, 149–50,
    155n21, 170, 172, 196, 217, 218,
    230, 234
meaningfulness 26, 209, 212, 213
Medina, J. 20
memory 83n10, 86n17, 123, 140
Mind Association 143
Moore, G. E. 8–11, 12, 56n4, 105

Narboux, J.-P. 26–7
negation 22, 63, 67, 204, 206–7, 214, 215–30,
    234, 236–8
  meta-linguistic 222n33, 225–6, 228
Nietzsche, F. 204n2,205n3, 219, 224n35
nonsense 166, 205, 206, 207–15, 220, 229
Nozick, R. 91n24
  Nozick's sensitivity requirement 85n16

objective 46, 200, 208, 210
occasion (occasion-sensitivity) 26, 93, 131, 135,
    139, 147, 152, 154–7, 176, 183, 187–203,
    220, 228n38, 236
ordinary (see also everyday) 6, 19, 21, 39, 53,
    59–60, 62–76, 78–83, 87–92, 103, 105,
    109–10, 115–16, 169, 206, 219, 221, 230,
    234–5
  language (use, usage, discourse) 1, 12, 14–15,
    38–41, 45–6, 48, 62–3, 69, 74–5, 78,
    89n22, 122, 130, 148, 166n38, 204, 214,
    220, 224, 231
  life 49, 56, 59–60, 67–8, 70, 73, 75–6, 78–9,
    82, 83
  practice 40, 67–8, 73–6, 78, 83, 96, 107,
    137–8, 140–2, 151
ordinary language philosophy 1, 2, 11, 17n14,
    20n17, 60n8, 150, 165–6, 171n45
other minds (see also knowledge; scepticism)
    23–4, 53, 89, 114–19, 129, 133–44
'Other Minds' (Austin's essay, mentioned and/or
    quoted) 3, 6, 10, 43n11, 52, 53, 54, 56, 58,
    59, 62, 65, 66, 75, 76, 78, 80, 84, 87, 88, 89,
    92n24, 93, 98, 99, 114, 115, 116, 117, 118,
    119, 120, 121, 123, 124, 125, 126, 130,
    131, 133, 134, 135, 136, 137, 138, 139,
    140n26, 143, 144, 148, 149, 161, 162, 167,
    168, 204, 238
'Other Minds' (symposium) 116
Oxford Austin archives 82n7

Passmore, J. 9
Pears, D. 11n11
perception 19–22, 24, 41–3, 49, 81, 84n10, 115,
    123, 133, 135, 140, 180, 181, 220, 231, 237
performative (performativity) 7, 9, 16, 22, 36n3,
    43, 44n11, 69, 123, 149, 196, 209–10,
    215n20, 219, 221–2, 225–6, 228, 234
'Performative Utterances' (Austin's essay,
    mentioned and/or quoted) 36, 42n8, 147
perlocution (perlocutionary) 18, 210n2
phenomenology 48–9
  linguistic 49, 231
  of dreaming (see also dream) 23, 80–7,
    99–104, 109–12
phenomenological 23, 49, 112, 231
  features 83n10, 84–5, 100–4
  states 99–104

Plato 5, 44, 216, 218, 219
pornography 18
possibility 40, 83, 84n12, 89–92, 94–107, 109,
    110, 112, 183, 189, 192, 205–6, 230
  conceptual 23, 83, 109–10, 112, 179
  logical 109–10, 112, 230
  metaphysical 23, 109–10, 112
pragmatic (pragmatics) 3, 16, 17, 25, 120, 154,
    165–9, 171
'Pretending' (Austin's essay, mentioned and/or
    quoted) 42n8, 216, 223, 226
Prichard, H. A. 3, 8–11, 12
promise (promising) 6, 23, 54, 115, 118,
    119–29, 211, 219, 225, 233
proof 56–7, 65
prove 22, 56n4, 57–8, 60, 62, 65n11, 67, 69–71,
    87
psychological state 115–16, 119, 130–7, 140–4
  expression of unconscious 134n21
  symptom/sign of 130–2, 137
Putnam, H. 30, 37n6

real 37–41, 59–60, 62, 92n24, 99, 184, 213–15,
    218–20, 228, 235
realism 8–10, 47
reality 26, 37, 39–40, 46, 48, 83n10, 210, 212,
    215, 223n34, 231
Recanati, F. 19
reference 146–7, 150–1, 201, 227, 228
relevant alternatives (relevant doubts) 91n24,
    152, 155–9, 161–3, 168–70
reliability 87n19, 88, 92–7, 102, 112, 118,
    138–41
representation 150–1, 176–8, 181, 187, 190,
    198–202
  words as instruments of 25, 146–7, 196,
    198–9
REM-sleep 83n10, 86n17
Ricks, C. 207n7
Rorty, R. 42n8
rule 1, 25, 38, 40, 45, 74, 114
Russell, B. 8, 17n14
Ryle, G. 11, 20n17

Sbisà, M. 17
scepticism 2, 25, 51–2, 60–3, 68, 73–4, 76, 79,
    91n24, 104–12, 155, 164–72, 205
Searle. J. 15–17, 211n13
second-personal cognitive relation to
    others 137–8, 142
Sedgwick, E. K. 16, 17
semantic (semantics) 2, 62, 155n21, 164–72,
    206, 209, 223–5, 227–8
  unity 216–17
sense 147, 176, 205n5, 207–15, 225m, 228–9
Sense and Sensibilia (Austin's lecture series,
    published version, mentioned and/or

quoted) 4, 20, 33, 34, 35, 37, 38, 39, 40,
    41, 42, 43, 46, 47, 48, 49, 74, 78, 80, 81, 82,
    84, 91, 93, 187, 205, 206, 213n15, 214,
    215, 216, 217, 218, 220, 221, 222, 230,
    231, 235, 236
Sense and Sensibilia (Austin's lecture series,
    unpublished UC Berkeley 1958 version,
    mentioned and/or quoted) 22, 82, 84n11, 85
sense-datum 42, 46–7, 78, 81, 218
Skinner, Q. 17
Solms, M. 83n10
Sosa, E. 19, 84n11, 171n45
speech act (see also illocution; performative;
    promising; testifying) 18, 120–9, 155n21,
    170, 211, 215, 225, 229, 233–4
  theory 1, 2, 16, 17, 18
Spinoza, B. 230
Stanley, J. 155n20
statement 22, 25, 43, 56, 93, 175, 184, 186–7,
    191, 195, 198–9, 210, 212, 221–3, 224,
    227–8, 230
Strawson, P. 11n11, 148n2, 226, 228
Stroud, B. 19, 23, 74, 79n2, 88n21, 106–11
subjective 46, 83n10, 85n16

testimony (testifying; see also knowledge,
    testimonial) 6, 23, 24, 26, 54, 114–29, 133,
    136–7, 140–1
  formal/informal 119n5
  reductionism about 140–2
'The Meaning of a Word' (Austin's essay,
    mentioned and/or quoted) 62, 75, 210,
    215, 217, 218, 224n35, 228, 230,
    231, 235
third-personal cognitive relation to others 137,
    142
thought (see also Frege, on thought) 25, 35,
    130n17, 149
'Three Ways of Spilling Ink' (Austin's essay,
    mentioned and/or quoted) 220, 222, 223,
    235
Tolstoy, L. 204
transcendental 205–6
  argument 213, 218
  philosophy 205
Travis, C. 19, 25–6, 27, 37n6, 146n1, 152–9,
    160, 169, 172
trust 54, 118n4, 119, 128
truth 19, 25, 26, 36, 67, 70n15, 72, 87–8, 93–4,
    96–7, 128, 148, 151, 158, 162, 164, 167–8,
    170–2, 175–203, 204n1, 204n2, 206n5,
    208–10, 212–14, 217, 220, 221, 223n34,
    224–8
'Truth' (Austin's essay, mentioned and/or
    quoted) 147, 164, 186, 187, 191, 204, 205,
    210, 212, 213n16, 214, 215, 225, 226, 227,
    228, 231n42, 234

'Unfair to Facts' (Austin's essay, mentioned and/or quoted) 212, 213n16, 215
University of California at Berkeley 22, 82, 84n11
Urmson, J. O. 9n8, 11n11, 12, 13, 44n12

verificationism 81–2

Warnock, G. J. 3–4, 6, 7, 11n11, 15, 22, 80, 82n7, 91n24, 120n6, 155n21
waking experience (see also dream) 23, 58, 80–6, 97–104, 106, 108–12

Williams, B. 5, 85n15
Williams, M. 74, 110, 152n14
Williamson, T. 152, 155n20, 171n44
Wilson, J. C. 8, 9, 10
Wisdom, J. 116n3, 130–1, 143
Wittgenstein, L. 20, 32, 33, 34, 41n8, 44n12, 52n2, 132, 136, 152n12, 158n25, 164, 172, 205n5, 206n6, 207, 208n10, 210n13, 215n21, 224n35, 236n47
Woolf, V. 143–4
Woozley, A. 10n9, 11n11

Ingram Content Group UK Ltd.
Milton Keynes UK
UKHW021847260323
419166UK00003B/148